T0345688

My Dear Molly

The
CIVIL WAR
LETTERS *of*
CAPTAIN
JAMES LOVE

Edited by *M. E. Kodner*

Missouri History Museum
St. Louis
Distributed by University of Chicago Press

To my parents, Ira and Barbara Kodner,
for always nurturing my love of history

In his letters, James frequently misspelled words, or used an incorrect word or grammar. In cases where these mistakes made it difficult to understand the content of the letter, we corrected the errors. Otherwise, original spelling and grammar have been retained.

There are words, phrases, and statements in these letters that may be offensive to the reader. At the time the letters were written, certain words and phrases were common and even acceptable. We wish it were otherwise. The words are those of the author, James Love, and the attitudes he expresses are those of the time period. We have retained the original language of the letters because we believe that, in spite of their faults, the letters provide an exceptional firsthand account of the attitudes and actions during this horrific period in our nation's history.

All photos are from the Missouri Historical Society unless otherwise noted.

Library of Congress Cataloging-in-Publication Data

Love, James Edwin, 1830-1905.

  My dear Molly : the Civil War letters of Captain James Love / edited by M.E. Kodner.

    pages cm

  Includes bibliographical references and index.

  Summary: "Consists of the 160 letters that St. Louisan James E. Love wrote to his fiancée during his Civil War service from 1861 to 1865. Introductory text and annotations place the letters in historical context"-- Provided by publisher.

  ISBN 978-1-883982-82-9 (hardcover : alk. paper)

  1. Love, James Edwin, 1830-1905--Correspondence. 2. United States. Army. Kansas Infantry Regiment, 8th (1861-1865) 3. United States--History--Civil War, 1861-1865--Personal narratives. 4. Missouri--History--Civil War, 1861-1865--Personal narratives. 5. Prisoners of war--United States--Correspondence. 6. Soldiers--United States--Correspondence. 7. Love, Molly, 1833-1924--Correspondence. 8. Saint Louis (Mo.)--Biography. I. Kodner, M. E. (Molly E.), 1974- editor.

  II. Title.

  E508.58th .L68 2015

  973.7'8092--dc23

  [B]

2014045141

Table of Contents

Prologue

James Edwin Love was an ordinary man. Most likely, no one outside his family would have ever heard of him, except that he left behind a collection of letters documenting four extraordinary and grueling years in both his life and the history of the United States.

He was born September 27, 1830, in Bushmills, County Antrim, in northern Ireland, the eldest of William and Esther Steel Love's four children. Sadly, by age twelve, James had lost both of his parents. In May 1849, James and his brother, Samuel, followed several of their aunts and uncles to America, settling first in Cincinnati, where they lived with their uncle Robert A. Love, an architect, for over a year. In December 1850, James arrived in St. Louis, where he worked as a clerk for various grocers until he opened his own grocery store on the southeast corner of Fourteenth and Market streets. Unfortunately, the store burned down in the spring of 1854, and James decided to follow the gold rush to California.

James and Samuel left St. Louis with a party of thirty and traveled to New York, the quickest route to California at the time. In New York, James heard many tales of failure and disease from men returning from California, so he engaged with a skipper loading a boat of supplies for Australia. After a voyage of 103 days, James and Samuel arrived in Australia and joined a party of miners. When that venture failed, James went to Melbourne, where he took a position as a porter with an importing firm and eventually became a shipping clerk and outdoor agent for the company.

When James's health started to decline in January 1858, he left Australia. Upon his return to St. Louis, he bought property at the corner of Ninth Street and Spring (now St. Louis) Avenue, where he opened a grocery store and lived above it.

At some point in the late 1850s, James met Eliza Mary "Molly" Wilson. She was born October 2, 1833, in Island Magee, County Antrim, the daughter of Alexander and Eliza Mary Murphy Wilson. In 1849, after the death of her father, Molly came to America with her mother, her aunt, several of her brothers, and her younger sister, and settled in St. Louis.

James E. Love and Eliza "Molly" Wilson, ca. 1863. James E. Love Papers, Missouri Historical Society, from originals in care of Dr. Arthur Love.

It is not known exactly when or how James and Molly met, but they had a family connection, and they lived in the same area of St. Louis. While James lived at the corner of Ninth and Spring, Molly lived about twenty blocks south at 75 N. Ninth Street with her mother, her aunt, her brothers Alexander and John, and her sister, Sallie. Molly's brother William C. Wilson married James's cousin Eliza Ann Adams in St. Louis in 1855, while James was in Australia. They lived a few blocks west of Molly on Morgan Street, with Eliza Ann's parents, James and Mary Jane Steel Adams; her siblings John, Mary E., and Ellen; their baby, James; and three servants. Mary Jane Steel Adams, James's mother's sister, had come to St. Louis with her husband in 1836. When James arrived in St. Louis in 1850, he lived with her, and he thought of her as a maternal figure since his mother had died when he was young.

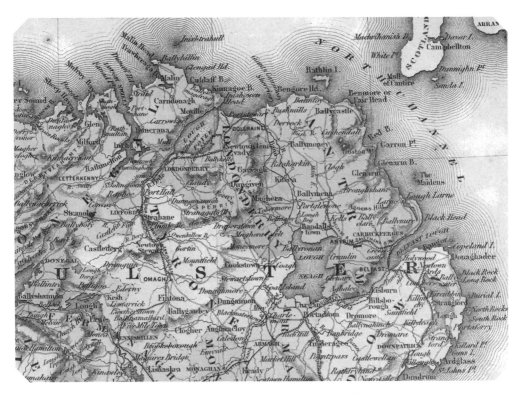

Map of County Antrim, Ireland, where Molly and James both were born. From George W. Colton, *Colton's Atlas of the World Illustrating Physical and Political Geography* (New York: J. H. Colton & Co., 1856), plate 6.

By 1861, James and Molly were secretly engaged, and in April of that year the nation erupted in civil war. James enlisted in May 1861 and left St. Louis the following month. The day after his departure from the city, he wrote his first letter to Molly, and he continued to write to her, 160 letters in total, throughout the four years of the war. James often mentions receiving letters from Molly in return, but, unfortunately, her letters did not survive. Through his letters, in his own words, James documented not only the marches, battles, and hardships of his military service, but also his undying love for his dear Molly.

Section 1

FIFTH UNITED STATES RESERVE CORPS

June 1861–February 1862

From the beginning of the Civil War, James ardently supported the Union. As the United States headed for war in 1861, he joined other Union men secretly drilling in cellars throughout the city of St. Louis. On May 11, 1861, James enlisted as a sergeant for three months of service with Company D, Fifth Regiment, United States Reserve Corps, Missouri Infantry, also known as Home Guards. The regiment was part of a force that Captain Nathaniel Lyon recruited to protect the U.S. Arsenal in St. Louis. At the time, tensions were high between Missouri citizens who supported the Union and those who supported Missouri's pro-Confederate governor, Claiborne Fox Jackson, and other Southern sympathizers. Governor Jackson supported secession by the state of Missouri, but a recent state convention had voted against it. James and the other members of his regiment remained in St. Louis until mid-June 1861. As tensions between the two sides rose, Governor Jackson asked for fifty thousand volunteers for the state militia. In order to prevent Jackson from forcing Missouri to secede, Lyon loaded a detachment of his troops onto steamboats and headed for Jefferson City, Missouri's capital. James and his regiment followed these first troops soon after on the steamboat *D. A. January*, which left St. Louis on June 15, 1861. The following day, he wrote his first letter to Molly.

James continued to write letters during the summer of 1861, beginning with his service in Jefferson City. The city had been the center of secessionists in Missouri, especially within the state government. After hearing that Lyon was on his way to Jefferson City with federal troops, Governor Jackson and other government officials fled to Boonville, Missouri, where militia troops led by Major General Sterling Price prepared for battle. Lyon, with part of his army, pursued Price's troops and left Colonel Henry Boernstein to defend the capital, restore order, and establish the necessary patrols into neighboring secessionist counties. James and his regiment remained in Jefferson City to help Boernstein. Throughout these first months of his service, James was not involved in the main battles in Missouri. As the troops led by Lyon and Price moved south and fought at Boonville, Wilson's Creek, and Lexington, and James and his company traveled on steamboats up and down the Missouri River on business for General Lyon. While James's early letters only briefly mention secondhand information about these battles, they provide a wonderful glimpse into life in the border state of Missouri, where the soldiers did not always know who supported the Union and who were rebels, or "secesh," as James called them.

By mid-August 1861, as James reached the end of his three months of service, he and his company traveled down the Missouri River from Lexington, skirmishing with parties of rebels along the way. In September, the men returned to St. Louis, where they mustered out and then tried to reorganize for three years of service. James started to recruit a company for the Fourteenth Regiment Missouri Infantry, a Home Guard unit organized by Colonel Robert White, lieutenant colonel of James's original company. After two months spent recruiting men, James headed to Fort Leavenworth, Kansas, where troops were gathering for an expedition to New Mexico to prevent an invasion of the territory by rebel troops.

This expedition never happened, and at the beginning of 1862, James had to deal with problems both personal and professional. In January 1862, he mentioned for the first time that his engagement was a secret, but he desperately wanted to tell Molly's family. At the same time, the future of James's unattached company remained uncertain. Finally, in early March 1862, James and his seventy-one recruits became Company K, Eighth Regiment Kansas Infantry, with Captain William S. Herd in command and James as first lieutenant. James's professional problem was quickly resolved, but the issue of the secret engagement would continue to trouble him, and become a constant topic of his letters, for the next two years.

On board Steamer "D. A. *January*"
Missouri River
June 16th 1861
My Dear Molly

We are at present near St. Charles & en route for Jefferson City. I shall write you again from there. At present I have only time to say how much I <u>love you</u>. All my hopes of Heaven & earth depend on you. I have tried to act through life so that neither my own, or my adopted country need be ashamed of me. I have a double incentive now! & with a little advice from you, I will try to never give you cause to Blush for me.

I hope & pray to return safe & soon – believe me ever truly yours in thought, word & deed.

James E. Love

James's view of St. Charles probably looked similar to this engraving. *City of St. Charles—On The Missouri River.* Colored wood engraving, 1856.

Steamer "*D. A. January*"
Jefferson City
June 18th 1861
My Dear Molly

After rather a pleasant trip we arrived last night at the Capital. I am pretty well & in good spirit but worked nearly to death. I guess I'll come round all right however. I hope you & all are well & that you are in better spirits than when I left you.

Dont fear for us. You know "Thrice is he armed who knows his Cause is just" & the fact is the Rebels dont, wont, have not yet stood before us in Missouri but run when even two to one without firing a Shot – but to begin.

We left our armory about five o'clock & march'd down 14th to Morgan thence to 11th down 11th to Washington Av. & so to the river. Our orders & stores were soon aboard & we started for the mouth which we reached without incident changing guards regularly every two hours. There we laid overnight. Next day being "Sunday" was nevertheless a very busy one with me & more or less so with all. We soon arrived at St. Charles & there met many friends & had a last farewell.

We found "Col Brown's" 4th Regt. (Williams) ahead of us & just crossing the river by ferry, we gave each other some rousing cheers, got some stores & started again.

St. Charles folks were very quiet & dress'd for Church & so it was for some time but gradually as we steamed gaily up the muddy river every Bluff & grocery & log cabin & settlement greeted us cheer on cheer – men women & children in emulation with handkerchiefs & flags waving, until we would round a turn & so lose sight of them. We also cheered ourselves hoarse & returned the Ladies' salutes. I was engaged writing all day & so could not note many of the incidents & I must leave them to the historian of the expedition. I notice that one of our boys is acting as special correspondent to the *St. Louis Christian Advocate* & I suppose will give all the items. We thus late at night reached Millers Landing, & laid over for Daylight.

Next Day Monday we passed rapidly up past Washington, Herman & the Gasconade &c, &c, &c, during which time we had a perfect ovation & the whole country as far as we could see swarmed with Home Guard. We saw the burnt bridges – all guarded now.[1] In the afternoon however we passed from thence to near Jefferson City through a rank secession district. We landed a mail at several places – found them & left them all as silent as the grave. We looked out closely for Prizes but could not secure even a secession Flag. However at St. Aubert's we saw tied up the Washington Ferry Boat which had conveyed up the river a few days before some secession troops. We took it in tow asking no questions, & no one objecting & brought it to Jefferson City where we laid up for the night awaiting orders.

We found old Boernstein in command of Cook County & the Capitol. All the Regulars & other troops having preceded us from this place in three steamers to Booneville & Arrow Rock where it was supposed the Old Fox would take it stand, but it proved to be only a run & they are yet after him. I hope they will yet surround him – but I fear not. We find a bad state of things here. A great many people left town & every man suspicious of his neighbor & Boernstein has kept us waiting orders until he hears further from Boonville fearing that if "<u>Lyon</u>" repulses them from there they may fall back on the Capitol again.

We had several false alarms during last night, & slept between hands on our arms, about one in the morning Boernsteins sentinels caught a spy from the Clarksville Rangers, & at once called us up to the Capitol on the double quick run, to be only at once sent back again.

This morning was wet, cold & disagreeable, but we had many duties to attend to <u>under cover</u>. At noon it cleared up & soon after one of the Penitentiary guards reported that the Prisoners had overpowered them, broke loose & were mining the walls. We were all under arms in one minute, though we suspected an ambush or a false alarm. We immediately surrounded the buildings or rather all the corners & outlets (for it is very large & covers sev-

---

1. Missouri governor Claiborne Fox Jackson ordered the burning of railroad bridges over the Gasconade and Osage rivers to break all railroad connections.

eral squares), 561 of these wretchs had mined a large hole in the wall, & were armed with Guns, Picks, Crowbars, Clubs, Hatchets, & Tools of all kinds.

The main body of their Guards had run away but now came back & we planted scaling ladders & sent them on the roof armed while we had the main gate opened & about 100 of us headed by Colonel White on horseback marched in, or rather rushed in charging bayonets. The poor devils at once scattering in dismay at the appearance of troops, they being quite unaware of our presence in their neighborhood.

Just as we thus rushed in, two companies of Boernsteins came down & stood guard outside to watch the secessionists while we quelled the riot.

The Guard on the roof fired & wounded several. We did not fire, & the poor fellows were quite thankful, although it took us over an hour to drive them from all the corners they had hid in after we arrived.

Our Colonel rode around as if on a holiday excursion & Comp. D with our Capt & your humble servant at its head were first inside.

Jefferson City has certainly something to thank us for.

In our absence 5 or 600 desperate men would have sacked the city. This alarm & duty detained this letter one day as I was writing & had got about half through when called on down stream & searched her thoroughly, but could find nothing contraband, except one of our Camp Jackson friends, (who is supposed to be a runaway from the Boonville fight) but who claims to be a good Union man & says he seceded as soon as the governor issued his last proclamation. He is accused however of casting Cannon Balls in the penitentiary here for the governor, & also in Boonville, where he went with the Governor. We've got him safe & have just placed him in the Capitol in Boernsteins charge.

And now my dear girl the reason of all this present haste is that we have just received the long looked for orders from General Lyon, & so Hurrah!! for Boonville. We start at daylight, & have got a large lot of camp equipage Tents, &c &c &c on board since dark. We either go in the Country or Garrison Boonville as necessity may dictate or General Lyon may order. He (the general) takes the field at once – if he has not done so already, so if you could address me a line care of Lieut Col White 5 Regt. U.S.R.C. at Boonville I would get it soon & receive it as a message from heaven.

but the mail closes
Goodbye
God Bless You
Yours Sincerely
James E. Love
Per J.C. *Swon*
via Herman

12 P.M. 19th June 1861
Thermometer 88 in the cabin
Love to all
Love

When James and his company arrived in Jefferson City, the state capital looked similar to this daguerreotype. State capitol building, Jefferson City, Missouri. Daguerreotype by Thomas M. Easterly, ca. 1850s.

19th 11 P.M.[1]

My Dear Molly

There has been enough of wars alarms all day but all foolish ones it seems. Everybody here is for the Union as soon as we come within half a mile of them & so it is peace, peace when there is no peace – but so mote it be. Men who have so little courage when it is required, & so much braggadocia when theres no danger wont break up the <u>Union</u> until they get a better cause for it.

We made a raid this morning into the county over the River that is on the North shore & recovered some Mail Coaches & horses that were seized by the secessionists from the mail agent. A company of 150 men that we hoped to meet ran away & disbanded.

We next stopped a boat coming.

8 o,clock P.M.

We are all badly famished for St. Louis News, but at this point the *J.C. Swon* just arrived from Herman & brought this mornings *Democrat*,[2] so we've just heard of the skirmish in your city so you see it is after all much as I said, we "Home Guard" are quite as safe out of town as in.

Keep in good spirits. The cause of the Union in "Missouri" & I expect in Virginia rolls along like an avalanche, & must prevail. We have just had glorious news from Boonville[3] which we send you by telegraph (I hope it is all true) to the effect that General Lyon, came & saw & conquered 4 times his own number – few of any troops killed – while of the State troop there was 300 killed & many prisoners. These numbers could have been much increased as General Lyon had just chased them into a ravine where his cannon was planted loaded with grape shot, & would have mowed them down by hundreds but he humanely at this point ordered his men to cease firing

---

1. It is not clear why the times in this letter are out of order.
2. *Daily Missouri Democrat* newspaper.
3. On June 17, 1861, Lyon's forces defeated Missouri State Guard troops at Boonville, Missouri.

& gave them a chance to run believing them to be fellow Citizens & even friends who were misled or compelled to fight in such an execrable cause.

We are all excitement & hope to be ordered to Booneville or some other point tomorrow as we are now no more required here. Home Guards have now commenced forming at many points, & the Union Men who were over-awed & scared can again speak & act according to their feeling, & sentiments.

Never fear for us. We only follow behind a good Leader who shoulders all the responsibility & faces all the greatest danger himself.

11 P.M. I must close tonight with Love to all & kisses to yourself, as I expect the mail to leave by boat again early in the morning, & I wish a sleep while I can, if it does not leave so soon & anything happens meanwhile, I will add a postscript.

Adieu My Dear Girl

Yours affectionately

James E. Love

Collision between the Federal Troops under Colonel [Kallmann] and the Citizens of St. Louis, Mo. – The Fire of the Troops Taking Effect upon the Recorder's Court, Which Was Then in Session. From Frank Leslie's Illustrated Newspaper, June 29, 1861, p. 97.

Boonville
on board Steamer *"D. A. January"*
June 21st 1861[1]
My Dear Molly

I again seize a favorable opportunity to drop you a line. I have not much to say however save that <u>I am well</u> though ennuyed to death with the confinement, heat, & Sameness of this <u>boat life</u>. I hope it soon may end. I have just rec'd a note from John Adams in answer to my St. Charles enclosure. So I suppose you got that Diminutive Billet Doux & the kisses enclosed all safe. Let me beg of you to accept a dozen more I wish to enclose just now. <u>Wont you return</u> <u>them</u> <u>by</u> <u>first Mail</u>?

I expect a note from you soon! Will I be disappointed?Not if you knew how I would prize it! How I prize any letter when from home – whether from a loved one or not! You know home is where the heart is & mine is all in St. Louis.

I was gratified with even the meagre news John sent, but surprised & even pained when I heard of Williams' leaving with his company.[2]

I hope God in his providence may send him safe back to you all as he is one of those who can not be spared just now.

I would be proud however to own such a brother who springs so at the call of duty – when every motive conspires to prevent him – not to speak of feminine persuasions innumerable.

I am so anxious now to know all the circumstances connected & how Eliza Ann, yourself & all the folks bear his absence on such a dangerous expedition.

I know you will never complain but would die from pure heart sickness first – but I hope he will be soon back with you & I may be soon back myself. There will soon be enough here without us, & it is broached even now to return <u>us</u> to St. Louis but candidly, now that this thing has gone so

---

1. This is the first of many letters in which James gets distracted and continues writing on subsequent days.

2. James's cousin John Adams informed James that Molly's brother William C. Wilson left St. Louis with the Fourth Regiment, United States Reserve Corps, Missouri Infantry.

far, we shall never return with my consent, nor with that of our Colonel, who is moving heaven & earth & General Lyon to get us in the van of the next fight. We lack discipline sadly but our boys are all as true as steel, & will never know when they are whipped. There will be an advance shortly. We have been waiting for munitions of war from St. Louis, which have been detained by the mistake of a stupid Dutch Captain at Herman who sent them down on the S.W. branch (after William) instead of here.

June 22d After writing so far we were disturbed by an order to get up steam for St. Louis to return as escorts for the Ammunition spoken of. This was afterward countermanded & we are here yet but <u>two</u> boats are going down this morning. They will take the <u>wounded</u> along & we may go too. We were out at five this morning up through Booneville City & boarded two boats just come from Lexington (our company I mean Comp. D.) we have brought them alongside as prizes as they carried Rebel Troops up the river, I believe by compulsion & if so we will release them at once. Events are transpiring so rapidly that I can give you no regular or connected account as my narrative is so often broken off & the excitement of the moment drives what I most wished to say out of my head. I can write but poorly at the best, & as these straggling sentences are penned everywhere from a drumhead to a desk, you must make liberal excuses for bad writing & any incoherency you may observe in the subject matter.

Yesterday there arrived two splendid regiments of Iowa Troops, one of them mounted. They came overland & got a good reception all along the route, & especially at <u>Macon City</u> where the Ladies presented them with a <u>flag</u> which they hoisted on a tall pole however & left the Home Guard to protect. They report the Secessionists as few in number but as having principally through the medium of false reports (about Dutch & freeing the Niggers) established a perfect reign of terror all over the state. This their conduct has dispelled in a great measure & life & property, nigger or otherwise is safer than ever in North Missouri. Why even the Secessionists in Booneville hail us now as deliverers & the Union Citizens, Ladies especially positively adore us & when we get a little Liberty ashore invite us into their houses & make us free to anything they have.

Booneville is a very pretty little city, much prettier & larger than Jefferson, & contains a fine population, though the rabid Secessionists have all left. There is a large number of German & Eastern citizens & these are the folks who are so frantic in their welcome. Most of them were under orders to leave when General Lyon came here last Monday & some had not dared to go out of their own doors openly for two weeks. One Lady offered to do any sewing I wanted but as we expected to be ordered off from here either up or down at any hour of the night or day we could not draw on her kindness. I brought some flowers aboard & the boys that were with me just then whatever flowers vegetables or Catawba wine they pleased to carry.

Two Regiments of our Boys are camped just alongside the Boats (of which there is now a fleet of Ten) on the fair grounds which are laid out on the pattern of the St. Louis very neat & tasty, not so large as the St. Louis ground but very large for the place.

I saw a St. Louis paper. The account of the fight is very meagre, but under present dislocated state of the mail arrangements, all you can expect.

They are just now bringing the wounded on board the "*J.C. Swon*" for St. Louis & now lying alongside us.

The Boats we captured this morning are the "*Emilie*" & the "*I.D. Bacon*". They report the Rebels all in motion, & that after fortyfying themselves first at Arrowrock & then at Lexington they are now on a full run down to the Arkansas line to join Ben McCullough & his Texas Rangers & Indians. I hope those who went out with & before William on the S.W. Branch are far enough ahead to intercept them & drive them back so that we may help catch them.

That poor Coward governor is always first to run. General Price is said to have resigned before the Booneville fight. The Rebels have followed the Governor three times & brought him back & some of the brave men has threatened to shoot him if he runs again, saying that he has brought them into this fix, & if he cant get them out he must at least stay & die with them.

Several companies of regulars left here on Wednesday & Thursday nights for various parts of the country around & we now hold it for a circuit of Fifty miles. The advance Guards arrived at Syracuse just in time to find the Rebels plundering & under orders to set it afire, they all ran however as our troops came in sight, & did not get time to carry out their designs.

There was also a skirmish of Two minutes duration at Tipton! Oh for that Ammunition! Wouldn't we be after them? There was but Two Union men killed in the Booneville fight & about Thirty slightly & Ten badly wounded, all expected to recover. There was but Five companies in the Action & but two companies (one of regulars & one of volunteers) done all the fighting & got all the wounds. These two companies no sooner fired & charged with the bayonets than the whole Three thousand Five hundred ran, led by the Governor. They most of them threw away their arms, & left horses tents, Boats everything even their coats behind them.

Hundreds of them swam the river which is here composed of narrow channels with Islands & bars between. The balance seized two steamers lying at the levee & made them take them across. They then ran 15 miles to opposite Arrow Rock before they formed.

The volunteer company that was first in the fight is commanded by Capt Yates & Lieut Manter, friends of Williams & have a dozen or two of my tenth ward friends in the ranks.

Adieu my dear dear girl

Yours Sincerely

James E. Love

Mail has closed per *J.C. Swon* & I must run after with this letter

Love

Love to all, not forgetting Sallie

Love

Steamer *Louisiana*
Booneville
July 2d 1861
My Dear Molly

I was about writing on Saturday, but the mail closed as I finished one to Alex, & one to Sally. I did manage to keep my promise so far as to send her one & you know a good commencement is often half the Battle.

I tried hard for some Illinois news! Will I get it?

But N'importe! How is your own dear self? I had a long weary day, after I left you waiting for <u>our</u> train which didn't start until 7 P.M. & then all night on the cars but I was all repaid Aye a thousand fold, by the reception from "My Own loved Molly Dear " & dreamt of sitting by her side again & again all night.

I return those kisses every morning & night!

I hope you are well Dear & that you have or will have good news from Willie for a Fourth of July Bonne Bouche & that you may have a pleasant time if such is possible now in St. Louis. I should like you to get this by that evening & you would if the mails went as usual but I know you wont, & I pray sharp eyes & Strong hearts may watch over you all & protect you, for if any trouble occurs of consequence in St. Louis, it is expected on the 4th ere you receive this it will be all past & gone but whatever happens, there can be but one result & that a triumph for the Union!

Providence overrules all for the best! & He wont allow the best government the World ever saw to be overturned unless for good reason. If this contest is as some say to be prolonged until Slavery is utterly overthrown may it not be a great gain to us & to mankind? I don't say it would! though I may believe it, but I dont see any other good to arise out of all this <u>Civil War & ruin</u> as Yet!

The South threw down the gauntlet on behalf of Slavery, & if such is the result, whose to blame?

But appropo – Have you seen the Comet? Is it not a grand sight? I certainly cant have been reading the papers lately! For it stole on my astonished vision on the 30th June without any preliminary telescopic introduction.

Just now 10 P.M. it shines like a flash of sunlight half across the heavens, or like one of the most brilliant streamers of the Northern lights. Its nucleus being low down in the red sun set of the N.West. while its tail extends to the Zenith or nearly overhead & sometimes I fancy I see wavy undulations rung along it, & even as if it was forked.

It is travelling towards the sun rapidly, & grows more brilliant nightly.

By the Bye! Did you get my last letter? I hope so. I dont like any of my correspondence to come up missing, especially since Ive got so lazy about it.

When I left & got on the "*January*" again we went right to Booneville again with 700 men on board & a large Cargo of Stores. We then while I was concluding my letter to Alex, were ordered on board the "*Louisiana*", & we immediately started down stream for Herman again. The trip was very eventless. We lay at Herman over Sunday & I went to two Dutch Churches a Lutheran & a Catholic, no English Churches in the Burg; I dont know whether I rec'd any benefit or not but it kept some of our rowdy boys quiet for two hours.

We left Herman with a load of Freight & here we are again, waiting orders. We were to start today but we aint gone yet. Now it is said all hands will start tomorrow, except the Irish Brigade who remain for guard here. We shall see.

3d July – 8 P.M.

The regulars & volunteers went this morning. We may go in the afternoon or not till the 5th. The others are gone to Springfield. We go to Lexington

Mail is closed

Steam up

Adieu

Yours Sincerely

James E. Love

Steamer A. McDowell

July 6th 1861[1]

My Dear Molly

We have just returned from a glorious flag raising in the secession town & county of Brunswick, but I will come to all that in due course.

I closed my last note in a hurry on the 3d & had to throw it aboard the mail boat. I hope you have received it. After that we passed a lazy day card playing &c but nothing would interest us. There was a strong under current of excitement in expectation of stirring events now at hand, and also of a perhaps dull 4th on board our boat, but still we did not move, & we at last concluded that we would probably lay over the 4th at Boonville. This we did.

In the morning bright & early we were up, ashore & had a drill returning at ½ past six.

Towards 8 oclock all the regiments & companies at Boonville turned out for a dress parade, together with the "Home Guards" of that pretty little city (a fine body of men about 200 in number) & had a rousting time. 2 of our men were quite exhausted & had to leave the ranks. <u>We thought</u> sun struck at first.

The Ladies & inhabitants generally turned out in large numbers, & we had plenty of Boquets &c &c not forgetting Beer.

We returned about 12 oclock. I comparatively cool, thanks to My Dear Molly, whose handsome Havelock I recd at daylight in the morning, & which I should have acknowledged & thanked her for first, it was so well shaped & pretty, that I got generally complimented, & it thus did honor to the 4th. Speculations are various as to where it came from. I answer invariably from a young Lady & the conclusion is general that she must reside near Boonville, so let it rest.

Well after Dinner we got some shore privileges, & soon found that there was a large <u>picnic</u> principally Ladies & children in the Fair grounds alongside by permission of Colonel Schaefer who is now chief in command at

---

1. James begins this letter on July 6, 1861. However, he gets interrupted repeatedly, so he makes additions to the letter over the next several days. The letter ends on July 10, 1861.

Boonville. It had been got up impromptu prompted I suppose by the wish to see some of the inner camp life of the Soldiers and the entrenchments. I mentioned in one of my former letters that General Lyon's command was encamped within the fair grounds & a pretty spot it is for a Picnic.

The Officers by permission of Colonel White, proceeded to cultivate their acquaintance & invited them on board to look at our quarters & to have a dance. I should say en passant that on all our boats up to this time we have had a piano & plenty of music & singing, several of the American Boys of our Company especially being quite proficient musicians, & especially strong on Nigger Melodies, & even Patriotic & sentimental songs.

Well we had a good dance for a couple of hours, but it was like dancing in an oven, & although we ran up the river for a couple of miles to see if we couldnt raise a breeze it was of no use. So we let the Ladies go ashore again, & we proceeded up town to see how the citizens celebrated the 4th. After we came aboard as there was still no signs of moving, it occured to us that we might get up a ball. We got the Colonels permission for this also, & canvassed all our acquaintances & the city generally. We got many rebuffs from Secession Ladies, but finally got by nine oclock both a large & pretty collection, & had a very pleasant Ball indeed. The excitement of the occasion, the place, & it being impromptu, took away all stiffness, & all went happy as a marriage bell up to a late hour.

But our men had had too much Beer & Whisky, & towards two oclock, they got mad at losing their sleep, while they did not share in the pleasures of the Ball & got pretty much into a state of mutiny, so we closed it abruptly at two oclock — few if any of the citizens knowing the cause. I made some pleasant acquaintances that I may cultivate again if I get an opportunity (I am invited). Among the rest a pretty Brunette Miss Ludovick & a Miss Miller each with sisters & a large circle of acquaintance.

Next morning at 4 oclock we ought to have started, but we did not turn out until six though the boat has had steam up for two days. We then had all our companies drawn up & gave them a sharp lecture on the question of

Mutiny – forgave all the past but the slightest offence for the future is to be visited with the most condign punishment.

We then started & at Ten oclock got to Brunswick. They had been expecting us for some time, & all the leading Secessionists with their companies (2) had left, so we had a good reception. Crowds of Ladies & Boquets again, but they had given Jackson's Army Boquets <u>as they passed</u> so we were not so much elated. However we had been presented with a large flag at Boonville, & as there had been none flying here since January last, & it would be a test of their peaceful feelings at the request of <u>the Union</u> Men & Ladies, we raised a tall pole & sent our flag 34 feet long to the breeze, with all military honors, & to the great joy of the population present, who assissted vigorously on the occasion. After stirring speeches from Cols Stiefel & White, breathing peace & the Olive Branch & forgiveness for past offences if they wished it but threatnings & Death to all future violations of the laws or insults to the flag, we again left. We made several calls as we came along & speeches of the same tenor <u>were delivered</u> during the evening & today. We tie up at a Wood Yard at night & so our progress is slow but interesting.

The A. *McDowell* came after us & overtook us. She is small & light draught & as the river is falling & the *Louisiana* is a large boat, it was judged better to change us, for fear of accidents, it wouldn't do to get stuck on a bar so now we are crowded on the A. *McDowell*. You must excuse this writing as she shakes so when running it is impossible not to have the shakes in such company.

I am in robust health but in changing boats this morning while carrying a heavy case, I stepd on a grease spot & had a bad fall. I was carried aboard the supposition being I must have broken a leg or a rib but thank heaven I was only stunned & am now pretty lame, but suffering a rapid recovery. Lame or not, whenever our company goes ashore on duty, I've been along, though I've not done any other duty.

I hope to hear from you soon. I am anxious indeed to get a good account of you all & as to how the 4th passed in the city, though we hope to see that first from the papers as soon as we get somewhere.

All the papers up here were secession & of course their publication is stop'd so news is scarce & we have to await the slow progress of the mail & the St. Louis papers of the 5th.

Brunswick where we raised the Flag is the residence of General Price, & he has taken two companies to the S.West with him. Five miles below, his son a boy of 17 I believe was on horseback & we at the time running very near shore, caused great excitement on board by several insulting demonstrations, & <u>hooraying</u> for Jeff Davis. We learnt afterwards in town who he was, & how badly he was skeered when the Pilot ran the Boat in shore for amusement. He galloped for home at his Horses best pace (Good Joke on him) & gave out that we were landing in pursuit. He was not at home today!

Adieu Mon Cher Ami! Duty calls.

July 7th 1861

We lay overnight at Hills landing some 20 miles above Brunswick, having called & speechified at a pleasant little place called <u>Miami</u> & just when starting an express came to us that the flag we had so much trouble in raising was torn down at nine oclock last night. The "*January*" has gone on slowly to Waverly, while we at once turned around & are now on a downward course for Brunswick again. Our boat carries the right wing of the Regiment so all these little expeditions fall to our share.

We will be there in an hour & preparations rather hurried is the order of the day so I must again bid you Adieu. We do not apprehend any fighting but there may be & so <u>may God defend</u> the right.

I do not know when the mail may go, & after this little escapade I may give you a little postscript yet.

With Love to all

I am my Dearest Girl

Yours affectionately

James E. Love

July 9th 1861

My Dear Molly

The Battle of Brunswick proved a very bloodless affair as the Union men together with the Mayor (a Secessionist) & the Police stood guard over it all night & raised it just as we came in sight. Colonel White went uptown had them salute it & then talked to them & had an influential delegation of the citizens headed by the mayor come on the boat & sign an agreement to defend it, & see that it flys to the breeze, as we will hold the lives & property of all the inhabitants responsible for its safety.

We then ran up as fast as we could to Waverly, & there found the "*January*" in a state of commotion & expecting an attack every hour.

This was at once dissipated by our presence. The secessionists at once ran away, & we could find nobody to attack. It is by far the worst place we have been yet & in fact is the worst in <u>Missouri</u> in proportion to population there being only ten Union men in the town. I should have mentioned that 150 Farmers anxious to enroll as home guards – residing in the adjoining county – Union men & true had walked down to Boonville over 80 miles in order to meet us & get arms & protection, leaving an equal number behind with all the rifles they could raise to protect their property <u>wives & children</u>. These men of course we welcomed & brought upon the "*January*". They disembarked them at Waverly on their arrival & sent 250 men to convoy them home as a guard of honor, through a secession county (so closely are the lines drawn here it is county against county man against man) to their headquarters 15 miles from here. So we had to lay over next day the 8th until their return in the evening when they brought a secession flag & some other small trophies & numerous sore feet. We in the meantime trying our mission of conciliation on all but open enemies with arms & flags in their hands or possession with poor success however.

We had numerous hunts by night & day for Cannons sunk in the river, for flags hid in the brush. We found a splendid large one & for powder we found the Magazine, but the powder had been removed two days before into the woods & we could not stay to prosecute further search at present but our Captain is in communication with several of the Union men left & if any of them can find its whereabouts they will ride over (35 miles) to let us know & we can go down for it, or take it as we go back.

We started for Lexington this morning at 4 o.clock & arrived at nine o.c. looking anxiously at every bluff & behind every tree for the valiant secesh, but they were found wanting & instead we found poor Union men & women who had walked miles down the river to meet, & who realizing that the reign of terror was over, were quite delirious with joy, & jumped (Ladies too) & danced & laughed & cryed with joy & so on up the banks until we reached the large & pretty city of Lexington. We saw several Flags hoisted as we neared the Levee & people crowding down the long steep hill (¼ of mile nearly) to give vent to one long hooray.

Lexington stands on a high bluff is the 3d city in size in Missouri. If fortified in the hands of good Troops would be nearly impregnable thence the importance of the situation.

Jackson got over 1000 men from this vicinity & got his Cannons Shot & Shell cast here & more aid & comfort, than in any other wealthy part of the state. But we found the Union men triumphant not through their own strength, but through the effect of our & the "Lyons" approach (<u>Aint we great warriors</u>).

We found four companies of Mounted "Home Guard" from the adjoining county of Johnson. The roughest <u>Hoosiers</u> youve ever seen <u>back woodsmen</u> each with the old rifle awaiting us for orders & advice, aid comfort & ammunition. We gave them plenty of all & a good dinner & the long train of dilapidated men & Horses with Wagons innumerable & some brave women with rifles too went on their way rejoicing, with some fine flags from the Ladies of Lexington, & one from General Lyon. They said they did not know day or night for months when their hour might come, & the sight of a friends face was worth more to them than all the wealth of the World. They had nearly despaired of the government giving them the assistance they required in this their great extremity. Indian varmints they didn't mind but that their fellow citizens should turn thus against them & the Old Flag of Washington while Foreigners had to step in to protect them, was beyond the reach of their philosophy.

We landed at once on our arrival & on the double quick step, although we apprehended no trouble. We had a Dress Parade on the Levee & then started up the whole regiment to see the town & be seen.

We had not reached the brow of the hill ere we saw a lady waving a large secession Flag & this for over 10 minutes before we could believe our eyes. Then our mounted officers started over to take, across some vacant ground half a square off our line of march. (We halted in battle array.) A crowd followed & surrounded our officers. The womens husband rushed out & pointed a double barrel'd rifle at the first, & for a moment there was every prospect of a row but our leading officer stood firm drew his revolver & grasped the flag. Our friend with the Rifle drop'd it, or he was a dead man in one second & so instead of a leaden warfare we had only a womens tongue – sharper than a two edged sword – to contend with. Our Colonel is not a gentleman it seems &c. Well we brought the trophy Home, & the belligerent Rifleman prisoner, & proceeded on our march through town, which finally proved a triumphant one, as the upper end of town was decorated with Flags & Ladies in bright colors. It was there too we came unexpectedly on our mounted country friends camp. We then returned after a detour, & got safe on board – directly after however two or three boys from our company were assaulted by a madman secessionist, whom they once disarmed of two five shooters one in his hand & one in a belt sheath & also a twelve inch bowie knife & marched him aboard. You should have seen the rush when the cry Company "D" to the rescue was raised it was no military cry & of course we had no right to take our arms which were stacked, so we fairly flew ashore with only our finger Nails.

Then we had him tried, & a saucy customer he is & glories in his treason. It proved that he & others only yesterday had attacked 5 of our Home Guard friends who were in town making purchases, & took their Horses Arms & money. They had afterward went to their camp outside town & tried to chop up their Cannon Wagon, & tear their flag. They could have shot them all down, but only disarmed them & then came in to town & had their Horses &c returned by some of the quiet citizens, who had an eye to our presence today.

Could you ask a better proof of their being worthy, & peaceful American Citizens than this. They would not commence the war, until sworn in by our Colonel, for U.S. Service.

So we've got a good prisoner you see. We are after many others. Our company (a part of it) has just returned after taking possession of the Iron Works & tracing from it hidden & sunken cannons, balls, grapeshot &c &c &c. When I sat down to write this the remainder of which I am one were under orders for another expedition after 3 wagon Loads of powder of which I got information, but were not started yet as I am still writing. Our Union friends, are scouting for further information, & as soon as they return we start be it night or Day.

Mrs. McCausland, who waved the Secession Flag is <u>quite a Lady</u> it seems & the right sort of a little woman besides being pretty. She is brave recklessly so, it seems but she has been on board with her sister & escorts for over two hours, trying with a smiling countenance & all a Womans Wiles to have her husband released. Her line of defense is rather untenable however.

June[2] 10th 1861

My Dear Molly

Information came in so plentiful & munitions of war left hid by the rebels are in such abundance that all our companies were busy digging & searching houses & carrying home the contraband up till after dark. We have already seized Two tons of Powder & other supplies by the Wagon Load. We expect to be so engaged for several days. It is not always a pleasant duty. If people are polite & assist it makes you feel ashamed almost. If on the contrary, they & their friends gather around in a mole with revolvers peeping out of side pockets & in number 10 to your one, it is still unpleasant to think that you may have in Self defense to charge on, or shoot into a

---

2. James incorrectly wrote June rather than July.

crowd of American Citizens, amongst which at any moment there is sure to be large numbers of friends & good Union men.

Such is life in the Army. At ½ past 9 last night our whole Company went on Patrol or picket duty up through the town & suburbs in squads of three's & four's, & so we remained up to near 4 o.clock

It was a fine cool night & the duties proved light & pleasant but working night & day is rather wearisome, except to <u>dance music</u>. The night passed quickly however having an active enemy to watch. All the boys were on the alert in hopes of more valuable plunder tomorrow! What pleases the boys most is finding these Secession Flags. But I find that events crowd upon us so, that lately I have to skip three fourths of the incidents & so condense the remainder as to render them comparatively uninteresting. I have just been taking testimony against our prisoner so as to let the witnesses go home. The exercise I've had has made me right smart again.

I hope you are as well & all the folks – Sally & William included & now with Love to all I must again abruptly close as we are ordered on an expedition to the country for a day or two.

I expect you are tired long since reading this scrawl

I am

My Dearest Girl

Yours Sincerely

James E. Love

Lexington
Steamer A. *McDowell*
July 14th 1861
My Dear Molly

I find this opportunity by the D.A. *January*. Ive sent you two or three long letters since I saw you but the strange reports that we are receiving & the knowledge that both mail & telegraph are tampered with by the Enemy between here & you makes me uneasy & I fear that you may not receive them.

Time is scant now as the D.A.J. goes off at five minutes notice.

I hope you & all are well & that all goes well in St. Louis. We understand it is so, & that troops are pouring in in abundance so as to stop these bridge burning vandals pretty soon.

I am well & in good spirits – hard marching & weariness succeed each other in regular order & hunting powder & watching the returned rebels from Jackson in the S.West our daily occupation & excitements. We are closely penned up, cannot carry books or reading matter with us, cannot buy any sterling literature on our way not even a newspaper later than the 4th of July.

So our minds are becoming so stagnant as to be scarcely equal to the effort of composition.

I wish I could Daguerreotype our daily life for you – time would not permit now if I could. Had I known yesterday of this opportunity – it was a fine cool day & we were resting – I might have. Our provisions have run out. That's what's the Matter! We've been expecting supplies & they didn't come. Writing letters with a crowd of 400 <u>noisy</u> men as it were packed in one room with you is not the best stimulant to composition & I find that most all I wished to say flies from my distracted head in this Babel. Were we in camp it would be different!

We sleep on our arms every night as the rebels are active all around & might attack us if they have weapons at any time. They have been very vainglorious & confident lately on the strength of news from the S.West, too extravagant & lying to repeat, but in which there might be grains enough of truth to make us feel serious. I fear we wont have any fight here however. If we do why I hope "we trust in Providence & keep our powder dry." I wouldn't like to say so much for all my Dutch friends. I can bear them (it has come to that) better than most folks but the fact is they do not improve on closer acquaintance. From what I've said you will see that we are perishing for lack of <u>News</u>, <u>News</u>, <u>News</u>. An old paper or a letter is a godsend we haven't had since the 4th – scarcely a telegram, as the lines are cut more than half time. If you or Alex would bless me with either or both & address to <u>me</u>, <u>care</u> Col. White 5 Regt. U.S.R.C. <u>Booneville or Elsewhere</u> I would get it sooner or later by boat.

　　With Love to all

　　I am my Dearest girl

　　Sincerely Yours

　　James E. Love

　　A thousand kisses & sweet thoughts.

　　J.E.L.

James's experience of life on steamer transports was probably similar to this image of Northern soldiers on the James River. "Home on Furlough" - Aboard the Army Transport." From Robert S. Lanier, ed., *The Photographic History of the Civil War in Ten Volumes*, Vol. 8 (New York: The Review of Reviews, 1911).

Lexington
Steamer A. *McDowell*
July 14th 1861[1]
My Dear Molly

I have been to Church this morning, (after writing you that <u>Pencil Scrape</u> before 6 A.M.) and I feel much better for it. It is such a great change from the vacuum & ennui of our boat life, or the weariness of our marches that it fell like oil on the troubled waters, or like dew on the grass. It was Communion Sunday too in an Old School Presbyterian Church & I never felt more like joining in.

Was it the contrast & relief from my card playing & Swearing Dutch friends only. I am afraid so as I know I am very impressible & like the Chameleon too often take my hue from surrounding circumstances & colors in some measure! Very wrong aint it? but so it is. How could a lazy man do otherwise than float with current? But I don't want to enter metaphysics. Well what have I been doing since I came from Church? Why I've been reading *Harpers Monthly*! Dont mention a chapter in the Bible! Smoking & dozing & now the Colonel having come home has Stopd these dutch boors from Card playing & as most of them have gone to sleep there is some quiet. So appropo a conversation, in which I do all the talking as usual with Ma Cher Ami. I have had no letter since I returned to duty! I believe you've written to me but that only makes me feel worse! Oh Dear! What <u>shall</u> I do? What do you think of *Harper* for July. I invested that much yesterday & consider myself fully repaid already. <u>Porte Crayon</u> is rich as usual in description & incident. Love's Messengers are sweet. Margeret Fuller Ossoli's story is so pitiful. Why is it that genius is always so unfortunate, & that the mere clods should progress & grow rich in this worlds goods?

All the other stories are well brought out! Thackeray in Phillip is in his best vein, but enough of *Harper*.

---

1. July 14 and 15 were sent as one letter.

July 15th

At this point I came to a sudden halt. One company that had been sent to work after dinner on the breast works came home in open mutiny. It rained a little & it was Sunday so they perjured themselves into a Mutiny. They had been playing cards all morning recollect so their religious scruples could not be very strong & as the remnants of Jacksons Army are coming back here a dozen at a time, poor, needy & desperate, we do not know what devilment they may commit at any moment, & Sunday & Monday require constant work & preparation.

Col White gave them a sharp lecture, disgraced them a little & got them to work again but Babel had broke loose again & I could no more.

I wished to tell what we were doing but there is <u>so much</u>, & so much plotting & counter plotting amongst ourselves too, that I find it totally impossible.

As a matter of course the Ladies are at the bottom of it & your humble servant is as deep in the mire as anybody else. Said Ladies at present being friends or wives of prisoners. These Dutch & the Americans & Irish in our regiment have several times come to blows or nearly so, as to what sort of treatment they should receive. Our Dutch Compatriots Officers & all with few exceptions, <u>wish to, & do when they can</u>, treat them as dogs or the vilest of humanity might be or is treated, while the others wish to treat them as <u>Ladies</u> or as their conduct deserves. So we quarrel & plot, & each day supplies unlooked for incidents.

We went in the country tother day & called at several Union houses & had a good dinner at one for 280 men served up in good style & at two hours notice. The Old Lady Mrs. White, as stout as a Dutch Beer Tub is the very essence of old Virginia, with that old fashioned kind of hospitality that could never make you comfortable enough but that considers that the very essence of comfort lies in stuffing you with good eating & drinking. At others we had refreshments – strong & weak – while at the Secessionists we had closed doors & sour looks. Nevertheless that day we brought home 4 Wagon Loads (ox teams) powder besides Shot, Shell, Haversacks, Cartridge

boxes, Cannon one or two & Artillery Carriages, also three Contraband darkies followed us which we have since delivered to the acting mayor of the
City (The Mayor has seceded).

These Darkies were shot by their master after we left because they
informed us where the Powder &c was secreted. Our Doctor took over sixty
pickles of shot out of the back of one – such is the result of a violent temper,
when disappointed.

Our Senior Captain – Captain Tannahill has his wife along & she pre-
sides in our boat. She was raised within Fortress Monroe in Virginia, &
seems quite at home. She is young not pretty, & more of a girlish hoyden
than a Lady – the consequence of camp life, a poor education & a bad head
piece – 10 P.M.

Got disturbed just here again – our company is on guard – but notwithstanding all hands not on Sentry duty had to go up hill & go to work on the
breastworks.

We have done so up to this time & now all hands 600 lay or stand by their
arms expecting an immediate attack. By our vigilance we expect to frighten
them off but they have gathered to near 1000 with pistols shot guns & bowie
knives & are desperate. All our plans are laid & though our fighting maybe
uphill work, we hope to make theirs more so.

I shall think of thee dearest in the hottest of it (if it comes) & it will nerve
my arm tenfold. Good bye. God bless us all

I am in haste
Yours ever
Sincerely
James E. Love
A thousand kisses & pleasant dreams to both of us –
J.E.L.

1 o clock in the morning. All quiet yet.
Goodnight Love
J.E.L.

Lexington – "Camp Fremont"
Steamer A. *McDowell*
July 20th 1861
My Dear Molly

Since last writing there have been no events of any note transpiring, half our Battalion is in camp at the Masonic College, where we have almost completed a fine fortification or breast works such as proved of so much service in the Crimea. Our companies alternate two hours each – each day – so that we have thus about 100 men employed 14 to 16 hours each day for over ten days, the balance of the time being actively employed foraging, standing guard, picket duty, patrol duty & in parading around under arms, overhauling steamboats & wagons, not to speak of Farm houses, private houses, stores & Foundries, so we are constantly employed, with but short sleep. The health of the company & Regiment has however been improving since we went actively to work, as I do believe if we had loafed on this hot steamboat another fortnight we would have been all sick. I've never had better health & never had half as good an appetite in my life. I'm only in fear that I'll overeat Pork one of these days & turn Hog for life. All this hard work is necessary because we are in the heart of the enemies country, and as eternal vigilance is the price of liberty, so Col White thinks that eternal vigilance is the best means of striking terror & preventing our craven foes around from attacking. Three men out of four in this city & county, pray night & day I do believe for a good chance to assassinate even one of us & plan daily to murder us all! This we know!!

But they dare not! They fancy our numbers two or three times what they are & we have established such a good name, & try to do so daily, that they can not trump up an excuse! Save that of searching houses without Warrant! And the amount of Powder &c that find justifies us a thousand fold. Discipline with us is now very strict, but not more so than necessary. Soldiers are not all Gentlemen even when well raised. There are many many <u>thieves & hogs</u>.

The men here – those whom we know well to be secesh – pretend the strongest Union <u>sentiments</u> (on the lips) but 5 minutes conversation, not to say argument proves their falsity. Jeff Davis, Jackson & Co are all Saints & Heros, while Lyon, Scott[1] & Lincoln are simply <u>Constitution breakers</u> &c &c &c &c.

Many regard us with black looks & stand aloof. I might say most. For of the Union men, one half of them with an eye to future consequences if we should be called away are even yet afraid to recognise us in public, but their hopes rise as their numbers increase daily & when we have armed & drilled them a little more, they will be able to stand alone as by that time their enemies will be all disarmed & without powder. We enrolled 180 in the city first day, all Germans. Of the Americans we may enroll 100 & of the Irish an equal number. We enrolled 200 in the County since that. This is Lafayette County, contains splendid farms & rich land, plenty of niggers who would all <u>stampede</u> if we say "go". It has a large & rich population – enterprising – & raises large quantities of Hemp & Tobacco. The city is built on & over very good coal mines which crop out of a High Bluff all along the river side & is thus easy loading on Steamboats or flats. So much for the city where <u>"only Man is Vile"</u>. In the adjoining county of Johnson, we have organized over 1000 men & <u>secesh</u> is virtually dead so in two or three adjoining counties, while across the River in Ray & Carroll counties it is just the same, though supposed to be all secesh. While the Rich Men of Lexington & Lafayette with Jackson's Army ruled the day, they now all come in daily to drill as Home Guard & arm & fight to save the Union & if we had arms enough so would it be with thousands, could we only say come one come all.

The "*January*" is now in Herman or St. Louis & we expect her to bring us a load of Stores & Guns.

We have just detained the "<u>*Emma*</u>" bound down stream on which we intend to send some Sick & some mutinous men & prisoners.

The Secessionists here have hit on the most ingenious plan of aggravation I've heard of yet, not being brave enough to fight their own battles or wishing to profess Union sentiments to us. They have set nearly all the Ladies to insulting & annoying us. Our good character galls them. They had

---

1. General Winfield Scott.

painted us in such black colors that even moderate good behavior shines by contrast & the fears of the ignorant fast wear off. This will never do say they & so if they could only get us to insult or shoot a few ladies or children in a crowd, they think they could thus manufacture plenty of fresh Sympathy for the poor persecuted &c &c.

This is why our discipline is so rigorous. Some men cant stand insult even from a Lady & our German Boors would wish nothing better than to war with women & children, & babes in the cradle "<u>so they say</u>" & its so, for we can scarce restrain them as it is & when Ladies, young Ladies, well dressed & of the F.F.Vs[2] step so far from their place as to speak to us, taunt us, sing Dixie at us in the street in open daylight & after night, as they promenade in sixes & seven's along the streets, it is too bad. It is such a desecration of the womanly delicacy of the sex & it is hard for some men to bear too. I don't say they aint boors because I think they are & the Ladies think so too, or I'm much mistaken if they would be prompted by their male friends to treat them so. You see I make a distinction. Well the Irish & Americans simply regard it as a good joke or rather treat it as such, & sometimes speak back, sing Dixie too, & so we've got acquainted with some nice Young Ladies without introduction. This is not what the Ladies expected though some of them seem quite pleased, but it is a natural consequence of their indiscretions & intended insults. Why if women of no character conducted themselves so for one hour, they would have a safe berth in the Calaboose & serve them right too.

I have made some friends & some of them think I could & wish me to get up an Irish American company for the war. There are many good men both from North & South & at present thrown out of business, who would go in, but I guess I wont commit myself in any way until I've seen you & old St. Louis again. There I wish to get a Washington commission. I can get it, but I wont until I see you. I happened to find Mr. McPheeters was on board the "*Emilie*", & I sent a note by him though I was called away before I could deliver it. Mails are among the things that were & writing is a sorry task.

---

2. First Families of Virginia.

I expect to hear from you by the *January*. When did you hear from <u>Sally</u>. Give my Love to her & all. I hope to hear that you are all well. I saw a late paper for a few minutes & I can do without for another week now.

This by the *Emma*. Paper is so scant so I cross it & now with all the best wishes of my heart for my Dear Dear Girl. I am counting the days to see her. There is only about three weeks now, but it seems an age to look forward.

I am, with only one sweet kiss & Good night

Sincerely Yours

James E. Love

"Camp Fremont"
Lexington
July 23d 1861
My Dear Molly

I recd your lost Epistle of the 7th only yesterday. It had lain at Boonville in the meantime & I suppose all since that has been lost, as our Sergeant Major made a clean sweep of all he could find at all the P.O's as he came along. I suppose mine get lost in the same way, but I must only keep on writing hoping some may get through. I was not aware on the 4th how much I was indebted to you for that Havelock. I thought it came not only quick but very prompt & here I find it had been <u>such a time</u> on the way & that I might have had it along hours before I left. What can I say to thank you? Since I wrote the other sheet, we have been scouting for <u>secesh</u>. Didn't find any! Though we heard of their threats & could see their caucus's at street corners that they would drive us away within <u>two days</u>! Their courage rises as our reinforcements delay! But thank God they have come at last & <u>brought your letter</u>! On Saturday we were to work & in the Evening a Review which brought out the Ladies in Force. Sunday was one of the wettest days I remember of it rained so heavy & so constantly for 36 hours as to raise the river here over 3 feet.

We had made arrangements to see some of the Ladies to Church, but <u>there was no service</u>. Yesterday afternoon our reinforcements came up & also three others boats, which kept us in a fever of excitement all day & especially because of the letters papers &c they brought. Work was at an end! No discipline could hold the famished officers or men. By the way I got 3 or 4 papers myself one as late as the 12th I judge from Alex & one of the 16th & 19th from a friend on board. The boats had a good deal of fun by <u>the way</u>.

When at Jefferson, they heard of Harris's runaway rebels coming to the River Bank & immediately landed some companies to intercept them from crossing. They had a shot at them several times, but nobody hurt. They took some prisoners, who had evidently thrown away their arms, & so having no proof, discharged them. Some they found quietly working in the fields who had evidently been in the muss ten minutes before, but what could they do? So they returned to the river & for 60 miles sunk or destroyed every skiff & Flatboat &c &c that they could see, & captured all the Ferry boats, that had ferried any of them over. So their retreat is cut off in this way. 800 men laid over for three days at Waverly to catch these boats, but when they arrived at nine o'clock of a dark night (Saturday) & saw the mortars, they all run away & couldn't catch them either, as they were all on horseback at Arrowrock. They also saw a crowd, but when they landed & surrounded the town out of the hundreds they seen half an hour before they couldn't find three. Everybody was at his work so busily, & nobody saw a Soldier until tapp'd on the shoulder.

Such is civil war, in its best phase, but if these folks wont learn a lesson, it will be impossible to keep our men from shooting them "innocent as they look" at their work

It is too easily done. Shoot a few soldiers or Union men from behind a tree or a fence, gallop home, turn your horse loose in the woods, throw your rifle in the fence corner, & get lost in tall corn, with a hoe in your hand &c &c.

Last night we went ten drinking, & then visiting the Ladies. We had plenty of music & singing & a dance, just as if there was no war, or with even more vim – stolen pleasures – all impromptu and talking all the time of our friends next door or over the way, whom we would take great pleasure in shooting or who had offered 50$ for a chance to shoot at any one of us if we went 10 miles in the country.

Tonight we go serenading, so as not to lose this fine moonlight. Several Ladies are on hand & we have a good band of minstrels in our company, but possibly we will make it more in the form of a surprise party, staying perhaps an hour at each house & doing the singing in doors with the aid of any pianos we can impress.

This morning we have just captured one of Claib Jackson's aid de Camp's.

I do hope they'll hang him (if he was in any of the fights), as I believe a little severity just now would save hundreds of useful lives hereafter, not one of them regards an oath. I find by letters received here that I have been wounded & poisoned, dead & buried (in St. Louis). I dont believe a word of it! Do you?

I dont expect to be in St. Louis until our time is out if even then? Thanks for all the news you send me! Dont try to tell me all! I hope to hear as much as I ought to sometime viva voce – but send me three lines & half as often as you can & by mail now. The cars run again on the Pacific to above Jefferson & a coach brings them here now in 3 days. I can only say that I pine for them & receive them all with rapturous kisses. Didnt I dream last night too? I should say so!!! try it next mail!! Love to all. I hope sometime to be able to get enough quietness to write you a letter that will be readable because I am ashamed of the incoherency & lack of thought displayed in these, nothing but a lot of disjointed incidents strung together & I expect lacking interest often to any but myself.

Let me have all your prayers & I hope I'm safe for even our short experience in Lexington makes all confess that womens wishes or actions control a mans destiny for weal or woe just now in the West – very much both in time & eternity.

I feel too as any good Catholic would that I require & need an intercessor "A la Sancta Maria" & will give all sincere adoration in return.

Yours Sincerely

James E. Love

Lexington

A. *McDowell*

July 25th 1861

My Dear Molly

I write at once fearing you may have some more exaggerated reports, as one of our boats has at last been in action, but I will commence from where I left off last, merely premising that <u>I am all safe</u> – though there is one killed, two dying & 10 or 12 more or less wounded. <u>It is too bad</u>! but it might be worse.

Well when I wrote last we were on guard, but even so when we learned that there were expeditions on foot, we were in such a state of excited expectancy that scarce any one lay down at the usual hour 9 o.c. But before this in the evening the *White Cloud* with 200 men had started up the river for Liberty or Kansas City for information & provisions. Thus leaving us with only 500 men here but relying on the terror of our name & knowing that there was gathered at least 800 secesh about 8 miles off! whose Colonel (Alf. Jones) & one of whose Captains (Mountjoy) had come <u>home</u> lately at night to their wives. We determined at dead of night to go & catch them, just before night fall.

A nigger brought news that one of "Claibs" aid de camp's had come in town in disguise & we sent 20 men of our company D, surrounded the house & brought him along, before his friends in the city knew of his presence. This caused some commotion, but nothing like the consternation visible yesterday, after these later arrests. So as we wouldn't go to sleep, our Capt. called us in line at Ten O'clock, & we <u>started on our night</u> march 4 miles in deep silence, & at places sneaking along the fences, trailing arms, in order to prevent their glancing in the moonlight. When we arrived near we divided the company in 4 Sections. I took the first & passed or crawled down the road past the house it stood back 20 or 30 yards & entered a large field or Kitchen Garden planted all my men along under cover of some scrubby fruit trees on the north side, & then waited. Two other sections passed through some tall corn, one to the rear or East side while one spread along the south behind the corn field fence. While this was done the Capt. waited & then advanced down the main road & entered at the front gate, & immediately surrounded the house guarding every door or window. Then we all closed in expecting to find 50 or 100 men on guard, while their Colonel slept, but we found none & all remained quiet but the Niggers, who expected us.

We searched all their huts, also the stables & out houses without noise & then we thundered at the front door. We did not burst it in, & so it was over half an hour ere the crying & screaming inmates admitted us & near an hour more ere our searches found the Colonel, all alone, with his fat sides squeezed <u>flat</u> in a clothes press, locked inside, among some Ladies dresses. We finally brought him along, it being now 3 o.c. We also brought his son in Law, an officer of some kind a stupid fellow, Jones himself being a courageous & really dangerous fighting man. We then made a rapid detour of two miles, & captured in the same way Capt. Mountjoy, only he came like a man to the window & dressed in five minutes & delivered himself up. We remained over half an hour after trying to comfort his screaming wife & then got to the boat at daybreak – safely. All day (the 24th) the city & country were in commotion, our companies patrolling around occasionally, we sleeping all the forenoon. In the evening dress parade in town, when at six oclock we heard something resembling cannonading. We scampered for the boat fearing a rescue of our prisoners, but could there hear nothing, so we went on extra guard all night, hearing distant rumbling occasionally, pronounced by the cannoniers, with practiced ears, a howitzer until 3 o.c. a.m. when a sudden call to arms revealed a boat rounding the bend. We thought an enemy sure & at full speed, but she proved our consort the *White Cloud*, come for more assistance. She had been attacked near Liberty at Blue Mills south side river by about 150 men who <u>lay</u> down on the top of a high bluff & fired into her several volleys & then before she could land ran like <u>deer</u>. In the meantime her howitzer fired 8 or 10 shots into or near where they were. They found some blood afterwards. They landed charged up the bluff took 4 prisoners & <u>fired</u> the houses (only 4 or 5) after carrying all the groceries in a store aboard the boat & then proceeded on their way two miles more when they were fired on from the North side, out of the woods & again with deadly effect to our men & the boat Carpenter. So they sent some shell on that side Jordan too & landing could find nobody. They continued on up, smashing & sinking all the flats, skiffs, ferry boats they could see from the time they left us until they returned, arriving at a Union wood yard on an Island they wooded up & were informed that at Liberty there was 800 men & 3 cannon waiting for them, part of these 800 however were among those who first attacked them & they had immediately run back to Liberty.

So it being 12 oclock by this time Col Stiefel concluded to turn back & as I stated at first arrived at Lexington at 3 oclock returning 50 miles in 3 hours, without accident.

Yesterday they stopped at Sibley & captured a Secession Flag & 10 kegs & some barrels of powder, rifles &c, & it was from here that they sent an express to Liberty, apprising the Secessionists of our coming & so the result I've stated. Well this fighting took place between 6 & 11 oclock at night the boat being a good mark for them while our men could only fire by guess, towards where they saw a flash & so ended our first battle. Col. Stiefel allowed himself to be surprised or we might have a better report to make & this after all our vigilance so far. We do not know whether any of the Rebels were killed, but we suppose there was. Mr. Stotman, a quiet young German was killed, Comp. A. The Carpenter & another American Comp. A are supposed to be dying.

I am in haste my Dear Molly, in good health & spirits & hope to give a good account of myself for some time yet.

Yours Sincerely

James E. Love

When shall I hear from you. I got Alex's letter within 3 days by mail! Love to all. Kindest Love to yourself.

Love

Lexington
July 27th 1861
My Dear Molly

Since I wrote last we have pursued the even tenor of our way, now cheered by good news, now despondent from bad. I might write of moonlight nights & starry skies but it seems as if all the poetry that was <u>ever in</u> my matter of fact brains has all seceded under the pressure of petty duties & constant risks. After several cool breezy days, we are today again scorching under an old fashioned July Sun.

The Comet has come & gone & yet fate & the times, are more portentous of war than ever, <u>all the World over</u>, & even Old Ireland, seems still bent upon seceding from her compulsory <u>Union</u> with England.

Meantime the mails still run in this much disturbed portion of Missouri, & I was much rejoiced yesterday on receiving your welcome letter of the 20th & also <u>John Adams</u> of the 23d. His contained good news from New York & Virginia, & I forgave the rest, though very unsatisfactory. I have written him a long letter in answer, & explained our situation more fully to him than I've done yet. Perhaps you may hear its contents. I wish you would, but if not, its news will keep until my return if that should be within any reasonable time & I expect to see you shortly after the 11th of August! & must for a few days anyhow! I look forward with impatience to the time, but time & space can not be annihilated except in Dreams & I dreamt long & pleasantly of you last night. What it may portend in an Irish point of view I leave for you to say, for I dont know, & knowing not my faith is small & weak.

It was very much mixed & involved & would require much more space to tell than I have left but the main facts were these! We had got Married!!! quietly & privately, all by ourselves! We had left a large company of Folks composed of your & my St. Louis friends, & also of my friends here & in this regiment! Gone out for half an hour in broad daylight, as if for a walk & come in again, sat down in a place which seemed alternately your parlor & this boat cabin, as if nothing had happened, while I kept inventing excuses to talk with you in a corner where you sat demurely near a bright fire or stove & at the same time I did not neglect any of the large company around in order not to attract attention to our past absence or present conduct. Among other things I went for a bucket of cannel coals & mended the fire, & fingered the coal & knelt on one knee over the bucket to talk to you! It seemed to me I was playing host to the company and I was in dreadful trouble as to how I was to break all the news to them, which I supposed I must needs to before nightfall, as we contemplated starting somewhere on the night train or boat! I believe to see the President & perhaps instruct him how to carry on the war, while you gave his wife lessons in deportment &c &c &c &c. Now what does it all mean? I being of little faith doubt very much if it means anything, but disturbed & often broken rest, a warm night & a hearty supper? But great is the power of curiosity & ancient superstition, over even the infallible J.E.L. & now pray what does it mean?

I spent all night over it, & it would take weeks to tell the scenes passed through. So I put this small part on paper ere I forget all.

I have just learned that the mail both coming here & going down was robbed day before yesterday, & if so some of my longest & most interesting letters are lost, two to you, one to Alex one to Eliza.

What is the use of writing under such circumstances

29th

I close this in haste. I had a pleasant day on Sunday amongst my friends here all day. Took two young Ladies to church. Last night stood to arms all night with breastworks formed of chairs, flour sacks & mattresses all around the boat expecting momentarily an attack from a large force, that was signalizing with Rockets &c in our neighborhood. This morning we start for a trip to hunt them up if possible, & to aid our Johnson Co. friends, who are threatened.

We expect a pleasant trip, perhaps some hard marching. Will write on return.

I am My Dearest Girl

Yours Sincerely

James E. Love

Lexington

August 3d 1861

My Dear Molly

I promised when I returned from our expedition to write again, but time has not permitted so far. We all got back however <u>safe</u> & <u>sound</u> but footsore, weary & dirty as sweeps.

We started on Monday afternoon expecting to make 16 miles before camping, but it proved so hot that when three miles out, we had to camp until sundown when we started again & made 7 more miles. Thermometer about 120 in the sun & no shade to be had. We all suffered dreadfully for water camped at 10 o.clock by a spring in the open prairie having in the meantime met a mounted company composed of the friends & neighbors of the men we were convoying.

This at once changed the character of our expedition, as they had scouted the whole country within a circuit of 80 miles, & had found several secession camps which they wished us to assist in breaking up. Some eight of their number were missing, about whom they were very anxious, as they had ascertained that the reports brought to us were all too true, & that there was five or six ambushes already planted for our friends destruction. Well we all started at 4 o.c. next morning in good spirits hoping to catch the enemy napping as now the tables were slightly turned. They did not expect us – the arrival of the Regulars as they call us was a surprise to them all. We got along quietly for over 6 miles to where the first ambush had been at Davis Creek, where a long bridge & a thick brush gave them an enormous advantage. We soon found however that they were not there. They had either left, or did not expect us so early our scouts & skirmishers had crossed the creek at half a dozen places above & below & hoped to surround them, but no the birds were flown.

We had not gone over a mile however & were just gaining the open prairie, when our advance guard sighted them. Our mounted friends immediately engaged them while we double quicked up hill, in time to see a pretty running skirmish, but too far off to join in. Whenever they got sight of us they galloped off at top of their speed, leaving one for dead (a Mr. Fleming) on the field. We got his arms but not his horse, & carried him home some half mile off, left him there, with two bad wounds in or about his chest. Now all was excitement. The principal camp being 4 miles ahead & our scouts reporting mounted men galloping in that direction from all points of the prairie & woods. We also heard that the 8 missing men were prisoners there so forward to the rescue was the cry.

On our way there we came suddenly on two or three squads & nearly surprised them at a Blacksmith shop but again they got away with one horse & one mule killed & two men wounded. This only whetted our appetite for what was to come, & with fresh vigor we pushed forward our two companies of 150 men being spread sometimes out in a line a mile long & again closed in to a solid square around our wagons, with our 40 or 50 Horsemen galloping every where back & forth, East, West, North & South. We at last found their whereabouts in a deep ravine on Tarboe Creek where a thick brush, several houses Orchards, Fences &c protected & hid them completely. There was again some sharp shooting on both sides, their guns however did not reach us, while our bullets at near half a mile distance whistled around their heads savagely, & rumor says we killed two more. Now again all our efforts were first directed toward surrounding them & in fifteen minutes more we would have done so. Our centre where was comp D, was in an open meadow with no protection, & only two hundred yards off them, laying down flat to fire, aim & load again then at a word rising running forward 20 yards or less, & again down flat in the grass. Comp K in a wheat field advancing under cover of the little ricks that were skattered all over it & our cavalry in the timber right & left crossing the creek.

At this point they ran again, but so quietly & under such close cover that we did not know it for perhaps ten minutes, when we at once made a rush surrounded the houses & got two prisoners with their arms & horses, all grimy with dust sweat & gunpowder, (as we also were). We found also that in their haste they had lost all their prisoners & seven of them now came in to us. The other they had put out as a target for us to shoot at in the woods

& on the road had ran the other way & we feared would be caught again. He had first taken refuge in one of the houses but when looking out at a window towards us, Capt. Tannahill saw him & fired at him breaking the window & the glass wounded one of the young Ladies of the house cutting her cheek slightly. This compliment skared him & he ran again three miles got home got another horse & came & met us some hours after.

We now searched the houses, the negroes, as usual giving us every assistance & information when their owners were not bye. We only found the Prisoners &c aforesaid & ten saddles besides several buckets of ice water & pans of Ice Milk prepared for & partly drank by secession lips. As we had had none for hours this we greedily drank at sight (fearing no poison). We meddled with nothing else, though the Ladies were very insulting & again & again cautioned us to let nothing stick to our fingers, suggesting that the plentiful supply of Crinoline to be seen in the closets would be useful to some of us when in the course of the day it would be our turn to run. Acting very bravely, one especially Miss Atkinson (whose cheek was wounded) talking & acting like a heroine, & when leaving with our prisoners she came towards them, & to one rather young & goodlooking, whom we suppose to be her sweetheart, she said, "Jemmy be firm let them do what they please, but never take the Oath, if you do I never want to see you again & to the other she said & you too Mr. Taylor but ere we had gone 100 yards, she could not help screaming & crying. When some of rear guard, not witnesses of the former scene asked her what was the matter, she said "You are taking "My friends"! "My friends"!! My dear friends!!!" & all this with such eloquent gestures & abandon, that it was too pitiful to look at, she evidently never expected to see them again? We could give her no hope, & most came away sorrowful, many with a tear in their eye, for the first time awakened to they full horrors of civil war.

But so evanescent are human emotions, that ere ten minutes were elapsed, we were all ten times more steeled & bent on exterminating or driving the Rebels from our soil, & so we ran, skirmishing occasionally until 4 o.c. in the afternoon, when arriving at a Union settlement, we could hear or see no more of them, & so we concluded to dine, but the inhabitants would not let us cook. We must rest in the shade & be waited on with water, whiskey, milk, peach brandy everything they had was ours, & within an hour every house produced such baskets & buckets of fricasseed chicken & ham, cornbread & biscuits, potatoes & bacon, butter & buttermilk churned for our use, that we felt ourselves, all kings, princes, Soldiers, American Citizens.

We had already ran & fought, if fighting it can be called, such a neck or nothing race as it was occasionally, over 18 miles, but there was still another camp in the woods, two miles off, that we wished to see before dark, & for this we started, but our scouts soon came in & reported them gone, & the camp broken up, so we marched two miles more to Hazlehill in Johnson Co. another Union settlement, to overawe which this Camp was formed. Here again we were in clover & enjoyed ourselves very well up to nine oclock. After a sound sleep, we next morning bade goodbye to our Johnson Co. & Hazlehill friends, & started on a forced march at 4 o.c. A.M. for Lexington which we reached after many stoppages & some alarm but no further adventures, at Eight oclock in the evening, as I said before footsore, weary & dirty.

Here we found them all anxiety both our Regimental friends & the citizens whether friends or foes, for Madame Rumor had magnified our exploits, & also the killed & wounded on both sides (we had none) our opponents only six, of which either 3 or 4 were killed, & she further affirmed that secesh would gather, & were gathering from far & wide to cut us off as we returned. So when after our forced march we reached town we found two more companies, coming to our assistance at their best pace, with Col White & Major Fischer at their head & what joyful reception we got, & what a relief to the secesh of Lexington who had already commenced fleeing from town with their household goods, expecting our friends here to shell & burn the town if we suffered.

The Union men had also been moving their families across the River. <u>We run the Ferry & tother side is Union</u>.

So all parties combined to give us a triumphal march to the boats, & immediately went to condole & attend to our crippled men in the wagons, whom they supposed wounded, & would not believe otherwise, even our repeated assurances of nobody hurt would not satisfy them, untill they saw their sore feet & we all limped aboard.

Our boat & us next night went up the river fifteen miles, to look after more flags, Secesh & powder. We had a hard night of it under arms, but found nothing save two prisoners. Got back safe last night.

Our boat looked rather queer, with breastworks formed of mattrasses strung around in the Pilot house & on the guards, & cord wood piled on the main deck for us to lay behind & shoot over but we did not need them.

My Oppossom Rug has proved a Godsend & I am in more robust health than ever with its aid. My feet will be all right by tomorrow & ready for another trip. We expect aid here directly & then we hope to run the gauntlet to St. Louis all safe.

You speak of Mr. McPheeters being tanned in yours of the 22d which I received when I returned on Wednesday night the 31st. Well we are all pretty much tanned, & this trip has not improved our color any, when in sight of the enemy we shifted our Havelocks in our pockets, as they would have made such good marks to shoot at, before this they had done good service.

I am glad to hear you received that old letter & hope the other missing ones may yet come to hand. A Soldiers letter if sent by the proper channel requires no stamp & I sent my <u>first so</u>, but now I send by mail, or by hand of friend, & so save delays.

Tell Alex not to scold Sally too much. I excused her or will do, after I've caught her some night, this fall as I hope too, & hear a long story from her & perhaps give as long a one in return.

I am glad to hear of Williams early return but has he not gone out to the Iron Mountain since. I saw something in the *Republican*[1] that looks much like it. I hope not. I cant see a word in your papers about our regiment, though there is letters from all the others. We feel neglected. I have just got the August *Harper* this morning. I've not cut it yet, but will when I close this

---

1. *St. Louis Daily Missouri Republican* newspaper.

tiresome yarn. I write so fast that I fear you will wish me to read it for you when I return, & so dose me with my own vanity & egotism never mind I haint said a word of myself yet. I'll tell you all that face to face, & then it wont raise up in judgment against, or I will refer you, as I did the Colonel to <u>Capt Hurd</u>, who eulogised me so <u>that I ran away</u>. I do wish I was alongside you. This letter has taken up but a short time, compared with what the subject would have claimed in conversation. I do wish to be <u>home too</u>, but we are quite in the dark. Know nothing as to all movements in the future even for half a day. <u>We</u> <u>cant leave</u> until government reinforces us strongly. <u>I also look</u> to the time when I can read again with you & you must not think that these letters require even an effort or exertion. I can sit & rest & refresh myself as I write, <u>as well as if I read or loaf</u>. I feel safe, shielded & protected by your prayers. I think I know why no presentiments of bullets ever crossed my mind. I dont think the secesh own one that can hurt me now, but goodbye –

God bless you, Give my love to all & believe me

Yours sincerely

James E. Love

While marching through Missouri, James and his company looked similar to these men from a New York regiment. "'Right Shoulder Shift' – Column of Fours – The Twenty-Second New York on the Road." From Robert S. Lanier, ed., *The Photographic History of the Civil War in Ten Volumes* (New York: The Review of Reviews, 1911).

Lexington

11 P.M. August 6th 1861

My Dear Molly

We start in an hour on a dangerous expedition, and although I believe I have a charmed life as far as secession bullets are concerned, yet should I be wounded I could not forgive myself if I did not write a line now.

Our secesh friends here are trying to enclose us in a net, so that when we wish to go down in a few days when our time is up & reinforcements have come in, we may get caught. We go tonight to catch them napping <u>if we can</u>, & so destroy the net, & the fishers who manage it. I know you wish us God Speed, & pray for us nightly, but even with a brilliant victory some few lives may & will be lost.

I hope to give a good account of myself as heretofore & refer to Capt Herd & my friends in Company D.

I leave what will have to do for a Will in my portmanteau.

And now my Dear, Dear Girl, I am with kindest Love to yourself & all.

Yours Sincerely

James E. Love

<u>A thousand kisses</u>

Letter from James in Lexington, Missouri, to Molly, August 6, 1861.

Lexington

August 9th 1861

My Dear Molly

I wrote you a short note on the sixth, just before starting on what was supposed to be a very dangerous expedition, it proved very much otherwise, but so much the better. We all feel better men for it. Many made their wills before they started. I for one had a few last words to say which I now suppress.

We had heard much of the Rebels, their entrenchments, & batteries. We went to see some last week but we could not come within half a mile of them, & saw none but pickets & stragglers whom we captured, & deserted camps, which in such state had no Interest for us. Then we went up the river but with the same success & only to find vacant secession farm houses & deserted farms. This we at first could scarcely account for but since that from the number of Union men they are driving out from down the river, we begin to understand. They have been threatening for a month past that we shall never go down the river, so now they were moving down to intercept us, & to fortify themselves on its banks.

In scouting around we found the whereabouts of four of these camps, & it was at once determined to attack the one most dangerous to us. We are too few in numbers to move around the country much, as it requires a large garrison here all the time. So at 12.0.clock at night or morning of the 7th 4 companies of <u>volunteers</u> started to march for Tarboe Creek where Joe Shelby had entrenched himself. We took with us one long six pounder, some shell & canister & about 20 mounted scouts who knew the country.

The boats at the same time got up steam & went down to the mouth of the Creek & landed one of our companies & a company of Home Guard to attack in the rear while we waited in front!! & the Howitzer on the boat threw shell a distance of ¾ of a mile, all to commence at about 5 o.c. in the morning. Three companies were still left in Camp Fremont to look after Lexington.

The boat & companies that went along executed their part of the programme in good time but unfortunately we who were expected to do most all the fighting were too late.

We marched slowly the weather hot & sultry as it has been for several days, for over 4 miles when all at once we stumbled on six mounted pickets. They must have been asleep & being a little way off the road our advance guard had passed them without observing them, & our main column was alongside, into which in their terror they dashed causing a little confusion in their fire, or rather in the fire of the first company which was all that had orders. We shot & took prisoners two of them, the other four got clean off. Meanwhile the second company seeing what had happened stood firm. It was as dark as pitch, but the continuous firing from our scouts spread out as they were all over the bush & field, caused some sort of a panic in the third company, & they at once broke & ran firing indiscriminately "a la Walnut Street" in all directions amongst our ranks. Our Company formed the Rear Guard & in front of us was the Cannon, they ran over the Cannoniers & many of us. I was amongst the rest, & it was over an hour, ere we got them formed again & ascertained what was the matter.

About this time came up the mail wagon, who reported the pickets galloping towards camp. He stopped them, & asked what was the matter! (We had fired our cannon after them without effect.) They said "Federals By God" & still galloped on. We knew this would spoil our surprise party, but pushed on again as fast as possible having sent our prisoners to town under guard on the Mail Wagon. We had another skirmish en route which amounted to nothing, & now at six oclock we approached the much talked of Camp.

Fancy a long hill nearly a mile gradually descending among trees to a deep ravine & still deeper creek, across which is thrown a long covered Bridge & on the opposite side of the creek a precipitous Bank of Blue Clay & slate about 60 feet high, through the face of which a road on a steep incline is cut towards the top of the bank. All along the top of this bank were dug rifle pits, with rests for to shoot from. These rifle pits commanded all this road. They could fire with their Rifles & Cannon, during all of our advance over a mile & through the bridge, while we could not see them, & they were perfectly protected. We were seen every step of the way, & a stockade & entrenchment right across the road commanded the bridge. You can see all their advantages, besides a large breastwork back on a high bluff commanding the Mississippi & the boats, but our shells waked them up at Sunrise & away they ran followed by the boys, who were still in chase when we came up, & made our advance on the camp, where all was stillness & silence, but the signs of work was so plentiful around, that this silence became oppressive, as at every step we expected a little volcano to break loose, so after feeling & exploring our way cautiously, until within pistol shot, we got the order to charge & away we went the Horsemen on a gallop & the men on a run to the Bridge & over it to find all deserted & naught but spades shovels & whisky to tell the tale, yes in a large farmhouse in the rear we found a plentiful Breakfast half eaten. Warm milk still standing in the wooden buckets & Ice Water, all very grateful to our dusty throats.

An Incident here shows how brave they are. We halted at their camp about an hour, while our scouts sought for information. After we had rested, I & two others started up the creek on a private road that led as it proved to some farm houses. When about a mile from Camp we saw five horsemen come out from one of these houses & mount. We took cover behind a large tree, to see who they were. They advanced within about 200 yards when they discovered us & <u>we</u> made them out to be strangers. Immediately they wheeled about & ran, thus proving them secesh. We fired wounding one & gave chase. When they took refuge in the same house, we advanced under cover of fences & trees, & could see them also skulking. We had them cornered & I sent one of the men back for reinforcements, but they met the adjutant & a small squad, looking for us. The regiment had gone to river & were embarking for Lexington in haste, why I dont know even now & so we had to leave <u>our prisoners</u>. The other companies had also embarked on the Boats at Berlin, one mile below, & reported a long run, some brisk shooting, two of the enemy wounded or killed they didn't know which & <u>nobody hurt on our side</u>.

I give you the full particulars of this you see but that is only one skirmish out of many, & as rumor said there was two cannon, & that it was headquarters for these 4 counties, we went in force & the hard work as usual fell to Comp. D & K, but last night again a part of our company went out 8 miles across the river, routed another camp of over 100 men, & captured three more pickets. You see we can rout & chase them easy enough, but we can't catch them & the next day, after we get to camp, why they also come back to their camp & go to work again & now the report is again this morning that they are lining both banks of the River at every safe & convenient Bluff for over 40 miles, on the way to Booneville.

I write this letter in great uncertainty as to what time we shall be relieved here. Our time is out tomorrow night, & I fear the boys will be in open mutiny on Sunday if nothing definite is known by that time.

We expect reinforcements every minute & we may be in St. Louis, as soon as this letter, but we may <u>not</u> for several weeks.

I will write again if we remain here next week. I am as anxious to go home as any one in the Regiment but it would be cold blooded murder to leave the Union men here one day without protection.

On returning night before last, I received a letter from Eliza Ann & one from William. I am glad to hear that William is at home, & so well after his fatigues. I am in the best of health, but getting as red in the face as an old toper. Eliza says Willie's nose is red, mine may be, it has got skinned so often, it ought to be, but looking glasses are so scarce I can hardly tell what change there may be. How dreadful hot it has been for a week. I dont think they can beat it even in the cotton fields. Dont fear for me. I lead a charmed life. I hope this will find you all well – believe me

My Dear, Dear Girl

Yours Sincerely

James E. Love

One sweet kiss good night

Love

Lexington

August 15th 1861

My Dear Molly

When last I wrote all was confusion & even mutiny, even now it is not much better, but the certainty that their commanders are doing their utmost for their release, is having a soothing effect on the men, before they thought themselves forgotten.

We have had a busy time too, on Friday a squad from our company went out about eleven miles & captured 80 kegs of Powder in a scrubby wooded defile or ravine, near where there is supposed to be a secesh camp, & then captured two wagons to carry it, & came home on a run for fear of rescue. Company C was out same day in the same neighborhood & took 2 prisoners & 18 kegs Powder. Saturday was a blazing hot & lazy day with nothing to do & nobody willing to do anything if it offered, when all at once great excitement was caused by the sudden appearance of two steamers round the bend & when we could see they were full of people we fired our Cannon, as an order for them to halt, & all flew to arms fearing a secession attack. They did halt & looking as if they wished to go back they thought us secesh in fact, not being aware of our presence in Lexington, but presently they saw our Flag, when they immediately spread the Stars & Stripes to the breeze, & by this time we could see that they were full of troops, which proved to be the first Nebraska Regiment, enroute for St. Louis. We at first supposed they would release us & excitement ran wild, but on finding the contrary there was as sudden a revulsion. They are fine looking fellows. They had had some fun at Independence & elsewhere & rescued some Union men held prisoners there.

On Sunday our Company was on guard & as I could not go ashore, & had much writing to do for the Company, I passed a busy day. So did the men, as Col White called on one company after another to volunteer to stop with him a few days longer. Only a few did so, three fourths of whom were from our company. Col White's body guard proving themselves worthy of their name. Several companies mutinied & would agree to nothing. On Monday the same scenes over again, men getting wilder, but finally as they found it impossible to go without money or provisions, or officers, they quieted down. The Colonel assuring them that he expected to be able to relieve them today.

In the evening again great excitement, took a Jew Prisoner, who had been robbing the mails of our letters & dispatches, & it was with difficulty the officers rescued him from being Lynched as it was he was very badly used, between brickbats sticks & fat pork, he had a hard time.

On Tuesday we started up the river for wood ostensibly, but it soon leaked out that our real purpose was after troops, wherever they could be found & as we expected some fighting by the way we all stood arms, but we passed quietly in succession Wellington, Camden, Richfield, Sibley & Blue Mills, where was the former attack, & a very dangerous ugly looking place too, & then feeling safe we went to supper. Soon we reached Liberty landing & Arsenal another bad place, then Independence where secesh has 800 armed friends, but see them we could not, so we passed on to Kansas City at Ten oclock at night. Here was a large & thriving Union City on the Kansas border, & we supposed some troops, but no all had gone to the seat of war in the S. West. So at midnight we again started further on our travels & at 3 oc in the morning found ourselves fast on a brush heap & our rudder smashed besides much other minor damage. This detained us to ten oclock, & here I made my first acquaintance with Kansas, verily it is a pleasant land to look at, & the appearances of thrift & prosperity on all sides are charming after the Lazy niggers look of the outside Missouri farms of this upper region.

We passed various villages until we reached Leavonworth City, another large, growing & busy place every thing is on the move, so different from the present state of all the Missouri towns.

Here we heard the news of Lyons battle & death,[1] & also that troops were few at the fort. Col White started for it overland, while the boat proceeded, soon we got there, & found the prettiest place & the prettiest location we

---

1. On August 10, 1861, General Nathaniel Lyon was killed in the Battle of Wilson's Creek, near Springfield, Missouri.

seen in the Western country. Nature <u>adorned</u>, & an almost English Landscape, with its meadow & clumps of trees, & clean officers quarters & barracks. Uncle Sam here farms three thousand acres & seems in a thriving way. We found a new company of Illinois Cavalry come to join Jim Lane, & as they were idle for the moment & waiting for Jim, they at once came with us & we turned our head down stream again.

The old boat had a hard time bumping along till midnight when we again reached Kansas City & tied up for fear of accidents. Today we started at daylight & have been running on & off Sandbars most ever since, making it impossible to write with a pen. It is still undecided depending as it does on the voluntary action of the men, whether we go to St. Louis tomorrow, or remain ten days more as per General Fremont's request. I wish to go down as bad as any man in the Regiment, but wish to go honorably, & have volunteered among the first to stay. However if the majority goes, I will have to go too, in order to see to the payrolls &c which duty falls to my share. We shall see.

I hope my dear girl keeps well & that she has nothing but good news for me. I count the hours now till I see you & dream both asleep & awake of you.

I am in the best of health & all goes well so far

With Love to you & all friends

I am Sincerely Yours

James E. Love

"Fort Leavenworth, Kansas, on Missouri River." From *Across the Continent on the Kansas Pacific Railroad (Route of the 35th Parallel)*. Plate No. 5. Albumen photograph by Alexander Gardner, 1867.

Steamer A. *McDowell*

Near Hermann, Missouri River

August 18th 1861

My Dear Molly

When last I wrote we were just in sight of Lexington. Since that we have passed the Rubicon, & had just as much excitement as we wanted.

We got into Lexington in good time before noon, & without any important incidents, but on arriving learned that our consort the "<u>White Cloud</u>" had been fired at opposite Independence while aground. This they returned with interest in the shape of Shell, Grape & Canister. This reached them & they ran, while all their bullets fell short.

When I reached Lexington, I went up town & bid good bye to the folks there, & then came on board where I found great excitement & preparations. We armed the Home Guards & several Independent companies from the country whom we left in "<u>Camp Fremont</u>", to protect it along with the Cavalry mentioned in my last & thus left behind ⅕ of our guns & several cannon. Finally all our preparations completed we started next morning at daylight & immediately stood to arms, but our "secesh" friends were too badly skeered to come & see us again & we passed quietly but slowly down the river past Berlin, Waverly, Miami & Brunswick where we found our old Flag flying, though turned very pale & ragged from exposure to sun & rain. Here we paused a few moments. We got aground in the bend a very long & ugly one full of snags & Sandbars. Water spread out for miles, just above & the "<u>White Cloud</u>" being ahead of us, as she was all the way, having the Chief Officer Col Stiefel aboard, went aground over an hour. When she came along we at once passed on our way, but grounded again both boats some six miles below in the next bend. We soon got off but as the *Cloud* was badly aground Col White concluded to lighten the boat & so he ordered us to march to the next point below, which we did passing out over half the dry bed of the river, being a sandbar half a mile wide. We marched through a thick timbered bottom 2 ½ miles, to the point where was a woodyard, a farm

& a large Melon patch &c. We regaled & rested ourselves for over Six hours when it got Dark & we marched back.

In the meantime the *Cloud* got off but the *McDowell* in going to her assistance got in a much worse fix & was till past midnight busily sparring before she got loose. We were ferried on board by the Yawl, got a grab supper & went on guard, put out a picket on the sandbar when we got there, while the *Cloud* did the same 2 ½ miles below, at the said Woodyard.

Started next morning (the 17th Saturday) bright & early & soon got to Glasgow, where we most unexpectedly heard of our secesh friends definitely as being six miles below on Buckhorn point where we had to pass close in shore, & remain within reach of their rifles & Shot guns for at least two miles. Glasgow is pretty much of a Union town for this region, & a good crowd surrounded us, & viewed us quietly. We all had 15 minutes leave from the boats & improved it in pursuit of Lager & Newspapers. The Union men clung to the officers & so it was we got our information. At once we started, & as soon as clear of town commenced our preparations, by building breastworks everywhere we could think of, & getting up ammunition in quantity. Every man took forty rounds to commence with, & more was got ready as a reserve. Whiteshell, Canister & Shot was piled around our cannon in increased quantities. It was told us Harris was crossing his men for the Southwest on every flat boat & skiff for a distance of 15 miles. Buckhorn point being his advance guard arranged for our especial benefit the day before though men had been flocking down the river for weeks to it & below. With these recruits he was said to have over 2000 men, most of his best men being already across & ready to march to the S.W.

With the "*White Cloud*" in advance we rapidly neared the point when all at once her Howitser commenced raining a storm of shell in upon them & within a minute our two mortars & six pounder also let fly as we rapidly steamed down.

Soon we could see the flashes in return from behind the magnificent sycamore trees with which the point was thickly covered, & we got orders to

65

fire away as fast as we could, our distance was still too great for their arms, but we could see & hear our strike the trees & the bank all the time. So as we could see the Rebels run from tree to tree & still our report nobody hurt, our boys got quite wild with excitement & yelled & cheered as their Officers cheered them on. Meantime the *White Cloud* was doing the same. Her Musketry incessant her howitzer & cannon ringing & clanging with shell & canister, & their explosing in the woods returning in a confused roar. While at the same time both boats floated lazily past on the current at long range for shot guns 2 or 300 yards around the point. Some of the Rebels stuck to their trees & fought like <u>men</u>, while others from the first we could see run like <u>Deer</u>, this only at a few intervals in the timber. As a general thing we saw nothing of them to in any way account for the torrent of bullets & shot fired toward us & which we could see fall in the water <u>mostly</u>, around us. Shortly we rounded the point, & as this flanked them, they had to choose whether to change their position for fresh trees or run away. Our boats were allowed by the pilots to round too, head up preparatory to landing, we all firing some 15 or 20 rounds, & at last they all ran that could carrying all the Dead & Wounded with them as they thought, but we found their flag, their camp clothing, fodder & provisions &c &c with 3 wounded (which we shot) & two good horses, & also one man wounded whom we overtook near his horse, & 5 or 6 Dead, these we left as they fell & after destroying all their plunder & their ferry boat, we left & pushed quickly down stream, so that they might not have time to ride forward & intercept us at points below. In this brush we had nobody hurt, & the *White Cloud* 3 wounded on slightly however. When we landed the other Companies broke through the woods as skirmishers, but as there was no enemy, & they did not calculate to follow them far, (they did in fact pursue them over a mile East, West & North) they merely acted as plunderers, while our Company much to their discontent had to stand in rank on the Bluff as a Reserve. As I said before we pushed on our way but were soon fired on from the other side just below & above Saline City. There was nobody at home in the city, nothing but a beggarly account of empty houses, so we could see, so we didnt land but ran on knocking over some houses on the outskirts sinking their Ferry boat & peppering the woods with Shell & Musketry as we ran along. Wherever we could see anybody, none of these skulking fellows fired more than one shot ere they ran, & now at every point for twenty miles, wherever the boat had to come within range, & sometimes from both sides at once we were fired on, said I not we had to run the gauntlet. We expected a cannon all the time & if they had had one & fired to any advantage they could have sank us all to the D_l, or a better Land, but we were well protected against Musketry, naught but Minie Muskets or cannon could reach us to do much execution, but the Minie Musket balls came occasionally, & we soon could tell them as they whistled & struck around us, but I believe providence protected us as after all was over we found our loss but small – only one killed & five wounded severely, with a few other scratches & bruises. We have since heard of over 30 of the Rebels being killed or badly wounded in one corn field where they were secreted behind some brush heaps. Just above & just below Arrow Rock they were in greatest force, in the town we could see nobody but two or three Union Men on the Levee. I believe they wanted to come aboard, expecting us to Land, which we ought to have done & burned the place, but no our Colonel kept straight ahead perhaps he feared an ambush & I believe his shells began to get scarce, as he fired none into the town, but gave it hotly to the Rebels just below. This was where we suffered most, where our man was killed, & here again we got the Minie balls. Here also was where we killed so many, as we had got mad & fearless & not a flash could come from the woods, without getting 20 to 50 balls in return. We fired now at every body we could see on Suspicion, the whole country was aroused, & all knew what was going on, in fact looked for it, for ten days ahead.

After we got 5 or 6 miles below Arrow Rock, we got fired at no longer, & from there into Boonville were cheered & waved at in the most enthusiastic manner by the folks along the Bank who had been hearing the Cannonade all day long as it is by river nearly 30 miles, it is not half that by land, and the numerous Secessionists at Boonville with our few Union friends all rushed to the Levee to see our safety or our partial ruin. Here we landed fearing much, but as we could command & sweep all the crowded Levee & town we risked finding Harris' there. However no "secesh" had come in, in force as yet, & after getting the news, & taking on a dozen or two Union passengers, fleeing from the Wrath to come with what they could carry we left for Rocheport.

Booneville was entirely at the mercy of the first comer, most all the Union men & Home Guard had run away to Jefferson City & parts unknown.

We expected another fight at & below Rocheport but no we had skeered them enough, quite as much as <u>they</u> skeered us. We sunk several flat boats for them & took a fine steam ferry boat along to Jefferson City.

During the fight at Buckhorn Point I & our Company were in the cabin firing over the mattresses around the guards, but after that I & about a dozen more were up on the Hurricane roof taking whatever shelter we could get & the point of danger dictated & firing away.

Here it was most exposed, but you could see best what you were doing. Col White remained here all the time & Capt Magennis of the boat, also most his Officers, Carpenter &c all with guns, & many of them think they killed their men. I dont know whether I did or not. <u>I tried too</u> right hard & for the first time. Many of their balls struck all around me several in the chimney stack behind which three of us stood, the Minies ploughing right through the others falling harmless on deck. Once while four of us sat on the side of the Texas, thinking of no danger – firing had ceased for some time, & we were in the wide river – a volley suddenly came from a grove ¼ of a mile off which we had just passed. The aim was good & intended for us. The man along side me was struck by two slugs, <u>about spent</u> however, while the next man had a Minie ball strike just over his shoulder, & go right through the Texas lodging in a mattress other side. One ball went through the skylight below where we sat into the cabin. Then through a Blanket rolled up, a pair of pants Ditto, through the sash of a glass door, through the cabin skin & the venetian shutters out side & so clean over board making over thirty holes in its passage.

It was a providential escape for all of us, as the balls were sent with best intention & aim for our destruction. The same can be said of a volley from four or five of our unseen assassins while out in front of the chimneys, these spattered all around our feet (& perhaps our heads), we afterwards picked up some of the balls.

About six oclock in the evening when ten miles below Rocheport we met the *Iatan & War Eagle* with the 5th Iowa Regiment on board, going along expecting no danger, without Cannon, shot or shell or ammunition. We stopd them, stated the case of our fighting all day, & the reception they must look for, as the papers had prepared the Rebels for them as well as us & so we tied up for the night & next morning, we all four boats started down for Jefferson City. When we arrived there, we gave them all our Cannon Mortars & Howitzer, also all our shot, shell & cartridges, besides which they telegraphed for more & also for Minie guns. Col White also went down by train to state their case more plainly to Gen Fremont, & they awaited the further orders. We reached there without accident or Incident except the kidnapping of another steam Ferry boat just below our camping place of the night before. This we also brought to Jefferson, remained at Jefferson, some hours say from 10 A.M. to 5 oc P.M. & then landed for the night after sundry stoppages on Sandbars & snags, at a woodyard above Herman from which point I date this long palaver. Now in the small hours of the morning of the 19th all safe & sound, never scathed by secesh or Minie balls so far. Thank the Lord & now with best wishes for you & all during the silent watches of the morning & committing self & all to the guardian hands of our Savior who alone can guard us safe till morning I am with sweet kisses yours dear girl

Good night – Love

In my haste about our perils I forgot to acknowledge your letter of the seventh Inst also Alex, note & paper, which I got on reaching Lexington & which I received with kisses, & put me in good humor with Lexington & all mankind – not to speak of Womankind. It was that, that put me in such good humor & gave such zest to my farewells, when bidding Adieu to my few young Lady friends there. Little did they know why I was so cordial & so emphatic in my last words

Goodnight – Love

19th

Made Hermann at 5 A.M. & after a short continued onwards rapidly more so than we expected considering the stage of the River, every thing looks green along here after the heavy rain of last night, for as I wrote the rain fell the lightning flashed, & Thunder pealed, & all this morning it continues. I dont know how it may be here but up Lexington way, <u>just so much</u> is very much wanted, received boisterous demonstrations of regard all the way down & at Washington, Southpoint & Augusta which we have just now passed at half past Ten.

Adio – Amigo Mio – Love

Washington, Mo.

September 20th 1861

My Dear Molly

I cant get along without a conversation this morning. I have been so excited over the Lexington news & so mad that our boys are having all the glory up there in my absence.[1]

I hope there is no doubt of their success, & that aid has reached them ere this, so that they be not forced to surrender.

I have a nice time up & down this road just now recruiting. I am going up to Jefferson City & to Rolla in a day or two, & may there see Ben McCullough & the war but I dont expect to get so close to his excellency & if there's any danger, of course I'll run away.

I wish you were along here to enjoy some of this beautiful scenery, & try the splendid grapes that are so plenty.

A rumor has just come along by the cars that Lexington has fallen. I hope not! If so it is too bad! too bad!! but if so I must just go to work & raise a company myself, & so I may not see you for a week or two.

I want to know in such case if I shall write you again. I wont <u>do so</u>, if from any reason of policy or otherwise you should not wish it?

That is what I called around on Tuesday to say!

But on the other hand if I raise a company & get a commission, why should we not go & do what Capt Herd & his wife has done, get married without ceremony. I want to argue the point when I see you & have a company.

I will try to see you soon. Try & write to me at Jefferson City, care 14th Regt. & now my dear girl, with much love

Yours Sincerely

James E. Love

---

1. After finishing his three months of service, James briefly returned to St. Louis, then traveled along the Missouri River to recruit troops for a new company. While recruiting troops, James heard about the Battle of Lexington, Missouri.

Osage City
Cole Co. Mo.
Sept 23d 1861
My Dear Molly

Whereever I take up a pen to write, I seem compelled to write a line to you. I wish to get alongside you in spirit if not in deed. Can you blame me? I wish I had something of importance to say, but you know I can talk of nothing but ill luck & nonsense. My budget in that way contains sometimes a perfect Niagara!

Who would not live in the country. If they could escape fever & ague. Here is now glorious times for Soldier or Citizen what with bushels of Pawpaw's, Hickory nuts, Hazel Nuts, Crab apples, Grapes, Pecans, Plums, besides apples & peaches by the Load for the gathering. It is a Paradise, & has been all summer. Then there is Persimmons just come in with Saturday nights frost. Did you see it? or did you not get up in time! I did for once!!!

On Friday last while at Franklin, a nice young man of my acquaintance, just after playing Billiards, got shot accidently almost along side me. His brother was along & took his body to St. Louis. He died in an hour. It was 11 .o.clock at night, & we had just spent a most pleasant evening. Very very sudden it was & a warning to us all of the uncertainty of life. The gun was in the hands of a soldier & nearly a square off! He & others were fooling & cutting up.

On Saturday I went from there to Westphalia 12 miles on foot, a most unmitigated green Dutch settlement, where I hoped to get some recruits. So I went to Mass on Sunday had a good sermon in Dutch & saw all the folks about 300 young men, found about one half secesh & that a friend Capt Ellsworth & Col Boomer had been specialyzing before me – so although I persuaded several to serve U. Sam they all concluded to go with Ellsworth instead of me. About 800 secesh are in camp 12 miles from there. I did not visit them, however so I came back as I went. I go to Franklin again today & to Jefferson tomorrow. What glorious news we had from Lexington Saturday. I saw the messenger & the plan of Battle ere the telegraph got it. It takes

<u>Irishmen</u> to charge Bayonets after all. Never mind I shall have a company yet, & then – & then – can you say no?

Think of Capt Herd! Why with My Molly to fight for I'd go to New Orleans on a pleasure trip with Fremont or even Colonel Mulligan who I see Fremont has made <u>Brigadier</u> for his bravery his Irish answer to Price & the "Black Flag".

My Dear Girl – I have a very pleasant time, but sometimes very discouraging to one with my small stock of patience & perseverance. I try to cultivate it however! Have been trying to a little for two years now & I hope next year you will find a better crop.

I have got promises for more than 250 men, but if I get 25 out of that number I will consider myself fortunate & be satisfied. There is such a famine of men, & such an extraordinary crop of officers from what I see. I ought to dispense with whatever stock of modesty I've got, & instead of Captain run for Major General. Such crowds of sap-heads do I see claiming to be Majors, Colonels &c, &c, &c, that it is ridiculous. Why their vanity makes them unfit to be even a high private, & in their bravery they need never emulate a vivandière or sutler.

When I may get to St. Louis I dont know. I would wish to be at that Irish Brigade meeting tonight & on the spur of the moment, I may carry this letter myself.

I must halt in my career just now ere I've had time to say anything sweet

That I love you, worship you, you know & yet you dont know half but need I say it. I hope I may have an opportunity of proving by deeds as I wish & not only in words. I write in much haste to you after writing on business to the Col. & Quartermaster on my bed in a country Shanty after my walk – for the present

Good Bye

Love

Love to Sally, Mother, & all your & my friends

More anon

Love

What is military glory! Here is poor Mulligan & his gallant Irishmen after covering themselves with glory are forced to surrender for the want of a little water after all.

Poor White is gone South too & I am left out in the cold just when prospects began to brighten. However it is only a little more work & to depend on my own resources instead of Capt. this or Col. that.

Jefferson City
Oct 4th 1861
My Dear Molly

I find I will not be able to be down on Sunday so I greet you with a kiss & embrace in return for your loving letter. Such a souvenir made my heart bound again.

I hope all goes well with you & yours.

Take care of yourself for my sake – if not for your own.

I feel a craving need of Love, & I confess it I need all of yours to cover my many sins & shortcomings, but if the service of a life, be it short or long, will repay you for the rich boon of yours, I will try!

In this place I will say how sorry I am that the Adams have played off on me so. With the exception of John I can not even try as I will get up a fit of virtuous indignation. John is <u>too mean</u>. I can forget him & despise him but the Old man I can excuse & Aunt has been always a mother to me, & would be now if she could. As to Eliza Ann, she has no soul above the baby & the wishes of her friends around![1]

I got your letter after much tribulation & search & a walk of two miles to the camp of the 14th Illinois Regt. where a Lieut of my name in Co. D. had it <u>unopened</u>. By the way, a nice young man, Irish by one remove & perhaps a 42d cousin of my own.

Alex had addressed it care (14th Regt.) & as there is only one 14th here the 14th Illinois & he of the same name, he got it but fortunately he has no middle name!

Pray dont continue to think me cold or precise. You may have to change your opinion agreeably. There is too much Irish blood in me, but something in our first acquaintance & the influences that then controld my destiny compelled me to appear so & I am such a creature of habit that Ive not yet got over it. I heard <u>too</u> that you were so precise & particular. (I dont believe it any more, or I would have had no chance, among so many better chances you have had.)

---

1. In several letters, James mentions an issue with his cousin John Adams and his uncle James Adams, the "Old man," regarding his property at Ninth and Spring in St. Louis.

Can you believe it? <u>after this</u> that I loved you almost from first sight & that for nearly or over two years there has been a patient effort for a position so as to place you as you deserve, to win you & wear you.

That I have been or will be with your loving assisstance successful in the last, is no thanks to any success Ive had in the financial part but I am still striving & still with small success. Things move a little better now in our company! but the news today is that Col. White will not live & that is worse than a Wet Blanket.

Had Col. White got down to St. Louis ere the siege (& he only stop'd by Col. Marshall's particular request) we would have been all in active service, I as Captain, but as it we are unattached. We have strained every nerve to raise his regiment, but his absence & his wound is a dead weight that works dreadfully against us, & his death will almost ruin us. We however have <u>now</u> some other Irons in the fire & some prospects. I think I have made warm friends who will not let me suffer & sticking to Col. White to the last will not injure us in military estimation.[2]

The word here this morning is forward & already 5 or 6 Regiments have left this place for the scene of action. Among the rest was prominent the bloody 7th or Col Stevenson's Irish Brigade need I say that it warmd my heart & excited me to look at them, with that elastic step that an Irishman has whether Celt or Saxon. They moved off proudly cheering to the tune of "The Girls I left behind me." It is the last sight many of them will have of Jeff. City.

I will write you again next week & see you too I hope.

Meantime I am in health, & as energetic & working harder than ever. I think it is near the dawning. You know the darkest hour is just before day & any hour if I can not command success. I will try for your sake to deserve it.

---

2. James was trying to recruit a company to serve under Colonel Robert White, who had recently been wounded during the battle in Lexington, Missouri. James worried about the possibility of recruiting a regiment with no leader.

I <u>guess</u> I go tomorrow or Sunday to Sedalia & Georgetown, near the seat of war. From there I will write. I wont be in any danger more than you are in St. Louis.

In much haste

Yours Sincerely

Love

Ambrotype of Robert White, Colonel, Fourteenth Missouri Home Guards Infantry, 1860s.

Georgetown

Oct 9th 1861

My Dear Molly

I have been here & in Sedalia for the last few days. There is no regular mails from or to this point so I take a hurried chance. I hope to see you in a week. I am in good health &c plenty of soldiers here also secesh, but no danger of attack from them as Price is on the full run for <u>Arkansas</u> or <u>St. Louis</u> & Fremont will soon be after him. He is watching him very closely & I see scouts from Lexington & all around every hour.

We are operating slowly but I hope to some purpose. I have had much pleasure & many discomforts by the way but there is some excitement & of course pleasure in being near or at the seat of war, & also in knowing that there is being something done.

There is no danger in St. Louis, unless from the citizen secessionists but there is more danger down near there than there is here, as Price has gone that way & South as fast as 20,000 horses can carry him, & will no doubt appear as usual where least expected. I hope you are well. Write to me at Jefferson if convenient!

Col. White is improving! He was dreadfully wounded & paralysed for two weeks but is now believed safe though crippled for two months to come. His Spinal column being sadly shocked by the crash of the ball which struck in the small of his back & pass up & out in front under his chin & alongside his jugular.

My Dear Girl, take care of yourself & keep in good Spirits & believe me trying to do so. This is as beautiful a country as man could wish to see & only man is vile.

It is good times for those who are bush whackey. Nuts of all kinds & pawpaws, persimmons &c &c are here in glorious profusion, & the air off the prairies feels as pure & exhilarating as <u>Champagne</u> <u>ought to</u> <u>be</u>. The woods look glorious & the colors come out richer daily, such splendid patches of red yellow & brown are only to be seen in the West, or in "<u>Churchs Heart of</u> <u>the Andes</u>". Would I were with thee? but just Hum me a tune in the evening hours occasionally & I will fancy I hear it borne on the Autumnal breeze & in anticipations of days to come which fancy paints in sweetest colors.

I am My Dear Girl with Love to you & all

Love

James compares the countryside around Georgetown, Missouri, to this painting. Church, Frederic Edwin (1826–1900). *Heart of the Andes*. 1859. Oil on canvas, 66 1/8 x 119 1/4 in. (168 x 302.9 cm). Bequest of Margaret E. Dows, 1909 (09.95). The Metropolitan Museum of Art. Image copyright © The Metropolitan Museum of Art. Image source: Art Resource, NY.

Sedalia

Oct 10th 1861

My Dear Molly

Yesterday I had to write in such a hurry that I wished I had put my former hours of Idleness to a better use, but perhaps I said all that was necessary & as my prospect of remaining here increases I will seize more promptly any opportunity that I may have.

I am just resting after a ride to & from Georgetown, where I saw Sigel, Fremont, Jeff C. Davis[1] & other notabilities. I saw also this morning some fine batteries. Major Backoff's & others maneuvering on the prairie west of here & every thing seemed to work to perfection quick & well. There are troops in quantity here & below, marching all over the country, with all the pride & pomp of glorious War & there are secessionists, who swear fidelity to the Union once a day to get passes &c, who ride hither & thither reporting our every movement to the prowling armed bands who are so ready to pounce when occasion offers, & to run when it don't. In fact there is treason in the camp & every where around. It stalks unseen & unmolested from here to the Presidential Mansion, in Fremont's body guard & Staff as well as in McClellan's. I cant understand what moral poison it is that has & yet does leaven the whole heart of society in these border & even in some of the Northern States.

Price & his men are "en retreate" badly scared & hundreds of squads are going or gone home that committed their quota of <u>robbery</u> & <u>murder</u> (I dont mean fighting) at Lexington & elsewhere all over the State, & for the present when seen are of course all good Union Men, who have been robbed &c by the secesh but when Fremont & Co go to Arkansas & South after the main body, these same Union Men will rob & steal & murder honest citizens worse than ever, & nothing that I can see now short of extermination will save <u>Mo.</u> from being soon a desert without <u>Slaves</u> anyhow. No army can ever catch these fellows unless it be an army of Jayhawkers say under Lane or some other competent spirit.[2]

---

1. A reference to Jefferson C. Davis, commander of Federal forces in Jefferson City, Missouri.
2. People in Missouri had to contend not only with Union and rebel forces, but also with

We must go down South & hold the poisoned chalice to their own lips down there.

Here we are only playing second best at their own chosen game, while there they enjoy the blessings of peace at least within their borders & the Union Men are under coercion such as the world has never seen except say in a French revolution.

I want to go on a pleasure trip to New Orleans under Fremont! Col White or even Jim Lane! I have been working for glory most long enough now, & prospects are brighter than they have been for that long expected Captaincy. I have got some 40 men this week & look for more. I wont believe it until I see it & have it in possession however so dont think I am building any castles in the air.

If you wish to fire my ambition however, I would inform you that the next step is Major & though my military education has been badly neglected, I will study to improve it as soon as time permits. I heard & seen much of Fremont's body guard at Jefferson but neither Mr. Rose, Willie W, or any of that clique of my acquaintancies. I had not time to go to camp, & I believe they are now somewhere up here. Their hard work will soon begin & with a man of Fremont's activity, who rides his 100 miles a day when pushed, they will have no sinecure! I wish them Luck!!!

I and my friends in council in this Regiment had & have yet I believe a fine opportunity of joining with our respective ranks assured to us & all our men in Elliss' Cavalry Regiment, but we decided to stand by Col White while he lives or longer if his Regiment becomes as we hope it will within a few days be a Reality. This unless something very unexpected turns up is how it stands now & meantime all hands & the cook work with renewed energy, many for Love & more if not all for Revenge.

The General opinion is that Col White will do to tie to & so much so that his name is a tower of strength to us when ever we can persuade people that he will recover.

---

armed bands on both sides who seized private property, burned towns, and even murdered private citizens. James is so horrified by the acts of these armed bands with rebel general Sterling Price, that he believes the only solution is Jim Lane and his brigade of Jayhawkers. However, Lane and his men committed equally atrocious acts in their efforts to defend Kansas at any cost and free the slaves.

This we assert he will though there 10 chances to 1 against us yet.

It is only his great vitality & tenacity of will that makes us hope. He just wont die – no more than he or Mulligan would take the oath or surrender at Lexington & if he ever can ride a horse again, you will soon hear of him as a Brigadier General, if any of his old energy & activity of person & brain remains with him. I hope so! both for his own sake & mine!

The Dutch are still in the ascendancy here, & will be our ruin in this State yet, if not checked. Because they have contributed Sigel & a few other good men, they think they are & of right ought to be the ruling powers & their own opinion of their bravery is certainly rather inflated! My opinion of their prowess is at present but small. I wish I had some of their assurance however & could use it to as good advantage.

Major Becker is here & has already got a position from Fremont, because he can talk so much fight, although it is known that had it not been for him & his Dutch & American Home Guards, Col's Mulligan & White could & would have held out for a week & dug wells, &c, & with the aid of Lane & Sturgis, who were at hand have perhaps in the end tired or whipped out Price & Co. but the Major must at the instance of his (brave?) countrymen & without a Council of War raise the White flag & so cause a truce for an hour & so the gallant garrison of Irish & Illinois braves were surrounded & closed in upon before they knew whose flag it was or what it meant.

I feel strongly tempted to stay here & turn Jayhawker. It is the best business just now. It has only one objection to me, & that is it looks too much like stealing. I have just secured however a good Secesh sword, that has seen some cowardly service, or it wouldn't be in my possession you may be sure & I expect to raise a horse ere I am much older. Uncle Sam & his friends sell such as do not suit them in size &c here at about 20$ a head & that is all profit, to them. Several regiments of regulars & home guards have been already fitted out with good ones & for the small cost of riding after them to secesh pastures or camps & with a good chance for a skirmish occasionally which does not always result in horses, but many times in Death to the Jayhawkers.

After all this is the only way to get back the thousands of horses they have impressed from the Union men of the State & some of those here in this way come back to their rightful owners. This occured with 20 fine horses under my own eyes the other day namely last Monday, but I have talked too much war have I not & you must not criticise my disjointed & rambling effusions.

You said I must write & I want to!! but the facilities are so poor, & the surroundings so distract my attention, that I cannot concentrate my Ideas enough to make the contents as interesting as I wish to.

Dont believe I criticise yours although I read them over 20 times. I see only on the page your sweet face & if every word were gems of eloquence they would not seem more so to me than they do. Gems of sweetness & love as they are!! Love is always eloquent you know, or seems so to the Lovers! & I kiss that last wanderer I reclaimd for you again & again. Speaking of your sweet face reminds me, I had not time to get those photographs, or to persuade you as I intended to, to go with me & sit for my benefit. I wish I had one as I ought to beside me now & it would remind me of many things that I ought to say but cant think of & instead of which I've filled these sheets with war speculations of which no doubt you get too much & which at any rate would keep till my return. Don't say nay?! But remind me of a fitting & convenient time when I return!

I suppose the sale on Spring St. took place on Tuesday would you believe it. I haint thought of it since I seen you until just now. I looked at an old paper. I am very much to be pitied I've no doubt, but while I've a cent in pocket (I've got a brass one yet) I won't find it out. I forgive them all freely & that is more than they can do to me. I am as happy as a King too & have no care!!! Save to gain a position so as to gratify the ambitious wishes my dear girl cherishes on my behalf?

I am only sorry to leave my room. That was home for a while where the store was shut out & nothing but laziness & comfort reigned.

I won't give it up without a struggle, but I expected to be in St. Louis on Tuesday to be on hand when the time was. Now I suppose it is too late & I forgot it till this present writing. It must take the chances of war for a week like its owner.

What of my Charming Sallie. Has she yet returned! <u>They do say</u> she aint coming back single. Just give her a kiss for me if you see her before I do & I'll pay you back & her too, if I can!

Goodbye & pleasant dreams until tomorrow

Love

Sunday morning Oct 13th 1861

Tomorrow & Tomorrow has passed into futurity & I am at Tipton. The forward movement has commenced & Price is 75 miles ahead in the race, everything is motion & excitement, except your humble servant & he is very dull & homesick, done nothing since Thursday but listen to the rain fall & trudge around in it & <u>mud</u> to the eyes. It is now a bright Sunday morning & I believe I will run down on the train 20 miles to Jefferson just to post this letter.

Fremont is here. I saw him & McKinstry yesterday. McKinstry was just starting ahead. Capt. Naughton of W. Avenue and Sigel went in the morning for Sedalia with 3 or 4 fine Regiments.

I saw Mr. Rose yesterday evening in camp. He seemed in low spirits & tired of Cavalry – very much so. He was all mud & grease from contact with horse flesh in his fatigue overall – very much like an overworked stable boy. This description will answer for all. The Mr. Rose of former days was non est. Willie I did not see but Forrester & others I did. Willie was out in the country buying & pressing oats & corn. The boys in camp were on an extensive hunt after Johnny (contraband?) Grunters, right under Fremont's nose.

I may start down to St. Louis at any moment & now with Love to you & all, I close

Yours Sincerely

James E. Love

Tipton

Oct 18th 1861

My Dear Molly

I have expected daily to be in St. Louis, but I now fear I may pass another Sunday up here some where in the bush or prairie.

I carried my last letter as far as Jefferson & had got on the cars for St. Louis when news I rec'd called me to Sedalia again – bad news. I have been there & at Georgetown since & now today I am here working St. Louis ward again. I fear all my work & expense may go for nothing. I mean of this last two weeks but I shall know tomorrow I expect positively so I wont touch on it now. Late reports to the effect that Col. White will be incapable of active exertion has nearly ruined us again, but we will have at least the satisfaction of sticking to a good man & a friend from disinterested motives, long after interested motives were played out. If he recovers soon we I suppose played our very best cards. He has very powerful influence & would be & is very largely indebted to us. If he dont recover, we have only lost so much time. Later accounts (2 days old from Lexington) say he is all right.

We had 800 mounted scouts sent up there 2 nights ago & expect to hear from them every moment with orders to release him & Col. Grover if fit to move at all hazard.

There were only 400 secesh in Lexington & these mostly a band of thieves, not Price's men, but led on by some of our perjured acquaintances up there, who have done the assassinating part of the business so I hope to hear a good account from there as robbers & assassins dont usually stand a fair fight – no reflections just now on Price & Co.

I expected to find some letters in Jefferson, but was much disappointed, as I got "nary" scrap. So I got on the cars, only to get off again & send a telegram instead.

Our orders for a month past led us to Kentucky that being now the post of honor, but our unfortunate slowness has interfered, & I believe our course will be to New Mexico. If you ask me how I know this? Why I cant tell!! but it is a shrewd surmise formed from being a little behind the scenes with

Fremont & Cameron – an eavesdropper if you will. Our Lieut. Col. (Graham) is the <u>wire</u> <u>puller</u> on this occasion & rumor says he will be breveted a Brigadier if we go, so he gains a great deal by the change & we <u>may</u> not lose in the <u>end</u>?

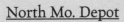

<u>North Mo. Depot</u>

12 M. – Decr 3rd/4th 1861

My Dear Molly

I dont wish to start without bidding you good bye.

I got orders to leave at 4 o.c. in the afternoon, & when I got out to camp & got the men down here it was near eleven. I expect to be down in a week or less, so it does not matter so much. Capt Herd is dangerously ill from congestive chills, which is the cause of my sudden change of plan. I have had charge of the Company since Monday morning & it thus added much to my duties, but dear me this change from killing <u>ennui</u> to action has renerved me, & I feel myself again. You shall see when I return what a flow of spirits I will have.

So we are for New Mexico at last notwithstanding your prophecies to the contrary last Sunday night & I had almost begun to look on your words as oracles & had only this morning given up all hope, & made up my mind to be disbanded – but no such luck.

I hope all is for the best. I wish to have a long conversation with you when I return. I've had many things to say for some time but in the unsettled not to say worse state in which I & all were in I could not begin did not know where to begin while I seemed so much on the downward grade.

I hope now Excelsior will be the Motto & the performance too.

My dearest girl I write in much haste & with sincerest love & esteem

I am

Ever yours

James E. Love

If Miss Wilson would kindly accept the accompanying trash, part of which came all the way from <u>Paris,</u> she would relieve my mind of a great embarrassment, "<u>What to do with it</u>," & confer a favor on

Love

for ever more

Amen

Kris Kringle presents his compliments to Miss Eliza M. Wilson and wishes her a Merry Christmas and a happy New Year, and many returns each more happy than the last

He pencils the list of contents so that it can be rewritten and rearranged at pleasure

He acknowledges having committed a breach of trust when acting as messenger for Col. Billy Wilson (whose Photograph appears tomorrow) in the matter of the Three first Photographs, but begs for mercy and a personal hearing of his case promising never to do so no more

Seventh Heaven)

Break O. Day)

Christmas 1861)

Saint Louis

January 3d 1862

My Dearest Eliza[1]

I only wish to outline what ought to be the subject of a serious conversation, or at least so it seems to me, for I am in doubt and fear and trembling.

I am running counter to all my preconceived opinions & notions, but while sustained by your constant suggestions, and the daily repeated knowledge that such was your wishes, I <u>blinded my eyes</u>! but now in my loneliness, can I call it ought else, I muse & chide myself for giving way so long to secrecy. I wish Miss Anna was a thousand miles away just for a few days or even hours (I don't dislike the foolish girl) so that we could have some of our old quiet meetings, which were the only heaven I sought or seek! To bask in the light of your smile awhile & look up in your soft eyes, & there read in prospect all the happiness & love of my fondest dreams & thus dreaming still look down the vista of a futurity, which sober common sense already tells me can possibly never be, but these dreams are sweet, & I am a sad dreamer & procrastinator, or I should have thought & said all this before.

Molly will you believe me mine was almost love at first sight, but I would not believe it. I know how much I enjoy & adore new faces for the time being, & then all the praises I heard showered on you rather repulsed me than otherwise, & so when I heard how fastidious & precise you were, I wrapped myself in a reserve heretofore foreign to my nature, & set myself to watch & dissect your every thought word & act, flirting with Sallie all the while, until I found myself entirely your slave.

I had entered the grocery business on a more extended scale than I otherwise would have done because I expected the earnest cooperation of my brother,[2] and as I wished riches for my wife's sake. If I could win her, as well as my own (I understood you had refused so many good offers, & you had a right to look above me) I worked hard to make my venture a successful one.

---

1. James addresses Molly by her given name, Eliza Mary.
2. James planned to run his grocery store with his brother, Samuel, who died in 1859 on his return voyage from Australia.

I could or at least did not succeed, & when I found you didn't like groceries, so you said! I lost heart, & so when these troubles changed the values of property so, & my loyal enthusiasm to the land! government of my early love drove me into the Home Guards. I thus drifted with your consent into the military business, & here I am disconsolate! Asking myself continually, am I such a weak purposeless, nerveless creature, that all my purposes come thus to naught?

But to explain, I would not ask your hand while my grocery scheme was an experiment, neither would I be in haste anyhow knowing your ideas of hasty matches, & then my courage failed me again & again whenever I thought of the consequences to me of a refusal & then the very day I had determined to plunge, you got news of the loss of your brother & so I had to postpone for months again so all our precious time was wasted which if I had seized on at first I might have been keeping store yet & had no fears of a long separation! & thus one castle in the air fell!!! bringing numerous others yet in its train I can foresee! and all through what I never approved of & what I never intended to be guilty of, a long courtship!

There is another long cherished opinion I have since done injustice too, that is in regard to a long engagement. I have always thought them wrong & bad in every sense of the term, yet what am I to do? I can't divine! Can you? Will you enlighten me? You know your word is law, or if you don't you ought to, as I never oppose anything, except by chaffing, in order to know your wishes & reasons.

But there is yet one thing that has been weighing heavily on my mind & that is as to the propriety of this secrecy as to our engagement!

That it is which has made me be so chary of my visits, to weigh & measure them out, with as it seemed to me, (& to you too) so much carefulness.

Now of course no others have any right to know it, but your mother, & perhaps William. Others might guess at it as much as they like, so they do now! but I do think that your Mother ought to have known long since, especially as things are at present if she can keep a secret. I suppose she can since you can keep one so well.

I often think that they all know, just as much as if we had told them, & others too, even <u>Anna</u> with her sharp eyes, & thoughtless cruelties.

Don't you think <u>they</u> do? Sallie & Alex especially! I know you get teased unmercifully, not to say painfully by <u>many</u>; & I would willingly give the last drop of my blood to release you sensitive as you are from such annoyances.

Would it not stop it in a great measure by acknowledging all.

We could then have such happy meetings & partings – free of constraint in a measure, & our pleasures would be so enhanced, over what they can be in the present guarded manner of conducting affairs, which presses on my mind all the time, & I have to be such a hypocrite in word & more especially looks that I get afraid of myself.

It is an injustice to me, but I don't complain of it, not at all, nor have I, & why because I feel I am so <u>poor</u> & <u>unfortunate</u> so far, that you had & have, all the right to dictate, but my life & energies are wearing away & I must grumble now, when I see you slaving so for the comfort of others, ever unmindful of self, (even at the risk of the engagement & with it my life) for it is far more of an injustice to you this secrecy, & must cause you unhappiness, as the longer it is postponed, the more terrible it seems to break the news, the harder to surmount maiden modesty.

But just here a thought strikes me, & I have often thought of asking you the question before.

Have you not a confidante? Have you not informed any of them. <u>Sallie</u> & <u>Alex</u> have both talked as if you had told them all about it; but of course I was mum!

And further Molly dear, if I am compelled to leave for New Mexico, without some change in our status – as at present – I will feel compelled, as it would be only simple justice to you to release you in the fullest sense of the word from any engagement or entanglement whatsoever.

We must be either more or less in the eyes of your family, if not of the world.

I cannot think of releasing you however, until <u>you</u>! present the dread alternative, as I must say in justice to myself, that I have considered it an engagement on my part perhaps long ere you dreamt of it, that I have lived up to it, & will do so to the end.

Now how would it do to say to the folks some day soon that we have been long engaged but that circumstances inexorably interfered as <u>they</u> know <u>partly</u>. That now I have got a certain income for a while, that I intend to save considerable out of it, & that when the war is over, if it is over soon I will thus be prepared to take hold of something else. If the war lasts as it promises to, why I can resign when a favorable opportunity offers! (<u>If such should be your</u> wish?)

That we wish to consummate our engagement, say in April or May ere I start for the plains, or if that is violently opposed, I could get a brief furlough next winter, & if everything is as agreeable as I expect to <u>make</u> it we could then make a wedding tour out that way, & making allowance for two or three days staging over the plains, perhaps as agreeable a one as even Lake Superior, or New Orleans, either of which by the way I wished formerly to propose but which as far as we can see at present are out of the question for me now.

Besides I wish to do something for you in case of accident to me, I have no other claim on me – and in such case there are pensions &c &c to be looked after, which if I remain single go to Uncle Sam's profit & of course my friend's loss. Now Uncle Sam owes me all I can make off him honestly & if I lose my life, I don't wish to these hard times lose everything else in the bargain, but to relieve myself from the imputation of having lived a useless life & die a useless death (perhaps?) by doing something at least for my friends!

I should return to my post at once for reasons of weight with a man of honor as well as with an eye to proficiency in my present profession, & thus with a much better chance of future profit, if I continue in it.

Now my dear girl, some of this may <u>seem</u> dictatorial, but I disclaim <u>here</u> all wish to dictate. Such is my opinion! I wish to ascertain yours! I have heretofore bowed to your wishes, the result over which we had little or no control, proves <u>you</u> right, but I still believe the principle of long engagements & secrecy wrong!!

I might go on enlarging. I ought to have touched on the thousand & one subjects often & then there would have been no need for this, but the uncertainty of my prospects deterred me time & again. Let us now if possible have a full understanding & decide at once in all love & kindness.

I believe that there is soon to be desperate fighting at many points!

I believe that I will not be in it; but wish to be safe in camp, learning my duties thoroughly during the Winter!

I believe that our expedition will be or can be made to me a very pleasant trip!

I believe I can save much!

I believe there are many opportunities of profit out there!

I believe that there is not much danger in the future.

I believe you could also have a very pleasant trip at the time mentioned or sooner.

I believe the sooner united, the more it would conduce to our happiness, present & future!

I believe that I could, nay, I know that I would do more for two than one!

I don't believe in long engagements!

I believe that I lack ambition, & that I thus require a "Jessie",[3] to give me fresh inspiration when interest flags, or novelty tempts!

I know I like variety, & that causes me to be accused of a lack of perseverance but I believe that all I want is a dear little wife at my side, to give her sage advice & cry excelsior!! & state the "Other Side" which I am prone to forget!

I believe that I am blessed beyond the power of words in your true love. No shade of doubt ever crossed my mind. I pray that I may ever return it – as you deserve – but if we cannot decide this question soon – I must leave you wholly free!

And now with the warmest love, and a profound regard for your best interests and happiness, as well as my own

---

3. Jessie Benton Frémont was a great supporter of her husband, Major General John C. Frémont.

I am My Dear Eliza

Sincerely Yours

James E. Love

P.S. Circumstances compel me to leave on Tuesday or Wednesday whether to return for months or not I can't say!

Camp Hunter
Fort Leavenworth
Jany 15th 1862
My Dear Molly

I arrived here last night all safe after a long & wearisome journey in good company however including some officers of the regular Army. One a South Carolinian & a very good fellow, some Ladies, a Kansas representative, fresh from Washington, & full of politics a la Jim Lane &c &c. So the time passed amid wars & rumors of wars, & we got some glimpses of secesh on horseback too. We passed on the Pioneer train over the new bridges, had to wait at Mexico half an hour until the large bridge there was finished for us, & in consequence did not make the connection at Hudson as we ought. After a while we got on a freight train which stopped at Brookfield, where there is a large hotel, nothing more & here we had to stop over Sunday, inasmuch as the Hotel keeper conspired with the Engineers of two freight trains that started to go without us and so the aforesaid company had to amuse one another on the wide prairie, nary church within 30 miles, which we did & got well acquainted had a sleigh ride as part of the bill of fare. On Monday we got on another freight train at Eight in the morning & at dark our company gained St. Joe where at the Pattee House, we revenged ourselves for past hard times.

It snowed most the day & was intensely cold both Sunday & Monday.

On Tuesday we again started in a snowstorm & arrived only at dark at the camp, thus taking over four days, to travel four hundred miles, which ought to have been done in 36 hours. I took it very easy, thinking I might probably be as well on the cars as in Camp, under the circumstances, & I rather think so, now that I see it.

Well here I am at last & just got into harness. I write this tonight because I will be officer of the day tomorrow.

And now as to news of the future, it is all too dim as yet to mention, but there is still some hopes of New Mexico being our destination.

The Colonel has had a proposition much to his & perhaps our advantage if we would join Jim Lane but he has for the present refused & in consequence there is already a great many obstacles being thrown in our way. Meanwhile my dear girl, I am in good health, & with care, which I can & will take, I expect to continue so, if Providence wills it. And now my dear Eliza, pray take care of yourself, & with Love & Patience I hope all will come right yet.

Yours,

Love

Camp Hunter
Jany 19th 1862
My Dear Molly

This fine cool Sunday Evening, I wish to have my usual tete-a-tete. I could have wished that I had Molly by my side but that I had put all that from me for 3 months & so no more of it.

I hope you Sally & Annie, & in fact all the folks are in good health, & enjoying yourselves sleighing and otherwise, now while it is so favorable, for I can hardly believe that the few miles I am West of you can make much difference.

You are really very <u>fragile</u>, more so than you are willing to believe, & if you knew how much pleasure it w'd give me, not to speak of all your friends, & their name is legion, to see you stout & healthy in the Spring, why you would not over exert yourself but take a leaf from Sallie's book & amuse yourself, <u>for my sake</u>. Now do! and I will promise to take so much care of myself & try to manage so that you will yet be proud of me.

Things here move very slowly & take such contradictory turns, that there is no accounting for them. The rumors founded seemingly on fact & authority are too numerous to mention. The facts so far as heard from are these

Jim Lane has failed to get his Major Generalship & M.G. Hunter reigns in his stead so we are not as yet attached to the Southern Expedition but the M.G. says he requires all the Kansas troops, & so we are under orders for Fort Scott down in S. East Kansas within 3 miles of Missouri & 20 miles of the Indian Territory – in other words on the border for which service we were recruited – while the remainder of the Kansas Troops & 20,000 others follow Hunter to N. Orleans or death. So much for this winter, & in the Spring we have the assurance that if any troops <u>can be spared</u> for New Mexico, we shall go.

The arrangements to fill our regiment with the Kansas 2d were all carried out as I informed you in St. Louis though not completed until the 17th Inst. There having been so many obstacles thrown in the way, & so many inducements held out to Major Cloud their commander to do otherwise, but it is now accomplished & as the more honorable number we are now the Kansas 2d & carry Springfield on our banners thus gaining a little cheap glory without any risk of life or limb. You dont believe in glory do you! gained in this or any battle field when any of the loved ones lives are at risk? I dont think you do! but strange to say masculine human nature craves for Glory as it does for money or any other supposed human good – <u>unless quite craven</u> – just as feminines do for dress or position in society for themselves or <u>husbands</u> but to return. We have many troubles still. I had to leave about 100 men in St. Louis by a special order of Gen. Halleck[1] dated the day I left & all of them had to go into St. Louis Regiments. 50 or 60 more had to be left in Illinois the same way. These men were part of our bargain in the consolidation, & a very important part; besides there had been a petition before Congress & the Sec. War, to make the 2d Kansas a Mounted Rifle Regiment. This had been often refused but the Petition was still pressed, & on the 17th was granted (the same day you will observe as we were consolidated by orders of the Governor & General here.)

Now either of these causes may wreck the whole enterprise, but it is at present under consideration at headquarters, and I expect it will come out all right.

I shall try & keep you posted as to the facts – not the rumors.

I have been very busy since I arrived here. Various matters & things claimed my immediate attention but among other things I have found time to pitch a splendid Tent, to improvise a good bed for two, & to inaugurate a roaring little stove, which keeps all as warm as your parlor with snow all around six inches deep, & frost such as you can imagine. It is very pleasant notwithstanding, and as it will be probably 3 or 4 weeks before we get our arms & get out of this imbroglio, & make necessary preparation to go South, we will in the meantime luxuriate here, & when I get a little more privacy, I will try to make my letters more racy & expect in return a flight of your usual charming little billet doux's.

---

1. Major General Henry W. Halleck, commander of U.S. forces in the western theater.

I will try & spare time ere I can post this to write to either Wm. or Alex & so enlighten the natives but I do so long to hear from you that I cant spare them a line until I can secure the wished for pleasure.

Love to yourself & all your & my friends. "Sub rosa" of course for the present.

Meantime I am as ever

Yours Sincerely

James E. Love

Camp Hunter
Fort Leavenworth, Kansas
Jany 30th 1862
My Dearest Eliza

I started to write you on Sunday night but got interrupted, & time & place have not been in accord since, besides I waited anxiously for one from you. I had that pleasure yesterday & kissed it as a proxie for your sweet self, and a thousand blessings on my guardian angel.

I have just read it over & over again. I knew there was a cause & a good one for any delay, & if I had to wait for six months, rest assured I would never tax you with the delay. No! No!! No!!! The mails, or the thousand & one accidents of flood & field & of conventional life w'd be anathema, I've no doubt, but doubt your action? Never!

On Sunday I went to Church in Leavenworth, & had a good sermon at the Congregational Church (another branch of the Universal Presbyterian Church). The preacher was opposed very much to the claims of the Baptists, but claimed that immersion, dipping, pouring, sprinkling were all valid forms, to be used according to convenience, or conscientious scruples, inasmuch as all forms were practiced in the New Testament & none in particular enjoined.

In such a belief, he agreed with what you may have heard me advocate, but N'importe! I enjoyed the walk immensely.

We had one or two days of thawing weather last week but it froze hard each night & on Sunday it again set in bitter cold with a slight fall of sleet at intervals. This continued with a high wind all Sunday night & on Monday morning Earth & air & trees were all covered & full of the most beautiful & fantastic forms of King Frost's creation. To explain, the moisture & fine snow as it fell, intermixed with hail had covered everything both on the upper & under surface with beautiful <u>Fern like</u> forms, leaves, branches, stalagmites & stalactites, miniature tracery & lace work. It was worth a journey to the North Pole to behold. Long & wary it hung from the trees in spider like tracery & moss like consistency. There is a winter scene at

Morgan St. much alike as far as the trees are concerned. Well since then every day has been cold, colder, coldest, up to this morning. Snow falling every few hours. Sun shining bright between, to the merry tune & jingle of the sleigh bells. Ambulances, carriages, wagons, and buggies being removed from <u>their wheels</u> & set on clumsy temporary wooden runners hewed out of Uncle Sam (or God's) free Lumber, & so the world runs on sleds improvised for the day. Cause why? The wheels wont turn without scraping & screeching. This morning it snowed heavily and now the sun shines hot, & the snow & ice does not melt exactly but evaporates or wastes insensibly. We have been famished for want of papers & reading matter, & it wont do to subscribe either, as our address maybe such a moving one, but yesterday I was in Leavenworth City, with a patrol to arrest absentees & deserters & brought back three such prisoners & also a good supply of old & new newspapers. So the hungry souls were made to sing with joy & ennui gave way to a pleasant excitement that in my case lasted to past 11 oclock. A very late hour in camp by the way where we rise at six, & should put out lights at 9 P.M. I read however two hours after Cap. & others had retired & until all my Chop'd wood gave out, & my eyes cried mercy. So I did not write you, but turned in thinking of all the bright things that I would & ought to say but that prove so evanescent when paper is spread or your actual presence gives the wished for opportunity & now this morning I have prolonged & dallied with the Loved task to its utmost thinking of the long week that may intervene before I can or dare tease you again!

This morning I have been to the Fort with 13 mutineers that refuse to do duty, & saw them safely ironed until they return to reason, & a sensible idea of the oath <u>they</u> have taken. They are some of our last recruits, and are inclined towards <u>Secesh</u>!

I am really getting stout again & do not ask for better quarters than I have for either health or comfort. We have scarcely room for all our company in comfort this cold weather, but that is our only drawback, and as long as the rain keeps off us, we ask no odds of Queen Vic herself. But the spring comes, & though this is a much drier climate than St. Louis still the rain will fall

& though our tents are dry above & below <u>still being much out of doors</u> wont be so pleasant; but even that is very trivial, if they only let us keep camp until April. But if we are marched down, down, down to Dixie, as is the fate of <u>most</u> our Kansas Copartners, it will be trying to weak constitutions, unless they are as careful as <u>I</u> am & <u>will be</u>. We hope not to go, but refer you while in suspense to Gen'l. Hunter's orders of Tuesday last wherein we are all ordered to get everything we want for use in camp or a march at once so as to be ready to march at an hours notice, & that as there is no surplus of transportation, Officers & men must prepare to carry all their clothes (one change & a blanket) together with two to four days rations each on their back between such Stations as Kansas, Arkansas or Missouri can afford us for depots; & to store all surplus luggage, in case of such necessity.

But per contra, our men have yet no arms, & many are new to the business, & whether we are or are not the 2d Kansas is an all absorbing question in our camp, in political circles in Kansas & also at Head Quarters at Washington. So we no doubt will linger here as a kind of Home Guard until the question is solved whether Governor Robinson & Genl Hunter can make us the 2d Kansas, or whether Jim Lane can kick us out & put in his pets, so mote it be! And now my Dear Molly I am so glad you are enjoying yourself & have so many beaus. Patronize them as much as you wish or can afford, to spite the gossips. You can not excite a jealous thought in me, by your own badinage or the gossips report, even if they bring proofs as strong as Holy Writ.

When I was a courtier with possible rivals who seemed to be on more intimate terms than I, it perhaps may have been different. I dont say but that I more than once went home groaning in spirit, but that is past! Is not your word your bond?

And now success in your <u>flirtations</u>, if <u>such you wish</u> Molly Dear & dont misunderstand me either! Dissipation is sometimes very wearing work on a delicate body!

I do remember "Bayard" & his Winter Tales, perhaps even mused of some of his word painting at the same time that you listened to his honeyed periods on the Am. People. I had seen his lecture advertised ere I started & wished to be there.[1]

Sorry to hear of Aunt Adams ill health. I cant afford to lose the only "Mother" I've claimed for years just yet. I pray she may continue to improve. She has not so much <u>devotion</u> & <u>moral</u> <u>courage</u> in her character as my mother had, but in most other points, she much resembles her – perhaps more so than I am willing to acknowledge – in my Ideal portrait of Mother.

I did wish to call at Mrs. Patricks. I had such a warm invitation. There was no mistaking the fact, that I must come if in town, & Miss McCall too invited me & you! with such impressment that I promised myself a good time in advance, & in such case it would have taken an avalanche of mishaps to change the current of feeling.

I suppose "Anna" has left you ere now. I hope John & her arrived safe & sound. What of her <u>conquest</u>? And did she return heart whole? I've no doubt however, for although I think her very fond of masculine society, I dont think her very impressible, & I do think she has too much of that peculiar country pride "or sensitiveness", to be Dead struck with any of her St. Louis Beaus on this her first entrée. May happiness attend her is my worst wish!

We do not get any pilot bread while in Camp so Wm's shipment must be for the traveler's southward & if we go on that pilgrimage, we may munch some of it.[2]

You wouldn't ridicule my stove if you sat beside it, or if you had tasted the toast & honey & coffee I warmed on it last night, with the thermometer outside 40° or 50° below freezing while inside it was as warm as "<u>Mrs. Rogers Kitchen</u>", and I enjoying Dolce far niente, in <u>half</u> <u>dress</u>.

I am glad you read those books. They are both good & the Margarets are both superior characters & with some happiness both had a large share of trouble. Margaret of the "Cloister"[3] being by far the best painted, & I should have thought much more after your own heart than her namesake, but

1. Bayard Taylor was an American poet and literary critic. On January 13, 1862, he gave a lecture on "The American People"at the Mercantile Library in St. Louis.
2. Molly's brother William C. Wilson was part of Wilson & Atwell, a Union steam bakery.
3. The book *The Cloister and the Hearth* was written by Charles Reade in 1861.

the tale is unsatisfactory. Though as a picture of life in the middle ages, I believe a very perfect one with a Flemish accuracy of detail as to all the Features, dress & household arrangements of the parties concerned, & therein consists much of its pleasure to me, being like a picture of one of the Old Masters, a glimpse into another world of which we know not of nowadays. Either Margaret will do for me as a heroine!

As to papers, all St. Louis news will be very welcome, but do not trouble or task yourself. As long as I stay here, I will have opportunities occasionally, but if we go further on the plains, I will then have to trust to you entirely as to the news. I'm afraid it might get lost by the way or stolen from the mail. Otherwise I would say, Do so if you love me.

With Love to yourself Sallie & all the folks I am ever

Sincerely yours,

James E. Love

James Love's aunt Mary Jane Adams, ca. 1862. James E. Love Papers, Missouri Historical Society, from originals in care of Dr. Arthur Love.

Camp Hunter
Ft. Leavenworth Kansas
Feby 2d 1862
My Dearest Eliza

I recd your dear & welcome note yesterday and to day being lazy day in camp, I must commence to answer.

I went to church this morning again, & heard a good old Presbyterian sermon, about obedience to the Powers that be, when legally constituted, and payment of taxes &c, &c, founded on the Text "Render unto Cesar the things which are Cesar's & unto God the things which are God's." It was quite refreshing to hear, after some of the fine spun St. Louis sophisms. It was cold bitter cold all the walk to town & back and commenced snowing again at noon & has snowed all afternoon since, thus keeping all hands in their tents, & quite spoiling our boys open air cookery. Poor fellows they suffer on such a day considerably! I got a paper in town of last Friday's & had quite a treat this afternoon reading it.

The War seems to move a little at last, & promises now I think a settlement of some kind this year. Our boys seem very anxious to be in it. I don't know how they would like its realities but this suspense wears upon all, & still more upon them now while inactive.

I look for that daguerreotype you <u>promised me</u> some time soon, but as long as you favor me with such pleasant heart Photographs as you promise, and as I have just received, I will hold you fully absolved of your promise.

I do certainly congratulate you on your heroism as I know what it is to break the Ice; I owe you several kisses for it, & hope I may be able to repay you soon.

I've had but little sleigh riding. I've no inducement, no lady friends – and you know that is the main charm after all – and besides Uncle Sam has not paid any of us a cent since last August so none of us could afford to be gallant under present circumstances in this a strange land even if our lady friends were present.

Alex says the girls have both got colds & he is in low spirits about losing his sleigh rides. Now pray take care of your cold as you have to fear it more than ought else. I am much more robust than you, and believe me I take my <u>own advice</u> & <u>yours</u>.

Your letters of Tuesday or Wednesday will just come in time for me to answer on Sunday and as I will go to church every Sunday morning while here, I think the Sin if any will be small. It will be only our old Sunday talks again.

I have studied little or no Spanish yet. I take some lessons in tactics, play some checkers & Backgammon, a little drill daily & half my time tinkering & fussing around for the benefit of the men, & my own amusement I might say, for the time passes really very fast & the only trials to my courage & endurance, consists in jumping out of bed in the morning with the thermometer at about zero, but I soon jump into Boots a yard long nearly & overcoat &c to match & touch a match to the stove. I am in ten minutes up to Summer heat. Then to roll call, & after that wash & dress for breakfast & dress parade at ½ past 8 oclock. Thus we have plenty of work & a good appetite and I am stout & bronzed though I see "nary" drop of Lager or Whisky, only an occasional Cigar, when I wish for amusement or when I think of you & my other dear friends ala *Reveries of a Bachelor*.[1] Dont you remember it! all the way from a cigar to a coal fire – ashes & all!

Do you begrudge me it? You see I confess it all! If so why I must quit it, & will if you say so when I've got you along side for consolation! Adio!

Tuesday 8 A.M.

I haint had time to mail this yet as you may see. All goes well & right. Weather very pleasant – exhilarating & cold.

The Kansas 1st came to town last night & there was a great reception. Your humble servant & his mates, could only catch a glimpse.

With Love to all friends & yourself

I am My Dear Girl

Yours Sincerely

James E. Love

---

1. *Reveries of a Bachelor* was written by Donald Grant Mitchell, under the pseudonym Ik Marvel, in 1850.

Camp Hunter
Fort Leavenworth Kansas
Feby 9th 1862
My Dear Molly

I rec'd yours as usual yesterday, and can I say how welcome it was! It is always the event of the week! It makes me wish so much that I could have something sweet to tell you each time in return, or if not some adventures or movements of interest to me, & that my vanity would make me hope would be interesting to you – but no, here we are on this beautiful hillside as heretofore, sheltered from the coldest blasts of the West & N.W. wind by the bluffs, back of which stretch in wintry coldness at present the illimitable prairie – or plains – so called. The whole situation is beautiful, & only man is vile. The weather too is, would you believe it, delicious, with a bright, clear, pleasant sun lately, in which the Ice & Snow wastes imperceptibly – sometimes in the afternoon a little slush – not much – as the air is keen & cold even after 24 hours south wind.

I am according to routine very busy most the time about the most insignificant duties; superintending & working myself, as our men have had so much to suffer, from this to them entirely unexpected cold spell, against which their experience in St. Louis or <u>South of it</u>, has never taught them to prepare or guard. I thus prefer showing them or leading them to driving them – as I would do old Soldiers, or say Wisconsin troops.

Then again I am a great carpenter with an axe, a penknife & saw. I have accumulated far more for comfort & convenience around our crowded Tent than any other in camp can boast of – don't expect any beauty. I'm not handy that way and don't study appearance, only comfort.

And then I have the tent full nights with chequers backgammon & cards. There is quite a furor over the camp about chequers, & over a dozen boards & men have been manufactured, but I have the only dice or cards, so we have some very pleasant & quiet games <u>(among the Officers</u>).

Mine is also the reading room at the expense of a paper occasionally. I have with some trouble & a great deal of running around established exchanges all over the camp, so that I have the reading of all the papers that come here & those who thus favor me, I see that <u>they</u> read in turn all I can offer. I find thus that I can now see the *Democrat* or *Republican* 2 or 3 days sooner than you could possibly send it, as it starts at one oclock in the morning by Express on the date of its publication & so I read Fridays *Democrat* last night (Saturday), but if I had the *Ill. L. News*[1] I would be a little <u>King</u> – I hate to say so – but I do wish to keep the run of English News & Sentiment under present excitement.

I mention again today that I was at church at the Epis. Methodist Church, where I saw a large crowd, heard a good sermon, sang some good old tunes in good old style, with the help of a very good large melodeon or small organ I don't know which & felt much at home only for the invariable & mendacious Methodist <u>whine</u>, that came in occasionally by the preacher, & the groans or amens with which the audience responded. It may be all right & many that do so are probably honest, but I don't like it & can't persuade myself that it ain't mostly hypocrisy. It smacks of the Pharisees against which he preached and now although I have made up my mind to attend church while in <u>camp</u>, that is in the Army, regularly as long as there is one within several miles of us I do not intend to bore you with it, & will only mention it when it is an event, that is a new church, or place or circumstance connected.

I am surprised about E.A. though I expected something would happen when I found Wm get so warm on the McPheeters question. By the bye, my predictions are coming true as to the treatment of Secesh, judging from the newspaper reports I see now. Mercantile Library, Preachers, Lawyers, Doctors & Institutions of all & every kind got to come up & take the Oath & live up to it when taken or suffer.[2] That is only right & simple justice their

---

1. The *Illustrated London News*, the world's first illustrated weekly newspaper, first published in 1842.

2. James's exact reference to his cousin Eliza Ann, "E. A.," is unclear. However, many citizens of St. Louis, including state employees, preachers, and teachers, had to sign loyalty oaths. Also, in January 1862, an assessment committee in St. Louis listed Dr. William M. McPheeters as a disloyal person. The provost marshal ordered a seizure of McPheeters's property, which was sold at auction on February 3, 1862.

traitorous proceedings & information given has already cost us more blood & treasure than all the armed secesh in the South will for years to come. Those who are not for us are against us in this life struggle of liberty or despotism & if they live & get protection, & make money, not to say fawn & lie & steal from our government, why they have a right to obey it in word & deed at least or bear the consequence. Yes even the Misses Secesh. We will be happy to exchange them all & every one for their betters in all that makes man loved & lovely & Godlike. The much persecuted, much abused Union men & <u>women</u> of Tennessee & the entire south – vide, letters found in Zollicoffer's camp. How the poor, heroes & heroines, I might say martyrs for conscience sake, have suffered & bled, & been hunted & shot like wild game in the mountains this cold winter, while we were so tender footed all fall as not to march an Army through Kentucky into Tennessee for their protection, by which we could have saved thousands of valuable lives (& property) but would not anger the Kentucky Secesh, giving them time for repentance which they have disdained to accept, while our friends who still worshipped the old flag of their Fathers, & the Constitution under which we have gained all our glory, were shot & imprisoned like dogs because they would not take up arms against their brothers – but enough of this. There is a speedy and dreadful reckoning preparing by both God & man for the author's of this horrid State of Affairs.[3]

Did you see in *Harper* of the 8th a piece entitled God's Soldier Now. I think there is a good deal in that & in many of its little articles on the 2d Page, but perhaps it was asking too much of the young lady, whether real or imaginary & so is painful even to read. I must repeat the statement that I increase in weight without the aid of Lager. All drinks are contraband, & entitle the possessor or drinker to a course of sprouts in the guard house & at wood chopping.

As to my being mistaken for Fremont, I esteem him too highly to ever venture a comparison, though circumstances & the fact of his having "Jes-

---

3. Most people in the eastern part of Tennessee remained loyal to the Union after the state seceded, and they had to fight the Confederate forces of General Felix Zollicoffer.

sie" for a wife and old "Bullion"[4] for a father in law might have much to do with it and I would mildly insinuate that it showed a great want of taste & perception on the part of the Young Ladies!! I wish I could help on the Scrap Book – with the privileges of a <u>brother</u> or <u>cousin</u>! even! Jim Lane is still Lord paramount here, though he has been denied the command. So we are no more the Kansas 2d!! but per contra Gen'l Hunter has declared we shall go to New Mexico or remain Kansas if he <u>himself</u> is not removed!

And now my dear dear Eliza, I hope all does go well (& will) with you & yours & all you <u>Love</u> & as this is about the only <u>Valentine</u> I can send this year, believe me My dear Girl I am ever yours –

Love

P.S. I must confess this whole letter is "Much ado about Nothing

Love

I recd a letter & some goods per Ex. from Alex. All O.K. and in good time

Love

When storms abroad beat o'er my way

I know who waits at home

To greet me with a warm caress,

And longs for me to come.

Her voice is full of melody,

Love's Melody, I mean

And Dark brown hair adorns the brow

Of my Loved Valentine!

How oft at night she softly comes

To kiss me in my Dreams;

I almost think I am awake,

So actual it seems:

---

4. Major General John C. Frémont's wife, Jessie, was the daughter of Senator Thomas Hart Benton, nicknamed "Old Bullion."

She moves around me all the day (in thought)
As graceful as a queen;
May no dark shadows ever cloud
Your path Sweet Valentine
Love!

Winter Quarters in Camp – The Inside of a Hut. From Harper's Weekly, January 24, 1863.

Fort Leavenworth
Sunday Evening
February 16th 1862
My Dear Molly
Twas a calm still night.
And the moons pale light &c

Only the moon has not yet arisen, as it will in an hour, but the thousand & one stars beam brightly, & the pale tremulous light of the milky way streaks the heavens and mingles with numerous lights from the watch fires & tents, while the buzz of many voices fills all the air around.

It is the end of a glorious day, well spent by the few, badly by the many. And so I sit me down to write, well pleased with all the world & the rest of mankind.

Have I not received yours of the 11th with all its treasured contents! A joyful surprise really you must take care! I fear I will become vain. If I am not already?

Your photograph is charmingly executed and looks every inch the lady; your very self and yet not half yourself.

I miss the ever changing smile & animation of course that go so much to make up our recollection of a loved face that we have studied! "You Start for soul is wanting there" & although the soul may & <u>does</u> look through the eyes, still you would wish to breathe the breath of life, into the dear dumb image & make the presence real! But no! Ah no! It will not cannot speak or move! It lacks the poetry of motion, and so pleased yet pained, you muse & dream on the times that have been and <u>the</u> <u>opportunities</u> <u>you</u> <u>have</u> not <u>improved</u> &c &c &c.

Well I am romancing again! Will I ever become practical, & put some of my vain romance in action? Echo answers it is late in the day! Verily the spirit is often willing but the flesh is weak.

A Valentine too! But a truce to blarney as I've no doubt you'll call it. I sent an informal one in a hurry myself! Hope you got it in time! I am sorry to hear you corroborate Alex's account of your cold. I can truly say of that, that only am I afraid, either as to myself or you. I wish I had you as safe under shelter of my robe, as I am often myself. Verily it is a shield to me as I would wish to be to a__hem.

When my brother officers & men are shivering under perhaps 5 Blankets, I am as warm as if in the old chimney corner (my grandmothers large one for instance).

But dont believe I would lose my kisses even for the dreaded cold. Why I think that w'd only be a fresh incitement.

"I'd kiss the place to make it well you know" &c if not out of sympathy!

Thanks for that Cigar! But I hope still to continue enough master of myself to give it up at any time, when I might fancy it disagreeable to you, or even to a lady I dislike from politeness.

Glad to hear you are still able to go around shopping. Guess you'll get over the swelled lips after all.

Nothing of very great importance has happened in the Interim. But we have been all very jubilant over the Kentucky and Roanoke victories and the cry is still the news comes in. Today we hear of the capture of Fort Donaldson and also of a victory by Sigel at Springfield. I hope they are all true, and in saying so I believe it w'd be for the best interests of the Seceders as well as ourselves. I am sorry to hear of the particular case of our friend Kelly, but I have heard him counsel much worse treatment for Union Men – myself included. That w'd be no reason, but we are at war – war to the Death & when the Leading Conspirators commenced the War at Sumter & elsewhere in Texas & New Mexico <u>they never thought</u> of all the Ten thousand Kelly's, Brown's & Jones both North & South. But as I said above, I hope all the energetic movements now going on will soon bring peace in its train & with peace, good will & trade & traffic & money as heretofore after all other wars – whether Civil or Uncivil – for believe me almost the only bad feeling left after this will be found in Missouri, Kentucky & Maryland. Far in the South, where the original Secesh have suffered, we will be received with open arms as deliverers, while in St. Louis, where Secesh had not the chance to ripen & bear fruit after its kind, the old grudge will rankle for years, & I fear often break out in Blood!

Our Snow wastes daily & the sun you begin to feel his rays, but winter even yet reigns supreme & the river is iron bound & contraband cross as of yore in squads, to this their promised Land. Poor Sambo! He is in a manner idolised here and yet his promised Land is like Jordan a very hard road to travel. What do you think? The other night a pack of Prairie Wolves – "coyotes" – ran some rabbits I supposed nearly into camp before they give up the chase. They had evidently got starved out on the prairie & had to come near the settlement in chase of the numerous Rabbits there <u>abounding</u>. They kept up their baying & howling all night, a most <u>infernal</u> <u>din</u>, the cowardly wretches make. Several times since we have heard them. Per consequence, I have been very curious to see Mr. "<u>Coyote</u>", & gone out to look for him more than once, but in daylight they are not visible, though we could see their lairs in the rock places (or holes) about the bluffs. In our travels yesterday, we tracked a large Bear over a mile up a ravine in the snow, where he was in the habit of going & coming to get water, but neither was Mr. "<u>Bruin</u>" visible to the naked eye of your humble servant his companions or the Dogs.

We did however get some fine views of Prairie, Bluff & River with its attendant cotton woods winding in the Near & Far distance in hazy laziness – or rather in icy bonds. The Bluffs reminded me much of headlands at sea, say the Irish Coast. I've seen just such. The furthest off – say 20 miles blue & misty – almost a cloud, then near, nearer, nearest in graceful lines until you can see every house Village & tree & so to where you stand, while the glorious Wild free Prairies stretch & roll and the Winds blow over them too just like the billows, with resistless sweep & with the same fresh, pure exhilarating feeling. These wintry days at least. These were my first slight experience of the endless plains that stretch from here in unending lines for near a thousand miles North, south & West. And I know as long as there is a <u>water</u> <u>prospect</u>, with perhaps a bluff in the distance I shall like them. That gives the Charm of Association of the <u>older</u> <u>time</u>. After the first Charm of novelty wears off them & <u>this</u> is absent, I fear they will become tiresome. Those in North Missouri seem so already and I've only passed over them three times. So mote it be.

But in exploring the Bluffs & Prairies I must not forget the Rabbit hunts we've had – great excitement, nary gun, all of us hollering like Wild Indians, Dogs Barking, Dogs & Men run up or down a plain or nearly a precipice as it may be quite recklessly & so with stick & rock & Dog, we've caught our Rabbits once & again.

And so the time passes & we can sit down & smoke the Calumet of Peace (as we did yesterday) on a snow bank & no man make us afraid. We have an artist with us too, who sketches for several of the Illustrated Papers & there has been several of our scenes in print already (one or two in *Harper*) & more you will see probably there or else where. He is one of the few <u>American Gentlemen</u> you meet with. He has traveled much in Europe & joined us in order to travel to New Mexico, but is contented where the Fortune of War leads us.

He is my particular friend. We have much in common to discuss, of travel &c. I wish you were alongside us sometimes. Really when I get away by myself I cant tell what I've seen, but when alongside another, it all comes back again. And so we travel France & Britain Sea & Land, & feel heroes for the Nonce.

But I must Good night. The Moon is high & near the witching hour. I've had many interruptions in the way of visitors & had to imprison two of our boys that got Drunk in town.

Remember me to Sallie, your mother & all & believe me Dear Eliza

Sincerely Yours

James E. Love

Alexander shall have a letter. The Dear boy shant be jealous of you.

Camp Hunter
Fort Leavenworth Kansas
Feby 24th 1862
My Dear Molly

I am a little behind time this week, caused through a dearth of news in these parts and an expectation of something important as far as we or even this department is concerned hourly but no! Our movements are postponed daily & our consolidation is not yet consummated. We have now I believe a certainty, that it will be done before the 1st of March and then comes our arms and pay.

As far as can be learned our number is the 8th Kansas. And on last Sunday (yesterday) Three Companies started for Fort Kearney. Two more have been located at the Fort. We & three other companies at present in camp with us will get our orders before or immediately after pay day and may go to Fort Scott, Fort Riley or most anywhere on the Kansas border, not out of the state at the present.

There is great activity manifested everywhere & in every Regiment but our unfortunate squad in this department and evidences before us go to prove that we will soon have the state of Kansas pretty much to ourselves, our duty being to look after straggling Jay-hawkers, Secesh & Indians, while General Hunter and his Expedition goes South if General Halleck does not require the remainder of his men.

There is not much glory in this programme for us and our boys grumble considerably at the prospect, but there is more safety, and we expect to see some wild country & Tame Indians. And then too New Mexico still looms in the distance like a mirage – further & further off each time – and contingent on how the War progresses both there & here, but we shall see if we live long enough what is to happen.

We had much excitement during the week caused by the news of Victory but no displays of any kind, and we all wished ourselves in St. Louis just for a day to see the fun.

Washington's birthday went off very quietly too, barring that quite a number of our men got drunk & got in the guard house, caused by an Irish fight in honor of the day.

I was in Camp all day. Most of the officers were in town but came back disappointed. There was quite a Ball & Supper at the Fort, but none of us went, reasons various, principally the want of money & arms.

I am in good health & will be in better spirits when I know my fate.

The War is not over yet, though we may go from success to success, there may be some unexpected reverses and especially in Arkansas (Price & Sigel) and all the way west of that to New Mexico & Texas, where the country is new & rough the War may be long.

I hope to hear however of the old & rich States giving up soon now that their Niggers are in danger.

I recd yours of the 18th in good time on Saturday night as usual.

Sorry to hear that any of your friends or acquaintances had friends lost in the fight. I see Col. Morrison's name in today's paper however as among the wounded.

It was a well fought fight where many brave fellows went to their last home.

Though ever thinking I find when I come to paper, I can find but little to say under present circumstances.

I hope to do better but wish to close for the mail, so with much Love to yourself and all friends I am my dear Molly

ever sincerely yours

James E. Love

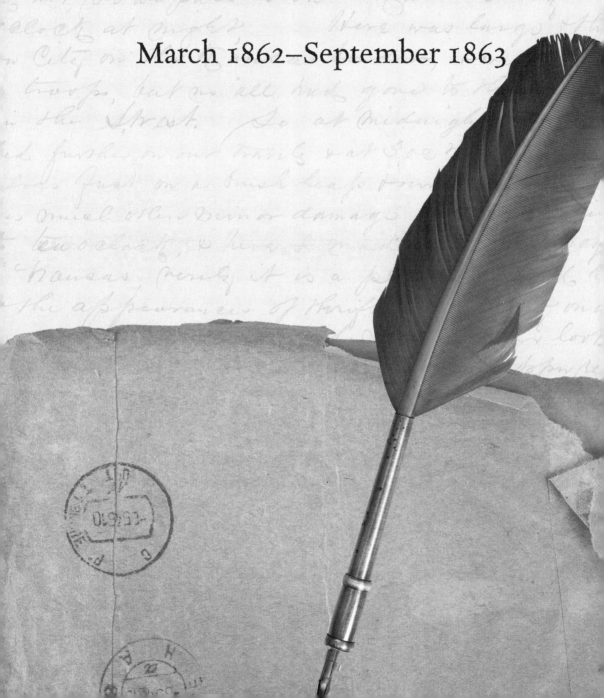

Section 2

EIGHTH KANSAS INFANTRY

March 1862–September 1863

During his eighteen months of active service with the Eighth Regiment, Kansas Infantry, as he endured strenuous marches and his first battle, as well as faced a devastating personal crisis, James continued to write letters to Molly. For the first few months of 1862, he remained in Kansas to defend the border against attacks by guerrillas. In late May 1862, five companies of the Eighth Kansas, including James's Company K, finally left Kansas and headed to the war. Over the next sixteen months, they marched and fought in many of the primary campaigns and battles in the western theater of the war, repeatedly pursuing and fighting the forces of Confederate general Braxton Bragg in Kentucky, Tennessee, and Georgia.

After several months of marching in pursuit of Bragg, who had invaded Kentucky, James fought in his first battle when his regiment, part of the Army of the Ohio commanded by Major General Don Carlos Buell, encountered Bragg's army at Perryville, Kentucky, on October 8, 1862. The battle was a draw, as Buell failed to order the movements that would have achieved a decisive victory, and Bragg realized that he was short on men and supplies and decided to retreat, eventually moving into Tennessee.

Largely due to his failure to defeat Bragg, Buell was relieved of his command, and the Eighth Kansas became part of the Army of the Cumberland, commanded by General William S. Rosecrans. The army followed Bragg into Tennessee, where the two sides continued to skirmish. In December, the regiment was ordered to report to Nashville for provost duty, and they set up camp near the State House. At the end of the month and into early January 1863, several regiments from James's brigade fought Bragg's army in the Battle of Stones River, or Murfreesboro. James and his regiment remained in Nashville to guard the city. The Confederates were driven back, and Bragg and his men retreated on January 3.

In June 1863, after six months of provost duty in Nashville, James's regiment rejoined Rosecrans's army as it embarked on the Tullahoma, or Middle Tennessee, Campaign to force Bragg out of the area. By early July, Rosecrans's army succeeded and Bragg's forces retreated to Chattanooga.

In the midst of these arduous military campaigns, James received a letter from Molly in which she ended their engagement. Since Molly's letters did not survive, the exact circumstances are not known. However, it appears that Molly's family learned about her secret engagement and influenced her decision. Shattered, James obtained a furlough and returned to St. Louis for the first time since June 1862. After meeting with Molly's family and visiting Molly in Washington, Illinois, he successfully renewed the engagement. He rejoined his regiment at the end of August.

By the time James returned, the men were in the midst of movements, now known as the Chickamauga Campaign, toward Bragg's army at Chattanooga. Rosecrans, wanting to force Bragg out of Chattanooga, decided to surround the city rather than attack it directly. The large army marched up and down through the mountains surrounding Chattanooga, in Tennessee, Georgia, and Alabama. They bravely crossed the Tennessee River in boats, expecting the enemy to shoot them at any moment. By mid-September, Rosecrans learned that Bragg had evacuated Chattanooga and was concentrating his army at Lafayette, Georgia. Rosecrans had to quickly gather his forces, which were spread out over forty miles between Chattanooga and Alpine, Georgia. The two armies began a series of constant movements, skirmishing often. By nightfall on September 18, 1863, the two armies were on opposite sides of the Lafayette Road, which led to Chattanooga—Bragg's army on the east side of the road, and Rosecrans's on the west. Due to the heavy woods along the road, neither army knew the exact location of the enemy. James was camped in a cornfield near Crawfish Spring, and on September 19 he wrote a letter from that camp before marching to the front lines of the Battle of Chickamauga.

During the two-day Battle of Chickamauga, Bragg's and Rosecrans's armies fought along several miles of the Lafayette Road. On the first day, Bragg's troops reached the road but were repeatedly forced back. The next day, September 20, in the afternoon, the Confederates charged just as a gap opened in Rosecrans's lines. Most of the Union army was forced to retreat, including Rosecrans and two of his corps commanders. One corps fought until after dark but eventually retreated. Bragg and the Confederates won the battle, but Rosecrans's army remained intact. The battle was the bloodiest in the western theater of the war. Of the 65,000 who fought on the Confederate side, the army counted 18,454 killed or wounded. On the Union side, 62,000 men fought, with 16,170 killed or wounded, including James. At 8:00 a.m. on September 19, his division left its camp at Crawfish Spring and marched eight miles, along a dusty road heavy with smoke from burning fence rails, toward the continuous thunder of cannon and artillery. After a brief rest at Rosecrans's headquarters, the brigade moved forward toward the heaviest fighting, with James's regiment in the center of the front line. After marching almost a mile through dense woods, the troops faced repeated charges by line after line of the Confederate army. According to Bill McFarland, in his history of the Eighth Kansas, the regiment lost "5 captains, 3 lieutenants, and over 150 men shot down in less than half an hour."[1] While on the extreme front, two balls hit James in the thigh, and he passed out. He awoke to the Confederates' second line marching over him, cannon fire hitting the trees around him, and an enemy soldier pressing a bayonet to his chest. Fortunately, a Confederate lieutenant from the Hospital Corps arrested the soldier, tied handkerchiefs above and below James's wounds, then moved James behind a tree and covered him with a rubber blanket. James remained on the field for twenty-six hours before he was moved to a Confederate field hospital. During the ten days he spent there, in a cotton field with no medical personnel, a soldier from his company, Private Fred Neiderbrocker, who was also wounded, tended to his wounds and most likely saved James's leg. After over two years of military service, James was wounded and a prisoner of the Confederates.

---

1. Bill McFarland, *Keep the Flag to the Front: The Story of the Eighth Kansas Volunteer Infantry* (Overland Park, KS: Leathers, 2008).

Fort Leavenworth

Kansas

March 2d 1862

My Dear Molly

Why my Dear Girl you have surpassed yourself! Two letters in one week! Wont it leak out!! What will the <u>world</u> say? Why I shall be afraid to come back to St. Louis! And then — what then? Do you think the mountain would come to Mahomet? Eh! But I think I hear you say, "Pshaw! The mans mad!" So I'll no more of it, but try if I can for once write a little sense.

Well I recd yours of Sunday last very quickly, and thereat was much surprised until I read the contents, and it proved to be the first news of what I thirsted for — that is of the great demonstration truly the old Mound City surpassed herself.[1] I hope it was all real & not <u>bogus</u> Union sentiment. I've just read last night the *Democrat* of the 24th and Oh! How I wish I was there. I would have so enjoyed besides all the reasons you have given & that you can imagine to have studied the faces and poked fun at some of my <u>former</u> "Secesh" friends. Talked about the war for instance or about driving the "Dutch" into the river &c, &c.

I am sorry I overlooked mentioning to have rec'd the I.L.N. all safe & in good condition. The first numbers were a long time on the way but I have just now rec'd the fifth number of which you speak & it you see has come through by express. I cannot thank you just now sufficiently! but that is not all my trouble. I fear they will get worn out. They are in such demand and I have such a poor place to keep them.

Apropo of that lecture though I fear I have made some maladroit assertion. I hope the gossips & prophets are all wrong for your sake and mine and at all events I won't argue the point just now, but we shall all see what we shall see, if we live long enough. I wish I could straighten myself. I thought the three months service would have done something for me in that way ere I entered but such expectations were falsified and I don't see much bet-

---

1. A reference to the recent celebration of President George Washington's birthday in St. Louis, which was sometimes called the Mound City.

ter prospect in this tent life, although there is much to do. There is in this weather so much to do <u>inside</u>, in such a confined & often inconvenient position & manner, that I won't wonder if its worse I'm getting.

Talking of the weather – I am glad to hear from you & the papers how fine you fare in that way in St. Louis. Here we have had some fine days & gradual thaws when the sod would be so saturated that water would churn out an inch deep & so wet feet & many colds. But all this is gone by. Yesterday it blew cold & rained & froze until all was in a glaze of Ice. So it continued all night; and all day to day it has snowed fine pieces like Mustard seed until it is now over four inches deep & old King Frost is monarch again. So we go in Kansas. While the Old Missouri that has been getting rather rotten lately for wagons is again frozen as solid as ever, & looks as if winter would last an age. I expect this is the last kick of the expiring season. So the boys don't grumble at it so much as you might expect. We had our usual bimonthly muster & inspection last Friday, & your humble servant had in consequence 4 or 5 days very hard writing to do, but that is all past & was rather a pleasure than a task, in consequence of the change & excitement. I've no further news of our future movements since last writing. I'm glad it does you a pleasure our location & inaction. I can't say I admire it so much myself and if you heard our boys talk of it, you would find the language more forcible than polite & would expect nothing but mutiny & desertion if they were not soon led into action. I fear some of them will desert to go to <u>Kentucky</u> or <u>home</u> when they get paid off – as they ought to & expect to soon – & even if <u>they</u> <u>don't</u>!

As I'm daily duty bound I've just paid my respects to your photograph (you'll find it in my inner vest pocket) but I would like to have been on hand to wear one of your rosettes! How I <u>envy</u> <u>Mr.</u> <u>Rogers</u> et al! I have not read "<u>Drakes</u>" oration yet, but I hope to tomorrow. We had but a quiet day, as you will have learnt by my last. I am glad to see from the papers that <u>Price</u> is chased out of Missouri at last. I hope it may be for the last time, both for his benefit & for that of Missouri. Poor Missouri has suffered enough and now that our "Secesh" friends have found out that one of them <u>cannot</u> <u>whip</u> 5 of us, I think that they might settle down in that Latitude at least <u>quietly</u> if not <u>crestfallen</u>.

Troops are moving here daily, as well as in Missouri. I pity the poor fellows from Wisconsin that left yesterday. I'm afraid they will have a cold night on the prairie. We have just excused our guard (so I learn) for the night, a most unusual course, & what we've never done before. As to myself what can I say – nothing new during the present monotony – except that I've had a slight bilious attack for the first time in my life. I'm all right but ever thinking of the time when wars alarms being over I'll have "My own loved Molly Dear Sitting by my Side" and <u>hope</u> that the "neer do well" will do better under the influence of a good example.

By the Bye, I infer from several references that Sallie, your Mother, &c all know of our correspondence fully, so I will not let my curiosity prompt me to enquire further? I am glad of it!

I wish I could map out some plans for the future, but I'm at fault, & cant. That's something new! I wonder what's going to happen considering my past <u>ill luck</u>. It ought to be of good augury. And now my Dear Eliza Pray remember me kindly to <u>all</u> – Mother, Mrs. Donnan, Sallie &c. I wont include Morgan St. but will sometime soon jog their memory myself. I am ever

Yours sincerely,

Love

Fort Leavenworth
March 9th 1862
My Dear Molly

Since I last wrote events have been progressing with us considerably and I have been strongly tempted to drop you a line, but I waited and here it is Sunday evening again. Well during the early part of the week there was much writing and excitement consequent on our consolidation into the Eighth Kansas Volunteers Comp. K, a long general order having been issued to that effect with Graham for Colonel and Provost Marshall General of State of Kansas, all of which is under Martial Law at present consequent on the large number of Indians, "Secesh" & Jayhawkers congregated and flourishing within our borders. These latter gentry especially have been committed to our tender care, with orders to shoot or string them up at a moments notice when found guilty or caught in the act. So perhaps you will soon hear of your humble servant playing Provost Marshall somewhere down on the borders, or scouting into Missouri after some of <u>your</u> benighted fellow citizens. We in fact expect to be located at West Point, away down on the border on the Osage River pretty soon. We move into Leavenworth City tomorrow, and thus break up our camp, where we have after all passed a pleasant winter as things go, and it passed quickly too, although each day seemed long. I don't like the city and will be glad to get out of it at once as it is the most God forsaken place I've ever seen yet. So both Capt. Herd & I are well pleased to get off by ourselves where we are & will be perfectly independent of all.

Well this news had no sooner stirred the monotony of camp life than a new excitement came in the shape of arms, the prettiest lightest little English Enfield Rifles you have ever seen, or I either. Warranted <u>death at 1100 yards</u>, and many of our boys are good shots too, so our secesh friends had better give us a wide berth. Well these were still as strange as a new baby when it was forward march up to the Fort for our six months pay. What joy in the camp that caused you can imagine! But our boys behaved well and sent large amounts home to their wives, fathers & friends, and there has been even less drunk than usual since, though there has been much traffic to town. There is much in the way of camp comforts to purchase and numerous daguerreotypes and other mementoes, not to speak of Pistols &c &c, which have so far proved a superior attraction to the usual dose of bad whisky.

Excitement is an epidemic you know when in a crowd. So I have shared in all this to a limited degree, not being so much interested as some to whom these same consolidations brought evil tidings. Several of our Officers got mustered out from various reasons, and near a dozen of the men too, who were unfit for active service, two of these from our company. Our Second Lieutenant for good and sufficient reasons was one of those who were compelled to resign. Still there is much of this changing around – both promotions & dismissions rather unjust, inasmuch as it goes not by merit, but like kissing "goes by favor". If I had a few friends at Governor Robinsons Court here, with a few thousand Dollars to spend in wine, dinners & bribes, I might soon be a Colonel or General. But as it is, I expect to continue for some time 1st Lieut. Company K 8th Kan. Vol., while some noodle who is 42d cousin to the aforesaid, mounts over my head without effort, service or work. So it is in Kansas.

But dont think I'm envious, it is only the injustice of the system I complain of as it presses on hard working & competent officers, and the injury to the cause by the acts of the incompetents that are thus foisted on the Nation!

I rec'd & enjoyed the fifth number of the *News*. It was really a fine number and from a passing glimpse I've just had of the Sixth, it is about equally good. I cannot deny myself the Luxury now, so I will post you at once of every change in our whereabouts, and as a soldiers letters or news follows him from camp to camp, I will I suppose get it as usual, especially if you mention the company and the Regiment.

I had quite a long and kind letter from Aunt Adams come to hand same time as your last, being a surprise it was right welcome. Bless her old soul it made me feel better all day and since I got both on Friday morning – very quick were they not, not half the usual time on the way. We had a welcome sight this morning – the movement of the Ice, under the influence of the warm March sun. And the strong March winds gracious don't it blow here. The changes from calm to hurricane & from heat to cold are more numerous, rapid & astonishing than I've seen yet. The River is all clear now from here to St. Louis, as the ice in this River don't gorge for any time, but sinks & melts at once on account of the Sand in it & the rapid current, so we expect to see boats directly. It is all hard & fast above this as yet, but must move in a day or two as the River rises and in time you ought to have a good flood after so much snow and cold weather in the mountains. I need not tell you that I am well. You will have inferred that long ere you read thus far. I expect to hear of you tearing some of these Epistles. It would serve me right for the many foolish & perhaps impertinent things I say. Don't you think a little quarrel would do us both good! Wouldn't it clear the atmosphere as a thunder storm does!? I don't know they say so however! But I don't want to try the experiment! Though I might confess to deserving it, if you would pick one? And so here goes to say it again. I wish I was in St. Louis just about one day, to get a look at your sweet face (and Sallies) in propria persona. There now! If that's treason make the most of it.

I'm afraid if I got one day that I would dawdle around so as to make three or four of it notwithstanding! I'd like to know why you thought me in low spirits. Why it's just the contrary, though I may grumble occasionally from one cause or another.

So I see my dear Sallie has been again dreaming about me. I don't know what's agoing to happen I'm sure, but they do say that part of every company in our regiment is to act as mounted Rifles say 10 or 20 men from each & I suppose your humble servant may mount a horse with the rest <u>if he</u> feels <u>like the expense</u>. Would that do for an interpretation.

But unfortunately that don't take me to St. Louis, so I think you'll just have to kiss her for me & tell her to try again! And some more potent spell may fetch me yet? So you begin to tell Telegrams too. That is a polite phrase nowadays for falsehoods, but I suppose yours is an oer true tale. Well all I've got to say about it is, just spank that Baby for me the first time you get a chance. I <u>don't like</u> boys, <u>never did</u> and I don't suppose that long expected phenomenon will be any exception, especially if its so like its Dad. I am glad to hear that William is as busy as usual for Uncle Sam and I suppose of course that also confines Alex, so I don't blame him for not patronizing me, & the more especially as he will have to correspond with Anna & his other Lady friends and he insinuates too that I get all the news without his assistance – the rogue – which discourages him. I am much beholden however to him & all for their good wishes, and their kind assistance when in their power and wish to be kindly remembered to Mr. and Mrs. Rogers, your mother, aunt, Sallie &c &c

And remain as ever

Yours Sincerely

James E. Love

Leavenworth Kansas

March 13th 1862

My Dear Molly

We are to move tomorrow, but I have not yet got the Official order so I don't know the particulars. I have waited for the latest opportunity to tell you, but as it is I must only guess.

Our company goes by itself to the border, just by West Point, Mo. and patrol back & forth for forty miles.

We are in the midst of preparation and part of our camp is struck. I shall write you from there, & give you the nearest Post Office as soon as I arrive, but it is over 8 days march, & if to that you add a few days for the letter to return, you will see that no matter how prompt I am you may not get a letter for two weeks.

I hope to hear from you sooner as I expect your letters to follow at once or perhaps precede us there.

I hope my dear girl, you will not feel uneasy. I am not going into any danger as yet that I know of. I see you are anxious that I should not, and so I hope not for your sake, but what little Presbyterianism I have left makes me something of a fatalist, i.e. I am in the hollow of <u>Gods</u> hand whether on the Field, in my Tent, or in your Parlor – equally safe – and so I won't <u>die</u> before my time comes, and my poor will won't defer the time! I say it in all love, I hope to live a long life yet, for <u>your</u> sake & my own, and so give you a chance if possible to be proud of the "Neer do Weel" yet?

I see by today's paper that we are once more under General Halleck's orders, that may <u>again</u> change all the programme out here, & I expect <u>it will</u> at once, to all but our Regiment, but as to us not just at <u>present</u> unless that it may give us a chance to go into Missouri but all is speculation, so I wont pursue it further.

We have had glorious news from all parts of the compass lately, excepting that naval engagement near Fortress Monroe, where we were evidently whipped by that mail clad vessel, although our brave sailors took their ships one after another to what seemed certain destruction, but that is only the beginning & sure as fate, we shall have her soon! We bide our time![1]

But things around are too prosaic to moralize & so I must close, with but little said & little to say

With Love to all, & the kindest love & wishes to yourself

I am as ever

My Dearest Eliza

Yours Sincerely

James E. Love

One kiss & goodnight

Love

"Deck View of the *Monitor* with her Crew." Photograph from Thomas Butler Gunn diary entry dated March 29, 1862, vol. 18, p. 91.

---

1. The naval engagement near Fort Monroe and Hampton Roads, Virginia, was the great battle between the *Monitor* and the *Merrimac* on March 9, 1862.

Leavenworth Kansas

March 15th 1862

My Dear Molly

We are yet as you see in the "Land of the Leal." My Tent as yet stands & almost alone, as all its companions have scattered & gone East, West, North & South and one of our companies that started last Tuesday, being better prepared with Wagons &c than us has had its fight already & two of its men wounded. They went in pursuit of the noted "Secesh" Jayhawker "Quantrel,"[1] who was in Kansas stealing horses &c, <u>found him</u>, pitched in and killed two & wounded two of his men, took some prisoners, & chased the balance into Missouri. Bravo! for the 8th Kansas!!

I commence to write just now as I have come across such a sweet scrap from Tom Hood the "<u>inimitable</u>" much <u>loving</u> & much loved Poet & Wit. It breathes the very essence of simplicity & love & I cant help copying it so that you enjoy it with me. We start about Monday and I thus fill up a leizure hour of almost the last night. Perhaps this scrap too comes home to me more as we had two deaths last Tuesday in our company. One our old cook Tom Southworth, one of the best old souls could live & the other our Teamsters Wife. Both died after 3 or 4 days illness from colds & exposure. Poor Tom had all due Military honors at the Fort Graveyard & the other had quite an aristocratic funeral to the city cemetery. I must now copy, or you will say too much preface

The Death Bed

We watched her breathing through the night,

Her breathing soft & low,

As in her breast the wave of life

Kept heaving to and fro.

So silently we seemed to speak,

So slowly moved about,

As we had lent her half our power,

To eke her living out

Our very hopes belied our fears

---

1. William Quantrill led a group of Confederate guerrillas.

Our fears our hopes belied –
We thought her dying when she slept,
And sleeping when she died.
For when the morn came dim & sad,
And chill with early showers,
Her quiet eyelids closed – she had
Another morn than ours.

but perhaps you have it by you so its only "Loves Labor Lost" but N'importe Goodnight

Love

March 16th 1862

Did you see a story in *Harper* of the 15th entitled the "Majors" Mittens. Quite a spicy little tale, aint it. Hope Bayne is another young Lady with great "force of character."

I have just recd this moment the L.N. of 15th Feby, but that of the 8th has not yet appeared. I hope it may yet.

Your letter of 12th March came to hand with it. I did not expect to be so fortunate as get it here. But while in a literary way, I want to know how it is I relish *Harper* for March so much. Is it the circumstances surrounding, or the stories Instance, Niagara, Cured, A Drawn Game, and a Soldiers letter – as good in their way especially the last. And then "Embarras des Riches". I feel I must read "Mistress & Maid by our old friend, the Authoress of "John Halifax &c & also in the *Weekly*, "No Name" by the author of "The Woman in White". See what a rich feast I spread for myself even under the shadow of a Great War. Will you accompany me in Spirit through the Tales, as you w'd if I was by your side & as I know you will in my little "role" in the great tragedy of war now enacting.

But I must leave literature for the present, & return to real life. Your letter Dear acts occasionally like a sniff from a flask of laughing gas or a Chinaman's pipe of opium. Molly Dear Molly Dear – you'll be the Death of me.

I'm so glad I thought of sending you two Billet Doux last week ere I read all your present <u>Badinage</u>. I'm repaid for all your teasing.

But I dont think you ever realized how much I enjoyed your teasing. I took such a pleasure, in <u>excusing</u> & <u>arguing</u> the point that I believe you mostly thought me in earnest & sometimes feared you would offend, when it suited me all better than the subtlest flattery.

But was it not flattery?

I recollect a long time since drawing good auguries as to the success of my suit! After you once interested yourself so much as to tease & lecture me. So again I say, was it not flattery?

Well I guess I wont publish anything about our affairs; I never believed there was much love lost when I heard a young man bragging about <u>his</u> Lady Love (not the future Lady Love) and at least common sense was scarce, so not to condemn myself. I guess I'll keep quiet, but they do say that I've been calling "Molly" in my sleep.

I don't believe it, but it mought be so?

I hope you think I've got over the blues. I'm sorry I sent that stupid note last Wednesday. It was so dull but I had written so much that I was drained of news & yet I didn't wish to start without goodbye, especially when I could find time to write so many pages on business.

Glad to hear of the fine weather. It has just reached us here today after 3 days cold rain, quite April weather or warmer today. I suppose plants & flowers will soon make their appearance here too, but as yet no sign.

Glad to hear of Sallie & Miss Burchard enjoying themselves hope they'll have much of it & that I may be there to see.

I guess what Ellen said about his (Johnnys) going to stay at St. Charles will prove true yet notwithstanding the Old Man curses and his disclaimers. At present I will bid you goodnight again with Love & remembrance to all but I wont post until I am "en route" through the city.

I am my dear girl

Yours Sincerely

James E. Love

Aubrey, Johnson Co.
Kansas
March 26th 1862
My Dear Molly

I have at last arrived at the Missouri Line & only 30 miles from Lexington, where I was last summer. I expect to have a pleasant time as I find the officers here more pleasant than those left behind. This is not first impressions either as I got acquainted with most of them during our winter in Camp Hunter, but these are <u>western</u> <u>men</u>, while <u>most</u> the other end of the Regt. are Illinois <u>Yankees</u>. A little too <u>Knavish</u> & <u>Pharasaical</u> for your humble servant to make bosom friends of though very pleasant passing acquaintances – exceptions there were of course, amongst which my artistic friend mentioned before. And a jolly <u>old</u> <u>Irish</u> <u>Gentleman</u> named Corker, from Cork, all the way, some 25 years gone bye. As you see we are here and a fine rolling prairie country it is. The town consists of about a dozen houses most of the owners have been driven away last fall by Price & Co, but now they are full of Union Refugees from Missouri who have fled here within two months in order to get protection from the Secesh Guerillas. This is the best place in the world for them while the Troops remain, as they have house room free, with feed for stock & firing ditto & Provisions dirt cheap – Potatoes 30¢ Corn 20¢ Eggs 5¢ Cabbages 5¢ a dozen & good & most other things as cheap as Cabbages. <u>We</u> live well just now & the spring sun shines bright & warm for two days. We had a hard journey though and found Kansas roads in spring time rather hard to travel <u>I believe</u>. Mush 10 inches deep & water on top nearly as much more was a common feature at the foot of each roll of the Prairie & especially in the bottoms by the sluggish Creeks which this sun will soon dry up.

But let me give you a leaf from my log, just for fun as I've half an hour to spare ere the mail goes & speaking of the mail they say it only comes & goes once a week & hasn't come at all all winter – nobody here to write or read letters. If it don't run however, <u>we</u> send a horse express to <u>Olathe</u> 12 miles & so connect with Uncle Sam & civilization. Yet as I said we are only 30 miles from Lexington 20 miles from Independence or "Liberty" or a dozen other <u>once</u>-thriving Missouri River towns but the vile spirit of secession & disunion has stopped the Mails, as well as all trade & even farming is at a stand still & so the poor ruined devils will almost starve to please a few hundred armed Guerilla bandits that rob & plunder & overawe both friends & foes.

But to my Journal —

We started last Tuesday & made but 5 miles, as we halted to finish our Supplies in Leavenworth City & many of our men were drunk & had to be tied to the rear of the wagon, rained most the time. Next day the 19th — We started ahead after a wet & stormy night and made the crossing of the "Stranger" through weighty Rain & had to dig the wagons out three times in 12 miles. Cold night & on the 20th snow an inch deep snowed all day — road wet & muddy — every body very miserable & wet. Camped at Wild Horse Creek — men in a "<u>Barn</u>" — Captain & I & about a dozen in a Shanty half a mile off — all in one loft. Got a good dinner & breakfast however so felt much better than our compatriots in the barn, who had to cook outside in the snow or rain made only 10 miles. Next morning 21st deep Snow — wagons stuck two hours at a creek, but we made Lawrence 7 miles after crossing the Kansas river, which is nearly as wide as the Missouri by a rope ferry boat pushed by the current each way by some patent Yankee Fixin. Camped in the main street in a tumble down store of a dirty old looking City — so new & yet so old is the Effect of the former Kansas War & the present Rebellion.

But I must close as the mail goes

Yours with much love

James E. Love

Address as before & I shall get it sometime

Love

"Massachusetts Avenue, Lawrence, Kansas. 38 Miles west of Missouri River." From *Across the Continent on the Kansas Pacific Railroad (Route of the 35th Parallel)*. Plate 10. Photograph by Alexander Gardner, 1867–1868.

Aubrey Johnson Co. Kansas
March 26th 1862
My Dear Molly

I aint half satisfied writing yet, so although the mail closed just now I mean to keep on writing a little longer, & so take up the thread of my narrative at Lawrence the muddy where our men got drunk again in order I suppose to forget their past hardships & prevent any ill effects from their late Exposure. We had thus the most miserable night of the trip, sober as we were of course. Next morning the 22d – got an extra wagon & some extra supplies & started at 10 oclock, but when 3 miles out in the "Wankerusha" bottom one of our wagons broke down & we had to camp until the teamster went back to town for another. A fine cold windy day, high grass on the prairie & on Fire in all directions. I accidentally raised a most extensive Fire from a match that I dropped after lighting a Cigar. It went off like a flash of powder and although I tried to put it out at once with some green bushes, & my big boots it defied my efforts – rather "<u>skared</u>" me & most burnt my whiskers off & proceeded roaring to Leeward of us at the rate of <u>15 or 20 mile an hour</u>. We camped on the "Wankarusha" Creek 4 ½ miles from town all night & had a fine view of the Fires for 20 miles up & down it. Next morning fine cool day. We started early & pushed over high ranges or bluffs for 20 miles with level prairie between – all prairie now between us & the rocky mountains or <u>Pikes Peak</u> – beautiful well settled country roads pretty hard as we took the "<u>range</u>" <u>road</u> & passed through half a dozen towns with high sounding names, though houses barely enough for a small settlement anywhere else – none of them over a dozen. Camped at Black Jack after a <u>pleasant</u> Sabbath days journey all before 2 oclock in the afternoon.

I intended writing all day but was too footsore & weary when the time came so I procrastinated until next day the 24th when we again made an early start & through a level rich prairie on the old & hard "Santa Fe" road. Made 20 miles more to Spring Hill – pleasant day & pleasant marching but hard work. So after calling on the Union folks & sparking some pretty girls –

besides going around at each village to see the Election – we slept sound & made an early start again under the inspiriting news of a fight just over & another impending – with seven miles to go, but we lost our road in the prairie & had to march 10 miles instead which we got through by ten oclock & camped at Aubrey under command of Major Schnieder a good specimen of a Knickerbocker or Pennsylvania Dutch Man.

That was yesterday the 25th & now already we begin to get our comforts around & I have been appointed "Adjutant" & Quartermaster to the Battalion. The Posts are no sinecure but the work is easy as I have a clerk to write while I sign my name & a Sergeant to scour the country for Beef &c while I do the Financial by signing my name. I've a horse at my service when I please to ride but my duties lay pretty much in camp and Capt. Herd has just bought a pony so I suppose I may probably do the same if time permits & I get a chance of a good trade. Capt. Herd expects his wife daily so he is preparing for her, hence the Pony.

I don't expect now to see much service here, as Quantrell the Leader here, has been wounded & seven of his man taken prisoners besides 8 more burned to death in their store houses where they had taken refuge & were firing on our troops.

One of our men was shot in the foot, the rest unhurt.

Quantrell has about 100 men & plenty of friends at his back in Missouri but is more of a jayhawker than a warrior & now that there is more troops here, he will give us a wide berth. But the Major calculates to go in search of him in a day or two & jayhawk the contents of his den or rendezvous if we can find it within 20 miles so there is fun ahead for somebody yet.

I guess he will run at any rate we will take wagons to pack the plunder.

He rides a fine horse & is another Dick Turpin in his way with his gallantry & chivalry & love's & hair breadth scapes & sometimes bloody deeds & is in consequence the great Hero of this section.

We shall see.

I have not heard from you later than the 12th Inst. But I suppose there is a couple on the way somewhere. So I hope you are in good health & spirits

& expect a feast in good time on the papers & letters that Molly the Dear Dear Girl has sent me lang syne.

I am better & better daily & if I had ten miles a day to walk for a month to come would feel all the better for it. I think I am safe over any spring fevers or such – nothing better than this walk could have occurred for my health or spirits – as even you divined that I was fast getting the "blues" from inaction & not I alone for it was epidemic in the camp and over 20 men deserted during February under the influence.

The prairie wind & sun here is cold but I get brown & bronzed daily & I believe health goes with it.

Look out for an account of our trip in the *Democrat*, if they only think worthwhile to publish it.

I see that at last troops must be sent to New Mexico. I wonder if "Halleck" will send us? If "Hunter" was here he would!

But I don't believe our Colonel will ask to go <u>now</u> that he is <u>Provost Marshall General of Kansas</u> & that he & half his officers have arranged to make their wives comfortable & especially now that there is fighting to be done out there & hard times ahead for the ladies at least if not for the soldiers – for according to the first ideas, both officers & men were to take their wives along – time will tell. I will take no step to urge Providence or the powers that be to send me there but I must say that in my heart I have still a sneaking wish to travel that way or perhaps it is only sorry that I am not there to help the Gallant Canby[1] & the few white folks out there for the cowardly "Greasers" can not be depended upon. So mote it be! Amen!!

I am a week behind the times now as to news, for so long I've not seen a paper & in these days within that time there sometimes occur great events. As soon as I close I intend taking some steps to get the "*Democrat*". Meantime goodnight my love & I expect to put a P.S. ere the Express leaves tomorrow. <u>Yours</u> <u>Love</u>

---

1. Brigadier General Edward R. S. Canby, Union commander in New Mexico.

28th Our men have just come back from that reconnaisance 7 miles into Missouri & across lots some 7 more making over 20 miles! & back by 2 oclock without seeing but one Irishmen, supposed to be a Union man. They found plenty of empty houses & deserted farms but could see nothing of "Quantrell" or his band. They rescued the stock of cattle hogs & chickens belonging to a Union man who went along as guide & picked up some nicknacks & packed home some eggs & chickens that were wild in hundreds on several farms. Thousands of <u>bushels</u> of corn, potatoes, turnips, cabbages & apples all rotting with no one to look after. Honey too & young colts & cattle – too poor to drive just now or they would have brought some too.

In short as there was no inhabitants & no guerillas they went a little on the jayhawk.

We may go back again next week! & if we are again unsuccessful in finding our opponent we will bring some wagon loads of Feed! I cannot leave camp until relieved unless as a spectator & on horseback.

I am My Dear Eliza –

With much love & kind remembrance to all <u>friends</u>

Ever Yours Sincerely

<u>Love</u>

<u>address for the present!</u>

Lieut. James E. Love

Co K. 8th Kansas Vol.

<u>Aubrey</u>

via Olathe

Johnson Co.

Kansas

"Waukerusa Valley, south from Lawrence, Kansas." From *Across the Continent on the Kansas Pacific Railroad (Route of the 35th Parallel).* Plate 12. Photograph by Alexander Gardner, 1867–1868.

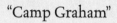

"Camp Graham"

Aubrey Johnson Co.

Olathe P. Office

Kansas April 3d 1862

My Dearest Molly

Yours of the 18th March only came to hand last night together with the I.L.N. for 22d Feby.

I suppose that both lay at Leavenworth for some days.

I had one from William same time & he spoke of your indisposition & returning convalescence. I hope my dear girl you take good care of yourself. You are far too <u>unselfish</u> for your own good, but I know it is your pleasure & happiness to be so & I've only to say you are not very strong & can easily over exert yourself.

Why not mention it? It only makes me think & fear the more when I hear of it thus indirectly.

Mrs. Capt. Herd came to camp two or three days since unexpectedly & although rather uncomfortable for her – in fact very much so – it has added considerably to <u>our</u> comfort. I mean Capt. Herd's & myself.

We have had a very wet rainy spell with a constant storm of wind from all points of the compass in succession & nothing for her but a cold tent. <u>I have a stove</u> I would have been gallant enough to give it up but it don't suit her tent. She lay at Kansas City for 3 or 4 days ere she could communicate with us or find our exact whereabouts & when the Capt. heard of it he started at once but missed her on the way as she started same time for here & so I had to play host & give up my warm quarters for the night to her & another married lady I hunted up to keep her company. All this in a dreadful rain storm & the water springing up inside the tents.

Capt. Herd returned next day, & I was relieved of my charge

I caught a slight cold by the operation but I've got over it again.

I mess with them for the present.

We send another expedition into Missouri to Monroe. I have to stay at home as before.

And so we've quarreled have we? <u>Well</u> you're veracity is unquestionable but I don't believe a word of it! I won't endorse it for the present, until I know more about it!

Molly dear Molly dear you'll be the death of me.

There will be such a long bill of kisses due. I fear I never can collect them all, unless I take a furlough for a day or two & call for part payment at once!!

I fear I cant get such a thing, but if things remain stagnant on the border here a month or two longer with a prospect of continuance, I shall at least ask for one! Now you musn't run away!

Am I become so exacting?

But if you <u>do</u> run, I shall run after, & so it will be a run away match after all! I know you admire such matches very much?

What do you say to it?

Well I wont be severe, but I think E.A. must be right, as I fear you are getting no better fast.

I think I attended those lectures myself with E.A. & other ladies for partners each night. There was generally quite a party of us in couples, if I am right in my conjecture. I don't know that they improved us much? Flirtations went on as usual going & returning, & even in church! Hope they'll have the same effect now!

I believe we had better quarrel after all! That is if you won't spank that horrid baby. I don't mind just for a change. I think Ellen will do it for me without much persuasion. You know or <u>I do</u> that I have some influence there, enough to make his <u>honor</u> jealous though you <u>won't believe it</u>.

Call it after me! eh! Well I hope they will. I always despised the horrid name & I want you to change mine! Pray what's your first choice "A rose by any other name is twice as sweet" – <u>Shakespeare</u>. If it was only the month of May, I would sacrifice all else in the world to have you here for a month.

With "Molly" by my side we could be as happy as two <u>doves</u>. I see such pretty (tame) ones around here occasionally. I mention a month because I fear in that time you would tire of camp life & me. In wet weather I pity a Lady caught in it, yes even a soldier. I pitied myself the other night when

Mrs. Herd arrived & would not have moved a peg – I fear – if the Capt. had been present.

I hope to get yours of the 20th tomorrow, as we send an express to Olathe P.O. three times a week. I send this with him to mail. I wouldn't sell them for their weight in Diamonds! O Pray don't stop the supplies! Now don't! There's a dear girl

I am sorry to hear of Miss Anna's troubles – express my regrets when you write & tell her I fear I won't get to plant that acorn or hickory in N.M.

Kind Love & remembrance to Sallie, your Mother, Aunt, &c I am dearest Yours Sincerely

Love

Aubrey
Olathe P.O.
Kansas April 6th 62
My Dearest Molly

It is Sunday night, and the Express leaves tomorrow and I am strongly tempted now that all have retired to say a word or two. I have not heard from you since the 18th & <u>that</u> I answered during the past week.

I <u>know</u> that it is the Mail that lags <u>not</u> you!

But conscience or <u>love</u> makes cowards of us all and did not <u>William</u> mention you twice in his last letters, and you said nary word of Indisposition.

I hope my Dear girl to hear by tomorrows mail of your complete recovery from what was perhaps after all only a little spring fever.

Well there is also more to trouble me. This uncertainty as to our New Mexican trip is not yet all removed & probably will not be until later news arrives from that now threatened point. That was the place by the bye where we were to have no fighting. Things have changed out there considerably and I expect to hear of much fighting yet out there & in Texas.

In the meantime we are mortified by seeing regiments brought from afar, go out there to win glory, while we raised for that service, lag in inactive & inglorious though sometimes dangerous home guard service. Don't say I'm grumbling. I only state the case & in fact I <u>almost</u> begin to wish to stay at <u>home</u> – even in <u>Kansas</u>. As I see by a new order in the *Republican* that I couldn't get a <u>furlough</u> unless under false pretenses & then only so as to allow me a day or two in St. Louis.

You can see it all much better than I can as I now see a paper but seldom, but selfish man that I am, I only run on my only troubles, when I wished to <u>talk all of you</u>. Accept my dear girl much love. Kiss Sallie for me – just to plague her you know. Kind love & remembrance to all. Wear a flower for me & I hope I will even yet soon hear your gentle voice.

So good night
Love

Aubrey
April 13th 1862
My Dear Molly

I recd your last kind epistle in due time I suppose. It was over a week, and as there was none the week before I was nearly crazy & feared you were too sick to write. I was supposing all the time too that we were under orders for N.M. & I had it arranged to go right down to St. Louis for a week ere we started. Being in suspense on both subjects was rather annoying & wearisome. All this is over now (I hope) and thank God for it. I am satisfied that our Regt. stops in Kansas and also that you are recovering (I had news to that effect from a very good friend of yours & mine).

But let me thank you for those pretty flowers Red White & Blue too – so tasty, quite a <u>boquet by</u> the way. I wrote to Alex yesterday in answer to one of his dated 17th ult. & stated that grass nor flowers had yet appeared, but I went out for a ride after, & on examination of a long southern roll of prairie, I really spied thousands of little bells, like Snow drops or Fuschias, just peering out of the ground & being thus ahead of the grass they were of a dirty white or rather a Pinky yellow tinge, but quite pretty & the first sign of spring here. Last night & today we have had a cool Southern breeze with Rain & thunder which will start the grass at once, so for a change I suppose I must say "Tis Spring time" the winter is past and the flowers appear on the Earth & the time of the singing of Birds is come. The Farmer goeth forth with his seeds, and the vegetable Kingdom arrayeth herself in a foliage of living green, and all seem to render praise to the God of Nature! Man alone is vile! How comforting are the promises. Seed time & harvest with every other blessing shall continue, while we can see the bow in the cloud, so let us be thankful, even if mans inhumanity to man will scarce let him put a crop in here.

But I will have to blush for myself. Yesterday as you will see no doubt, I indited a political rhapsody to A.D.W. & now I must needs moralize or sermonize?

However I can't help it. I am rejoiced without measure at the glorious victories that reward the just for their long suffering and consign at the same time the political swindlers whose ambition brought on all this ruin & death to perdition in this life if not in the next. God may pardon them, but the execrations of mankind will pursue them a long way into futurity!

What a glorious list of events about New Madrid No 10 & Pittsburgh Landing[1] are now grouped. The last a dreadful slaughter on both sides, caused more by carelessness after the late successes on our side than for any other reason. It came near being a disaster to us, but a little severe fighting just now is all for the best (of course I mean if it must come) as it will teach each of the combatants a proper respect for each other & lead to more mutual kindly feelings in the future. These inevitable runaway battles settle nothing if the Southern people are honest in their opposition. They will only blame & execrate their Generals, join Guerilla bands & try again first chance. I think much of the running away however comes of a concealed Union Sentiment that never dare show itself before, until we confronted it in the field, & thus gave them a chance to care! It certainly proves that <u>they</u> mistrust their <u>Leaders</u> somehow as no one ever supposed them <u>cowards</u>. I didn't! A Bad conscience needs no accusers however and starts & fly's at a Shadow!!

But I am satisfied, if you are only well & round again my dear girl, as patriotism even the most sublimated expects its reward – be it in cash in political power & the Love of a people or in the smiles & Love of a Fair Lady. The latter be my portion if I can choose is the fervent prayer of

Yours Sincerely
James E. Love

14th April 1862
Molly dear I can't close until the mail closes, & though last night I wrote a letter I did not say goodbye only goodnight. I heard you in my dreams say call again so I appear, if only to pass the compliments of the Season, and ask

---

1. The Battle of Shiloh, or Pittsburg Landing, lasted for two days and cost tens of thousands of lives. The Union forced the Confederates out of Tennessee and back to Corinth, Mississippi.

to be remembered to Sallie, your Mother & Aunt &c &c. I must thank them too for the care you say they take of you. I think you require it all, for I don't believe you would take any care of yourself under ordinary circumstances except by compulsion, so the little coercion they use will be a pleasure to all I hope.

And now I want you to write to me whear my gurl is mart yet or not, I reckon she's fur the union so tell that gurl I wuld like to sea hur, and tell hur if she wants to come to Aubrey, tell hur to write to me and i will cum after hur.

but I beg to enclose in full a copy of a letter that came to camp some days since, & has been the laughing stock since accidently. I quote the above paragraph so you can laugh at the whole of it. I wish you had seen the original. No copy can do justice to it![2]

I am in good health, and as I wish for a long lease of life yet, will act accordingly never fear – although "I <u>am a Solger</u> <u>of war</u>, as soon as pece is made I am cooming to sea you"

We have just had a dreadful storm of thunder & lightning & wind lasting nearly 24 hours & it has washed most of us out, because the Prairie where we are camped is a little too level.

I see there is a letter advertised for me in Leavenworth City which I have sent after. Where can it be from. I recd the *Illustrated News* yesterday, and I am in hopes of something else today.

At present goodbye

My Dear Girl

Yours Sincerely

James E. Love

Ceredo Wane Co Va Mach the 30 1862

Much Respeced Sur I em brace this optunity of Derecten you a few lines

---

2. James quotes the text of a letter from John Facemire, a private in Company H, Fourth Regiment, West Virginia Infantry. At the time, this regiment was stationed at Ceredo, West Virginia, and Facemire mailed the letter to Joseph Duffle in Johnson County, Kansas. The letter somehow ended up in the hands of James's company.

to let you no that I havant for goten you and to let you no that I am well at the presant and I am in hopes that thes few lines will fine you well Craxon is buuurnt up the famely is oll well I am a Solger of war and as soon as pece is made I am cooming to sea you wee have plenety to doo hear write and let me now how all of the peopel are in that contery and how the times is and what the peopel are doing give my best Respect to oll of the peopel that left Crascon write to me whear my gurl is mart yet or not I Reckon you oll are fur the union tell that gurl that I wuld like to sea hur and tell hur if She wonts to coin to Craxton tell hur to write to me and i will com after hur

I will clos at the presant time Derect your leters to company H. 4 va. Redgement Ceredo Wain Co va as I hant eny thnig of eny emportant to write I will close

John facemiers to Joeph Dufel

Mr. Joseph Duffle

Oldathy

Jonson Co.

Kansas

Aubrey
Olathe P.O.
April 22d 1862
My Dear Molly

I am still anxiously waiting for a letter from your dear self.

I have no doubt at all but that it is on the way somewheres and that not by your will is the detention.

I hope you are long ere this reaches fully recovered.

We have the first spring day here, it is at last warm & comfortable, storm & rain & cold winds remained with us continuously up to yesterday. The oldest inhabitant never heard of such a spring and the prairie is wet & cold as in December.

It may be for the best on this border, as confidence ought to return gradually from the constant presence of the troops. I see you are enjoying fine warm weather in St. Louis.

I hope you <u>do</u> enjoy it. Alex says in his last that he has the Horse & Buggy fever as bad as in former years. I hope your experience proves it; How I should like to have at least one good ride with you in the coming May time, but I fear the fates are not propitious & then those Soldiers are such a bad lot, that I further fear you wouldn't ride unless I disguised myself as citizen Love.

What a dreadful mortality list from that last battle at Shiloh. It must be a mournful & painful sight to see the long lines of wounded on their way to the hospital & many the graves! War is a dreadful thing!! What punishment then is sufficient for those who bring it on, & to whom all these deaths, pain & misery is attributable!!! <u>Treason</u> <u>thus</u> is always responsible for thousands of <u>deaths</u>.

All honor to those brave men & women who have so freely volunteered to attend the wounded in the field & Hospitals.

When you are writing next let me know whether you have written weekly or not since I came here, so that I may know what to <u>blame</u> <u>the mails for</u>. I don't receive any St. Louis papers, & for that at least I know they are in fault, also one copy of the *Ill.L.N.* I got the last No. without the cold supplement that of course you detained according to my request originally express'd.

It is as usual very interesting & of course it will daily become more so after the opening of the great Exhibition.[1] I would be sadly at a lost for it, if it failed me, as it is the only pictorial seen within a hundred miles of this point.

I must apologize here Molly Dear for the scraps of paper I seem to write on in camp – large small & mixed. The fact is I'm particular <u>sometimes</u> when within hail of a Store, but on the <u>Prairie</u> just now Paper & many other <u>little</u> things are scarce – and and – why my constitutional laziness you know, interferes with my fastidiousness thus many times & oft. Oh Molly Dear, why didn't you take me in hand long ago & infuse some of your own quiet energy into me. I feel when I think seriously that I have great powers but from pure lack of <u>ambition</u> & <u>will</u> they <u>lay dormant</u>, and I dream away life in fact satisfied with mere comfort when thousands around <u>mere dolts</u> strike out & seize out of pure impudence the great parts & prizes of life. Out of what fools do they make Colonels now a days, out of what ninny's Captains, out of what Knave's sometimes Generals, but so it is, & why moralize. Well its a fine dreamy lazy day, & I'm lazy, & this is a lazy life, but even this has its opportunities that can & are oft times neglected by lazy people, but I've just had a treat in the shape of Drake's oration on the Anniversary of "Sumter". Eloquent is he not. Thoughts sublime & words that burn. You heard him on the 22d Feby. We had some late arrivals in camp that brot us a complete budget of late papers from Kansas City. Quite an oasis of excitement in the desert of camp dullness at present.

What do we do now in Camp? Why we play cards & backgammon & Chess & Smoke – day after day early & late – while whisky is almost a forgotten beverage. We spilled it out as fast as seen for a week after we came here until all the Stores were <u>out of it</u> & Beer is too cold as yet to cause it to flow down our mainly Irish & American throats & so "<u>order reigns in War-</u>

---

1. The London World Exposition of 1862 was held from May 1 to November 1.

<u>saw.</u>" Then we take a turn at foot ball & base ball & quoits[2] and then theres guard nights & dress parade in the morning & drill & target practice twice a day, and then our daily (now!) patrol into Missouri to see that there's peace & quietness, at which times we usually do a very little quiet jayhawking if it comes in our way. These patrols consist of from 20 to 40 men & 3 or 4 times a week take a wagon along to return with a load of Hay or Corn to feed our stock or rails to feed our fires, or sometimes chickens or Eggs to feed ourselves, as the country & farmhouses is all uninhabited, we only use thus what is at present without owners & will rot ere long on the ground, so we reconcile our consciences, that nobody loses by us & <u>Uncle</u> <u>Sam</u> & his boys are the gainers. Then we seize "Secesh" Stock & Horses, when we meet them which we advertise & if not claimed in a reasonable time sell for the benefit of our said Uncle. I being Quartermaster, all these things pass through my hands or are disposed of, or executed by my orders at present, so I am busy enough sometimes, but as you see quite outside of the line of regular military duty unless we should meet "Quantrell" of which there is just now but little danger.

Only yesterday we had quite a sale of these Horses &c many of which I had been riding occasionally for days past. They were mostly colts however & young unbroken stock, but I bid Forty Dollars for one nice little pony without success – plenty of fun we had. Today we captured two "Secesh" from Prices Army – with Horses – & so we will soon perhaps gather enough for another sale. I was out at the Shawnee Settlement today & contracted with the Indians to chop some wood for us which they gladly & in quite business style proceeded to do – poor fellows – they will work when they can get money but the prejudice of color & their own sturdy independence stand in their way & so they pass away from the face of the earth & the place that once knew them knows them no more. All that I've said goes to prove that I am well in body if the mind does stagnate a little sometimes & for that blessing at least thank heaven & if I only had you dear by my side, I think I'd be as contented as a pig in a barn, but "mea culpa." It is over three months

---

2. A game similar to horseshoes.

since I've seen your dear face, save this photogram before me – let me kiss it (in parenthesis) for its original! There now! let it rest again next my heart until again called for.

As the moon's soft Splendor streaming
Oer the dark & trembling sea –
Light, bright light through darkness beaming,
Is thy Smile, dear one to me.

Take it all back. I've no other poetry at hand so I must needs quote your own – but pardon me – the guard signs ½ past 11 oclock & alls well. <u>So good night</u>

Love

I kept this over today expecting a letter from you. I have just received it and find I have answered most of its contents. I still think the mail is at fault as this is dated 15th & the last I got was the 2d – let me know.

I volunteered this morning for a scout into <u>Missouri</u> & have just returned after riding nearly 50 miles & had considerable fun & am nearly tired to death as well as my horse, so I must goodbye

My dear girl
Yours Sincerely
James E. Love
April 23, 1862

Aubrey
May 1st 1862
Morning
My Dear Gal

I am and have been thundering busy & I aint agoing to bore you with a long letter this time that I know of at present.

The 1st of the month always brings its toil in the shape of an immense amount of calligraphy & calculating. So it has been for a week of preparation but that it is over now, and yesterday it also brought muster day in due course, & in time again the paymaster comes around.

Since writing last I have received quite a number of papers I.L.N., *Democrats*, besides a bundle of Irish & American do from Mr. Kinnear. I got your letter just as I mailed my last & found I suppose by some clairvoyant operation that I had answered or anticipated the most of it ere I read it! What say you? Don't the world move. My ride in "Dixie" I mean <u>Mo</u>. just put me in good trim for the since then weeks confinement. I hope to have another good ride perhaps today as I've a good horse or two at command – "Secesh" – and the sun smiles a mild May morn approval. We have had April weather since, everything by turns, but mostly pleasant. No ploughing begun in Kansas yet, ground too wet, and yet this is May day. Neither flowers nor grass an inch long here yet, and so <u>we'll</u> have no maying; How is it in St. Louis. Is't warm enough for the old time school picnics. I think I see in the old room the Boquets you've gathered in the market, and at the farm Ditto as to Heliotrope, Tuberose or Monthly. Now pray just inhale a whiff of their perfume each time you look at them & think of me, & forward it by some such spiritual telegraph as you did the news in that last letter, and who knows but we may get up yet such a spiritual communion of souls as will convert me from an unbeliever to a devotee in Dreams, Spiritual rappings, clairvoyance &c. There are things in both Heaven & Earth not dreamt of in my philosophy I know.

For the Present "<u>Excusez Moi</u>." Love

<u>May 1st 11 P.M.</u>

Dearest Molly

Oh that I could take unto myself wings like a dove & fly to you for I am a weary, aweary positively for a sight of your pleasant face – aweary of hard work under the depressing influence of this lazy camp life. When <u>shall</u> I see you? When shall we meet to part no more? (in life) Questions often asked in though ever recurring, but echo only answers <u>when</u>?

Verily! Home is where the heart is! and mine is not here. Neither is it in the Highlands, chasing the Deer, but it is in St. Louis haunting My Dear! Do they miss me at home? I needn't ask, for have you not confessed "You thought of me several times today". Perhaps like all <u>mankind</u> I would like a little heart ache on my account – causeless heart ache – but I don't wish you have such a heart ache as I've had for a month past. Nary time. I talk like a woman! do I? Well, I was always a little effeminate in some respects, and proud of it too! Mothers Boy! &c &c Call me so & I'd move mountains for you. Pattern Boy I wasnt, I had too much self will, ere I earn'd the name I'd run into mischief & break the spell. "The Vanity of the Man" So you say! & I wouldn't contradict you for the world, but that aint whats the matter. It is when shall I, can I, will I, claim my Molly Dear? I left it all in your hands – must I remind you monthly or quarterly – which.

Will you condemn me to single blessedness during the war (say 3 or 5 years) during the year, or during the summer?

Either one may be for ever! Not a forever of separation I truly hope.

I <u>hope</u> I grow not "<u>reckless</u>", & I pray sometimes I grow better. There is no church here & Sunday is the most quiet & uneventful of days. On the whole it is <u>well</u> kept. We are on the prairie recollect, & but little temptation. But how long Ma Belle Eliza. How long am I to inhabit a solitary Chamber (tent). It is not good for a man to be alone you know. His thoughts & actions too are only evil & that continually! & even your humble servant, perfect as <u>you</u> say he is, needs some humanizing influence around him, as well as any other man!

I am quite wolfish to night, & if you were by, I fear I'd eat you up with kisses & caresses to make up for lost time. Capt. Herd has his Lady here, keeping house in an empty house – military fashion – but they seem to like it, & to all appearances (They are not demonstrative) bill & coo like any turtle Doves. Everybody else has got his wife here but I and the Major & even he – example is contagious – threatens to go off & get married at once. He showed me a Daguerreotype only today, a very pretty young lady too. I must look at mine. Its much more beautiful in my eyes. The soul is there I flatter not & I know not what to do with the great treasure I've found. Will the owner kindly inform. I want to know? Do tell! Recollect tis the "ne'er do weel" enquires and tis not for a day, but for all times. I tremble at my temerity.

My heart feels chokin'-like & weak

And drops o' sweat run down my cheek

Confound me for a dunce! &c

And now I've just got your letter of the 23d April for which a thousand thanks and I want to say, <u>I wrote every week</u>. I was not very regular lately as to the day – <u>I could not be!</u> – but I wrote each week. I suppose I needn't pity you – appropo of house cleaning &c. It will be all over ere now & then I am glad to hear that you are so spry again. I wrote to you two days before I wrote to Alex. I have not left room to answer your letter in detail but it has done me good – much good – do not stint me. It is the only oxygen I breathe here & is better than all the medicine in the Pharmacopiae. I mean your love, whether conveyed in papers, pellets or in propria persona or in spiritual communion, Dreams &c.

Love to all – much Love to yourself

Sincerely

Love

12 P.M.

This starts at once by our express to Leavenworth so you will have it soon –

Love

Love and Molly
There's only one I'm after,
And she's the one, I vow!
If she was here, and standin' by,
She is a gal so neat and spry,
So neat and spry,
I'd be in glory now!
It's so, I'm hankerin' for her,
And want to have her, too.
Her temper's always gay and bright,
Her face like posies red and white,
Both red and white,
And eyes like posies blue.
And when I see her comin',
My face gets red at once;
My heart feels chokin'-like, and weak
And drop's o' sweat run down my cheek,
Yes, down my cheek,
Confound me for a dunce!
She spoke so kind, last Tuesday,
When at the ball we met
"Love, now your arm! What ails you? Say!
I see that somethin's wrong to-day
What's wrong to day?"
No, that I can't forget!
I know I'd ought to tell her,
And wish I'd told her then;
And if I wasn't poor and low,
And sayin' it didn't choke me so,
(It chokes me so,)
I'd find a chance again.
Well, up and off I'm goin';

She's in the <u>garden</u>; so
I'll try and let her know my mind;
And if her answer isn't kind,
If 't isn't kind.
I'll jine the ranks <u>and go</u>!
I'm but a poor young fellow,
Yes, poor enough, no doubt.
But ha'n't, thank God, done <u>nothin'</u> wrong,
And <u>be</u> a man as stout and strong,
As stout and strong,
As any round about.
What's rustlin' in the bushes?
I see a movin Stalk:
The leaves is openin': there's a dress!
O Lord, forbid it! but I guess
I guess – I guess
<u>Somebody's</u> heard me talk!
"Ha! here I am! you've got me!
So keep me, if you can!
I've <u>guessed it</u> ever since last <u>Fall</u>,
And Tuesday night I saw it all,
I saw it all!
Speak out, then, like a man!
"Though rich you ain't in money.
Nor rich in goods to sell,
An honest heart is more than gold,
And hands you've got for field and fold,
For house and fold,
And – Love – I love you well!"
"O Molly, say it over!
O Molly, is it so?
I couldn't longer bear the doubt;

T'was hell, but now you've drawed me out,
You've drawed me out!
And <u>will I</u>? <u>Wont</u> I, though!
Love
You like "Burns"[1] dont you? Well above is a half Irish half Yankee imitation of his style, which you can laugh at, destroy, or discuss and show to (Sallie)? as you will.
I want to know?
Love
May 1862

---

1. Robert Burns, a Scottish poet.

Olathe P.O.

May 4th 1862

My Dearest Molly

When last I wrote twas May Day & a fine day it was. I took the ride I spoke of & enjoyed it much. We extended it to Olathe say 12 or 14 miles & found that the entire village had been a Maying & were all preparing for a ball, then & there to come of. We at once concluded to stay, & so we danced all night & enjoyed ourselves very much. There were some very fine Young Ladies, & a very designing widow &c, & so forth & we came home rejoicing next morning, with fine weather then & since. Today we had camp meeting & a very good sermon, for the first time here in a year, that being one of the fruits of secession, as prior to that time there had been preaching weekly in the school house which Yankee like you find in every settlement here. But we were interrupted in the midst of the sermon, by a report that 5 or 6 Secesh were within a couple of miles driving some ponies mules & colts. Everyone who had a horse at command at once started in pursuit. Six of us, of which I was one, & soon overtook them or rather the stock, for they <u>ran</u> at sight & we came home rejoicing, with what is probably some Indian property which they had just <u>stolen</u> (or jayhawked). We have them safely corralled, for the owners if they are <u>Union</u> & call for them, if not for Uncle Sam. And this brings me to the secondly. Your long lost letter of the 9th April, has just arrived (from Fort Kearney) & in it I find the scolding you speak of. Well now I'll tell you two truths, & the first is, I like to hear you scold either Viva voce, or by letter. The second is that I <u>never have</u> or never would profit by any of these things. I don't know what I might be tempted to do in the dark but (Love of approbation large) I could never look anybody in the face, that knew of me owning such ill gotten gains, & I would fancy <u>everybody</u> knew. So I acted in <u>Mo</u>. last year. So I act here, & those motives are sufficient with me I assure you to withstand any temptation, leaving all <u>higher</u> ones out of the question. I write this not because I fear for one moment that you have really accused me or suspected me, but because I fear

I have written between jest & earnest what would seem like self accusation & I may do so in future, so I put this on record.

There is much taken from Rebels here daily, & we also take some <u>rebels</u> as well but it is all done under cover of civil as well as military law & our Regiment is specially stationed on the border to stop jayhawking either in <u>Mo.</u> or <u>Kan.</u> We caught six jayhawkers three nights since & they are by this time in the <u>Fort.</u> So whatever we do is done according to order, generally property going to ruin on deserted farms, that Uncle Sam will have for sale to or settlement by Union men as soon as the war is over. It is done under my signature, & when stock, forage or ought else is taken it <u>lays</u> in my charge; but I have no responsibility in the matter, more than safe keeping until the owner calls & proves himself to <u>have been</u> a Union man, or until I can advertise it & sell by auction for <u>cash</u> to the highest bidder, which cash goes directly into the public treasury & helps to pay the expense of the war, besides do I not know how strictly conscientious you are, and also what would please you. And at present need I say that to please you is my pleasure!

And now Molly dear I <u>thirdly</u> must answer all these letters, four of them, for though I wrote weekly, yet it so happened that I just posted mine ere yours arrive. So imprimis, I all the time take very good care of myself, though of course I can't tell you about it all the time, & it is only when I do a little out of the every day routine as today or <u>once</u> before that you hear of it & for the future I intend riding a little daily, so as to counteract the confinement I have been condemned to so far. I guessed you would be going to the farm & so forth now that the flowers have come. I do wish I was there. Glad to hear of all your pleasures, I hope you wont stint them & also of the Morgan St. folks & the other news all of which is like food to a starving man, greedily devoured.

By the bye, what could you expect of Miss Annie, but such gossip as you speak of, fortunately everybody knows what a tease she is, so her tongue's no scandal.

I hope you <u>will</u> go up to Illinois[1] & see them all. I'm sure it would do you a world of good, more than you will admit of & then you know you can tease her in turn, & tell her how I think of her all the time. And then there's that dear little Minx Sallie. I don't mind her hard words a bit; prefer them in fact to compliments. I don't know how to thank her for her kind care of me present & absent; I think I ought to have one of those pretty photographs. If she don't give me or send one, I'm afraid I'll steal one the next time I see her. The temptation is so great you see. I can't withstand it. She feels you know much more like young America & wouldn't mind it as you would. I wish particularly to be remembered with love to her, your Aunt & Mother &c &c

I have just seen the *Harper* you spoke of containing that Poem & the uprising of the North &c. I get the *Democrat* regularly or <u>rather</u> <u>irregularly</u> at last, (like the letters) some in five days some in 15 days, & I do expect another letter and a I.L.N. tomorrow from you until which time I will detain this missive.

I sent my last by an express <u>we</u> <u>sent</u> to Leavenworth, so you ought to get it much sooner than usual & so I come in course to peruse your letter of the 23d which left you all in dirt & confusion. Well that's all over long ago I suppose & I intend to thank you trebly for the letter notwithstanding your disclaimer, but as I can't come paddling in, I wish to do it now, so I make my best bow.

I gathered a boquet just before church. It looked pretty & does now on the table at my side, but there's not much variety principally wild violets. I expect if this weather continues & gets warmer that we will move our camp very soon out of town to a creek. I go prospecting a good place tomorrow probably. Our P.O. will be the same <u>"Olathe"</u> & in fact "Aubrey" might be left out in the address altogether.

Goodnight

Love

---

1. Molly's brother Dr. Robert B. M. Wilson lived in Illinois with his family.

May 7th 1862

And so we have taken Yorktown & New Orleans & Fort Macon &c &c &c too numerous to mention? <u>Is it not glorious</u> & do not the Yankees, the western mudsill[2], aye & even the poor Celts & d---d Dutch fight well & worthy of a good cause. Verily I fear after all history will record that the poor foreigners – who fled from oppression at home – also saved Liberty in America. That they valued the blessings they enjoyed here more than the native born. Oh I have had such a surfeit of news, such an avalanche of papers came to camp at once, that for the first time in life, I wish a day to digest what is past, ere I get any more. Among the rest that *Leslie*[3] of yours (half a dozen more kisses) & then the I.L.N. & such a good No. of both. Have not the English got a big scare at last! IO! Triompe!! Johnny Bull.[4] The day of reckoning is at hand and America will yet knock you off your pedestal, & possibly without striking you a blow, step Father though you are. Poor John. No Nary left, & your <u>adored</u> Armstrongs mere pop guns after all. Vide *Harper* 3d May & the I.L.N. This is the same John who four short months ago was going to wipe us out as a nation from the Earth and yet he talks of <u>our</u> Braggadocia. After all, <u>Providence</u> rules this earth for good, for if Jonathan & John had fought both would have been ruined, but John would seen by what passes now have been like ancient Carthage & Liberty for a reason w'd have fled the earth affrighted. Excuse this rhapsody – put in you will say to fill up.

Well my Dear Molly – its ever of thee &c & if you never have a chance to be proud of the "ne'er do weel", I will at least try to manage that you shant be ashamed of him.

Amen

Yours Sincerely

Love

---

2. "Western mudsill" was a term of pride used by Northern soldiers fighting in the western theater of war.
3. *Frank Leslie's Illustrated Newspaper.*
4. A popular personification of England.

Aubrey
May 17th 1862
My Dear Molly

It seems late in the day to answer yours of the 30th ult. but so it is. I received it on the same day as I wrote last, & I have been real busy since so now I greet you, last night I rec'd yours of the 6th along with a pile of others including two from Alex, two from Ireland inclosed by Wm. &c. Alex mentioned another he had for me, so I wrote him at once, and now if I can find time I intend to write all my other friends.

I am in good health, <u>tanned as red</u> <u>as a beet</u>, & so I suppose open air, & occasional exercise agrees with me, it is only occasional though. In my capacity as Q.M. I have a dozen of horses (U.S.) at my disposal all the time. I rode day before yesterday over 50 miles & had a good time, visiting our Missouri friends to gain information of guerilla or Jayhawking parties supposed to be lurking around. Don't suppose I was alone. I was one of a party of Ten mounted scouts (mostly officers) while we had 70 or 80 infantry <u>along</u>, in <u>reserve</u>.

It is glorious galloping over the prairies just now, so fresh & green they are, & we regard not the road, but go straight as we can from house to house, or whatever our destination. The whole expanse is carpeted with flowers, all hues & sizes. Violets have gone, and now sweet Williams are in the ascendant. They are of all colors red, pink, purple & striped or nearly white, & look as tame as possible. Then in places there miles & miles of Strawberry patches all now in flower & within two weeks in fruit, much of it is found now. So with the apple trees in the orchards we pass, just one mass of snowy blossoms. The Peaches came & went two weeks ago & so the whole land is full of beauty, yet the treachery of man to man has made it nigh a desert.

I have a fresh boquet all the time & it makes the old table look like home when I gaze. I hope the glorious victories that we gain daily will soon cause many to experience the realities instead of the mere look.

What do you think? folks in Belfast & elsewhere in the Old World will have it I'm a dead man! Do you believe it likely?

Some of my best friends there say that they've written me two or three times within the last two years, & several of the letters have went back from the <u>dead letter</u> <u>office</u>, while mine to them, they've not recd. I can't understand it, unless it all happened since I went to Lexington. While gone that time, & <u>since</u> <u>recruiting</u>, I had requested some of my <u>dear friends</u> to enquire for me each time at the office. I suppose <u>they</u> didn't!! My letters at that time were all addressed to James A. these last were addressed to W.C.W.

And now to <u>your</u> letter. Glad to hear that Sallie had her laugh at that poetry. It was enough to make any one smile that was <u>not a lovesick</u> swain. He would have had a dewy eye I'm afraid. As to your <u>Beau</u> the "Prince of Wales" – I've seen late papers but observed nothing concerning his marriage. Won't you kindly let your fancy run in a less elevated channel for the future. I've no ambition, & if you can't, Why! "I want to know!" & then as to the very good friend of yours who done me the pleasure to write & mention your recovery why it was Mr. Kinnear.[1] I've got to answer his letter yet.

Thanks for all the Morgan St. news. John seems to have lost all energy. He never was, nor ever will be as good a man, as the Old Man, bad as <u>he is</u>. I can truly sympathize with Mrs. Wm. Barr, & fervently hope that her other brothers may return to her unscathed. I hope you enjoyed your flowers at Old Shaws.[2] <u>I do now</u> in imagination, such is the power of a letter from one you love next to their face & voice, a talisman of pleasure hope & happiness.

So Mrs. Rogers is still opposed to the "neer do weel". I'm very sorry. I like Mrs. Rogers very much, respect her very much, but I was always a very poor hand to make friends & I fear I have failed with her. I know for some time that I have but I'll try again, yet as I can't change my thriftless way, as I do know that I lack energy somewhat, and as I fear she measures worth somewhat by success – I fear I'll fail again – & then! what then?

If I can only please my Molly who I know measures by another standard though I don't say <u>that</u> (success) is a bad one, I am impervious to the frowns

---

1. Oliver Kinnear was married to Lucinda Allison. Molly's brother Alexander would eventually marry Lucinda's sister, Lucretia Allison.
2. Shaw's Garden, which today is the Missouri Botanical Garden.

of for time & the contempt for such cause of the world. & so to scenes & pastures new, you wind up by saying my rose bush will soon be in bloom. That at least does well. Thanks to your care however! Might I not do well under the same auspices? So much in answer to the 30th ult. & now apropo of May 6th, so long & interesting & so the hopeful boy thrives, & my favorite keeps in perpetual motion up in Morgan St. Long may <u>they</u> wave! but my favorite once my favorite still. I hold a long time with old friends & pets, just as long as they will let me! & often longer than is to my advantage. Didn't Fowler say I had "Adhesiveness" large, very large in fact. Love of <u>a</u> home too, & that notwithstanding that I am such a rolling stone? When Ellen plagues you! I know she will! Just tell her I ask for her often! I really do like to hear of her, for somehow, with all her faults she interested me from the first, & even when I supposed she might be acting deceitfully by me, (false & fair I know she is, when she chooses) I could not help liking her & treating her well as I knew how!? That aint much?

Tell Sallie I wish to send my love again. There is a virtue you know in perseverance, & as I can't stop writing, I fear I must come down & take all her abuse. Can I not propitiate her. Give her a kiss for me or ask her shall I fetch one. I'm her most devoted slave you know? but I wouldn't dare tell her.

And now you dear dear girl how can I answer the rest of your letter. I can not now. I can only answer a small part at a time, but I can enshrine it in my heart & let my life be an answer to it as far as poor human nature will allow. I mean especially this imperfect specimen.

I have said before about long engagements I don't think they are for <u>good</u>, but in our case it is possibly for the best. I don't see what I could do to give you anything like the comfort & happiness that I hope & suppose you enjoy now & that is just what is fretting me. So until the Grand Army melts away, I suppose that idea must remain in Dreamland! I feared as much & would not dare to make a movement, for which you or yours would afterward blame me (under present circumstances) so I wish'd to know what you thought. I know my comfort would be <u>enhanced incalculably</u> if you were here but I also know that yours would not, & so ere I asked you seriously to come I would tell you & such is the contradiction existing in Human nature, that if you had said yes, I would at once began to paint the dangers & <u>perplexities</u> of camp life in dismal colors, but why speak of it. I <u>knew</u> you were aware of it all & feared much more.

As to the consents to be obtained, & other troublesome matters you mention I usually cut all those things very short. They are generally disagreeable to me & so left to the last, to be hurried over & not thought of, but acted on – but I give them all credit for being sensible people, & though they may do all they can to control such matters yet when they find it is no use & our minds are made up <u>for good</u> some time since, I believe they will all turn round & make things as comfortable & agreeable as possible, & try to prove to you that all such fears were in your own mind. I do hope so & believe it! I think such treatment & far better than the best of them, ever can or will give you, you deserve from them. <u>If I do not</u>. This I say without disrespect to any one, & in the kindest spirit, pray understand it so.

I think of course you are the flower of the flock – old & young – and I am not alone in such opinion, for I've heard it from a hundred sources, before I was supposed to be interested – that is before the searcher of all hearts my deliberate opinion, & <u>no flattery intended or implied</u>. I need not begin to make any Protestations. I don't believe in them & they are generally of little account as fate or Providence puts events above our control & so all promises for the far future are vain but do I not talk & write enough for to answer many of your other questions. I have generally tried to be as open & as candid in statement as poor human can or can afford to be. I will continue so & try allay all your doubts, or I should say perhaps those so sedulously instilled into you by others.

I am very impulsive, & easily tempted but with a good angel by my side I think – nay I am certain you are not mistaken in me, unless you have built a fanciful ideal, where knowledge you had not in regard to my honor & virtue. As to both I believe I can show cleaner hands than ninety-nine in a hundred. As to the second, I have strict Ideas & live up to them in action. As to the first most every man & woman carries their own standards in their conscience. I try to live up to mine. I find that in many cases it holds me to stricter account than many pillars of the Church, allow theirs to do, while in others they would call me culpable because I cannot admit their standard of action.

If I was a member of the Church I would just act the same. I could not nor would not be a hypocrite and subscribe to any of their narrow views, (say in regard to dancing). I could not, of that character I have more honor than of sinning openly.

Do not hesitate to express your feelings in your letters in any way, I <u>shall not misunderstand you</u>.

Never has or shall any other eye see them, unless you request their return. <u>After that come Death!</u>

If I die & it comes not too suddenly, I shall return or destroy them anyhow, as it seems best; That w'd be a point of honor with me.

Anything you have said only heightens my love & regard, & my determination to deserve you in future.

In the past my conscience accuses me of nothing in which I was willfully unworthy of you, or of which I would be ashamed to have truth told – save only in being a poor hand at a bargain. I can not in conscience "sometimes" <u>act smart</u>.

Do you recollect me arguing with "John" at the supper table concerning shipping corn by rail. From what he said, he considers it right to take more latitude than I should in order to come out even. <u>So he</u> is good at a trade. I am not and now I suppose as usual I've talked too long & said too much, so with kindest love & wishes to yourself & all friends

I am

Yours sincerely

James E. Love

Please address to "Olathe P.O." & leave Aubrey out

Yours

Love

I expect to have a letter & paper from you tomorrow, & also to write you very soon again on other matters. Since writing the first half of this long epistle, I have been to Olathe to another dance, remaining until next afternoon, & enjoying myself much, as did several other of the officers. The Major (Schneider) who was in command of this post was there also, & proceeded from there to Leavenworth, on what is supposed to be important business.

Yours ever

James E. Love

The Prince of Wales and his Intended Bride, the Princess Alexandra of Denmark. From *Harper's Weekly*, December 6, 1862.

Aubrey
May 19th 1862
My Dear Molly

In my last I spoke of writing about some other matters, nothing of much importance, but to fill a page, & first I have not before mentioned that I sent that deed for Land in St. Francois Co. Mo. for record <u>in your name</u>, in due time, & have got it safe returned. I will keep it in my trunk (as it is so bulky) for the present, along with my other valuables – will, &c. Money is not safe to keep so last pay day, I sent to William through "Alex" $400.00 and I expect to send more soon. How had I better dispose of it all? Let it remain on interest with William? or invest otherwise in St. Louis or Kansas? I can purchase cheap <u>homesteads</u> here all improved, gardens, houses, fences &c, that will be worth & easily sold at 3 or 4 times the money whenever this war is over! They are now deserted as their owners dare not live here, for fear of being shot, burned out, or their stock jayhawked, by the opposing party, be they Secesh or Union! Strangers who have no enemies here can settle without danger even now, are doing so daily & so <u>the late owners</u> will sell for half what they cost 5 years ago.

I must choose a course soon to pursue after the war. I would as soon farm in Kansas, New Mexico, or California as any where else sooner than in Missouri.

I always preferred farming to store keeping & was only deterred by my want of knowledge & fear of hard work in the sun. Now I have the last opportunity of free choice offered me.

If I go storekeeping again, it would probably be for life. St. Louis & Missouri will be dreadfully overtaxed for our lifetime & longer, & that will work very much against all new beginners there. I mention all this to elicit your opinion, as I have no definite purpose yet, but it may be necessary to strike soon, and I would wish to know your positive ideas before hand as to these eventualities which are possibly two years in the distance yet.

I don't say that I've made up my mind to farm – not by any means, perhaps never will, but I have a penchant that way if I could do so (as a gentleman & an amateur). Will that ever be? Or could you endure it near a city even near St. Louis? All this I'm aware I've said or hinted at before. So how would it do to speculate.

I don't expect to be out of the army unless by resignation for two years! I don't look for promotion now unless by accident or the battlefield! By the Bye we had a narrow escape, from being ordered to <u>Corinth</u>. Four Regiments are detail to assist Halleck from here, ours was on the list, but finally was permitted to remain as it is home guard for Kansas. It is a very inactive & sometimes disagreeable life, and both men & officers dislike it, with some exceptions, especially those who by their duties are kept busy, I for one! I had too much to do, & the Major of whom I've made a warm friend, has today relieved me from part of my duties. I sold all our "stray" Horses & Colts over 40 head & I bought a fine young mare, of which I've already made quite a pet, & have her nearly broken to the saddle. She is a pretty bay with white feet. I've called her "<u>Fanny</u>", only three years old. Almost too young to ride, but she will already come & eat corn from my hand, when I visit her out at pasture. So we go!

Since writing the above, I've rec'd yours of the 13th short & sweet, many thanks. I'm glad to hear that your learning the machine, it is such an assistance to work & <u>to health</u>, & I don't believe sewing so much as you have done is good for your health. I should like to be remembered to Miss Nelly & others in the Tenth Ward, but that I suppose I must send through Alex! Very glad to hear of Wm's recovery. I hope he will take more care of himself. His life is too valuable to his friends to be thrown away. I wish I could say as much for mine, but I can't, unless I might make an exception in regard to Uncle Sam! I got the I.L.N. & *Leslie* & find them as interesting as usual. Johnny Bull is evidently a little hurt at our neglect of him. He respects us more day by day however, & when we have a fleet of "*Monitors*", at our disposal we may be able to live in peace with him – not before. He's too jealous to love us & so to be safe he must fear us.[1]

---

1. The *Illustrated London News* contained numerous articles about the naval engagement between the *Monitor* and the *Merrimac*, including one that asked, "What is the first effect of this news upon English interests? . . . There is not now a ship in the English Navy . . . that it would not be madness to trust to an engagement with that little *Monitor*."

I'll forego my spite towards him when the Union is safe & we are the arbiters of this continent as before, & when Columbia in the name of peace, progress, trade & humanity rules the Seas – as Johnny Bull pretends to – but is in hourly agonies & fears of losing. John claimed that the *Merrimac* was the better ship as it was the largest. What will he say now. As usual he also claims our invention, after we have put it in practical use. Well we can afford to gratify his vanity even more than that soon as he will find that *Monitors* are no use without our Parrotts & Columbiads on board & even *Monitors* will get a bad hole, if hit fair by one of those deadly missiles. And now as Johnny likes nobility, as for that reason he has adopted our Slaveocracy & Chivalry I wonder how this blow up will suit him. If it had been one of our ships (or his own) every officer on board would have been court martialed & shot, because he did not fight to death, go down in honest warfare the night as the *Cumberland* did with the Stars & Stripes flying when 10 Fathoms deep, but commit suicide in that way! Never!! Never!! Never!!!

More anon
Love

May 21st Mail closes ere I can say more, but with much love & kind regards to yourself & all
I am my dear girl
Yours Sincerely
James E. Love

After a ride on the prairie & to the creek, I send you a sprig of the red white & blue that I've got to beautify my table & perfume my tent.
Love

Leavenworth

12 P.M. May 27th 62

My Dearest Molly

I have just got here after a forced march. We are en route for Corinth. So I hope to call & see you all as I pass. I intend to try & get ahead of the command somehow but I may be disappointed. I think however we will get a chance to land as we pass St. Louis. It is all very sudden, though the air was rife with it for some weeks yet we couldn't believe it. Madam rumor is such a Jade, but so it is & why complain – if the country calls, I obey.

I have scarcely time to address you & if I can't send this by tomorrow's mail it will be of no avail as I expect not to be far behind, but I wish to let you know as soon as I do myself in a measure & so I write.

I wrote to Alex as an advertisement to my friends at large. I got yours of the 20th at Olathe as I passed.

My dear dear girl. I fear I shall never be able to repay a tithe of the love you lavish on me, even if I live to threescore years & ten, but the ne'er do weel Loves notwithstanding & if he is called to account ere such a ripe age will if he knows himself murmur your name as a last word.

But enough until I see you or until I get a better pen & more time.

With much love to yourself & all friends

I am

Yours Sincerely

James E. Love

General Buell's Army Crossing Lick Creek on the Way to Corinth. From Harper's Weekly, June 7, 1862.

Columbus[1]
June 4th 1862
My Dear Dear Molly

I am so sorry and pained to see you so thin weary & careworn, that I must as the least I can do write at once. I wish I could do something more positively useful to your health & spirits, & I need not assure you that if I could no sacrifice would be too great for me. I think change of scene & place w'd do you a world of good. If you were only out among your friends I think they would make you sit & rest awhile, & I do think that is what you want as much as anything else.

And now I want you to call on me at all times and places for any service I can do. Will you do that as a favor to me? But I fear you wont, you are so independent of the outside world & yet you dont know what a pleasure it is to serve you, but I have had so little opportunity to pay attention to Ladies through life, sisters, cousins or others that I must appear to disadvantage with others – your brothers for instance who have had such chances to learn their wants & practice. Wont you instruct me. I will be an apt scholar.

I sent for my horse ere I left St. Louis. I found one of Major Schneiders had been left behind, so I wrote for it and my own same time, & if not sold it will I hope soon be under Sandy's care. Now if it comes & its feet is better as I expect they will be when shod, will you ride it occasionally for me. It is very gentle & very fast, & with two days training by a competent person will be a fine pacer. I put it under Sandy's charge and I wish him to use her (Fanny) & to see that you do also. I expect to write you very soon again, after I get to camp & perhaps may forward all together with one for Sandy. I left at 5 oclock after two or three abortive attempts & got here at six oclock this evening. It is now near midnight, & rains heavily but we have not finished unloading yet, & Ive been on the stretch driving up sneaks all that time. I suppose it will take us all night & I wont get to camp ere morning, so I seize this moment ere the boat leaves to greet you again.

---

1. After writing the last letter, James and his company traveled to St. Louis, where he finally saw Molly. The men arrived in Columbus, Kentucky, on June 2.

What shall I say about being so tongue tied while in your presence or vicinity. I mean about subjects of interest to ourselves alone. I wish'd to talk so much of many things, & yet I never said a word, but so it is through life – with me I never think to speak of things that are often the most necessary – unless asked – Yankee fashion – and then you say I tell too much, but then looking to the end of this war is looking a long way ahead.

I pray that it may have a happy termination and soon. I mean both the war & our suspense, and that I may come back to you safe & soon & find you renovated in body & spirits & not near so ethereal. I always believed I'd got an angel, but I wish her to appear in good health & flesh for some time to come & when she must return to her native heaven, I wish to have lived so as to accompany or follow fast.

We expect orders very soon. Several boat loads of troops have just come down the Tennessee from Pittsburgh & now lay at Cairo.

This is a very nice place for a camp, & everything is in apple pie order – made so by the rebels. I should like to stop awhile but some of us will certainly go ahead in a day or two. Address for the present

Co. K 8th Kan. Vol.

Union City

Tennessee

Care Lieut. Col. Martin

Mitchells Brigade

for the present goodnight

Love

June 5th 1862

I got into camp all safe this morning and now we are under orders for Union City Tennessee tomorrow. We have a very nice camp here, with fine fortifications all left by the rebels with guns & munitions of war in quantity, & so I'd like to stop a while, but forward march into secessia is the order of the day.

So with much love to you & remembrance to all
I am my dear dear girl
Yours Sincerely,
James E. Love

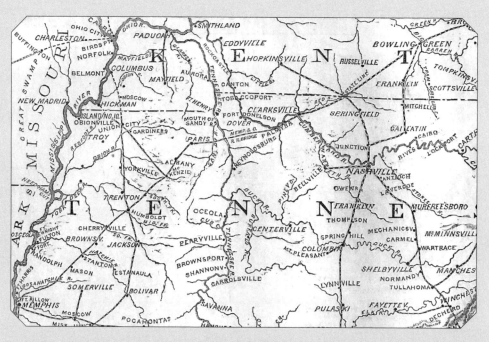

After a brief stop in St. Louis, James traveled to Cairo, Illinois, and Columbus, Kentucky, which are both shown in the upper left corner of this map. *Map of the Seat of War in Tennessee and Mississippi, Showing the Present Positions of the Union and Rebel Armies.* From *Harper's Weekly,* April 12, 1862.

Union City, Tennessee

June 11th 1862

My Dearest Eliza

I seize the earliest moment to write again, it seems only yesterday since I wrote before. I've been so busy & time moves so fast. We made but a slow march, our wagons being overloaded, as transportation is scarce, but we are all here now & safe. We were bound for Fort Pillow & Memphis, but low & behold the news meets us that both have surrendered, & so we may chance to remain for some time here or else go as garrison some place away down South that needs our protection more.

I find it very warm here by day, though cool & damp by night, so as to make double blankets a necessity, as the men are very careless concerning the dew &c. I expect we shall report numbers sick soon, as others have done before us. It is so different from the dry warm climate of Kansas in Summer.

I think I need not fear it, as I am cautious & careful as usual.

We had but a short & busy time at Columbus scarcely time to see one fourth the defences, & prepare for this march. The march itself was slow & pleasant through a fine heavy timbered country, worthy of Old Kaintucks renown, people mostly secesh, some few Union but <u>no young men</u> to be seen – <u>not one</u>. All gone to the war on one side or other. Such is the pressure of public opinion here that the veriest coward, out of pure cowardice <u>must</u> go, & so you see old men "Secesh", who hadn't time to run, or who wish'd to save their property & young & old ladies, who do not scruple to express their sentiments by word & deed. Secesh ladies who act as if our touch or presence was contamination, & Union ladies who can not do enough for us or for the weary soldiers, & whose glad looks give evidence of the heavy weight that has borne down their weary hearts for <u>months</u> & so we got into Tennessee. The evidences of wealth & cultivation increasing as we went, fine farms & fine orchards. The owners almost afraid to cultivate fearing the ravages of war, <u>so far</u> & lately the want of a market, New Orleans & the coast being the only market they have ever had. I gladdened the hearts of many by telling them that the river would be open in a week, & so it is in much less time but have <u>they</u> money to buy down there. I dont mean in N.O. alone. It takes several states down there to make said market, of which the city is only the Market Place or <u>entrepot</u>, & so we will probably not join in a great fight after all. Aint you glad?

I hope my dearest girl, that you are in health or spirits (not fretting) or in the fair way to be in health soon, & that you take good care of yourself. I was so refreshed by the short visit I had to the city, that I wish more than ever to have another one, and I nearly succeeded in obtaining it right away, but such hopes are dashed again, and I must await my turn for a furlough as I best may.

How about Charlie & Mrs. R. Wilson. Of course you have heard of them since, & all the other folks I saw. Love & Remembrance to them all.

I hope you will receive that young horse of mine quite renovated by this time, & that you will exercise it & yourself daily or often for my sake. If you don't I wont forgive you – there.

This nigger question comes up in all shapes as the chief nuisance. Coming down on the boat, we had quite a little excitement about a jet black lady, in which I as officer in charge of the boat took the liberty of putting her ashore at Cairo, in charge of the Provost Marshal there, & also in confining as punishment & to save their lives (from the hot heads aboard) the Kidnappers who brought her from St. Louis. I let them remain on the boat & go on home to New Madrid when we left it. They grit their teeth & wished to shoot somebody very badly at first but soon got badly skeered, & were glad to go home safe, when so permitted, and now on the march, another muss occurs passing a wheat field, where several Niggers with an old white headed <u>Secesh</u> (who has taken the Oath however) were at work with a reaping machine, cutting the wheat. Some of our Niggers went over the fence. Old whitehead & his Niggers were gazing at us and started a conversation with them, & soon marched towards us arm in arm with the Old Mans Niggers. Several men from Co H with arms then went & took another light colored slave off the reaper, & at once confusion reigned. Our Colonel being an abolitionist, said let the niggers come if they wanted to, & some were for taking them on & fell in ranks with the Niggers guarded. Others wouldnt move & I am proud to say our Whole Co. were among them until such a <u>mean theft</u> was wiped out & the Niggers returned. Now if these same Niggers had left their work & came after us I w'd have protected them in their strike for freedom, but as long as it is the law, I will not countenance stealing a <u>Nigger</u> or a <u>horse</u>. I wont raise a finger to coax them off, or to drive them back if <u>they will</u> be free. Am I right?[1]

I am my dear Molly with much love, & prayers for your continued health & safety

Yours Sincerely,

James E. Love

---

1. Union officers and troops had their own opinions about what to do with runaway slaves that crossed into Union lines. The officers issued dozens of conflicting orders and proclamations, and there was often disagreement among the soldiers of a regiment—as well as between the soldiers and their commanding officers—as to whether the Union troops should assist the runaway slaves or return them, as property, to their owners.

Headquarters
Eighth Regiment Kansas Volunteers
Trenton, Tennessee

June 23d 1862

My Dear Molly

I have waited until I could report that I had safely joined the company. I done so this morning all safe after a long ride through Tennessee all by myself. I had a pleasant trip on the boat. Stopped some time at Cairo & got to Columbus early on Sunday morning & then to Hickman.

Columbus June 24th When I got so far I got an order to start for this point forth with which I did by <u>handcar</u> on the railroad & here I am. I got a detail of eight men to run me down & we made the trip of 80 miles in 9 hours, so you see I pursue my devious way, & in the fullest sense of word cannot tell what a day may bring forth. Well to begin again, from Hickman I rode 60 miles to Trenton, through a very rough country & found plenty of Secesh & plenty Union folks. I was told by many folks that I was the first "<u>Yankee</u>" that passed that way (our troops had went another road) & they wanted to know how many more were coming & when, & seemed to think that they were innumerable. Ladies would glance out the door to see the passing horseman, & start in again in fear, such vandals they have been lead to believe we are. Children looked in open mouthed astonishment at me & shouted theres a Yankee – O, here's a Yankee. I got lost in a cypress swamp 2 hours, & expected to kill my horse every minute, & remain there myself a monument to all future time – of what? but I got in all safe – though not as I expected in one day. I stopped overnight with a secesh & done my best to convert them. They led me to believe that I succeeded, especially the young ladies. Ladies down here all talk politics, but I wouldn't trust them much. I slept sound with my pistol under my head, & rode on next morning. I got complimented for returning so soon & as I said sent off here in two hours after for reward with a good chance for another visit to your city, but not so. I go back tomorrow, having transacted my business already. So I shall surprise them again I hope tomorrow, unless they start for Humboldt in my absence, which I fear they will. We do not go much further south until the fall, unless something happens to Beauregard[1] & Co. Our Brigade (3000) men has fixed all the Bridges along this road from Columbus to Memphis & as we had just landed to day two locomotives from Louisville, we expect to run the cars tomorrow.

In the meantime I am well & enjoying myself, though it is hard work & the Thermometer is about 90 in the shade with a scorching sun; I can now say positively there are plenty of good Union folks in old Tennessee in fact sometimes for 5 miles, you would find nothing else. I hope you are taking good care of yourself and not spoiling those bright eyes of yours. I got your letter, it arrived at camp only a few hours before me & for it many thanks my Dear Girl & now with much love, I must postpone any further for the present.

I am ever sincerely <u>yours</u>,

Love

The bridges James's brigade fixed probably looked similar to this bridge across Bull Run in Virginia. "Rapid Repairs." From Robert S. Lanier, ed., *The Photographic History of the Civil War in Ten Volumes*, Vol. 2 (New York: The Review of Reviews, 1911).

---

1. Confederate general P. G. T. Beauregard.

Humboldt, Tenn.
July 1st 1862
My Dear Molly

I have been anxious to write every day since I wrote last, but each day found the wish vain. I wrote the last letter under difficulties in a crowd & I was so dissatisfied with it when finished I would have torn it up, but I did not see any chance of writing another, & so I sent it. I do not know what success I may have to day for I sit in the sun, on the platform of the depot, with 500 men marching up & down & I must needs assist in the conversation of the passers by occasionally.

We have had rather a stirring time since. Day after I wrote I started for Humboldt, but had a sudden attack of the "cholera" & had to stop half way. It tried me severely for about 10 hours, but by Friday (Two days) I was all right & started again. When I got to camp, I spent a day in writing & mustering the men for pay – next day we struck camp packed up & waited for the cars to go to "Corinth" – ere night that order was countermanded, & we pitched our Tents – next day orders came to go north to "Union City" & from thence to "Vicksburgh" – during the day rumors of "McClellan's" defeat leaked along the wires & it was said we were ordered to Richmond but this is all contradicted <u>& we lay</u> at the depot, for fresh orders – all night. Today it is said we go to "Corinth" but nothing is certain, except that we have not found our place in the programme yet, & are seated on the ruins of our camp, arms in hand waiting on <u>Providence</u> or "<u>Halleck</u>".

All this w'd not seem worth putting on paper, but it has made us such a deal of work & excitement, that I could not have written a coherent letter even if I could have found the time. I am not quite "en rapport" even yet but the <u>will</u> is present if I am a little "<u>bothered</u>". I believe I mentioned that I received your missing letter on my return here, but none of the papers sent have come to hand. I would not send more than two or three until there is more safety. I get the *Democrat & Republican* but in the I.L.N. in this wilderness of literature, there is too much temptation for safety at present. I am in good condition again able to fulfill all my duties here & as strong as ever. I had eaten heartily of some fine ripe plums both at dinner & at supper (cooked) & lay all the blame to them, though perhaps a little bilious before.

We shall be glad when we join the grand army & get a little settled, as our present erratic movements are more tiresome than marching.

I hope to hear from you soon, letter mails come safe, & did come regularly until the last three days. I suppose it is not known at Cairo or Columbus where to send them, in consequence of so many contradictory orders. That is only temporary however & so I long for one of your cherished epistles, as the parched traveller does for water in the desert.

"Morn, noon & night
Where e' er I may be
Fondly I'm dreaming
Ever of Thee"

I fear from causes afore said your patience may be tried ere you get this but as the distance increases over such uncertain lines of travel as these railroads we have been building, we must expect delay in transit.

I wish to hear that you look as bright as ever, that you get strong & weighty & that you let not your bright eyes tell tales of ought but happiness.

Do so my Dear Eliza and you love me, just throw fretting & fine sewing to the winds for a season. You know I looked long for perfection. You wont let me say I found it, but if I choose to think so, pray do so much to encourage me in the delusion.

And now what about the 4th. It is at hand but I fear a dull time unless we get to "Corinth" in the meantime, when we might have a review & some salutes from the artillery. I hope you may have a happy time, as it will be all over ere you see this scrawl. I believe you are to have a procession of some kind & then to the country. I had a little pleasure last night. I went with a Capt Kidd to visit some "secesh" young Ladies – F.F.V's to whom he had extended protection, (or rather to their father & his property). The Ladies tried to be very agreeable & were so, though I could see evidences of constraint occasionally. We remained nearly three hours & had music from a fine piano most the time. They sang well too, & I got them to sing all the secesh tunes – The Bony Blue Flag – Dixie &c – which they did with much vim & afterwards favored Capt. Kidd with the Red, White & Blue as a compromise – result we were invited to call again, & may do so if we remain. Their father Dr. Stillwell is well informed & agreeable, & not near so much infected with secesh doctrine as the Ladies.

I hope for the sake of civilization & peace that all these rumors of McClellans defeat at Richmond are untrue, as if true it will prolong this war at least Three years (more than it w'd be otherwise & also get us into a row with England & France with nothing but ruin & destruction of life to look forward to all that time.

Our people with the knowledge of their strength now gained & such a long course of victories w'd not give up until desolation reigned, & so the only hope of speedy peace both North & South is in the South's being whipped there, which bids fair to be the last ditch.

We have been capturing quantities of property belonging to the secesh army when here, in the shape of officers trunks, letters swords &c – also a large mail, which has given us great amusement in the reading. The spelling & sentiments are so rich – many of the letters too are to young men from their sisters & others at home, expressing Union sentiment, & requesting them to leave the secesh Army – & now I suppose I must write to Alex for the information of the community at large & close for the present so give my love to Sallie to your Mother, Aunt, Mrs. Rogers &c &c & with much love to yourself

I am my Dearest Girl
Yours Sincerely
James E. Love

10 Miles South of Corinth, Miss. 4th July 1862
My Dear Molly
We have been on the tramp in a scorching sun ever since until 10 oclock last night when we arrived here 90 miles south of where I commenced this letter. We did not halt at Corinth longer than an hour but kept on to the

front. We rest here two or three days & then go Southeast again 40 miles more as I understand it to Rienzi & there if Beauregard or Bragg allows us, I suppose we repose for the summer.

We are now camped on a fine high ridge in the piny woods, the air being perfumed & heavy with the dense vegetation.

We are now in the sunny South, most as far as we can go & it is past mid-summer so it can not get much warmer. I stood the march quite as well as any man in the Regiment, & feel well today – but expect a quiet 4th – as there is nothing to be seen here & no whisky or Beer. I hope to see this off now at once & so with much love my ever dear Eliza

I am
Sincerely Yours
James E. Love
Address
8th Kansas Vol
Care Genl R. B. Mitchell
Corinth
or elsewhere
Many happy returns
Love

Camp Near Rienzi

July 8th 1862

My Dearest Eliza

The silver moon shines above & soon our immense camp will be rapt in sleep, securely so, though supposed to be facing the enemy. But we have been diligently searching for said enemy & found him not.

They have all gone to Richmond leaving scarcely a corporals guard behind to watch us, for say they "Our independence is to be gained or lost there, & on the present battle we stake the result," so they have left their Southern homes unguarded save by a hot sun, a swampy soil, & all the diseases, so brought forth & I believe our commanders here wont attempt to combat such opponents ere October next & we have every prospect of going no further South ere that time. We may march much from place to place, as the ever changing requirements of this game of war, as of Chess may dictate but not South of us, but at Richmond is the life blood of the Rebellion to flow. God send that it may do so!! is my fervent prayer, and that in all Charity & Kindness on both sides, as if we are defeated at Richmond (as we came near being) it would be only the commencement of the bloodiest time the World ever saw.

So I hope they have reinforced McClellan & that he is now or soon will be in Richmond, where we started to go, but are here – in the advance & look with intense anxiety for news. We get the St. Louis & Chicago dailies when two or three days old, but have had no letters for ten days. We have moved camp & marched every three days or oftener & so they could not overtake us, & many have no doubt gone down to Major General Mitchell at Chattanooga. So put Genl Mitchells name on no more – simply 8th Kansas Vol – Corinth or Rienzi.

We are now directly under "Halleck" & perceive many advantages already from so being. We have been all very anxious for a fight, but as we have no enemies but the heat at present, we are & expect too conduct ourselves valiently even against such odds.

We have all the vantage ground of a good airy camp, high & covered sparsely with tall trees enough for shelter & not enough to stop the circulation of any air stirring. We have also at 200 yards distance, a deep ravine full of the <u>finest</u> springs & the <u>coolest</u> water I have had since I entered the service. We are on the southern slope of the Tishimingo hills, splendid rolling timbered land, but entirely wild, as it wont grow enough cotton – by nigger labor – to pay.

& So the great fight progresses at Richmond, & we lay here in peace, enjoying the heat even while we can – but hungry for a fight when comes the cool breezes of October – if there should be by that time any secesh left to fight. I fear there will be, as "<u>they</u>" threaten to tender their allegiance to France or England if whip'd at Richmond & thus become a <u>province</u> of one of those powers rather than succumb to the cursed <u>Yankees</u> offering to free their slaves gradually, & to trade freely with them, in return for their protection & <u>rule</u>.

Well if <u>they</u> do so, there will be much fighting yet, & so much money spent, there will not be much to fight for – "but never give up the ship" is a time tried motto & though time that tried mens souls may have come back again, why we must only, hope on, hope ever, & <u>worry through</u>.

So God grant McClellan is in Richmond & that thus I may have a chance to see my Molly well & hearty ere I grow gray.

I enjoy better health than Ive had for years. The Sun scorches, but I stay as much in the shade as possible from 9 to 4 o.c. & exercise before or after those hours, & I've felt the sun as much in St. Louis & more in Australia. I believe now if fate favors me, I will get through this campaign healthier then before & now what of my darling. I look for a heavy mail when it comes. It is now 18 days since I left the city & yet not a word, but I have no doubt 2 or 3 missives are on the way.

I wish you could for a day even visit our camp among the ever waving pines.

Our men got paid off up to 1st May yesterday & are in the best of spirits. In our company only two sick one from typhoid fever & one from the effects of a former sun stroke. Other Companies have 8 or 10 each, but our <u>city boys</u> – whisky heads though some of them are – are impervious to disease to all appearance. They are a little lazy perhaps, but they attend to their comforts, live well & reverence a good shady bower or tree. So different from our country cousins around.

I enclose a scrap I cut from a Chicago paper that I believe is correct & gives some details that will save me writing.

I have a nice tent well fixed up – all save a writing table, which I suppose we must do without for the future. We have a table for common use but it is barely two foot high, & so I write this on my knee sitting on my bunk.

I will enclose this along with a scrap to Alex, in the morning & will then close it. I could find much more to say but it seems as if I must tire you sooner or later with all these details & I find it almost impossible to fix my mind on other themes – the present interest & occupation of our movements are so overpowering.

So with much love to all & the kindest wishes, love & thoughts toward your dear self, I kiss you, by proxy wish you pleasant dreams & goodnight.

Love

July 9th 1862

My Dear Molly

I hasten to close this straggling epistle & the more so that I have nothing new to communicate. We have no news of any kind in camp. All is quiet along the lines & naught remains but that surcharged Thunder Cloud at Richmond. Will it break with our destruction or our salvation or will it only cripple both parties & prolong the war indefinitely. That is the only question we are capable of thinking of discussing.

We wait an answer as patiently as we can & meantime Madam Rumor is busily at work romancing wildly. I hew her not but look for a paper anxiously.

A mail has just come in but nothing for me yet better luck tomorrow I hope

I am my dear Girl

Yours Sincerely

James E. Love

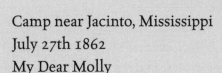

Camp near Jacinto, Mississippi

July 27th 1862

My Dear Molly

I seize on Sunday night again as the charmed moment to renew our tete-a-tete. It is a fine cool night, and a thousand twinkling stars overhead repay us for the loss of the "ladye" moon while the Bull Frogs croak melodiously in the swamp near by, & the thousand & one Locusts & Katydids answer one another from tree to tree on the hill side – all will soon be silent else – for Tattoo sounded ere I commenced & Taps is sounding now. It is only half past eight & yet it has been dark in this land of Dixie one hour & a half & so I wishing to turn night into day, to bring sunshine near to midnight renew herewith our conversation & if I can not hear a response I can fancy one in keeping with your quiet face & loving Character knowing also that one is or soon will be enroute if not on the wings of Love or the wind, why dawdling along somewhere on a government steam engine.

Oh! I have wanted to hear from you so bad during the last few days – every thing seems to be going backward with us as if all the fiends of hell were let loose on our beloved country again for a season, but a brighter day is coming when guerrilla raids will be talked of as things of the past & folks will wonder at the folly & fiendishness of man in this the much vaunted 19th Century.

Judging from the papers (I have just read those of the 23d inst) folks in St. Louis and <u>Missouri</u> must be as much <u>skeered</u> as their Louisville & Cincinnati friends – how is it? We had not guessed it from the papers until we saw those orders about the militia – all had been mum – but a deep excitement must have been in your midst, do tell me?[1] How it appears to you or to William, has he got a company? And then I dont understand this militia arrangement; I know the state pays them – when they are paid at all – generally not! But what place will they fill as regards Home Guards, Volunteers, State Guards &c &c &c. I am in the dark.

---

1. On July 22, 1862, Missouri governor Hamilton R. Gamble ordered the organization of the entire state militia to protect the state against "bands of guerrillas in different parts of the State, who are engaged in robbing and murdering peaceable citizens, for no other cause than that such citizens are loyal to the Government."

Is Alexander in the levy? or John Adams?

Truly I am perplexed, astonished this night. Now I'll tell you what we've done – Capt. Herd & I. We have petitioned Frank Blair & Governor Gamble to use their influence to have us & our Co transferred into one of Frank's new Brigades or into any Missouri Regt. in the field. I hope we shall be successful. There are good Missouri Regts down here & if transfer'd into even one of them, we would have a good chance to be sent home to recruit which we never expect to do while in a Kansas Regt. We sent our petitions through a friend to James Archer for presentation. I think they are in St. Louis today if not before.

We are located on a pleasant hill side – where none had encamped before – still in the piny woods – fine springs & bathing & washing places around. We have had considerable rain lately with weather occasionally cool for July & it has brought out some flowers but it is almost useless to gather them, as they fade & wither ere 15 minutes pass & they are all very modest & colorless too, generally small unless the swamp products, which are on a gigantic scale. Occasionally I see many pretty wild peas, also sweet peas. I'll enclose one if I can. I am in good health & better spirits. We are in a much richer country than that around Corinth. Jacinto is the county seat of Tishimingo County Miss & is a nucleus for the few F.F.Vs in the Co. Strange to say we see scarcely any men & not one really pretty girl since we left Kentucky, but I had not such a good opportunity to prospect as some of the other officers as I travel'd hurriedly – alone – and unacquainted. I heard of Belles here & there, reputed Beauties but they w'd be second or third rate even in St. Louis. I strolled towards town today purposely to get a sight of one of the local Belles and I had a talk with her on chickens, green corn, &c &c – but I was disappointed as usual. She could not be more than 17 or 20, but seemed fading fast already. A very clear complexion, but with that suspicious & to me disagreeable dark shade below the eyes that some young ladies have acquired from dissipation, foolish eating & other causes. So I bought some chickens at 50 cents a piece, cabbages in proportion, hooked some very green apples & peaches & came home to my quiet tent, to find a letter awaiting me from Leavenworth. Sorry it was not from the <u>Mound City</u>!

I hope my dear girl yourself, Mother, Aunt, Sallie & all the folks are well as can be expected under a July sun, if you only enjoy the weather and stand the effects of the sun & heat half as well as I do, all will be well, but it requires sometimes a veritable salamander so to do.

Well now that we have left Corinth – as we did last Tuesday & marched here 14 miles – I may I suppose say a word of it though I saw very little of it or of the camps around it. It was so warm while we lay there, & the locality was so uninteresting in any but a historical point of view, and had from the numerous camps & consequent destruction of timber become so denuded of shade that I ventured on but little perambulation & what I did see was not agreeable to my Optic or <u>Olfactory</u> nerves.

We were encamped as far away from the scene of the late battles, & from the Union & Secesh entrenched camps as possible, quite on the other side of town.

We saw some earth Works but not near so strong as you w'd or I did expect. I did see numerous graves "Secesh" some of them, right in town around the depot & Hotel, the poor white trash seem to have been chucked in any where by their live companions or lordly masters, when they died from fevers, caused by exposure & lack of medicine or from wounds, but now that lifes turmoil & fitful fever is over, I've no doubt they sleep well – as well as their masters, nigger owners though they be, will do in a metallic case or a Mahogany Coffin – and will start at the sound of the last trump with as much alacrity when Earth & Sea – Land & Water – Swamp & Hill-side give up their dead.

May we all be prepared to welcome the Archangels blast!

But to return to Corinth. I was disappointed. Its a vile place – at all times. Still more so now, when so much dead horse & unfortunate overworked mules lay bleaching in a tropical sun. Trophies, there was none to be had & historical points had not yet the mould of age on them nor the romance of History or poesy attached as they will have in future years. All was bare red earth hot & tiresome to behold & painful on the eyes from the glare, on the lungs & nasal organs from the vile effluvias spoken of & those incident on a camp of a hundred thousand dirty men – secesh & Union in turn. There is however very strict sanitary and police regulations in all our camps – much more so – evidently – than there was in that of the Chivalry. So I am not sorry that we are twelve miles further removed from it, in the 1st Brigade 1st Division of the army of the Mississippi, which of course is one of the advance posts of the Grand Army.

Things go very much by contraries down here. Our Republican General is carefully guarding secesh property, while guerillas are ravaging the fair fields of Missouri, Kentucky & Tennessee & Democrats but lately hand & glove with their Southern brethren swear that it is all wrong & they are willing to free even the blessed nigger if it will end the War.

When last I wrote I begun to think we would not move but no sooner had I said so, but we came down here.

Since two weeks we have been looking for a fight but it dont come, & our scouts cant find any one to fight with, & yet occasionally a body of horse swoop down & capture a company on picket when least expected & so the world really does move though which way, just now it w'd take a philosopher to tell. I intend writing tomorrow to Alex. I had an answer from him to mine of the 2d a few days since. I think you will all get tired of my letters after a while unless I have a little more variety to flavor the <u>incidents</u>. I will soon have to come down to a business letter of three or four lines.

Alex tells me of a rather good story of his friend Dr. B. who has been among the list of "Secesh British Subjects" but who now along with others of our friends wish to become American Citizens, <u>from pecuniary reasons</u>.

I hope they can none of them find (friends?) willing to perjure themselves willfully or unwittingly.

Oaths that as in the case of thousands of our Irish, English & Canadian fellow citizens have been broken once are not worth patching up again and I would scorn to call the perpetrators of any such double sublimated perjury my friends. True they dont look on it, so though what text of Scripture or what Dogma of religion excuses them from an oath once taken in good faith, I dont know – except the Jesuit one "That the end justifies the means."

If they have thought that in order to break up the American they were justified in perjuring themselves – So be it!

But all honest men, women & patriots differ from them – whether American or otherwise.

I need not say take good care of yourself. I hope you continue so to do. And now with much love to yourself, give a modicum to Sallie & the rest

I am my Dear Eliza

Yours Sincerely

James E. Love

28th

Yours of the 22d to hand this moment, very much pleased with the news – will attend to all your requests.

Thanks a thousand times

Love & Kisses

from

Yours Ever

Love

Colonel Frank P. Blair.
Photograph by E. Anthony,
New York, 1861–1865.

In the field near Jacinto
August 2d 1862
My Dear Molly

After a week of peace and quietness & when just in a fair way to have all creature comforts around us, we again leave our summer quarters tomorrow.

We have had a very wet week but we only worked the harder for our comfort, in the shape of bowers &c &c &c & now when finished, Jeff. C. Davis[1] at whose mercy our summers peace lay (I said before) raises a perfect nest of hornets about our ears, & we start for Alabama, to protect General Buell's rear from Guerilla attacks. So mote it be. I am well as you see. I was just commencing a letter to you this morning when we had an alarm in camp & the result is we took 16 of Jeff's scouts prisoners. Nobody hurt on our side "seriously." We are all packed & ready for the road. Continue addressing me all the same as our letters will follow us & I expect must come through Corinth anyhow. I will write of course as soon as settled again. I think we will be near the Tennessee. I hope so, if it is not swampy.

I recd your last letter & the I.L.N. for June 28th yesterday. I see the excitement in St. Louis continues, but I dont clearly understand yet. I suppose light will break on me gradually.

Glad to hear of all those horseback rides & also of your enjoyments at "Old Shaws." I hope you'll continue such dissipation as long as it improves your health.

I am very careful & a very good boy always! You know that surely?

I thought all the folks up Morgan St. wanted boy's. I hope the last one has a good constitution, and promises to continue the name with more certainty than its elder's. I suppose the mother is well?

Your letters all came safe sooner or later. It requires no apologies, & probably your mistake did not detain them, as our General is already well known & the other has gone to Washington.

---

1. James's reference to "Jeff. C. Davis" is unclear. The Eighth Kansas was part of Union general Jefferson C. Davis's division. However, based on the context of the letter, it appears that James is referring to Jefferson F. Davis, president of the Confederacy.

I am my dearest Girl ever sincerely yours. With much Love to yourself Sallie & <u>all the folks</u>.

James E. Love

A dozen kisses & Embraces if you please from your

Love

James says he is happy to hear that Molly has visited "Old Shaws," a reference to today's Missouri Botanical Garden in St. Louis. View looking across Shaw's Garden toward the Conservatory. Photograph, ca. 1906.

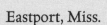

Eastport, Miss.

on

Tennessee River

August 6th 1862

My Dear Eliza

I did not get this note off as I was too late for the mail, & so it is yet in my hands. We got into camp yesterday on "la belle Tennessee" 50 or 60 miles above Pittsburgh Landing. We can throw a stone or fire a pistol into Tennessee on one side or Alabama on the other but we are yet in "Mississippi".

The town of Eastport is dilapidated & deserted.

We are encamped on a high ridge or bluff overlooking it & the river. We have a fine view of rolling bluffs, of timber & prairie land, thickly dotted with fine farm houses & good farms on the lazy Southern plan. Item – there is scarcely an apple or peach ripe yet, & it is now far in August. The trees are all old standards, no grafting or improvements in specie or cultivation of any kind being given to them. On the contrary there is generally a crop of corn, sweet potatoes & melons raised on the same ground, & so the trees dwindle along, raising apples not much better then the original crab, & peaches not better than plums.

We marched through a fine well watered country thickly settled & found it all the same.

We have scarcely seen a young man since we entered west Tennessee. All were pressed for the War ere the rebels retreated, many of them being for the Union firmly & all the time though not having the constancy to become martyrs in what seemed a hopeless quarrel. They desert to us occasionally.

A few miles from us in Alabama the commander had a message from the Union men, that they were being pressed & had all run to the mountains rather than fight for the accursed Confed. So he sent a Regiment down 40 miles south, at the risk of its total capture, & in the march of seven days making a circuit around. The Ladies hunted for their husbands & brothers & sons to the number of over 200 who are now enlisted as volunteers in an Illinois Regt. for the Union or Death. They have thus left their families to the tender mercies of the secesh troops & to the danger of starvation rather than fight against the good old flag. On the other hand the "Secesh" are quite as much in earnest, in fact more so than we of the north. Here for instance is a secesh belle advertising for Beauregard & she is not alone for women are if not the first by far the worst secessionists & was it not for their influence making it so fashionable it would have been over ere this. We passed through a fine Mississippi watering place yesterday, a perfect Paradise named I-U-Ka or Iuka.

There are five springs containing Iron & Sulphur & reported very healthy. The Soldiers stationed there are recovering health.

The whole place is well arranged with walks seats & bowers and has several hotels & numerous private residences with flowers, ornamental trees & shrubs. One large bushy shrub or tree from its beauty drew my attention, such a delicate pink & such a delicate crimped up crazy flower, it does not grow in the north unless under protection and as it is indescribable I will try & send you a sprig. It wont look right under pressure either, as its beauty lies in its wary gossamer lightness, & its color which like all southern flowers fade so soon when pulled unless in a vase.

We expect to have a stirring time, looking after suspicious characters & two or three expeditions are in prospect already. There are four Steamers at the landing & we wish to skeer our friends the would be assassins who are skulking around.

I am so delighted at having a water prospect again that this camp pleases me much, but for real pleasure I would take I-U-Ka for the Summer.

I suppose I must close, compelled by heat & scarcity of paper. The thermometer has been as high as 111 deg in the Shade & over a 100 deg for several afternoons. We have cool mornings & nights, & we started at three o'clock each morning & got into camp at 11 or 12 o'clock.

I hope you are still in health & enjoyment. So with much love to yourself & Love & Remembrance to all the folks

I am as ever

Yours sincerely
James E. Love
Address
Eastport
near Corinth
Mississippi

James included a
small flower with
this letter. The
flower left a mark
on page 7.

Camp at Eastport Miss
August 10th 1862
My Dearest Molly

I have just recd yours of the 30th ult. I suppose long ere this you have got some of mine. I hope the rebels have not confiscated them, poor as they are I cant do better in this dull & to all eyes transparent camp life, where heat & ennui goes hand in hand or alternates with excitement & severe exercise. As I anticipated in my last, we have had some hard marches & scouts in the sun. The enemy is near at hand in "Guerilla Bands" and active. It was only on Friday one of our Companies at daylight was in "Chicasaw" and saw some salt, cotton, &c. They came back to report & I with others was sent out to fetch it in. We got there in the early afternoon, & found that the Guerillas had come in the meantime & stole half of it.

We gave them chase. They cross'd the river, & we had some very pretty shooting at over ½ a mile distance, nobody hurt, secesh skeduddling very fast. We then arrested the owners of the store, & took the goods, but even while in chase of the rebs the inhabitants stole all the light goods. Today there was a shooting scrape in camp. I am on as "Officer of the Guard", Capt Greelish as "Officer of the Day." Two of our men (Co.K) went down town & got drunk, they were followed by a sutler who accused one of them of stealing & Cap. Greelish went to arrest them, "they" resisted & attacked him, took his sword & so in self defence shot one & brought the other to Calaboose. Whitehill who was shot is in the Hospital now in a dangerous condition – resisting the "Off. of the day" is one of the highest crimes in the army, so he has few to pity. He has every care & much sympathy however, such is life. Whisky & its indiscretions are worse to be feared it seems than our (Southern Chivalry?)

Need I reiterate I am well. Have no fear. I am careful. What do you think? I have a strange shaped chest & shoulders. My chest is narrow but very deep & in going around with my shirt unbuttoned at the neck, somebody noticed it & called the Doctor's attention (as a consumptive or formed by disease). I challenged it & the Doctor says, I have as good lungs as any man in the

Battalion & have had a good constitution, very good, for it is good now "he says" & I have abused it or been exposed. Two other Doctors said likewise. I said I had been much exposed, & found I could stand it, so my lungs & chest are found useful & good, & my round shoulders are attributable to my own folly. I have written about once a week. I might write oftener, but sometimes opportunity, sometimes the lack of news or the heat of the weather prevents, & so it goes. Do I not bore you sometimes, I fear so. I know I write both too much & too little! I get all yours I believe; & I hope you will get mine soon! I would not have a line less from you. I am always ravenous for more. I wish I was eloquent enough to say in words or on paper how much good your lines do me, how I long for them, & appreciate them. I would fail miserably if I tried today, so I wont! There is or has been no disturbance in our Regt. As to the other Kansas Regts I know not. "Ours" is all right, & with this new policy of the war fully inaugurated, they will feel better daily.

I dont expect ever to see John Adams fight for the Union, & the day is past when he would have fought for the South, (if he dared??) He thought then money was to be made? Now he thinks they are Bankrupt, Ive no doubt

Well if they are out of money those in the field fight out of pure courage or cowardice still & take their chances for pay. That he wont do!

Glad to hear of Mrs. Wightman & Mr. Kinnear keeping memory green, but dont compromise yourself – eh!

You dear little, loving, warm hearted piece of frigidity. Do you know it is prophesied that you will be a martyr yet on the altar of friendship? That is sacrifice yourself in looking after the comfort &c of those you love? You'd better not!

Sorry for Mrs. Armstrong Unfortunate that she is!

Glad to hear your residence is in St. Louis still, so is mine but my address is as before.

Goodbye

Love

August 12th

Mail goes out this morning, all goes well but we have heard nothing of the outer world for over a week except our mail with dates of the 1st from St. Louis. We have had dreadful rumors from secesh sources, good ones from Union sources concerning General Pope. It is also said the President proposes to draft 600,000 men. I hope it is so & that this war may end ere the whole country is ruined.

I have no pity for our fearful Irish or Secesh friends. Their policy you can see has prolonged the war a year or two. We are now in a land flowing with milk & honey at fair prices. Union women come 4 or 5 miles & sell cheap – not so the Secesh. We can have nothing except by force or at ten prices. These are poor white trash of course "Mudsills", but everlasting glory to the mudsills, who while all the powers of earth & hell seemed leagued against the Union, stood true at peril of life & property & all they held dear.

The warmest Love to your Dear Self & all

I am My Dear Girl

Yours Sincerely,

James E. Love

Captain John Greelish. Photograph by T. M. Schleier, Nashville, 1861–1865.

Camp near Waterloo, Alabama
August 20th 1862
My Dear Molly

I have been rather delayed in writing this time from lack of opportunity. I have been busied in such a way & in such places as to prevent it, neither have I received anything from the North either paper or letter later than yours of the 30th so I reckon there is a stoppage in the mail somewhere, & if so besides my deprivation, you will likely have lost my flowery epistles somewhere, also. I hope not, cause I cant replace them in any way. The Newspaper folks manage to get them through occasionally somehow, so I read a *Democrat* to day of the 16th and have thus got pretty well posted with regard to matters & things North of us, in all of which especially as regards St. Louis Missouri & Tennessee, I am much interested. I say Tennessee because of the frequent & <u>important</u> Military movements taking place there all the time now both within & <u>without</u> the reach of newspaper reporters.

As to what is <u>without</u> their <u>ken</u>, all the movements down here are so at present. The Rebels are moving men back & forth looking for an opening to recapture Tennessee, while 70,000 men on our side are marching more or less daily to prevent their entrance. They dont wish to fight us in Alabama or Mississip, but to steal in and plunder & burn Tennessee & so compel us to go back.

We (our Regiment, Brigade, & Division) are marching now so as to be able to go to the relief of either <u>Nashville</u>, Huntsville, or <u>Chattanooga</u>, whichever is threatened by them, as their movements indicate an attack on some or all of those places, each about 100 miles from us in different directions. We are not alone either as many thousands besides are marching in the same direction from various points.

All this means strategy & it dont get into the papers now. I should like to get to Nashville. I would feel in a much more friendly country & also so much nearer to you, in space & time. I hope you are still improving in health & enjoying yourself abroad as when last heard from.

I am pretty well I thank you, as I said in my last we are living well now and it seems to agree with me wonderfully. Weather here is for the present cool and rainy, and in that respect pleasant while we have our Tents to take refuge in, but the other night it caught us out in the cold. I didnt catch any cold however, and can feel no bad effects whatsoever. We had also much wading in water consequent on our ferry boat going aground in a creek, & it took us several days to get it off but the water & the sun were both hot & we didn't mind! Wet feet dont hurt on the march if you dry them when you come to a halt or to camp, such is my experience. We have much strange experience in camp which could not by any possibility be got within the bounds of a letter, & though it might serve for Newspaper gossip, much of it is probably only interesting to us the participators only & so I spare you the infliction generally, but I wish heartily now that I was out of a Kansas Regt. & why because this Battalion of Kansans is persecuted for reasons political, & they are not <u>guilty</u>, still less do we as <u>Missourians</u> relish being persecuted because we are in a Kansas Regt, this doubles the injury to us. The last case is an order from H'd Q'ts stopping $1053.50 from our pay because somebody has charged some of our men with stealing at Trenton two months ago some sugar &c. We <u>know our</u> men are innocent.

We never heard of the matter until the paymaster got an order to stop it from our pay. No trial, no notification of an accusation. We have just been penning an indignant protest, a copy of which we or I may send to the St. Louis papers. Such is the last instance. But this is all professional & camp news – as to general news we hear but little that dont get into the papers. In other words most of the news of movements come to us through the papers. Our movements as you know are frequent, but there are no correspondents or reporters allowed in our camp, and now all movements are contraband news. Beauregard & Grant are playing a game of chess & cheating all they can, & outsiders are not allowed to pass any remarks, or state the intentions of the combatants. What news we do hear is rather discouraging, barring Pope's small success we are under a cloud, but "We are coming Father Abram 600 thousand more." This encourages me. It is the "silver "lining" and <u>then</u> too Newspapers live on <u>exaggerations</u>.

I think this winter after all will settle the war. Jeff has got every man in the South in the field, he can get no more save niggers, & we can get as many of them as he can so if we are true to ourselves these 600,000 fresh men will soon settle it. But this is only news so I'll no more of it. We have a stirring winter before us all in the sunny South I hope, & until that is <u>past safe</u>, I grieve to say I cannot hope to see you. Stern fate is upon us now! Do I repine at that! No! No! No! though I would sell my dearest hopes to bask in your presence to live in the light of your eyes the beattitude of your love & presence. Repine No! I rejoice that I was among the first Volunteers on principle of patriotism to the Country of my early love and adoption. My country needs me more than ever & if at home now, I would fly to the rescue, nor wait for a draft, but here I am in the advance, with the new volunteers & the militia behind the enemy in front and now if we march again & our communications are cut off, dont think for a moment that I dont write. I shall write as before or oftener & if the mails are insecure wait until we get to <u>Nashville</u> or elsewhere with a base line open. We are tortured occasionally with audacious Secesh rumors, but now I give no credence to any of them. It is the only safe rule.

And now my dear girl My Guardian Angel (as per wood-cut) I feel strong in your presence in your prayers & in your Love. I fear not for myself. Fear not for me, if letters come not believe it not as a sign of evil.

Give my Love & remembrance to Sallie, mother Aunt & all the folks.

I am my dear Molly

Sincerely Yours

James E. Love

August 22

My Dear Molly

Mail haint gone yet & so I add a P.S. and first I wish to mention I had a letter from a friend who gives me all the gossip of the city and including most my friends. You are mentioned, as "looking like patience on a monument," "as sighing inwardly my Jamies far awa frae me", and again I'm told not to let the secesh get hold of me for my numerous friends sakes & especially "for the sake of her who prefers" "Love to Roses"! What does it all mean? I dont know! Folks will talk somehow! I wont tell you who it is just now, for fear you might pull "<u>her</u>" wool out at sight.

We are now camped in an apple orchard, a very nice clean shady place & living on Fruit & milk and vegetable diet.

23d August
4 oclock A.M.

I have not been to bed & the drum beats for the march, where I dont know, & the result is in the hand of the power who rules all things, to him I confide it.

The mail goes soon. I am with Love & a thousand kisses

Yours as ever

My dear dear girl

James E. Love

Co. K. 8th Kan. Vol.

Corinth or Elsewhere

James calls Molly his "Guardian Angel (as per wood-cut)," a reference to the illustrated stationery he used for part of this letter (page 9).

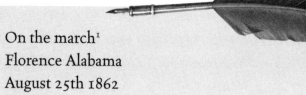

On the march[1]
Florence Alabama
August 25th 1862

My Dear Molly

Here we are at the prettiest town in Alabama, so reputed, & I have no doubt it is worthy, as it is a very pretty place. We marched from Waterloo on Saturday morning through a fine country & over a dusty road. Made only twelve miles on account of bad roads & weightily loaded wagons. Camped at Gravelly Springs. I was on picket all night & captured only [illegible] three nights in succession & in a very bad humor, inclined to get sick out of spite, but didn't however Ive got two large boils on my haunch instead that interfere with my locomotion very much & I will have to ride tomorrow. On Sunday we started early & passed through the garden of Alabama, a well improved delightful country, had a good time as I was not on duty with the company. Dined with a very pleasant <u>young lady</u> & had some interesting arguments & conversation. On arriving at Cypress Mills we found the whole population turned out to see us & some to welcome us. They consisted in large part of young girls – it being a large factory village. This county <u>Lauderdale</u> has 23 factories in it – a great many for Ala. Got to Florence in good time (4 o'clock) to see it & camped in the city on some fine lawns overlooking the river (Tennessee) which is wide shallow here & crossed by a very long rail road & wagon bridge – of which at present but the stone piers remain as General Mitchell burned it when he made a descent here before "Corinth" was evacuated. I had a swim in the river, & felt much better for it, as we were just loaded with dust. We made only 14 miles, & expected a large force from "Buells" Army to join us, but there has none crossed the river neither can we hear of them.

I rambled around Florence on Monday a little (to day) as I am quite lame & was much pleased. The streets are very wide, & well shaded with old Trees, houses very Luxurious on large lots set far back, & garden or green-

---

1. From August 18 to September 4, the Eighth Kansas marched more than 240 miles with few rations, hardly any tents, and little time to rest.

ery's in front, flowers & fruits in profusion. <u>It is</u> quite old for a western town. I found old graves in a family enclosure of Judge McKinley (U. S. Supreme) 50 years back – very interesting as historical & family mementoes they were. The enclosure is a late erection surrounding older ones & a vault. His wife died I believe in 1812. He died lately.

Mount Pleasant Tenn.
August 28th 1862

Got so far all safe anyhow but the guerrillas pitched into our train this evening and were quietly making off with at least a dozen wagons when the rear guard came up unexpectedly to them & chased them good, killing some, capturing two & recovering all our property & some of theirs. Such is life in the Army – mighty uncertain. He that sows dont always reap, but to return to Florence. We got up to start for "<u>Nashville</u>" over 110 miles next morning at 3 o'clock but shortly after came fresh orders for a forced march & to turn in all our Tents & extra baggage at once to <u>Tuscumbia</u>, a railroad station 5 miles across the river. We did so & consumed half a day. Still our reinforcements & provisions did not come. At 4 o'clock came our stores & then it was decided to wait for midnight & if nobody came, start soon after. We did so at 3 o'clock & made 20 miles to Blue Creek, where we camped again after a days horrid dust & heat. I in the ambulance crippled with a couple of boils, came cool & safe. On Wednesday we started same time & passed over a rough mountain rocky country, plenty of poor white trash. I rode half the time or more made 20 miles to Lawrenceburgh got in late, our wagons later. Camped by the creek in town with little to eat & up early in the morning again & off when we had the hottest & dustiest march yet – country still rough & when passing a long rocky ravine steep down hill the guerrillas got us as I said. When we got in camp, some men (seven) from the 22d Indiana went out foraging & came not back again. The wild <u>Gorillas</u> picked them up so we heard – that is all we know. The country is alive & Union men have to keep very quiet, & soldiers are not safe out of camp. Still they go – on folly or business.

Columbia Tenn.

Friday 29th

Started at dawn this morning & passed over a fine Turnpike road all day. Lawrenceburgh is a fair sized county town but in an alarming state of dilapidation. A general shiftlessness, as Harriet Beecher would call it prevails. There is a fine obelisk monument in the public square in memory of a large number of citizens of the county & state that <u>died</u> &c in the Mexican War at Monterey & in California. It looked mournful & rebellious all together & we left without regret and passed through the garden of Tennessee. Very aristocratic it was all the way to Columbia, each side the road fine residences & lawns with a very superior style of Architecture – cottage & otherwise set along way back from the road, & porticos, terraces &c all covered with blooming beauties – fine old walnut trees, poplar, oaks & cedars scattered over the beautiful blue grass of Kentucky. Much surprised & gratified we were all day. The change was so pleased from the bleak hills & ravines & poor white trash to all the beauties of an almost English landscape – ornamental trees & all more like that than anything else I've seen since. We made a very quick march into Columbia 15 miles & found General Negley in command, reported to him but found he intended to stay a while & judged it better for us to go on. So we go again in the morning over 40 miles yet & General Bragg somewhere around.

I saw a late paper today 25th six days later than we've had before. I see they are making a desperate struggle ere our new Vol. can get into the field. It says Buell has evacuated Huntsville & Tuscambia. I don't believe it, as we left them all there. I have no doubt however but they intend getting into Corinth as quick as possible and now the fight is about to become general, both East & West. After a few more strategic moves look out for hot times. We found Columbia a large & bustling business town with good stores, good houses, & Aristocratic residences. A large river runs through named the Duck River. This we passed and are in camp one mile this side. I eat to day the first really fine large ripe peaches & apples I've seen in the Southern Confed. If we get safe to Nashville, & it is possible to send anything, I will send some valuable enclosures along with this to you & William. If anything happens to me, I reckon they will come anyhow – as Capt Herd or Lieut Babcock will attend to it for me.

I am not fully prepared yet, but will be I hope by tomorrow night & God willing I will try to worry through, so far my presentiments are all of the happiest. There is no secesh ball cast yet for me. I'm not so predestined or if I am so be it. God wills. Taint my fault, but a thousand kisses when we met in happier times.

My dearly loved girl goodnight

Camp near Franklin Tenn
August 30th 62
My Dearest Molly

I closed writing last night at 9 o'clock & jumped up this morning as fresh as a squirrel anticipating a long days march but alas for presentiments, I was no sooner up than I fell down again & an iron spike ran in my back. I was stunned & fainted, but they bundled me into the ambulance & marched along. I suffered some from the shaking of the Wagon, but feel quite fresh now after some hours rest. We got into camp about noon, & rested again under fresh orders. We find considerable Union sentiment around and the Planters brought in delicacies for the hospital. News more cheering. Buell is after Bragg with a sharp stick & General Rosseau at Nashville says he is no danger now. We make a short march again tomorrow (Sunday) & then a review & muster in the Evening. We are only 25 miles from Nashville now having made 17m to day. I see communication is open with Louisville again by stagecoaches. Unless inflammation sets in tomorrow or next day, I hope to send you a clean bill of health on arrival at town. Our march today was through a fine agricultural & planting country. The cotton is in blossom & looks pretty with its flowers some lilac, pink or purple & some white much like morning glory. Some of the bolls are already open & picking will begin next month & continue all through. We have seen much of it growing in Alabama since wherever the ground was not too rough, & now Au revoir take good care of yourself. I am good for marches of 25 miles a day yet.

31st August

Started early this morning riding as before & soon reached Franklin – found the prettiest little town we have passed yet, not so aristocratic as Columbia, no marble palaces, but pretty clean cottage houses set far back with trim front gardens full of flowers & shrubs & walks made with white & black gravel & shells on the borders, quite a little gem of a town. I understand however it is not singular in Tennessee. At Franklin fresh orders. Murfreesboro is again in danger & so we turned off toward that bone of contention over such a miserable rough rocky road up & down hill as the Rocky Mountains or the Highlands of Scotland would be ashamed to show. Made 17 miles to camp.

September 1st

Had several alarms from Cavalry during the night, nobody hurt on either side, but seven of our men were taken prisoners while eating supper at a farm house about dark. Men were up mostly all the night but we made an early start as usual & found the road much the same, so our wagon train got along slowly & we had to halt & march slow while it came up as the guerrillas cavalry was in sight all day. We sent a few shell after them once & they skedaddled at the Double Quick. The day was cool & showery & we got in to Murfreesboro before dark. 19 miles

September 2d

Murfreesboro is a fine town, much like Franklin in parts, but is getting quite dilapidated from the curse of an army – now Union, now Secesh. Many of the inhabitants have left & many of the stores are closed. Those that are open sell nothing but whisky bread & <u>Shoes</u>. This morning after cleaning clothes & arms we had a review & muster & looked very fierce after our Trip. There are about 15,000 Troops in town, 7000 of which came with us & belong to our Division. Some of the others came in after us from different points & more are coming. We do not stop, as our secesh friends have run already & we may be sent after them or else to Nashville. Bragg is 70 miles off yet. Gen'l Buell has arrived with his staff but his troops are pretty near the same places maneuvering daily as the enemy changes its position. General Rosseau is in command at Nashville & we are in his district, having left the Dept of the Mississippi when we left Florence, or rather when we got to Florence as that is in Buell's Dept. of the Ohio. Our men are all washing their clothes & preparing for the future. I have been busy all day seeing the Muster Rolls made out, notwithstanding my stiff back. Consequently I have had no time to post this or make up my packets for express

September 3d
Occupied much as yesterday, very busy, expect to march somewhere tonight or tomorrow morning. I am feeling quite well today after resting in camp yesterday. Everybody is in good spirits & think that some hard fighting this fall & winter must finish the war. I will mail this & put in a P.S. ere I leave stating all I know & so I finish this journal now. It has interested me in the writing & I hope it may not bore you in the reading. It would be impossible to write any other form of letter under the prevailing fatigue & excitement.

So with Love to you, Sallie & all I am dear Eliza
Yours Sincerely,
James E. Love

Sept. 4th
My Dear Molly
Half an hour after writing last night, we were on the march, not for the south nor after Bragg, but to Nashville. I could not even add a P.S. nor post this. We moved so suddenly & now we are camped by the Capital & find the Enemy still North of us in Kentucky. Probably we will go there tomorrow, but I am determined to mail this in town, whether I can send anything else or not. We marched most all night halting from 3 to 5 A.M. to get Breakfast. Our Regt. had none to get, so we went without until after we reached here at one o'clock. It was near 5 o.c. when our wagons came up & we got

supper cooked. We thus made 35 miles in 19 hours, including over 4 hours we rested by different springs. We came over a good pike & through a fine country. All our Division is along safe.

Good night
With Love

James and his regiment marched from Florence, in the northwest corner of Alabama, to Mount Pleasant, Columbia, Franklin, and Murfreesboro, Tennessee, in the center of the state. Section of Plate 38: Map of Kentucky and Tennessee. From George W. Colton, *Colton's Atlas of the World Illustrating Physical and Political Geography, Volume 1: North and South America* (New York: J. H. Colton and Company, 1856).

Camp near Nashville
Sept 9th 1862
My Dear Molly

I hear just now that the mail going North was captured, if so I fear my last extracts from my journal was captured with it. Well I wont risk going into detail again, but we had a hard march from Eastport Miss to Florence Ala, thence to Lawrenceburgh Tenn. & so thro' Columbia Franklin & Murfreesboro to Nashville. Near Nashville we lay 3 or 4 days expecting a fight but finding none. On Sunday I went to town to see it, the churches, the Ladies, the Capitol & monuments &c &c & to get something to eat. I saw all & was pleased with the location of the city & the Capitol. The Capitol is a real gem of beauty but the city proper is a poor narrow, dirty place – up & down hill – with fine residences around however. The city & Capitol looks well at a distance.

We passed through it yesterday & crossed the Cumberland on the Railroad Bridge, expecting to go on a forced march again to Bowling Green or Louisville but not so. There is some misunderstanding between Buell & Andy Johnson, so we went into camp one mile this side the river. It has taken over three days to cross all our army & baggage & they are crossing still without halt, & would seem to do so indefinitely. It is an immense host now for all Buell's Army is at last here, & some of Grant's. Where we go we know not, but the enemy in small squads is all around, so we cant go far wrong to find them.

Rumor says Buell is a traitor, reasons given – numerous ones too. Why does he abandon Tennessee cry indignant loyalists, Andrew Johnson at their head – that he & Buell have quarreled is certain & so we are almost like sheep without a Shepherd and even now the rumor is that 8,000 rebels are near by but I write to you in a new capacity. I am under arrest. I was placed so yesterday morning because I had been in town the day previous. I have got 27 companions in misery all officers, & all the rest pretty much were in town before or since, so I am easy in conscience of any misdemeanor, or if I am guilty, <u>all are</u> or <u>were</u>.

As I said, I went to get something to eat & wear. Gen'l Buell issued an order day before that none should come to the city & published it in Sundays paper. None of us saw the paper. None of us were arrested in town but a circular letter was sent to all the Colonels to enquire if any of their officers were in town & their names – names were given of some – mine with the rest.

I have had a good lazy time. I am not confined & I have no duties to perform. I can do as I please except go out the camp line without permission. The lines extend miles around, so I can ramble & bathe & loll under a tree & so I do so & write to you under one.

We have no tents, & so we live in the woods & have a continual picnic. All very fine, pleasant and romantic until it rains. Then the romance fades into a muddy reality. Sleeping out in the moonlight is also very pleasant when it dont shine in your eyes – then it is worse than the sun. But the leaves are falling and September is at hand and rain will come occasionally & soon the winter of our discontent will be at hand again.

I have recovered from my wound altogether. I am a convalescent & a prisoner at large. I wish I was certain of our mails & telegrams. It is such an ungracious task to write after all when you dont know whether it will reach or not.

I hope you are in good health & spirits. I have just reread for the ___ time yours of the 15th ult. I have no doubt but you have written since but I doubt whether I will ever receive them. Pray write on receipt of this & let me know about my last posted at Nashville along with one to Wm. For all these favors receive ten thousand thanks.

Give my love to Sallie, your Mother, Aunt, yourself &c &c &c.

You tell me to return thanks to U. Sam for moving me around so. I would & do when the roads are so I can breathe but Oh, dear when an army passes you cant recognize your next neighbor & then the sun beams down while you march & sweat & burn until it seems unendurable & you fling your <u>body</u> every <u>chance for a moment</u> under any passing shelter or crawl into any muddy spot for coolness, regardless of after consequences. Towards the end of your march you only stagger along because everybody else does & when you get to camp generally it is two or three hours before you have energy enough to return to the duties of washing yourself & looking after your supper & bed. Your day is divided, with the exception of luncheon at Springs when you are so fortunate as to have secured it to carry, into getting up before daylight to Breakfast, marching all day, eating supper & sleep.

I hope Sallie is quite recovered lang syne, & that John got his color back ere he left. That Mrs. Rogers is as active as ever in well doing & that they have drafted all our secesh friends, Irish & American, especially those who used to be a little better than anybody else because they had been so long here – pretended when in strange company to be American born – but are now only British subjects.

Sept 11th

No mail has went out for two days. We have been detailed to defend Nashville, 4 Divisions, 10,000 men or more. The rest have gone North towards Bowling Green. Bragg is North of us. Buell is yet here. We are so glad to be out of his immediate command. He is a traitor & has tried to sell us all to the Confed. As soon as proofs of which there are volumes can go to Washington he will be arrested or superseded if he dont get shot by his own soldiers first – numbers of Generals even are crazy to do it.

None here can arrest him or speak in his presence even. He has arrested a Brigadier because he told him if he obeyed a certain order his Brigade w'd be captured or starved for water & provisions – grass. It was so as his brigade was sent & came back in two days at an expense of $50,000.00 to the government in Dead Horses. Mr. Brigadier had to be released, the facts were too strong even for the Traitor to cover it, from the dullest soldier.

He is a Traitor. It is spoken of openly in the streets, by his own staff & by all the secesh fools that they are.

We will never give up Nashville if our generals are only plucky enough. Such a state of facts has made every soldier a general in his own Ideas on whom the country salvation depends & especially the State of Tennessee. It is too bad – long lines of wagons containing refugees. Ladies in satin & lace on their knees begging us not to desert them to the damd guerillas.

No more
Sincerely,
Love

Above: *General View of the City of Nashville, Tennessee.* From Harper's Weekly, March 8, 1862. Right: General Don Carlos Buell. Steel engraving by Brady, 1865.

Camp at Bowling Green, Ky.

Sept. 16th 62

My Dear Molly

When last I wrote I told you <u>we were to defend Nashville</u>, <u>but</u> necessity has no law and here we are at Bowling Green & with a probability of going further ere we stop, for Bragg & Co. are still North of us and on our railroad too, and if we dont drive them off soon, we will have nothing to eat. There has two more divisions of the Army of the Mississippi come to the relief of Nashville from the south since we left.

We get no news, or newspapers. Our last mail came in a month ago now.

I can scarcely expect that you will get my letters but I will keep on trying & hope you may soon – if lost I scarce know how I can replace them, for time was so scant & I was so tired generally, that I kept but little other record. Of course you will get all the Ky news from your papers, but we do not. We have heard however that there has been a fight at or near Lebanon & also at or near Mumfordsville, so I guess thats our route next.

I cant imagine what is the state of affairs North in St. Louis. I am afraid you are despondent. It is not time to despond however. We must all be desperately determined or soon be destroyed.

It is said here I dont know how truly, that Jackson is already in Pennsylvania marching on Baltimore & Philadelphia.[1] I hope not though if he is, I expect to hear he is caught soon. We must do it.

We all look for & wish for a desperate fight here. I dont say that I do, but that is the prevailing thought & I suppose it must come unless Bragg & Smith run which I dont expect.

Truth to tell we must fight or starve, for we have been on half rations for some time & soon will have none as far as the government is concerned. We get enough so far from the enemy but we soon eat up everything where ever we go. An army of 50 or 60,000 men marching requires more eatables than all the inhabitants of St. Louis.

---

1. Confederate major general Thomas J. "Stonewall" Jackson seized Harpers Ferry and moved north into Maryland as part of Robert E. Lee's campaign culminating in the battle of Antietam on September 17, 1862.

Rumors have just come to camp that Nashville has been evacuated for want of provisions, & that all the troops will be here tomorrow. If that is so, & I believe it, we will all soon be up to the Ohio River.

But I need fill my paper no more with what the Newspapers will tell you far better, so now to things more personal. I hope my dearest girl you are in good health & keep in good spirits, dont borrow care – "hope on hope ever" – "The darkest hour &c." Think of that & dont fear for me. I have got a charm at my heart, in the shape of your last letter (rec'd) & your photograph, besides your ring on my finger. Think you that harm can come nigh me. I dont, but you will tell me that is only my superstition and that you wonder at me professing to be such an unbeliever in Dreams for instance – but has it not been so. I have been in much danger, but thank the Lord am safe – from bullets fevers or colds so far & from all this fatigue I come fresh as from a long snooze in your old arm chair of a Sunday night of Old – if such things could be. What w'd I not give for only one Sunday night with you. Well most anything I value. A thousand kisses for instance. W'd you value them much. Perhaps not.

Well what shall it be then, but dont be worse than Laban to Jacob, when he worked for Rachel, neither when I work for Rachel, can I afford to be fooled & take to her not by any means. I am too old you know & getting very gray – while Jacob could double his Threescore years & ten. I cant expect to. All this means that I am coming home from the War, sound in mind. Though perhaps wanting a limb or two in something less than seven years & that I expect to do something desperate about or before that time if I can! Soothsayer say shall it be so or not? Look at the bright side! It is so much more pleasant & conducive to long life & even prosperity.

I grant that I have looked much at the Dark side, but I grow more hopeful daily as times grow more unkind & was I to marry as Paddy does, without a cent to pay the priest, I believe it w'd be a bright day for me & still more so – even a year or two stolen from heaven if with Molly!!

Now nuff-sed, or you will chide me again for flattery. But I dont wish to try any such experiment. I wish for my Molly's sake $20,000 & a Colonel's

Commission – that's all! Unless you make me ambitious in the future! But my Molly must keep her spirits up & so secure as good lungs as mine at least & as robust as possible under such circumstances. Will she try this for me – Pray do!! & believe me that I try to do as near as you w'd wish me to as circumstances ever changing will allow.

Well to change the subject again I will take up the thread of travel where I last left off that was at Nashville. Well next day I went to town again on <u>leave</u>, & there posted that missive containing a long palaver or three days gossip & much also that I overlooked previously. Also as to my <u>arrest</u> & <u>Buell's</u> treason. I went with the same companion as before & had such a pleasant time shopping and visiting. I like shopping about as well as ladies are said to do. Well at 4 o'clock before we were quite ready to return we heard our Brigade had got marching orders so we hurried to camp & found all gone but the rear guard & sick. We went town again with some of the sick in an ambulance & could not return without new passes & so we went to the Provost Marshall – thence to the governor – thence to General Thomas – & ere this it was pitch dark & raining a torrent such as I've not seen for years. So General Thomas ordered us to remain & he would send an escort of Cavalry & dispatch tomorrow. We did so & had a pleasant night with our friends & at the Hotel. While the Brigade stood up in the road in the dark in the rain – no shelter & when the worst was over lay down in the wet & drizzle & slept. Next day Friday 12th at noon we started & found our friends 10 miles out, just ready to start again. We marched 12 miles & camped at 10 at night. Started again at six in the morning (Saturday) & got along quickly 14 miles when we turned back two miles & camped in the afternoon under orders we supposed for Nashville but not so. At 10 P.M. we started again & marched all night through Mitchellville & Franklin Kentucky, orders met us at 8 in the morning to camp awhile. We did so & slept all day & remained until 2 o'clock Monday morning when we made another start to Bowling Green where we now are making 30 miles more – had they not stopd us we would have made 75 miles in about 3 days or 48 miles almost without sleep or camping. We halted of course to water & cook some coffee, nothing more – many slept at every halt – I <u>did at most</u>. On the way we had some fine views, & mostly good road. Some curiosities in the shape of caves & springs & a pretty country well settled all the way. We passed up through a gap in one of the ranges some miles before we left Tennessee. Near Bowling Green we stopd a while at the Lost River, a spring quite a River boils up runs 300 yards, turns a mill, now partly ruined, & then enters a cave, & has been traced it is said under ground from 3 to 7 miles but never comes to the surface. Imagine one of those large hollows or sink holes 100 yards wide 100 yards deep & 400 yards long. This spring boils up at one end runs the whole length & then runs in a cave with a mouth as wide & as high as one side of the courthouse in your town, sides all around nearly perpendicular & the ruined mill I spoke of just at the mouth of the cave. This mill used to make Kentucky Jeans, flour & corn meal & was run by this Spring (River?).

Bowling Green is well located in a Big Bend of the Big Barron River very suitable for defense & hard to attack, it will be such a pity to evacuate it quite as much so as Nashville. I dont know what the poor Union people of both places will do. Their lives & property are in much danger. Probably they will lose or both, unless they go in the Southern Army or run away as thousands are doing – poor Refugees & join ours.

Good by – More anon – ere the mail closes. Love to you & all. This is my only pleasure now – let me make the most of it.

Love

On Tuesday we remained in camp all day but were distracted with contradictory orders. We started next morning Wednesday the 17th & went 7 miles down the river to a ford & crossed, while other divisions were crossing at different points above us, besides the Bridge in town. It blew a hurricane all day & raised more dust than I ever saw out of Australia. This wound up with a thunderstorm & so we got in camp wet & as our wagons did not come up, we remained wet & hungry too & had to sleep as best we could in the rain. This we did & started at daylight again in the same way. We had only gone a few miles on Wednesday when we turned off to the East towards

Glasgow & made 17 miles on our devious way ere we camped. We had been often & cruelly detained by the long wagon trains of Divisions ahead & behind us & so it was late & so we lost our wagons. Well as I said we started hungry & still bound to Glasgow but in a few miles we turned N. West again & camped on the Northern road again making about 18 miles more. It was late ere our teams came, but meantime we raised a lunch by various means, & so the day closed after various alarms & expected skirmishes which did not come off, with a good supper and the news that the secesh had retreated from Glasgow & left us some prisoners that is the Division in advance of us. Slept sound & arose refreshed this morning at 4 o'clock to renew our march, but we soon found the enemy in force in front of us & can now hear occasional skirmishing. We made but 5 miles & then took the open field batteries & all in position before this we met 4 or 5 Regiments of our Troops returning with drooping heads – reporting that after a siege of a week and a hard fight of three days they had surrendered to superior numbers at Mumfordsville, and been paroled until exchanged & so our worst fears were confirmed. Mumfordsville & the Bridge is taken, our supplies cut off by from 50 to 75,000 Secesh under Bragg, Kirby Smith, Morgan, Forrest & others.[2] All the Guerilla Bands united for one more grand struggle. We have been waiting since morning movements ahead & hear occasional skirmishing in which it is reported we have the advantage & have driven in their pickets several miles, but that is of no importance. Our loss at Mumfordsville was very small – only 13 killed & 18 wounded. The enemies over 800 killed & wounded but our men fought behind a good stockade & entrenchments.

Good bye

Much Love

---

2. Confederate officers Major General E. Kirby Smith, Colonel John Hunt Morgan, and Brigadier General Nathan Bedford Forrest.

Camp at Pilot Knob Kentucky
Sept 20th 1862
My Dearest Molly

When I closed my crowded paper last night I did not expect to be here in quietness still but so it is. It is a lovely September day & to live & love & camp out even as we are doing would be the height of human felicity if the one you love was nigh, as it is I assure you we enjoy it & all the more because it is spiced by the belief that ere tomorrows sunset, many a poor fellow in either Army will fall to pass below the sod of some of the beautiful prairies or groves around.

It is a solemn thought on the eve of a battle such as we expect, as Bragg with 30,000 is reported behind the entrenchments that we must take or die dishonored and this beautiful Kentucky, the dark & bloody ground as it has been, be lost to our beloved Union forever – forever. We all stand on the boundaries of forever – or Eternity – who can say which of us shall first cross the to us gloomy portals, for earth will remain, and is very dear to all at least to me. I have got many castles built I know. They are in a ruined state just now, & I may never rebuilt, but I pray fervently that I may be allowed to try with "Molly" for a mentor & helper.

So I go tomorrow under the hope of a charmed life – to live & love on future Sept. days when the sun shines as bright as now & the air is as mellow as pure & as calm when I can recall my wigwam of boughs & blankets hung around with my opposum skin carpet on which I am seated a la Grand Turk. We are in a classic land – beautiful mountains, prairies & groves, wonderful caves, & a proud people with brave liberty loving sons & daughters graceful as princesses & lovely as the queen of the morning. The Mammoth Cave is Nine miles off near the scene of strife – a little down the Green River, for the possession of the bridge over which we fight & gaining which we gain Ky & something to eat, which is of much present importance to us. 3 miles from here is Cave City – near which is a dry tunnel or cave, at the bottom of which is a roaring river cold & pure & of large volume in which is placed an undershot wheel which pumps up all the water needed for town & country –

while the river that comes from darkness, rushes on to the same coming none know whither going none knows where.

But we cannot see as yet even these wonders. It is not safe, until after the battle – & then? What then? Even if successful & alive, the pursuit may hurry us on God knows where. But we have plenty of men & I fear not, but rest confident of victory if Buell allows us to do our duty.

Well that is talking of the future, but the present is ours, see how I improve it. After we camped yesterday the prisoners on parole spoken of passed back again towards the enemy, reason unknown – a mournful procession & a hungry one & we lay in expectancy just by Buell's head quarters on Pilot Knob – watching all day the telegraping by flags from point to point, from the general to the pickets & other Generals. After night this still continued with lights & so we slept. Troops moving forward all the day & all the night & we in reserve. This morning we got up early & still no move, but as I was released from arrest yesterday, I was made "Off. of the Day" & so busied about camp. We waited, men cooking three days rations to carry with them as no wagons go with us tomorrow, only ambulance & now my Dear Molly, I will leave this in such a way that at any time if any thing should happen to me you will get it all safe, also my trunk, the contents of which you can dispose of as you please. There are your letters & other matters you would wish to have I know, but on this I will not dwell. There is also a deed in it for you. Of course as long as I live, I will add P.S. until the way is cleared.

So goodbye
God bless you
Love

Sept. 25, 1862
After writing last we started on Sunday morning & made 4 miles. We were there drawn up in line of battle by the cave I have spoken of I went down. We lay on our arms all day skirmishing going on in front & at night made a forced march of 12 miles over a country road up & down mountains & got to Munfordsville or Green River just in time to find that our cavalry

& artillery had driven Bragg across. We camped very tired & disappointed & passed Monday morning walking over the different battlefields – very interesting they were, & the stories of the different eye witness. Four fights or more have occured here & I saw many of the bloody memorials. I had to return to dinner tired and at once marched down to the river 3 miles & forded it. It took us a long time & was near dark. When we again started we marched in hot pursuit along the Railroad track 12 miles & then camped in an open plain en masse.

The sight of so many forces was glorious but we could get no supper on account of the delay of our provision wagon. We slept by the fire on the grass & it being midnight some rested ere we marched again without breakfast. We hurried along all day over a hot & dusty road & still could not catch the runaways, although we marched 26 miles ere dark into Elizabethtown and all the way through intensely Union settlements.

Sept. 25
West Point, Ky.
We left Elizabethtown yesterday at Daylight & marched to this place 24 miles got in here at 9 o'clock having travelled all day over a hard & dusty road with only one halt at 2 o'clock, long enough to make coffee. We found at Elizabethtown that Bragg had taken the Lebanon road & our advance went after him, our center kept along the Louisville road while some 25,000 men comprising the left wing turned off this way in order to flank Bragg. We all felt tired but marched very well, singing all the way after dark & feeling quite elated at the prospect of seeing the Ohio River & getting once more in communication with the North where we would have a chance to get a mail. I wonder if you will ever get my former letters since we left Eastport on the 20th of last month. I wrote most every day & as I was in better spirits then & not so tired I wrote a better Letter. I am in robust health now however, a little footsore from old & new Shoes & from half cooked food & alternate starvation & repletion, but one days rest & a good dinner will improve all that. My wound left only a scar on my back & no effects remain-

ing, though I had a very narrow escape from paralysis & lockjaw.

We expect to get to day or tomorrow to Louisville & the prospects for a fight are very good as Bragg seems still driving that way but of that hereafter. Pray write me to Louisville as if you hadn't written for a month, & I do hope to hear good news of all, & especially of yourself.

Good bye

Love

Greenwood, Ky.

Sept 26th 1862

Left West Point yesterday morning & had a hard & dusty march to this place, a great deal of obstruction on the Louisville Road & scanty water as it has not rained for near two months & so after trying hard all day we turned off here to the river to rest & water. We got plenty of water & a good swim, but little or nothing to eat, & no rest as we had several alarms during the night & had to fall in line without any cause that we could afterwards ascertain. So yesterday was our hardest days work – although we only marched 16 miles, today I suppose we will go a little nearer Louisville & then get supplies of clothing & rations. We are camped in a splendid Beechwood Forest. I cannot say grove because it extends for miles & we have for several days passed through a beautiful but rather mountain country over a finely graded road. As long as we stopped on the main pike – we passed thus through long gorges in the hills getting fine views of the dark & bloody grounds – scenes of old Indian fights – also some of the French skirmishes before the revolution, now a finely settled country though the hardy sons of the soil are mostly gone to the war but its daughters turned out at nearly every house to do us honor & invited the soldiers in to eat cooking day & night.

I am Love

in much haste

Yours ever

James E. Love

Louisville

Sept. 28th 1862

My Dear Molly

I closed my last letter at Greenwood & mailed it as soon as I came in town. Since I arrived I have been busy & also crippled. I am only surprised I aint sick, as most of the men are, not so much from marching as from want of food & proper food.

We have much to complain of, & now that we have been under Buell for a few days we also believe him a traitor.

Had he wished it, we need not have starved, need not have marched so far – as we could have fought <u>and</u> <u>captured</u> Bragg at Mumfordsville. But of all this hereafter. I only wish to state that Buell is at least doing all he can to prolong the war. Is that not Treason?

Well his last order is more atrocious than ever as we (were/are) commanded to move today at 6 A.M. with 3 days rations cooked & carry on our Back every thing we want.

For the men the items are specified, making a reasonable load for a mule, including Coffee Pots & Stew Pans. For the officers, I suppose they may go without clothes or eatables, to a place where probably none are to be got.

Now we wish, all of us to leave "Buell's" Army unless it would suit the country's honor & purse better that he should be superseded, court martialed or something else.

I have bought a small valise yesterday & given away my trunk & much of its contents (old clothes &c). A small parcel containing letters & other articles of little value to any but the owner, I will send by Express to William or you to be out of harms way. In it are your letters & also a deed in your name.

If the Officers under Buell cannot get an equal or a little superior treatment to the men, it is expected that over a thousand of them will resign at once. The threat has been made & the papers signed.

Sept. 30th

My Dear Girl

My Eyes have been at last gladdened by a sight of your delicate writing. After an interregnum of 6 weeks our Regt. got a mail again yesterday and I got the *London News* of the 23d, an Irish paper & your letters of the 2d & 10th Sept. We expect our August mails soon & as I suppose you have got some of my later letters if not all, I expect something later from you.

Just as I got into camp & read these letters, who should I see sitting alongside me but William. I couldn't believe my eyes, so rubbed them & opened them wider but there he was in Propria Persona, and was I not right glad to see him. From what he tells, somebody heard from me at Nashville but as to who or what letters got through I did not too curiously enquire, expecting to hear all in good time. I had quite a conversation as you may imagine, & soon after voted myself a nights leave of absence (what I have never got before) and went to the hotel with him forth with, remaining until after breakfast this morning. I heard in the meantime much of the news, but not as much as I wish, yet I had to hurry to camp & he had to attend to business so I promised to dine with him again if duty permitted which it did not & he on the other hand promised to join me in camp in the afternoon if I did not.

I now await him & employ my time scribbling.

I expect our missing mail is at Corinth yet.

It is said Buell is or will be removed. I hope so. Most any change would cause an improvement in the morale of the Army! I wish they would send us Burnside or Sigel. We had a sad occurrence yesterday resulting in the death of a good General (Nelson) by the hands of our General of Division Jeff. C. Davis. He is now under arrest and another reigns in his stead, so we lose for the present when so badly wanted the service of two good generals.

It is very warm again today

I am nearly ready for the road again, & feel quite hopeful that if our generals only let us fight, the war can soon be ended both in Kentucky & in Virginia.

It might have been over in Ky now, but that is past and many of our men will die of fatigue or its resulting exposure, that had far better died in battle & so been of service to the cause.

Love to all & especially yourself my dear girl

I am as ever

Sincerely yours

Love

Address

Louisville, etc.

The Assassination of General Nelson by General Jefferson C. Davis. From Harper's Weekly, October 18, 1862.

Camp near Mount Washington

Oct. 2d 1862

My Dear Molly

Just after William left, we got marching orders & so we started yesterday at daylight. We made but a short distance from various causes always incident to commencing a march with a large army. Today we are facing the enemy, but we are the reserve, these new conscript have done the fighting. Yes we were near enough to hear the cannon & musketry & we advance tomorrow, if they're not run away to take them on a charge.

Tis said they're gone. I hope they wont run far as I dont wish to follow them to Alabama again.

William came to see me per agreement, and I had a very pleasant afternoon though quiet sitting on my blankets. We discussed a bottle of wine on the auspicious occasion. I was strongly tempted to run away for two days with him & see you & to see if I could not manage to get in a Missouri Regt. but duty held me fast. I feared this move.

Now my dear Molly take care of yourself. I am doing so – although it has been a wet day & is a wet night and all the command is wet too. I am dry – as you see & expect to be.

I am with Love & Kisses

Yours Sincerely

Love

James was part of a large force that was in pursuit of Braxton Bragg in the state of Kentucky. General Braxton Bragg. Photograph, 1861–1865. Library of Congress Prints and Photographs Division, LC-USZC4-7984.

Camp near Danville
Oct 10th 1862
My Dear Molly

I scarcely know where to begin now, but we have seen the end of one bloody episode which may be called the battle of Perryville perhaps – though I dont know, it being a General Engagement & covers so much ground. The hardest fighting was just on our left, under McCook, but we were in the Centre & took Perryville, so I will call it so until I hear what General Buell (who knows the ground as I do not) calls it.

It was impossible to write before between the rain & the marching & the laying in line of battle, especially where we had no paper or pencil. We have been out now 10 days as we left Louisville on the 1st Oct. That day we made but little progress, as the streets were so crowded up till 1 o.clock but after that time even with our drunken crowd we made about 10 miles to Newberg, a most hot and disagreeable march. On the 2d at 3 A.M. we were under arms & remained to daylight when after a hearty breakfast we started & left the road & marched as it were all over the country, first towards Shephardsville, then towards Mount Washington & then as friends the secesh ran off again & again after each skirmish we turned towards the Bardstown Pike. Camped that night near Mount Washington, from which place after a wet day & a wet night, I sent off a note to you that I had commenced in the city, & here as you may occasionally not receive my letters I wish to say that when I could not forward to you on the march I wrote nearly every night or morning, & posted every opportunity making an average of at least one a week, <u>save once</u> when you had two in one.

I hope to live through the horrors ahead & after this chase is over receive a whole cord of letters from you at once, but always recollect that from me, no news is generally good news, as if anything happens to me, you will hear soon enough by letter or in the papers. I have it so arranged however. Thus on the 2d we made about 12 miles, on the 3d we marched towards Bardstown but we only made Salt River, as the roads were dreadful rocky, & hills steep so the wagons could not get along – part of our way was through the fields. We made 8 miles, day warm & sunny, skirmishing still in front & dead horses in the road & field, dead & wounded men reported in the houses. Next day the 4th it took us nearly all day to cross Salt river, but we went 6 miles after dark, again it rained on us & no cover, nor no dry clothes, not even a fire. Our road after dark was up a creek or rather a crooked ravine with a flat rocky bottom. The rock consisted of a curious deposit of Sea shells just such as I or you have often gathered on the coast of Ireland, mostly of the small & delicate sort however, thin as Gossamer, & fine as piercers, where the current washed or the travel ground it. There was a fine shell road same as youve seen on the shore often, & moreover the farmers put it on their corn & tobacco fields, as we would on our wheat or potatoes. That night we camped in a Burr patch almost impossible to sleep as Blankets & clothes were covered with them. On the 5th we made a wrong start & had to come back to the same old creek again for miles, followed it until we got on the Bardstown Pike 5 miles from town into which place & through which we drove the enemy, who were cheered by the presence of Bragg in person. We passed through & camped at the creek 1 mile towards Springfield. At this place Buell came out & took command in person, greater part of the command took the Lexington road & some the Danville. We in the center took the Springfield road, our Division being on the front on the 6th. We had made 14 miles that day & passed a cold night without Blankets, heavy frosty dew. We lay by the fire, but had little sleep as we wanted, much turning. Our camp was we understood on Rolling Fork. On the 6th we made an early start & as the enemy was reported in full retreat by the cavalry we made a forced march of 25 miles after him. Got in early & camped on Beech Fork 5 miles on this side Springfield, our cavalry skirmishing & driving their rear guard all day. As we had travelled the Pike, our wagons came up in good time, so after a good supper, we got our Blankets & slept well.

On the 7th we started at 7 A.M. but at the Bridge 1 mile off we found the enemies pickets which we drove off & went again in full chase through several villages full of badly skared people mostly women & children however, some Union, some secesh, all very outspoken, to us & amongst themselves.

Most of the men were out with their guns. Secesh had joined Braggs new Regiment. They dared not go as Guerillas here. Old Kaintuck would annihilate them. The <u>Union men</u> had started out also, & where ever a "Grayback" left his ranks to get water or to rest behind the main body, there our brave Home Guards pounced on them, made them prisoners & brought them in to the nearest troops rejoicing, when off they would with their long six foot rifles on another chase & as they know every mountain path, soon are in ambush again & thus until the foes leaves their doors & firesides far behind. When they at once go home again to their wives & sweethearts, after a hunt much more exciting than chasing the wild deer.

Well as I said we chased their rear & skirmished heavily all day. All our troops coming up on one side or other & amid ominous preparations, with naught but ammunition, wagons & cannon. We suddenly found ourselves in front of Braggs whole army drawn up in Battle array & the fight begun by the Artillery <u>on our side</u>. We were all hidden away in ravines so that we could not see or be seen & also in the timber wherever possible & we thus did not see a road for the next three days, & dare not go up on the hills even to look at the enemy. Towards 4 o,clock although General Mitchell had had strict orders to <u>evade</u> a general engagement, the firing became fast & furious & our companies had to be sent out as skirmishers to deter the enemy from taking our cannon. So it went on momentarily getting hotter as we found out the position of the enemy, they keeping very quiet as if waiting to see where we were. Soon they seemed as if they wished to silence our cannon, the shots from which was annoying them very much, when we were at once formed in line of battle first just behind the crest of the hill a few yards off the battery, then we were moved into the woods on the left of it & away in front, but we did not get a shot as another battery began to give them a cross fire of grape & canister, while they lay or marched through corn fields & mowed them down so fast that it got too hot for them & they retired double quick & also took their battery out of sight on the hill beyond. Such was what passed on the center. On the wings, it was much the same, both parties getting close together & trying to find out the force & position of the others. They were well posted however, & it was only their advance & skirmishers we could see, but we drove these back within their line of battle all along the line before morning, as our Division or Corps D'Armie had done early in the afternoon in the center. It was now seven o'clock, a clear moonlight night & our Brigade was withdrawn from its position shortly after (I had in the meantime fell asleep laying down in ranks as we all were) to the ravine where we had been before commencing the action, that is half a mile in the rear, leaving the ground to the regular pickets & to the advance vedettes of cavalry. They ventured nearly half a mile beyond our advance & so we lay in line of battle all night listening to the continuous roar of the cannon, which at intervals bayed from every battery along the whole line, directing their fire at any point where our pickets or skirmishers were attacked, & shelling thus the woods in every direction.

So we slept, tired & exhausted from a new excitement. We slept sound too, I did. We were not allowed to light our usual camp fires, neither to make any noise & each one also wanted to make the best of his time, so the night passed quickly. I believe with all on our side, as we had but few if any wounded or killed on our side as yet, though there must have been many of the enemy. We all dreamt & feared for the morning, for Buell had said the enemy were in force & well posted, being thus equal or superior to us, & such being the case he wished to bring up all our reserves & send word to Crittenden, Thomas & McCook, & also perhaps Lew Wallace, who is on the Cincinnati side or North of Bragg. Tomorrow he would let us fight & so we awaited the morrows sun, which was to set in Blood for thousands on both sides. Before daylight on the 8th we were in line of battle, but all hands were allowed to make small fires before sunrise so as to boil coffee. This we drank & eat from our haversacks, enjoying it much being hungry. All this to still deceive the enemy as to our numbers. Then what was the rear of our Division yesterday marched at once to the front & soon after Sunrise the fight begun at once both fast & furious. Our Divisions all formed in three lines of battle. We were in the third line today but the fight was so hotly contested all along for ten miles or more that even our reserves were soon in it or so close as to <u>resist</u> or <u>charge</u> themselves at any moment. So it went all day with varied fortunes, sometimes we gaining, sometimes the enemy, bloody work it was, every where, batteries charged on, taken & retaken, death in a thousand shapes, & worse than Death to many. The next Regiment to us the 2d Missouri took two cannon that were annoying us just in front. They were to be supported by a Michigan Regt. but Michigan didn't come to the scratch, so they fought over it by themselves, took it & lost it, & took it again & finally brought off two pieces & lost 80 men in that charge. All this before our eyes. Just then we were in reserve to defend our battery. Soon our Division took Perryville & drove these batteries through the town at the point of the bayonet, but had to leave again suddenly as Bragg began to shell us out. We retired out of range there to the top of the hill where secesh battery had stood just before & played across at them again on the bluff beyond the town from there & other points. We shelled them until night closed in & we remained on the field, shifting our position to the right or left, & advancing all the time as the enemy moved up till 10 oclock, the day being ours & gloriously so – with but little loss to us & with much to the enemy, their dead & much of their wounded being piled & scattered all around us. Our's were all spirited away at once, so much so that I have not seen a single dead Union soldier. I have seen many wounded however & that is more horrible to me.

I hear of over 1400 wounded on our side perhaps much more but these were mostly on the right & left of us as I said very few in the Centre, but just so we had to go to sleep, lunching from our haversacks or going to sleep without, our guns quiet at last, but the enemy still sullenly firing at us from a distance. Meanwhile on our right Crittenden had been fighting hard & had been driven back over a mile at one time, but when his reserves came up he regained all this & more & late at night was in line with us having also driven them across the creek, with much loss on both sides – so far so good, but on our Left was the Chamber of horrors par excellence where McCook & Thomas had been trying to flank them. They threw all their available force on McCook & threatened for hours to overwhelm him – his reserves one after another came up until all were in the fight but still they drove him back & took his best battery after a dreadful fight, the slaughter of thousands, before leaving it our men choppd the spokes off the wheels of the cannon & wagons, so that they might not carry them away, his horses & cannoniers being nearly all killed, so he had to leave it. This bloody field was contested all night & after dark part of our Division was ordered over to assist. We were but fortunately were not at hand at the time, having just advanced but the remainder were taken & got very soon badly cut up & so the night closed, a small corner here being forced to be left in the hands of the enemy.

But I must close as the mail leaves.

With much love my dear dear girl good bye I hope not forever

Yours Sincerely

James E. Love

Perryville Battlefield State Historic Site in Kentucky, where James fought with his regiment. Photograph by M. E. Kodner, 2012.

Camp at Goodnight Spring
Oct 10th 1862
My Dear Molly

I had to stop in the middle of my story much as the *New York Ledger* does at the most interesting part, but I will improve a rainy hour under a wagon to finish it if possible.

It is a wet cold day & as Bragg has retreated, & the fight is stop'd we are lying in camp until it clears up, while details are searching the woods & corn fields & burying the Dead & bringing in the wounded. It is a sad & awful occupation. Its horrors I cannot look at, & will not repeat now, so I will go back to where I left off. McCook had left his battery & a corner of the field in Braggs possession. They skirmished & cannonaded each other all night & at daybreak charged again & took all back again, driving Bragg in a total rout at this point, taking many prisoners. 4 or 5 Regts. threw down their arms, & ran away leaving everything. We took many of them prisoners, with all their arms & effects, also all their wounded & dead amounting to thousands. The gallant men then rested from their work of slaughter, gathered up our wounded & dead & soon after marched over the creek & took possession, by this time Bragg was in full retreat from all parts for 20 miles & we on this day the ninth had no fighting, only our cannon shelling Braggs retreating columns as they passed. Then from all parts we marched over to where McCook had been & camped among the dead for the night.

I had a good wash, first one for two or three days & took a short survey of the wounded but it was too horrid. This morning the 10th McCook started in pursuit, also Thomas, Rosseau, Wood, Crittenden & others, while we remain here in the rain to bury the dead & bring up the rear. Oh it is a horrid scene, covering the woods & fields for miles, naught but poor dead & wounded Graybacks, the wounded some for two days without water & the dead with the maggots already at work. We can hear cannonading still going on & I suppose there is much more hard work in store for us. Buell & Bragg will I hope make this the final fight here, & if they do, there is dreadful fighting to be done yet.

I do hope you will get my letter ere you have seen any bad accounts in the paper. There has as usual been dreadful slaughter among the officers as well as the men, but our Battalion came out very safe. We done the secesh a good deal of damage, but as none of their cannon played on the spot where we were & their musketry could not harm us, we are all here Thank God. Good night.

Excuse these letters. They are written on secesh paper & in secesh envelopes. We have no other in camp. We have nothing but what we carry on our backs or in our hands – even to our rations.

J.E.L.

The Battle of Perryville, Kentucky, Fought October 8, 1862. From Harper's Weekly, *November 1, 1862.*

Oct 12th 1862

Camp at a creek bet Harrodsburgh and Danville, Ky.

My Dear Molly

I wish to tell you here our present place in the "Army of the Ohio". We constitute part of the 32d Brigade – Col Colwell[1] commanding – which is part of the 9th Division General Mitchell commanding (instead of Jeff C. Davis) which is part of General Gilberts 3d Corp. D'Armee. Now if you see any of these Corps mentioned with killed or wounded or marching it includes the 8th Kansas whether we are along or not.

As to the past I will also say a word for myself. I have been very weak with Diarhea, but am now recovering as quickly as cold & wet will allow. I rode in the ambulance for two days before the battle, but when we fell in line, & the fighting begun I joined the company & have been with it since, though really getting weaker daily. I only suffer from a severe cold in the head at present & expect to be all the better for this little spell of biliousness, if I can protect myself from the weather.

I got the cold on the field of battle. I had to lay all night without blankets, coat or overcoat, in rain & wind. This last two nights were the worst but I managed to buy an overcoat from a wounded soldier & I sent back my "nigger" several miles after one blanket, all I can carry & all he could get out of the wagon. The wagons have to keep a good distance behind, as we require all the room in the road, woods or fields to manuevere.

Well after I closed on the 10th we had supper still in the heavy rain. We built shelters & thatched them with Secesh wheat & went to sleep about 8 o,clock but at ½ past ten, orders to march arrived, & in 15 minutes we commenced a darksome march over creeks, & ravines & fields for 5 or 6 miles bringing up in line of battle at Oneida or Nevada, I dont know which, where we stood till morning listening to the cannon of Woods Division, who were skirmishing with Bragg in force. It rained all night & on the 11th was cold & frosty. We kept moving around all day anticipating a fight hourly, but it gradually got fierce & loud in front, & then it moved off into the distance.

---

1. Colonel W. W. Caldwell.

At dark we again marched 3 miles toward Harrodsburgh, where Woods Division was said to be attacking Bragg's entrenchments, but the news met us on the way that Bragg had fled again, leaving more arms & 500 prisoners in our hands & taken the route to Danville. Now as it was a fine moonlight night we turned around & marched to a creek on the Danville road 7 miles from where we were & camped where we now are, had a quiet night & a good sleep, well wrapped by a warm fire. Troops are moving out now, over 20,000 have gone & we are just about to follow. I think Bragg will soon have to leave Kentuck or be taken prisoner with his whole army. I hope so.

My Dear Molly – I am so glad to hear that you & all are well as I did from Alex yesterday. Take care of yourself my Dear girl for my sake & believe me ever

Yours Sincerely

James E. Love

Camp near Mount Vernon Kentucky
October 16, 1862
My Dear Molly

I closed most all my late letters in a hurry & I dont know but this may be the same but I hope not as the enemy has finally gone on a full run for Cumberland Gap (it is supposed) & the advanced Divisions are peppering his rear, his advance is at least 2 days or 40 miles ahead of us.

He broke yesterday morning after we attacked him at Lancaster while Crittenden's Division attacked him at Crab Orchard Hardcastle Co. & after some brilliant skirmishing on our side & good running on his with but small loss of life on either, though a good many wounded & sick & lazy secesh fell into our hands all protesting that they were tired of the war, & that their comrades would soon all desert if it wasn't soon ended. They are in fact much demoralized.

But to return on the 12th I wrote you & ere I could well close we marched – at the next halt I begun to answer a letter to Alex but that I couldn't finish as I found the messenger with the mail was starting, & our Regt. marched on & left me ere I could hand him the letter. We were then in camp between Harrodsburgh & Danville – that day we marched towards Camp Dick Robinson where Bragg was said to be entrenched with his main Army, that was Sunday last. We could hear cannon all day, & we afterwards heard that McCook had driven them on that day out of Danville, & was close on them at Camp Dick. We lay at night after a march of 12 miles half way from each place about 5 miles. After a fine warm night we marched next morning to Danville expecting to follow McCook but not so. We countermarched to the South East of the Camp & lay over night, hearing the cannon roar constantly, & next morning news came that Camp Dick Robinson was also evacuated so we countermarched again on the 14th into Danville & made a rapid march through it & out on the Lancaster Pike some 20 miles where we suddenly were attacked by Morgan & the forces under Kirby Smith into the very camp of which we ran without notice on either side, & to the equal astonishment I believe of both – for Bragg had taken the other road

& McCook after him. Well we had to rush up hills & over ravines under fire, so as to gain a good Position. This we did within 5 minutes our Regt. leading as skirmishers but not before the 8th Wisconsin battery had lost two guns in their haste turning in the road to escape Morgan's Cavalry, but immediately Genl Mitchells body guard the 2d Kansas Cavalry rushed upon it, & put new horses to it with drag ropes & brought it away, the secesh having skedaddled <u>without fight</u>. We gave them a good lesson & the night closed on both parties in line. We had driven them into town & took a few prisoners – so we returned to the creek about a mile to camp, posting pickets to watch any movement in our direction. We could hear movements all night but could devise what it meant, as it is so dangerous to enter a town after night, unless it is doomed to fire or total destruction & this being a Union town we wished to save it from even a fight in the streets if possible. Well next morning we ascertained it was some of Bragg's men coming in off another road whom we could have taken prisoners if we had known, as we had them cut off at the time we fought. We started early through all the roads & fields leading to town & at once found their pickets. Our cavalry charged on them & drove them on a gallop through town while we all charged like Wild Indians after, up one street & down another. On the hills about a mile beyond, we found their cannon posted & we had to stop our race until our cannon could pass us & face them just at the edge of town, which they soon did. We had such a grand reception by the inhabitants, ladies & children flocked around regardless of danger & blessed us with tears in their eyes as their preservers from death & destruction. Old men & young could not do enough for us, fetched us everything out in the field, & fetched out their old rifles to have a pop at the runaways, even the niggers were in extasy as the Rebels had been running many of them down south & numbers of those here had escaped from their clutches in the haste of leaving. So the time passed, a rebel shell dropping occasionally while we lay in line & our batteries took position in front. As soon as they were placed they soon silenced our opponents. We could see them run out of the corn fields & from behind the fences, their battery left also, & our Battalion was again sent out to feel the ground as skirmishers under cover of the artillery & with a cloud of cavalry in our rear. We advanced about a mile crawling in open order & took their positions one after another, & found only deserted camp fires where lately were cannon. Soon our whole charged after them. Cavalry first, cannon after & we after being recalled after them until they found what road they had taken. Then we had to advance again & skirmish & examine all the fields & houses on both sides of the road for ten miles along & one mile wide. We marched about 12 miles in all beside the ground we skirmished over & camped last night at the creek by Crab Orchard near Mount Vernon. All along the road we found traces of Secesh camps & took many prisoners & stragglers & sick, but ere we got here we found that the rebels had left the road & as we had no orders to follow them east (other troops of ours being in that direction) we camped here.

The fates are unpropitious
The mail closes again
in haste Good bye
With much love
Yours ever,
Love

Camp near Mount Vernon
Oct 17th 1862
My Dear Molly

I got an unexpected chance to send off my letter yesterday by Gen'l Anderson & so it went out – that ending the introduction. I wish to commence now where I left off, but I suppose this must assume the form of a journal, & be continued daily as there is no regular mail from here & no mail at all comes here. I have got but two letters from you and one from Alexander since the 12th of August but <u>I know</u> that they must be awaiting me somewhere, so I am just as well satisfied that they are not in my haversack if I get them when this chase is over. So my dear girl, I hope you are in good health & spirits. Keep up a good heart, for as I said before that secesh bullet aint run yet, and as to my depending on your prayers I still think I ought to, only as an additional help to my own however I hope for jesting aside I do pray occasionally – not so often as I ought I know, but more lately than usual – even on the battlefield – it may be from fear of a hereafter – but I hope not altogether so. I felt calmer & clearer in mind after, lost sight of danger altogether & only thought of doing my own duty according to orders, for the best interest of the <u>success</u> of the cause, & seeing that all the men in my charge did the same. Some officers were excused not half so sick as I was. I would not take an excuse while there was danger else my conscience would have accused me, if other men had not – but of that enough. I am alive <u>and well</u> <u>thank</u> <u>God</u> for it, save a very slight cold in my head.

Well we got to this camp & found that Crittenden had come in by another road at Crab Orchard ahead of us & after a brisk little fight drove Braggs main army out of it.

The news of this was what had turned Kirby & Morgan out of our road, so we had nothing to do but go in camp. We sent all the rations we had after the advancing army & waited here ourselves (J.E. Mitchells Division) until more would come up. This gave us yesterday a much needed rest which we improved washing & getting a change of clothes from our trunks which came up last evening, so the day passed quickly & lazily & now today we are quiescent yet. Our rations came up this morning & what detains us I now know not.

It is said General Mitchell goes to Kansas tomorrow & that if Bragg runs into East Tennessee that we will go back to Kansas also. In that case I can get leave of absence, but of this hereafter. The rumor is from good authority or I should not mention it.

I have not seen a late paper, but it is also rumored that there are changes among our commanders & that "Halleck" has come back to us. I hope so, for I am tired of Buell, his confounded orders has prevented us once more from capturing Bragg. <u>He wants</u> <u>the war to last</u>!! <u>We do not</u>!!! Neither does many of the best Generals under him – but whenever we have overtaken our enemies and there is a good chance for a fight, Buell has prevented to the intense disgust of all those who were in earnest & those who wished to make a reputation & a name.

There is no doubt but that he is a traitor & that thus the services of 200,000 men are lost to the country, that an immense unnecessary expense is incurred in marching us over the country & that thousands of valuable lives are lost through fatigue, privation & poor & scanty diet, all contrary to the laws & regulations of the United States. We could have taken Bragg at Perryville & since, but <u>He</u> would not let us.

With much Love
My Dear Girl
Goodbye
Love

Camp near Lebanon Kentucky
Oct 24th 1862
My Dear Molly
I commence again after a weeks interval and a march of 60 miles within 3 days to this place very much fatigued again. We are of course, besides being dirty, dusty, dry & tired for again this time without reason we have been put on short rations, in order I suppose to line the better the pockets of some

knavish contractor or commissary, for of course Uncle Sam generously finds us every thing we require & worse than all pays cash for it too, as we shall find out if ever this war ends in our time.

Need I say that I am well and with a mind pretty easy & free from care and that I fervently pray that when our mail comes in if it ever does that I shall hear of your continued health & strength, and enjoyment of all the blessings that can be expected during these dark days of our beloved though distracted adopted country – <u>long may it wave</u> & long may peace of mind & comfort bless its adopted or native citizens & especially yourself and humble servants.

Well I need not bore you with the dry details of how we lay in camp at Crab Orchard near Mount Vernon, how we went on picket & got a glimpse of the mountains nearly 50 miles off, & it is said were as near the Gap for all practical purposes as if within a mile of it (this I dont believe for Bragg was between us & the Gap, & Morgan too & if we had went <u>too</u> near we might have caught them. <u>Now</u> they are both safe, & Morgan has already followed us here & stole 500 of <u>our</u> Mules & 81 of <u>our</u> wagons).

Neither need I describe how fine & hazy & foggy the days are & were, how cold & frosty the nights, (for those who like us sleep out of doors on the prairies or under a tree) how we proceeded the afternoon before we left to build shelter sheds, expecting to remain at least a week but to our surprise we were waked before daylight in the morning, with orders to march in an hour on Lebanon with three days rations (rations that we could find nobody to issue, but we had to march all the same) & fast, buy, or steal, all of which we done, even in the loyal state of Kentucky. Yes time & again have we been compelled to steal both on this march & the last from Nashville, & why <u>it is said</u>, because it is wished by Buell to disgust the Kentuckians & force them to turn secesh or at least go against Old <u>Abe</u>'s government certain it is. Buell never allowed such things in Tennessee or <u>Alabama</u>, but bought & paid the highest prices for every thing the soldiers did or did not want.

Neither need I say how pretty the little & great hills with mountains in the distance looked all clothed in living green, yellow & golden fading in heavenly blue as distance lent enchantment to them but I will come down to mention simply the facts that we found good Union people in plenty along all our road – that they suffered much from both our army & the secesh, but that they generally grudged us nothing unless it was taken in too forcible or insulting a manner, or <u>they</u> had nothing else to live upon.

Of the prisoners we took most of whom were disgusted with the secesh army and its Officers and also that Morgan had got behind us even to Bardstown & threatened to cut off our supplies as he did one of our empty wagon train, & so as I said on the morning of the 20th 50 or 60,000 men marched back again through Lancaster & Danville to this point, leaving more than as many more as an army of observation at that point still.

We made 16 miles slowly the first day without any adventures – on the 21st we made 23 miles to water on this side of Danville, here I treated myself to a half pound of good oolong tea. I have been so much poisoned by drinking strong coffee for the last month or two that it has injured my health, so I am now drinking strong Tea instead & feel quite rehabilitated already, however on the 22d late at night we made this point which is on the Rolling Fork of Green river 6 miles south of Lebanon. We had to come here for water as there has been no rain in this country since Spring and as a consequence all the creeks & springs are dried up. We are now on the line of the Louisville & Nashville railroad – that is to say <u>Lebanon is</u>, & so we are very near where we marched up – but there is still no rain & such a dusty God forsaken looking country, you would not wish to see – even before it was plagued with the horrors of War.

I sent some letters by our Brigade Quartermaster from Crab Orchard to post at Louisville & the report is that he is captured along with all his train & letters of course. I hope not as he had at least one for you.

It is a very hilly, slaty, but still a beautiful country here reminds me much of some parts of Antrim, Derry, or Down but better looking as there is an abundance of rich foliage & an absence of the <u>omnipresent</u> <u>bogs</u>. There are many good residences, thick settlements & expensive improvements with the usual splendid Kentucky Turnpikes – equaled only by English or Irish ones but all looks cursed for want of the needful rain & the presence of unholy war.

Lt. Col Martin has gone to Louisville today by way of Lebanon & the railroad. There was Lt. Washer & 20 men with him & they took over 100 secesh prisoners along. They will bring all our Tents, Camp & Garrison outfit for the winter back with them, so I suppose for a little while my address will be as per the heading of this letter.

I saw a letter today that left St. Louis on the 21st and I am getting very anxious indeed to know whether you ever get these epistles of James or not – and how it is I cant get yours.

I was so disappointed even today, a large mail came in & none for me. I feel inclined to run away for a week or two, & I believe I will whenever we go in Winter Quarters, if not sooner certainly at Christmas. Remember me at Auld Halloween, & the other fete days <u>that used to was</u> of the coming winter.

Love to Sallie, your Mother, Aunt &c &c & especially yourself My Dear Dear Girl

With a thousand caresses & the hope of happy days to come

I am as ever

Yours Sincerely

James E. Love

General John H. Morgan. Photograph by E. and H. T. Anthony, New York, 1861–1865.

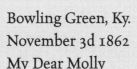

Bowling Green, Ky.

November 3d 1862

My Dear Molly

I had just headed this letter, & was about to tell you how broken hearted I was for want of news, when my eyes were gladdened by your missive of the 25th Oct. I could scarce have told you however, how much my heart has sunk, & how lonely I felt when the mail came in once or twice (as it did lately) without a missive for me. We have only had three or four mails within the last 3 months & of course then I did not think so much of it while communication was interrupted, but as soon as it opened, I looked for an avalanche from all parts & of course from you, but none came, save two of yours, which I mentioned before, 2d & 10th Sept. Do not Dream for a moment that I ever reproached you or will on that score. I hope I know better. No! No! I always gave you credit for writing when you could <u>once a week</u>. I know it would be hard to do so, while you were so long without hearing from me but I thought & <u>do now</u>, that many of yours are awaiting me somewhere in the <u>Offices</u> that are cut off, (if not robbed). I hope to get some of them when we go to Nashville if you did so. I still miss yours of the 21st & 28th August & of the 17th 24th & 31st September. Did you write on or about those dates or since? I merely ask to know what <u>I have lost</u>!!

And now when on the subject of letters in your answer to this pray tell me! Did you get all mine as if so you will have almost a daily record of what I've done? And if not what dates are missing?

I am sorry to say that I have but little other record left, & if lost, it is lost for good – in most part.

I could & <u>would</u> have made all the <u>journal</u> more interesting, if I had had any certainty that you would ever get its detached sheets for after all it was only a journal & not worthy of the name of <u>letters</u>.

Will you satisfy my curiosity on these points, on which I have been a long time anxious and not think me too inquisitive or exacting.

And now let me return to your present letter! A thousand thanks for it!

And its contents, all & every word of it! My Dear Dear Girl, <u>I am</u> <u>only too</u> <u>happy</u> in this distracting time when I sit and think of it. What have I done that I should be blessed in your love so? Is what I often ask myself! The happiness & blessing seems almost too great on contemplation for such a scapegrace as I am and if half <u>our plans</u> or <u>Dreams</u> (<u>or my dreams</u>) should ever come to pass in the future when the war, which has now become such an <u>earnest</u>, <u>dreadful</u>, fact is over, I will bless God that he has rewarded me far above my deserving, and try with your assistance to be <u>contented!</u> And now as I know I often break promises from forgetfulness, if in <u>that</u> future I should forget this pray preserve it, & bring it to my recollection, so that I may resolutely strive for that content which is <u>I know</u> the only happiness in this world!

I wish to say so much that pen & ink fails me, and I would fill more paper than the law allows. I dont wish any credit for writing! It is not a labor! It is one of the very few pleasures left to me! For we have seen and are seeing hard times. Truly Gods providence is Great and all powerful! or I would not be alive!

I begin to feel the fatigues some as the weather gets colder, for <u>we</u> too had our 4 inches of snow, and <u>sleeping out in it</u>, after marching all day, breakfasting before light, and supping after dark, <u>with no dinner</u>, is no holiday work.

We are all so much pleased however that the "Old Man of the Mountain" is removed from us (I mean Buell) and that our favorite Rosecrans is <u>with</u> us, that we are precluded from grumbling any more for some time to come even if worked hard.

We have still some hopes of going to Kansas! That is being allowed to rest a little, so as to be joined by our sick (half our number) & by the other half our Regt. which remained in Kansas when we left!

Buell had consented to grant our petition in some way (how I don't know) for rest! But he is gone now & his orders & ideas with him. And Rosecrans reigns in his stead, and so we must talk to him about it, and as I said we have grounds to believe he will not refuse us the boon we crave – a rest. I want a rest very bad myself but I am not anxious <u>like others</u> to return to

Kansas this winter. After <u>resting</u>, and paying you a visit, I would choose to return to Rosecrans department & under Generals McCook & Mitchell – all of whom we adore – so to say – proceed (<u>as they are going too</u>) to purge East Tennessee & all <u>cottondom</u> of traitors even down to Mobile & New Orleans. It is said you know that Bragg is gone to Richmond to reinforce <u>Lee</u>. Now if so – there is no large Army anywhere in the South. All their men are near Richmond & if McClelland, Burnside & Sigel can only keep them busy as they seem to be trying to do, why it will be easy work to conquer the whole south.

Now Rosecrans has already made us a speech & this is just what he is about trying to do with the splendid army of 200,000 men now in Kentucky & Tennessee.

I wish them all success. We shall know soon I hope what is our destination, as far as it is allowable for <u>junior</u> officers to know. We know already that our Division is ordered to march to McMinnville, <u>Tenn</u>, as soon as <u>Bread</u>, Provisions & Tents can be procured for us from St. Louis or Louisville, & thence to <u>Georgia</u>. The Question is do we go along now, or in the future, or do we go to Kansas!?

Gen'l Mitchell did go through your city, as he is on furlough for 20 days, & proceeded to Kansas & may not return to us. We are temporarily under Genl Woodruff, a good general, a Kentuckian, & one whom we like very much. In fact we have every confidence in all our Generals in this Army now since Buell & Gilbert's removal.

As the country is pretty well cleared of guerillas, (we are driving Morgan & them all before us, as this grand army goes South) we expect to be in daily communication with the North by mail as of Old at Jacinto or Eastport – even if at McMinnville or away down in <u>Georgia</u>.

So if we do go you shall hear from me weekly as of old & I hope to hear in return. I will try for ten days furlough if I go – either at or before Christmas.

That poetry you enclose is a sweet, true to nature, & loving production, and coming as it does, is doubly dear to me & will be prized as one of the sweetest mementoes I have.

"Dearest, remember that I love you more, Oh, more a thousand times than all the rest"! And yet I can talk of but little but <u>war</u>, & Bragg & Buell & <u>Self</u>. That's so – but it is of dreadful interest to us all now, since we are worked so hard. Both the Rebels & us have become so dreadfully in earnest, & then, we read no more favorite Books or <u>stories</u>, or papers, seldom see even a <u>daily</u> & then over a week old. So nothing else have we to talk or write about – our old subjects of gossip all seem so, <u>Old</u> & <u>lang syne</u> – new subjects we have none. We hear so <u>little news</u>, of anything out of our own <u>Division</u> of the Army, & our daily cares & troubles engross us all the hours of the day & some of the night but I must put them away from me & try to answer your letter as it ought to be, and in passing let me say we are now in <u>McCook's</u> Corp D'Armee – since Gilbert was removed – so when you see his name mentioned in the papers, you will have a further clew to the movements of our Regt. This whole Army however will be reorganized as soon as it gets to <u>Nashville</u> by Gen'l Rosecrans & that may change it all again! I hope not!

I wish to be remembered to that dear little teasing friend of mine, Sallie. She must think I have forgotten her. I would write her a letter once in a while if <u>I dared</u> but I <u>am</u> too <u>skeered</u>, from the threats she made when last I saw her and also her <u>threats</u> regarding <u>these</u> epistles. Remember me if you can also to your Mother, Aunt & all the others. I will try to write Alex soon, so as to send some news by another channel, & if I remain here a day or two as we may I must finish up some of my other St. Louis correspondence that lags sadly behind.

Thanks for your care of my parcel, from the unlucky detention of the mails, I feared Alex or William might not get my letters concerning it, & to my mortification open it to see what was inside it.

Glad indeed am I to hear of the <u>general</u> good health of the folks on Sixth, on Ninth & on Morgan Streets including the babies boys though they be! Also of the safe return of William from St. Paul where I hope he was successful. If not Rosecrans wishes to send 3 months bread with us to McMinnville at once, so that if anything happens we will have plenty to eat. So there's work for all the bakers for a while – only about 5 or 10,000,000 pounds.

Oh! how I wish I could have joined you and Sallie over the fire, that snowy day & night, don't you think it was cruel to mention it; I think enough of those pleasant chats in your cozy parlor and I've got so much to hear & to tell, I dont believe I could learn half the St. Louis changes & new subjects of gossip in <u>Ten days</u>! much less <u>one</u>! Wouldn't I cross question you. I cant really cant on paper. But above all I want to see & hear of yourself in these long weary days, that have sometimes so tried my patience & yet you wont, positively wont tell <u>me of yourself</u>.

Put me off with a piece of poetry indeed – instead of particularizing in the manner of the most <u>approved</u> <u>Novel</u>.

Well I'm coming sometime to see for myself!

See if I don't!

I wont wear the willow neither for any <u>old</u> <u>Widow</u>!

If I had expected to leave Louisville so soon <u>after</u>, I would have extracted more news out of William.

And if I had known, we would have remained there so long as we did, I would have ran over to St. Louis even for one day. We know not what an hour may bring forth is true of the army as of life! & so in both cases we lose golden opportunities never to be recalled!

I try to be careful of myself, & though my constitution is not of the best I have escaped so far, better than stouter men – disease has thinned our ranks terribly as you say.

I will bid you goodnight & reserve the story as to how we got <u>here</u> for the morning. All the folks <u>are to</u> bed & it is a calm frosty night. I am wrapped & rewrapped over the fire & yet cold.

I am my dearest girl

Yours

Love

This morning we have marching orders, and I will only say in the hurry that I think I wrote you last at Lebanon. We remained in camp there for two or three days <u>during</u> which it snowed. We started on our march down here on the 27th & made 15 miles the first day camping in a fine Bush thicket at Pittsfield Creek. On the 28th we crossed the almost dry bed of the Green River, marched about 15 miles more and camped on the little Barron River, pleasant but cool marches both. Next day 29th it took half of to make a bridge at the ford & cross the troops & trains so we made but 8 or 10 miles. On the 30th marched again & struck the Pike soon, bringing us on to the road we marched over before when skirmishing with Bragg's Rear Guard. All the spots we've looked at with interest especially Pilot Knob, from the top of which there was so much signaling for two or three days. We camped for the day & went to work writing out muster rolls far into the night. I did & the majority, but a large party was made up to visit the Mammoth Cave & pass the night there as it was only 8 miles off. They enjoyed themselves – <u>so did we</u> however resting & doing needful writing. Next day we marched 15 miles towards this point & there we mustered & inspected the Regt. & on the 1st of November we marched in here, where we have been since writing early & late in order to get our papers in order before marching further. We are in the old camp ground, which we left on the 17th Sept.

Goodbye with love & kisses my Dear Girl

I am ever sincerely yours

James E. Love

Camp at Nashville

Nov 9th 1862

My Dearest Molly

Here we are at Nashville again, & I take the earliest opportunity to write you again for fear of accidents! <u>We may go</u> <u>further</u>, and the mail is and will be irregular for a little yet until we clean out our guerilla friends.

I wrote from Bowling Green last a long rambling letter and at its close gave you a very hasty sketch of our march from Lebanon. Although got over in few words it was full of interest to us, first from being a new road and a bye road taking us among the poor whites and towards the close at Pilot Knob we came on our old stomping ground where our Army had many skirmishes with Bragg's rear though as my correspondence informs you we the 8th K.V. had but few, and so we got to Bowling Green & its extensive fortifications – which thanks to the Kentucky Cavalry under Wolford never left Uncle Sam's possession. Indeed with 2000 true men all fighting for their hearths & homes, he done more than all Buell's immense army to check guerillas & take prisoners & save the Union folks from plunder by Bragg & others. A few minutes after closing that letter in the morning we started once more on our travels and now ere I tell of our adventures let me tell you that on arriving here I found part of the lost mail. My share proved to be a *Frank Leslie*, an *E. News* and three copies of the *I.L.N.* Also two letters concerning which I enquired & dated the 20th & 27th of August, all of these from you! truly I was delighted and will not pretend to thank you now. These letters &c came to Eastport after we left, & came up in charge of the last division Generals Paine & Negley – arriving here after we left, and as they were pretty much in a state of Siege since the letters remained here for safety – <u>so we now get</u> <u>them</u>. I expect <u>these</u> account for nearly all your missing letters mentioned in my last? Now it only remains for <u>me</u> to know! Have you got all mine so as <u>to make a connected narrative</u> if at any time you should not get this for the <u>future</u> you will know that a letter is mislaid by the Post Office folks!

Well we started in a dust storm & made some marching through town. A fine thriving town it is so as to show ourselves – and then put out again – but it was hard work – very – it got warm too after such frosty nights as we have. So we soon passed Lost River again & its queer ruin'd mill in the <u>cave</u> and got out to a pool 11 miles out where we camped for the night.

On the 5th started again & pass'd the Lost Spring another <u>bottomless</u> spring running off into a crack in the limestone away down in a sink hole. Soon we passed through the thriving town of Franklin, then on through the <u>dust</u> to Mitchellsville & so to camp just on the state line. All these places interested us as we passed them on one of our night marches on the road up, & especially one little village of which I never learnt the name where at midnight, we had our first welcome to Kentucky. A young lady up in a Balcony waved a flag over us as we passed while regiment after regiment tired & weary as they were cheered & cheered again as they saw it. We found her & <u>others</u> at her post again with the same old flag – notwithstanding all the dangers from rebel & guerilla rule since passed through. We found her also young & pretty with a very sharp nose & countenance, & a sharp tongue in which she advised us how to treat them to hemp – shot &c & so to camp 15 miles.

On the 6th off again in a terrific dust storm – men had to scatter & get through the fields as best they could – it was almost dark as night. I was lame from a slight rheumatic affection in my left ankle & knee so I rode in the ambulance 16 miles to our old camp at Tyree springs. Country seemed all deserted houses & villages going to ruin, where was smiling peace & plenty when we passed before – secesh & Union had suffered pretty near alike from the guerilla thieves of Morgan, Forrest & <u>others</u> of <u>lesser</u> note but more <u>devilish</u> minds. That has Buell to answer for in this world or the next if he let Bragg & these Band's a hundred times worse come in <u>when he</u> <u>could</u> <u>have</u> <u>kept</u> <u>them</u> <u>out</u>. So the leading generals under him say & then too we would have been saved all this dreadful hard marching without shelter & the sickness & <u>death</u> that has followed in our track & used up the weary worn out pilgrims once the conquering soldiers of Buell's Union Army – now gone from our gaze – without even the poor satisfaction of having died in Battle for the good of their country.

This is a dry and parched land, it was so when we passed before & but little rain have they had since, so our marches have to be regulated entirely by the distance to water.

On the 7th we had to make the Cumberland river 22 or 23 miles. The springs in the intermediate country having all dried up since we passed before & to commence with we had to pass a spur of the Cumberland Mountains in the morning. We started at 6 A.M. marching very quickly morning frosty & a cold North wind blowing. We got to the top of the crooked winding road that leads through the Gap all safe – our Brigade & Regiment being in the front & commenced to descend when all at once a sudden popping in front! which we could not understand. We concluded however that General Negley must have sent a picket out from Nashville to guard this pass for us, since he heard of Bragg's retreat, & that his men as is wont were firing of the guns that were exposed to the dew, after guard mount. Still we hurried forward. It is a dangerous place where 1000 men could keep at bay & badly slaughter 50,000 for a while, & we found a band of guerillas, who had attacked some sutlers & others who had gone ahead of us, & were already plundering them. Seeing our advance – consisting of about 50 Cavalry – followed by General Woodruff & his staff & body guard perhaps 50 more they fired at them fortunately too high as only one was wounded in the cheek. Then they ran taking the sutlers wagons with them. Our men pursued & almost immediately killed 11 which we found dead or dying besides more wounded that escaped. We had a good chase after them & were very glad to find so few of them only about 100 men & horses. We recovered the sutlers wagon but they took all the Horses & two prisoners with them. We got several of their horses but no prisoners except the aforesaid dying & dead. All was over in a minute – almost before the general had time to give an order or unlimber a cannon. We were very fortunate, & the whole command escaped as I said with only a big scare. So we passed down the hills after a while carefully watching every overhanging rock or frowning cliff while the cold increased as the North wind got stronger & then it commenced to snow, & now we made some of the quickest marching we have yet done to our old camp on this north side the river. We got over 19 miles in a little over six hours. Our Doctor being sick I rode his horse & though I nearly froze I consider I fared well & was very fortunate in so doing.

Monday Nov 10th 1862
My Dear Girl
We are still in camp where we arrived on Friday night. On Saturday & Sunday (yesterday) we remained – <u>resting</u> – <u>washing</u> & <u>mending</u> – both clothes, limbs and constitutions. Today we propose to do the same! Who knows?

Yesterday – as an old Sunday custom now I commenced this letter but got so sadly & often interrupted, that I have to finish if possible today.

Saturday passed without incident but on Saturday night a sad accident occured to a St. Louis boy in our Co – Martin Cochran. He was on guard – and as you know, guards are <u>2 hours on post</u>, & <u>4 hours off</u>; during which they generally sleep. Well when he was relieved, he went to sleep in front of the fire – at his head was a large tree cut into lengths for rails & trim'd of its branches. Somebody set a fire agoing on the other side & <u>soon it rolled</u> a little & smashed his scull. He never breathed spoke or moved. Those laying almost alongside didn't know it for some moments but soon they observed his position rolled back the weighty log & carried him to camp – Dead. We buried him yesterday afternoon. He was a Catholic, & we had a Priest Chaplain to the <u>25 Ill's</u> in our Brigade to read a service over him. I attended of course & heard just such as any Protestant Minister would say – short, pithy & to the point, principally readings from the Douay Bible (not our version) a short prayer & the sad service was over. We returned sorrowfully to camp, much more so than if a bullet had laid him low, very much more so than if we had left him in an hospital behind. We got him a good coffin, what a soldier can seldom have & thus my letter was interrupted. I dont care for writing or reading too much now by firelight & candles we have none. When we have, it is hard to keep them alight in the wind – if I could – I would always when not too tired or sleepy plenty of time these long nights for writing or reading, whether on the march or not, as it is I have to economise daylight.

I have been rather under the weather of late since I left Louisville & strange to say it commenced with dyspepsia, & proceeded to "Engorgement of the Liver". I have been taking strong medicine since I came in camp and am now better. A little rest in a good tent or house and I will be again a hardened "Sinner" I suppose. This work you know either kills or cure's – so that no exposure or fatigue in future need be feared.

I got that sketch of our Irish friend claiming protection among the papers it is rather good – a good joke both on Miss Brittania & on Paddye.

I can see that they are rich in sketches &c &c – but with the exception of the *Ev. News*, I have not perused or examined them yet. I hope you can read my hieroglyphical writing. It is the best I can do squatting on the ground & writing on my knee. If I dont bore you it wont be for want of trying.

I have re-read your letters but I cannot find much that needs notice in this. It is all so old to you now – though new & very interesting to me.

It is now Dinner time & we have just got orders to move camp so as usual I must close for the present in haste.

I hope to hear from you soon, & I will also write soon again. I will try not to be so long winded unless I can find something new to interest you. I have not been to Nashville yet. I hope you will get this soon. I am with much love my dearest Molly

Yours ever

James E. Love

Address for the future to

Nashville or elsewhere

Nashville

Nov 16th 1862

My Dear Molly

I commence as usual on a Sunday, and a wet one with all its depressing influences. I have been in camp here all the time since I wrote last. We moved camp after I closed your letter to this place about a mile, just on the bank of the river below Nashville. We can go over easily daily if we wish to get a pass countersigned by half a dozen generals, but as we have little money, and there is but little to buy or see in town if we had, why we stay at home. I have gone to duty again, a weeks rest has made me a new man, together with plenty of Quinine.

There are hope's of our staying here for a little while now. Our request to be transferred to Kansas has been refused and General Rosecrans has sent to Kansas for the rest of our Regiment. He wishes us for the present to remain in town, and perhaps so continue either in the fortifications or on Provost Duty.

We are all in good spirits on account of the anticipation of a rest, and that was the principal reason why we wish'd to go, expecting of course as we passed St. Louis to have or take a furlough.

If we stay here as Genl R thinks we will, (and orders us too) when the road gets safe, I will try for leave for Ten days. It will be hard to get, unless we go in winter quarters. I fear the fighting is becoming too much in earnest to expect it, but somebody must stay here, so if good luck is with us <u>we</u> <u>will</u>.

Mails are coming this way pretty freely just now, and the R.R. will be open in a day or two, so I hope to hear from you soon. We have got late papers & the times are exciting & full of important events, from all parts of the compass. The Army of the Cumberland of which we are now a part is concentrating here rapidly as it scours the country side above us and it is fast being outfitted with clothing, Tents & Wagons for a Southern campaign. It is said to Chattanooga, East Tennessee & even Mobile.

I see you have had an exciting contested election once again with Frank Blair in the field, this time beat I suppose by a new man. So mote it be, for the sake of poetical justice. I care very little, so as Missouri becomes soon a free state.

I have no hairbreadth scapes nor startling incidents this time to relate, & I'm glad of it. I hope all may soon be peace & quietness for a generation.

I am with much love to you & all

My dear dear girl

Yours Sincerely

Love

General William Rosecrans. Photograph, 1861–1865.

Nashville
November 26th 1862
My Dear Alex[1]

We have been here for some time but have again rec'd marching orders to go where I don't know. South I suppose.

This is as usual unexpected to us. I have been getting right smart, and have been particularly busy in trying to obtain Leave of absence from Rosecrans now or next month, but with no effect. I talked of resigning but with no effect. However as a set off, I was offered position as Brigade Quartermaster, as there was not much permanency or promotion in this, & no benefit unless pecunniarily, I refused it. I was then offered position in the Pioneers or Topographical Engineers, but that fell through from one cause or another, and now I am acting as Adjutant. This suits me very well & were I in a Missouri or Illinois Regt. I would soon step higher but in Kansas some swindle of a politician may jump me and so prove slow on the path to Major &c.

You will think I have been dissatisfied. Well I have with Buell & with Kansas & with our <u>Lazy</u> Captain whom I could never shove out of my way as long as I remained in the Co – any other man would have been a Colonel with his opportunities. So I hope I have got rid of the dead weight. I haint got my commission yet, but I expect it daily. I have been so busy that I couldnt easily steal time to write before and so I write as usual at high pressure.

I intended as I said to come to see you or send for some things. I have been robbed within a few days of my Trunk and all its contents stolen from our sleeping quarters 6 feet by 2 of a tent during the night and rifled all my clothes, letters, papers, everything.

There is at Mrs. Morris's some Trunks and Valizes of mine. I wish you would go see them & the contents, (I know not what) & if there is any <u>winter outfit</u> worth sending express it to me to Nashville to be left at the <u>Commercial Hotel</u> not to exceed however 3 or 4 Shirts, undershirts, drawers, Stockings, Handkerchfs, a pair of gloves – & other &c – that you think I want.

---

1. Molly's brother Alexander D. Wilson.

I also wish you to look at some papers in the valise & enclose one a receipt from Sergeant Fisk 8th K.V. for some monies & vouchers handed to him at Aubrey Kansas.

This I must have as it is of importance. <u>Enclose in your letter soon</u>. There has been some <u>defalcations</u> & I must exchange it for another & enclose to Washington so as I can show clean hands.

Dont send to weighty a parcel or Trunk. <u>I have one here</u> but for most things it is impossible to buy beg borrow or steal so I have to send and when you are so doing if you can send 2 lb Tea & 5 or 6 lbs Butter it will also fill an important vacuum in our eatables.

I am in haste

My dear fellow

Yours as Ever

James E. Love

Charge these last items to me if you purchase them and remember me to all the folks.

Love

Nashville
Nov 27th 1862
My Dear Molly

I have waited, <u>waited</u> until Sunday has come and gone, and still the usual epistle is unwritten and yours of the 9th & 16th recd together a day or two since unanswered.

It is too bad, but what could I write – only Surmises a hint of which I gave you in my last.

I wished to get leave of absence now or before spring. I failed. I wished to resign for reasons too long to explain, the principal being that I could never get preferment or gain a name as long as our lazy friend <u>Capt "Herd" ranked me</u>. Although all my friends here knew I have done <u>all the work</u>, until lately that we have a first rate 2d Lieut. – who is my warmest friend – and who has relieved me much. I expect he will in a day or two take my place as 1st.

But anyhow my action spurred my friends up, & I soon had an offer from the Genl of a position as Brigade Quartermaster or in a Pioneer or Engineer Corps. I refused the first, and ere I closed with the 2d it was otherwise filled by a friend of mine.

I was at the same time offered by Col. Martin the position of Adjutant, this I accepted and I expect daily to have my commission. It is as good as Captain, and in fact suits me better, and the chances of promotion are as good or better. All I want now is to have some political influence to bring to bear on the Governor of Kansas. That I can little expect but patience & opportunity will overcome even that, and then if providence favors me, I mean to seize.

You will think I've become ambitious all at once, not so however, but I got tired of driving a man, who from pure laziness couldn't be driven, and I see others above me, not so competent as I am. I can say so without vanity or boasting even to Brig. Generals. While I will also acknowledge that privates in the ranks would make and are now <u>better soldiers than I am</u>.

I have been delayed also from business. The office work is behind and I wish to finish it up to date, so does the Co, so I am at it all my spare time. I wrote Alex yesterday & mentioned much of this – also of a loss I sustained. My trunk and all its contents everything I had clothing letters &c &c &c being stolen. I recovered the trunk in the woods but of the rest I can get no clue and as there is nothing to buy here yet – I am in a ackward predicament.

The railroad opened through yesterday however and soon stocks of goods will be here & so will the Paymaster. We had marching orders today but they are countermanded for the present. We have <u>no abiding place</u> until the war is over – that is certain no matter what temporary stops we may make – even if they last for months in a place. We are at the mercy of an order to move at five minutes notice and act accordingly. We will be in communication with <u>Nashville</u> however, & I wish you would write just as if I was stationed there as long as we are in this <u>Department</u>.

I will have an outfit before anything can reach me but I have asked Alex to look through my wardrobe in St. Louis & send me anything available. I dont know whether I done wisely or not but so I did – transportation is so limited, we can only carry articles of necessity and not much over a change of anything.

I have recovered rapidly during the present rest here. As rest it is from marching & exposure – though so busy otherwise. I feel myself again. I hope you do also <u>my dear sister of Charity</u> in good offices. I know you often overdo your strength, pray be careful. You <u>owe</u> that much to <u>yourself</u> & <u>others</u>.

I hope Morgan St. however is less of an hospital and that all goes well with them and you long ere you receive this. Your last 3 or 4 letters that I recd went with the rest, but my Valentine including poetry & Photograph was in my breast pocket as usual – also that gem "A Womans Answer"[1] – "<u>expressing your sentiments</u>". When I lose these and the ring I am lost.

Let me congratulate you on your new business, I mean dressing the babies. How do you think you succeed. I know you do well, as patience & love of the little dears are the only necessary accomplishments to succeed.

Glad to hear that Ellen poor thing is satisfied. I hope it has been the dawn of a better day for her – but I forget where the place was – if I ever heard of it?

---

1. Poem by Adelaide Anne Procter.

I am glad you have got all my letters, written under the circumstances. They are dry enough – but if you get them I am repaid if you are bored. I guess I have got all yours – so as the Regiment is on – I will get them – sooner or later. The place specified does not matter. I write this as usual in a corner on my knee – not but that I have a tent now and an office, but the crowd & confusion drive me away and the wish to look at your sweet enclosure again.

Sorry indeed am I to hear of the dying out of the good old custom at Halloween. More sorry at the cause of it. The case is hopeless I fear, as long as the sorrowful memories connected with them & other holidays are in the ascendant.

If Robert or John are down at Christmas pray keep my memory green, give my love as usual to Sallie & the folks. I haint got the papers you mention yet but I suppose I will. I got a *Democrat* & a *I.L.N.* about a week ago however.

I went to hear Parson Brownlow and Horace Maynard speak, both from East Tennessee and was much pleased especially with Maynard who is an old man eloquent, with Brownlow I was before acquainted & he is the same old Brownlow but the rare intellectual treat to us made or would have made even a second rate speech agreeable.[2]

We were reviewed by Genl Rosecrans on Sunday last & appearing to very good advantage as our Battalion always does. We got highly complimented.

The inspector General also inspected us this week and gave us a No. 1 certificate so we rest easy – expecting favorable notice and treatment either before the enemy or otherwise. Our Colonel is very particular to make all the men keep themselves their clothes & arms in good order & clean and as appearance goes so far in this world – it helps us.

I am, as ever, dearest Eliza

Yours,

Love

---

2. William Gannaway "Parson" Brownlow and Horace Maynard both defended slavery but supported the Union.

Head Qts.8th Ks. Vols.
Camp at Nashville
Nov. 30th 1862
My Dear Molly

It is a rainy Sunday Afternoon, and I must needs improve it! Would you believe it? I have actually been to church this morning, almost the first opportunity I have had in Dixie! It was an episcopal church with its gorgeous worship windows, & music. I entered into it fully & with feeling even to the responses, but was miserably disappointed in the sermon. It only lasted 10 or 15 minutes & there was literally & truly nothing in it. It treated of the season of Advent, of which this is the first Sunday & explained what was good <u>"Church"</u>? doctrine on that head. Neither did I hear a word of the war. Now when the war is left out in Nashville, now the very center of a great war & all its havoc & devastation, where all the people thereof flew from the presence of both Armies as from a plague – all the Sermon & <u>prayers</u> had better been left out. He might have even prayed for peace & every hated foe he had (the hypocrite) would have prayed with him, but he didn't even do that, but let him rest. I enjoyed the <u>meeting</u>, & not less so that there was numerous pretty girls there.

Well as I said, it is raining and all nature looks muddy & desolate. I feel it, for I got wet coming from church, & the rain had put out our fire, so I sat for a while in the Tent the charity of the Doctor has vouchsafed to me – not the care of Uncle Sam – for he now pleads poverty & expects of us hard work in return for few comforts.

Such is our experience. I speak for thousands of officers, the working men of the army not the butterfly grubs, who lay around great cities, devouring the substance of the government & making the very name of an officer at home a stench in the eyes of the people – but I could not stand it & I came to head Qts. where I found newspapers & correspondence hold sway, & I joined as you see the majority. It is the first time in three weeks I've been here that I could get the time or the quietness to write to you – or any other private matter, so it is the more welcome. I have had such a busy time since my health allowed me to go to work – that my promotion, I fear will not promote it – writing is a sickly position, & when every thing has to be just so as red tape & precision & figures will have it. It is even worse. I have a stove, & hot air inside, while frost & rain & sunshine hold revel outside.

But the day is breaking & ere the New Year – old scores of work will be cleared off & new I hope will not accumulate – if I can help it. Then I can enjoy myself in camp & have a horse on the march. I have already had time for many pleasant round games of Cards, & much literature in the shape of the daily papers in the evening. So much for Hd. Qts. & an open railroad.

I said nature looked gloomy. The leaves have been falling slowly but surely with most the colors of the rainbow, ere & after they fell. Cotton has been picked or burnt & so the seasons travel and tomorrow is the first of December, or the beginning of Winter. Although we have been laying here – our men have been working hard in guard duty & fatigue duties their time is filled up building fortifications & guarding forage trains while the rest of our Div. has been marching & chasing after guerillas & the advance of the enemy who are still entrenched at Murfreesboro 40 miles off just where we were three months ago. We will soon be fully outfitted for a Southern campaign, & I suppose we must travel as light as the "secesh" if we wish to catch them, so we wont be over burthened with tents or clothing, (on the Wagons) on the contrary it must be on our <u>backs</u>, aye both our house our cooking utensils and our rations, such is life in the Army now. I pity those of weak constitution – even under a southern winter, but I prefer a Southern to a Kansas one myself although we were comfortably fixed there – and as I said I expect now to have a horse, & a servant & the concomitant chances for comfort.

I looked for a letter from you today, but as I was dissapointed I revenge myself characteristically.

I hope you are all as well as heart could wish you – in body & mind. I wish you well through the holidays, & all your fatigues in the soldiers cause or that of their destitute better halves. May they prosper & you achieve a success. I hope Sallie & all the rest are well. I am so sorry that I cant join you.

My present position precludes it altogether so I may have to run another year if the exigencies of the war last so long, but there is no use speculating. A fortunate chance might send me on the way tomorrow.

I will send you a Journal that if you change names of Divisions & Regts will give a better account than I can of our movements for Nov.

I will also try and send you a Nashville paper occasionally & now with love & kisses for the present for Christmas & New Years – good night.

I am my dear Molly

Yours Sincerely

James E. Love

Camp South of Nashville
Hd. Qts. 8th Ks. Vols.
Decr 6th 1862
My Dear Dear Molly

It is all chill & bleak December here at last. We have again got a real live snow storm, after a time of delightful Indian Summer weather, with frosty nights. We moved camp 5 miles to the prettiest place you could wish for, on the Franklin Pike. A fine lawn, or rather Blue Grass sod with a sprinkling of grand old trees, just enough for a good shade, so it is for miles on each side of a rolling country. The Bluffs of the Cumberland river on the one side & on the other in the far blue distance the Cumberland Mountains that stand guard forever over the Loyal vales of East Tennessee – between us just outside our lines, lies an army of rebel <u>guerillas</u> & regulars of from 20 to 50,000 men, probably the former.

We keep mutually a very strict watch over one another and have daily a modest skirmish either with pickets or sometimes a Regiment or two out foraging. So times are thus more lively than they were. We could soon drive them out of this if we were ready to advance as we are well aware through our spies, that they do not intend to stand this side Chattanooga, where they are building strong Earthworks. They only wish to hang on our flanks & bother us, keep us back as much as possible & if possible to get behind us & tear up the railroad again; Genl Rosecrans does not intend to be caught in any such way – but says he must have 3 months supply of bacon & Crackers in Nashville ere he leaves it for his whole army – so that if Mr. Guerilla (in this country all supposed to under John Morgan) should take up a rail, his boys should have plenty to eat.

You ought to be in camp a while just to see how comfortable we make ourselves under the chilly circumstances. I mean scarcity of Tents &c. We have to put over 20 men in a Tent at night, if not on duty. Then you should see & hear the constant crash of falling trees, & the glorious old log fires that light up the camp all night & all day. There is but one stove in camp, that at Head Quarters & so officers & men build fires from 6 to 10 feet in front the opening to their tents so as to throw the heat inside.

Goodbye

Love

8th Decr.

I have just got a letter from Wm. dated the 1st Decr. which I have answered in full & also send remembrance.

I have received nothing as yet from you or Alex later than the 16th.

Love

Hd. Qts. 8th Ks. Vols.

Camp South of Nashville

8th Decr 62

My Dear Molly

Just as I finished or closed my first note, the Paymaster came, and occupied most the day. In the evening I went to town & got clothed. I remained & went to church yesterday & again heard good music & a good sermon by a Scotchman – <u>Secesh</u>. He wouldnt pray for the president either by the way. I have just finished reading that sermon of Dr. Elliott's you sent me. I need only say – Thems my Sentiments, though as you are aware of how weak human nature is, I might be unable in the crush to live up to it.

Well I passed a pleasant night in town. I went to the Theatre too and saw "Kate Kearney" played & sung very well. It is a fairy extravaganza, and I called & supped at a friends who fortunate man has his wife along, a dainty little bit of a New England <u>feminine</u> and do you know, the sight so strange to me just now of a lady in her sphere at home, gracing & adorning it as a good housekeeper always does – made me very very home sick. Well it did – and I even told her so – flatterer that I know I was – but it was not to gain her good graces only her sympathy. I believe I got it warmly not for myself alone, but for all the poor boys in the Army whether married or single. I made some purchases, very hastily & came back with a new fit out.

It is but seldom we will get to town now, as we go further away daily

Tomorrow we go on a 3 days reconnaisance in force – say 20,000 men. It will cause a brisk skirmish ere we go 3 miles & if we go to Franklin must cause a fight with Bragg or Johnson's left wing, there posted. I see in the *Republican* of the 4th that there is some Nashville correspondence in it. When you see any news from here – in it or the *Democrat* – you will always get fuller particulars, than you ever can from my letters, & even if there is no news of our Regt. Division or Corps we are all on similar duty.

I got a *Democrat* of the 5th also, which has for a time satisfied thirst for local news.

I should like to send you a souvenir of the season in some way & will if I can. But you can scarce imagine how impossible it is to procure anything beyond provisions & clothes.

I know how useless it is to ask you to remember me to outsiders & yet I cant help repeating the phrase. However wish a Merry Christmas & a happy New Year to as many as you can for me.

Love to yourself – Sallie, Mother & Aunt

I am ever yours

Love

James says he finished reading the sermon of "Dr. Elliott," most likely a reference to William Greenleaf Eliot, shown here. Daguerreotype by Thomas M. Easterly, ca. 1850.

Hd. Qts. 8th Ks. Vols.

Camp at Nashville

Decr 21st 1862

My Dear Molly

I scarcely know where to begin. I have been through such a fever of business & excitement since last I wrote it seems an age and I have so much to tell that it seems impossible to compress it, but to the point!

I received the valize sent all safe three days ago, & for which as a whole or parts I can not sufficiently express my thanks or gratification, will you kindly put it in words for me. The Portfolio is a little gem, too neat & complete for a soldier. The peaches <u>we</u> have already discussed, & found them most as sweet as Sallies dear little self (excuse my blushes) three cans however from rough usage "en route" lost their tops & came near spoiling all, but thanks to the newspapers enclosed only spoiled the said papers, & the pasteboard division in the Valize. I have had it coopered up with a wooden one in camp. The tea is still unopened, it is a "Corp de Reserve"; a thousand thanks for all including Alex's trouble as regarding clothing & papers. I will write him further. I could not sooner. I had not time to open the valize for two days. I last wrote on or about the 10th since that we have had constant alarms. The enemy meddling in heavy force with our pickets, say just about a mile from our camp, & we in turn with theirs, right into & through Franklin some 15 miles off – but I will give you a leaf from my note book.

We began on the 8th to fall in line of battle every morning to guard against surprise. It was very cold & we would occasionally stack arms to warm up. On the 10th we could hear heavy firing just in front which caused some excitement because we could not join in the muss. Just at daylight, the relief an extra picket came in, which gave us the idea that they had been driven in, & so the assembly was sounded & preparations made for immediate battle, but all passed off quietly & we were dismissed out of the frost & snow which had fallen the day before. On the 11th under arms as usual but nothing of Interest transpired though Genl McCook & Davis expected an attack momentarily.

We are waiting by the bye for a rise in the rivers, as the railroad cannot bring us rations & supplies fast enough, and it is all the time in danger of being stoppd by guerillas. We have had some heavy rain, but the season has been so dry that it seems to have no effect.

On the 12th some 2500 Cavalry & 1000 pioneers went to the front & drove the rebels into & through Franklin without difficulty. The thousands heretofore troubling us had strangely disappeared. Shelter tents – mere thin calico covers without sides or ends – were issued to us & we expected some scouting & fighting again if not marching but this was dissipated next day by the information I have given above. It is only part of the preparations. We were much dissapointed however as we considered that our long cherished hopes of remaining in town with Genl Mitchell had flown – we made up our minds for marching.

I had hoped for a quiet time & chance to write you a good letter, but I have commenced this so often already that I am almost discouraged.

On the morning of the 13th Genl Woodruff was ordered away & as Col. Martin was the ranking officer, he had to take command of the Brigade. So we went over there bright & early. I say we, for he apptd me A.A.Adjt. Genl 32nd Brig & this was the sea of trouble untried & unknown into which I sailed, & good gracious it as it happened took me from before sunrise to after midnight for over a week to get thro' the work.[1] The orders were so out of proportion numerous & the movements of Regts, detachments & Batteries so constant, besides Genl Woodruff took all his clerks, tents, paper & papers with him, & I had as much trouble finding out how to do it, as to accomplish when I ascertained the way. It didn't last however, so I proceed with my notes incomplete though they be. I had to commence with signing 200 or 300 passes then to mount Brig. Guards & instruct the officers of the day Capts or Majors. Then an interminable amount of routine business & copying of orders. I finally got two good clerks a little posted & the Col. who is well posted helped me manfully for his own credit but I got into such a

---

1. As acting assistant adjutant general for his brigade, James's duties included writing and transmitting orders, working on reports and returns, corresponding with other administrative departments, mustering troops, and arranging the records of the brigade.

nervous fit to have every thing right that I could neither eat drink or sleep. Then I had all the details for guard (Officers & men) to arrange & make out & forward & finally the countersigns to issue I enclose you one – but that is a small business. I only mention to show the routine, every command large or small in Rosecrans dept. has the same countersign nightly & so with all other orders & papers, & all go through the hands of the A.A.A.Gs of Brigades. Our Brigade has consisted since we left <u>Corinth</u> of the 25th & 35th Ills. the 22d Ind. the 8th Wisconsin Battery & the 2d Ky. Cavalry & since we left Louisville a new Regt. the 81st Indiana thrown in. Then besides that all the reports from these Regts. & every paper of any kind from them goes through Hd. Qts. on its way to Division, Corp. or Dept. Hd. Qts. – or to Washington & so red tape ties you up. But it is all necessary to the proper disposal of business.

Next day 14th was Sunday & it was passed just so, all day writing & fussing, & no time to write a letter to you as usual & I wishd to far more than ever just because I couldn't. I note it in my tablet as the busiest day I ever passed.

On the 15th orders came for all hands to have 3 days cooked rations in their haversacks from henceforth, & officers detailed to take all our tents & every thing inside the entrenchments if we moved & to keep our horses saddled mine inclusive. Why we didnt know – but it since transpired that a large body 20,000 of the enemy came up & looked at us & marched away to the West. Genl McCook issued the most minute instructions to every officer & man what to do. He means fight & to waste no powder or lead – all must hit & kill if possible. Just then news of Burnsides crossing the Rappahannock put us all in high spirits, to be dashed since by his sad repulse. So it remained all afternoon but 10 P.M. came & no fight – so to bed weary.

The 16th passed in much the same way – but being used to it, quietly & busily. On the 17th all was quiet again, & as business in camp did not press so much, I went to town & did up a large amount of necessary business there, having to call on old Rosy to force it through. Got his signature, & as it happened he was not very busy, & my impetuosity in pushing my case, led to a long conversation, that is to say 15 or 20 minutes. I gained my points, but I had ran the risk of being arrested, as it is not allowable to approach him in that way, by an officer so low in rank. I found my valize at the express office same time & got back to camp at sunset, had to work later for it when I came back so much waited. I found my Commission as Adjutant had come in the meantime & several other long looked for commissions.

The Governor wanted badly to put in one of his friends but justice prevailed at last, through the influence of the old Adjutant a warm friend of mine now in Kansas & influential. I found when I got thro' that all the officers save the Colonel & myself were on a tall spree or celebration at the expense of the newly appointed, so at midnight business over we were compelled to join in, & I had to find my share of oysters &c &c &c &c & Brandy – remained an hour or two & did the honors, & had a slight headache next morning but the Colonel & I were the only officers out of 40 not tight – business was our excuse – or we couldn't have escaped.

On the 18th the Camp fell in as usual at 5 A.M. but of course I am out of that scrape now. I get up however, & get ready for the coming labors as usual.

The enemy are out of sight however again as our cavalry are reported in Franklin again only having to skirmish slightly to get there – so it changes from day to day. Many supposed we would now go and hold Franklin, but it proves a mistake. Rosy our respected commander wont be tempted out of here until he's ready.

You remember what a pretty place I described Franklin as when I passed through it on our way north. I hear it is much dilapidated now.

On the 19th we sent out half our Brigade with our Forage train & they came in safe & well loaded having been within three miles of Franklin – could see nothing but the enemies mounted Vedettes who retreated faster than they could follow. When just coming into camp again a man fell off a wagon & his gun exploded & wounded more or less 5 men his comrades – such the results of carelessness or awkwardness. Late at night at last came the long looked for order to go to town & relieve the 1st Tennessee from Provost duty.

Here was a sudden change. As sudden & unlooked for just at that moment as death from appoplexy or drowning, but welcome to all myself included. Here I said is rest – whether it is so or how long remains to be seen in the future. Well we had to go to work & finish up all business & pack up by 8 o.clock next morning, turn all this business over to raw hands again. A new Adjt. a new Col. neither of which knew anything about it & so it took <u>all</u> night, & shortly after the given time we marched out of camp with colors flying in splendid order & good appearance. Very much regretting & regretted by our old & tried friends in battle & in dreary hot & cold marches. We were feted & cheered. We the <u>despised</u> Kansans of it seemed only yesterday had got by <u>compulsion probably</u> the best name of any Regiment in this army, & we could see were sincerely regretted & respected. So the wheel of fortune turns & it is to this good name we are here now. We got in town by noon, & soon camped on a fine hill in rear of the Capitol where we have a good view of the city & hills around. We had a busy day. I have joined the Colonels mess, & now sleep at Hd. Qts. a great improvement I assure you, an increase in expense too, & I must have a horse &c so the money goes.

Today Sunday again. I was up early, & as I said before had a rush of business & interruptions to my letter writing, quite unexpectedly all of a temporary character however & I got time in the morning with a few Catholic friends to attend Mass. I there saw Genl Rosecrans & his Adjt. Genl. Col. Garesche both Catholics & regular attenders I understand. Hadn't I better get converted & get on the staff. Its the shortest cut I can see just now – but to be successful I had better study a little more military books first and if my resolution holds I will too & so my notes are down to date, but I fear I have compressed all the sense & pleasure to you out of them & still left them long enough to bore you. I wished to give you another instance of the uncertainty of military life & orders. It makes a man – if he is a good obedient soldier or officer – a fatalist & almost a slave – so accustomed becomes he to surprises – to not getting what he wants & to obeying orders without knowing the reason <u>why?</u> Well now its about time to answer your letters if possible. I find I have one of the 3d which must have arrived since I wrote you. I haint been able to catch the suspected nigger, so that you could kindly knock him on the head as yet, but I'll try to accommodate, if the Provo when found dont finish him!

I got your note in the valize of course & I have also got your last of the 12th – Alexanders likewise & Williams of some time previous are to hand.

And now as to what I said in Wm's letter, it may have been foolish, but it was intended & probably will have a different construction from what you think.

It was in reply to one of his in which he said Alex & you had or would give me all the gossip, & I intended simply to disclaim receiving any letters from you lately.

I dont apologise you see & I wont offend you by trying too, but I'll try to do better in future. If a poor devil who is so ackward in speech & action as I can do so.

I really think that our philanthropy is taxed enough at present by the wounded & destitute soldiers, & their wives & children, & also by the widows & orphans of the killed & although the niggers are no doubt in a bad way, & <u>in need</u> as long as a large party in the country wont let them fight for their rights, but insist that white men shall do it for them, & so bring poverty & death into so many house-holds of our white brethren, I would let them wait, until the said whites are served. At any rate their democratic friends should lead the way & if any body else does – they will raise such a howl as will obstruct the vigorous prosecution of the war.

It is about time both sides of politicians should halt & give & take a little for the country's sake. If they dont it will go to ruin in spite of victorious armies but excuse me, I ought to keep politics out, & just say that its time enough to sew for the niggers after the wars over, & the poor soldiers & their families are served. [2]

---

2. In September, President Lincoln issued his preliminary Emancipation Proclamation, and many former slaves moved to northern cities, becoming refugees or contraband. Providing aid to the former slaves became an issue, which James clearly did not support.

Decr 23d – I have commenced these sheets so often that I have almost made a vow against long letters about the army. When I try it, as Ive done this time I fail unless done daily & that was impossible this time. Since writing the foregoing, I read in a paper that there is now about 6,000 contrabands in St. Louis! Is that another Democratic – or secesh lie?

I got last night a letter of yours dated 25th Nov. It has been down in Arkansas or Mississippi. You see they all turn up in time, sometimes after travelling as in this case thousands of miles.

Here let me say, I crave for your letters all the time! I know you write as often as possible! I would not have you write oftener! When they dont come to hand I blame the mail! Never you! But I cant help talking about it when I write! and thinking about it daily when the mail comes in! As to visiting Ellen, I aint going to make any such remarks as you suggest about it. I think Ellen deserves a visit; until she proves in her own house that she is as unworthy as her <u>old man</u>.

You must recollect that men are far more charitable of a ladies failings than her feminine acquaintance are whether justly or unjustly!

Cant you send me the *Harper* you speak of? What about the caricature?

I have a letter of the same date of yours, come to hand same time, from a friend in the 10th ward & in it I am told that the 8th is mentioned as not doing well before the enemy? Seeing St. Louis & New York papers so seldom we are all anxious to know and the more so, as we are not aware of anything that could by possibility be discreditable! Buell mentioned us favorably in his official report! If you read it you will find on the 7th Oct. the evening before McCooks great fight, "He says" – "that two regiments advanced under fire & supported a battery in the most handsome manner" &c, &c. These regiments consisted of the 35th Ill. & the 8th Kansas – not over 500 men in all – while the enemy before us were at least 5,000, & that they did not attack & surround us was only because it was so late in the evening & probably the supposition that we had strong supports which we had not!! This and the rapid firing of the battery! If we had <u>nobody hurt</u>, the enemy had hundreds, and it certainly wasnt our fault? Buells praise to two abolition Regts, is better testimony in our favor the 500 Abolition news-papers but we have no correspondent for the press in our camp – save to an obscure Kansas paper, & we thus scarcely get justice done us! Our good deeds go unmentioned.

All this is unnecessary to you, save to show how much I and others wish to know whats the matter? Our honor is all thats left us, so far in this campaign. We have no friends in Congress to make Brigadiers from our numbers – neither have we in the newspapers – but those who have trav-eled with us as officers, soldiers, & commanders know that there has not been an officer or man, absent from duty, save from sickness since January last, while other Regts have got 4 or 5 officers <u>absent without</u> <u>leave</u>, all the time. Genl Rosecrans has dismissed & disgraced 30 or 40 already and will do so with 50 or 60 more very soon. A court of enquiry is sitting now, and will soon be heard from. You will find none of our officers in the list. The incapables were compelled to resign long ago.

Dont I require to retort "take care of yourself". In rereading all your let-ters, I find you invariably working hard for the soldiers or somebody else besides the usual round of gossip & dissipation, visits day & evening – truly I think you task yourself about as much as I do, probably more in proportion to your strength. What do you think about it? I think no wonder you recoil from the latest phaze of the nigger question.

We have had fine warm weather since Sunday, quite spring like, & yet we dont acknowledge to any winter as yet. It looks like rain now. I hope to God it will & raise the river – the secesh here say God is on their side now and he has condemned the Gunboats to inactivity. We are still <u>provosting</u> – but of that more in my next. I am well and if you dont return this rubbish I will write soon again.

Love

Much Love to you and all – with all the compliments of the Season added.

I am my dearest girl ever sincerely yours

James E. Love

I send you two papers same time
Address – 8th Kansas – Nashville

Copy of Countersign enclosed with letter
Hd Quarters 14th Army Corps
December 18 1862
Parol
Lill

Countersign
Iuka
By Command
Maj Genl Rosecrans
C. Goddard Maj & A.A.G.
Official
James E. Love
Lt. & A.A.A.G.

Hd. Qts. 8th Ks. Vol
Camp at Nashville
Decr 26th 1862
My Dearest Molly

How is it with you? I bid you good evening Love! I've just steppd in for an evening call to your own dear self, and being so far from <u>home</u>! and in sentimental mood for a wonder I've been worshiping at your shrine incog, present in spirit I would say, but with only your photograph before me in person! It is nine of the clock. The musical horns in our band has some time since chimed tattoo, my work is done, & my spirit is at leizure to take a flight to old St. Louis in thought and on paper! What cheer do you give me? What welcome? I look at your sweet face alongside smiling on me and a – I dont flatter! Dont you dare to say it or think it! And a – I read & reread that "Valentine" and that "Womans Answer" & think & muse for the fiftieth time as to how you are passing Christmas & New Years! Tell me about it, of course you will so I need not ask but I will only say that I have passed a quiet & not unpleasant Christmas, stopping at home in my tent and busily at work all day – for Uncle Sam – had I been idle I'd been miserable and so the shades of evening fell, but I could not though I wished it settle down to write and so instead of it read in *Harpers Weekly* Dickens new story <u>all of it</u> and in the monthly I finished "Orley Farm" and "Madeleine" "Schaeffer" and so filled up the night to 12 M, & drowned all thought in the Lethean bowl of light reading all of which I had succeeded in purchasing just the day before – so opportune.

We had a plain but good dinner for camp – Fresh oysters & chicken roast with Sweet & Irish Potatoes Fresh Eggs & Butter &c &c, and we had no indigestion Eggnogg or even Whisky after it, only some good cigars & so to work again.

I hope after all you have been as happy as Ive been.

God tempers the wind to the Shorn Lamb! You know I dont know that I'm very lamblike. I fear the contrary! But may I apply it? It has been worse gouted!

I am here! Shorn of Liberty – Shorn of Home – Shorn of your company – Shorn of those pleasant Evening calls, that were in a sense my only pastime ad infinitum &c. Well! Well!! Dont chide me! I'm getting old & gray I fear & I'll never be any wiser. I fear you'll rue the bad bargain you made, long before you can reform me and steady me down – like staid money making brother William for instance. I'll stop at home enough never fear too much perhaps – but financially I'm not lucky. Thats an easy way of shifting your fault onto Providence or Fate or Luck! Aint it?

But Shade of Mahomet! Whats the use of talking? When can these things be? The vista is so long. I fear to look down it! Wont you cast a horoscope & say for me fair Lady Enchantress? Or are the "Ifs" too many, the war and its chances too vague, the future too dark. I grant you much of that & it need not you repeat it – as much as you wish – but still after all it resolves itself into a long, secret, engagement and although I have & do assent to it, my reason aint convinced.

I am so selfish as to say it aint what I want. I want an anchor! I want something to provide for! Then I can do, what I cant do for myself. I can try to compel luck to make a sport of fortune. So out of much love, I am compelled to sing an old tune, and say When! When! Fair Lady! When! When can I revel in possession? When can we come down to practicalities? How? What? Where? The war may last its Three years that I enlisted for! Is its foundation not to be laid until after that? I tell you Nay! I shall contest & protest (on paper) occasionally all the time! though acknowledging with a bad grace that you must decide & dictate! Let me call you mine? Say when? But do not for Pity sake say when the wars over and after a year or so you are started in a steady business, then so and so. Will that time be? When?

Procrastination will make havoc of our happiness! We become more & more set in our way – more & more dissimilar – less & less able to be

"Two hearts with but a single thought

Two souls thats joined in one

Again selfish shall I say. I feel at times alone! Alone in the world! I have been so much alone! I fear or rather I cant believe any better fate at times is open to me – nought but possession can make me a believer in Home! in Happiness in my wife & her Love an ever present refuge in time of trouble.

Well I hear you say. Its about time you were interrupted – so I have been several times & so Ill change the subject. I have a chance to live a little longer you see. The Army has moved a fight must soon come off. We skirmish forward daily and I am safe in town. I am much pleased until the wet weather is over. Then I want to go again. There is something wrong with the railroad too, & you may not see this for some time if ever. I hear the cannon roar again. I have got to close for tonight.

With prayers for your safety & love to you & all

Good night

Love

Hd. Qts. 8th Ks. Vols.
Camp at Nashville
Jany 3d 1863
My Dearest Molly

After a long and busy interregnum I wish to greet you again. The road has been interrupted, it reopens tomorrow and I wish to fly to you on the wings of the mail & fulfill the law and the prophets that is, that if "No News is Good News", "Good news is better." I fetch you good news I hope in this pacquet!

I don't excuse myself so! My excuse is much shorter, simply "business." I've been very busy! Good for me? Aint it? Well I think so. It has been on pleasant duties, & pleasures that should have been more pleasant, but that as pleasures often do, "turned to ashes when tasted".

I speak in parables? Well with the explanation in Rosecrans words that there has been a Big fight for 5 days or more, and that we slowly gain against (strange to say) <u>as usual</u> the overpowering force of the enemy – that our Battalion with 4 or 5 exceptions are all safe, as a reserve to defend the Capital that we are daily arresting crowds of stragglers & cowards from the front, & sending them back to fight again – that there has been great slaughter on both sides and the end is not yet. I will now resume my notes for a connected story of events so exciting that my pen is unequal, & that in passing the last sensation follows what has gone before so rapidly, that the particulars are even driven from your mind?

The present lays with the wounded fast coming in in the rain & cold "en route" or on the field. God help them, and in fact all our brave men without tents without food, perhaps a bloody death before, certainly a cowards name if in the rear.

Old Rosy is a perfect war horse, whereever disaster threatens us – omnipresent in danger foremost? And it required it all!

It is another Fredericksburgh this "Murfreesboro" & no mistake – yet we will never gain laurels before the world as the armies in the east do. The correspondents of the press of the world are not with us. But the dead &

wounded will tell the tale of horror on both sides, to satisfy the most morbid tastes but from generalities to particulars.

On the 26th ult. the day I commenced, the Army moved out on the Murfreesboro road and left us and others about 10,000 to guard this city and vicinity including the road to the battlefield. We and the 1st Tennessee in case of an attack to fall back on & defend the Capitol. The cannonnading heard in the evening was our army skirmishing and advancing. This continued daily up to the 30th when our men reached within 4 miles of Murfreesboro where the right wing under McCook encountered the enemy strongly entrenched on a rocky creek & pass & got badly whipped and driven back four miles. They have been fighting ever since and yesterday had not crossed that creek yet though they have in turn whipped the rebels driving them back daily with great slaughter on both sides. On the 30th the enemy captured and burnt all their train, wagons, tents & provisions – a force under Col Wheeler having ridden 70 miles around & come in, in the rear so to do. Our men were in dreadful confusion, nothing but defeat and death or a Southern prison seemed possible, when late at night Rosecrans formed the 4th U. S. Cavalry & led them <u>himself</u> to their relief, & soon <u>annihilated</u> the rebels driving them like sheep 10 or 20 miles leaving but few to tell the tale except 3 or 400 prisoners which he sent in here. They had to march two days without anything to eat, & so appeared rather forlorn on arrival.

Meantime the right & center had better luck but hard fighting. They drove the enemy steadily from the first & finally got in their rear in turn, & into Murfreesboro. They found the inhabitants all left and in that place and four miles south their fight has raged ever since, so the line of battle extends 8 miles now. It commenced 25 miles this side of, that is North of Murfreesboro and is now right wing 4 miles this side – center in Murfreesboro & left wing 4 miles beyond it.

It is a dreadful hilly rocky country, splendid for defence and hard to attack. The rebels are getting reinforcements daily from Richmond & Chattanooga while we are today being reinforced from Gallatin & Mumfordsville.

O God for a success!

It is rumored that our cavalry is playing "Morgan" on them. Genl Stanley is said to have played havoc & torn up rail between them and Chattanooga. While Genl Carter is said to be in Knoxville & to have cut their communication with Louisville, Richmond. I hope so but I doubt. If it is so Rosecrans deserves much credit as it is the first time we have tried anything of the kind though they do it on us all the time. It is not fighting – but it is very annoying – and sometimes paralizes a large army for want of supplies. Many Generals, Colonels, & Officers known to me & to fame have been killed – more wounded – & men by thousands.

I find the mail goes out so I will send thus much and give you the balance tonight.

Much love to all

Yours

Love

On December 31, 1862, Confederate forces attacked the Union army's right flank, which included troops from James's brigade commanded by Union colonel William E. Woodruff, starting the Battle of Stones River. During the first day of the battle, Union troops established a line of artillery where the fence is today, along the Nashville Pike. Photograph by M. E. Kodner, 2012.

Hd. Qts. 8th Kans. Vols.

Jany 3d 1863

My Dear Molly

In my last just this moment mailed, I proposed to begin my notes several times but each time got lead away in the wish to give you a connected account of the battle &c &c.

Oh it is a horrid affair. Our Brigade the 32d & our Divn was under McCook and in the front, and it suffered the worst. We had just left it to come to town, so imagine the escape we had. They fought bravely, & Genl Woodruff their commander who has just come to town sick from the exposure & loss of sleep compliments them highly but that he wished often and often for the little 8th when they were so much overpowered. There is a dreadful loss of officers in their ranks. All parties unite in saying that the Genl (Woodruff) fought like a tiger – while his adjt. was wounded and taken prisoner almost from beside him. He cried on the field while encouraging his men and rallying stragglers – at the time that his battery was taken the Capt & most of its men killed or prisoners, and he states that where his men fought he could walk all over the field and step from one corpse to another.

The dead of the six days fight are mostly unburied yet – scattered over the ground 8 or 10 miles from right to left & the same from front to rear and still the fight progresses.

Jany 4th 1863

My Dear Girl

It is true of army as in civil life, that "In the midst of life, we are in death." Just as I wrote the foregoing yesterday an order came to fall in, as the enemy had attacked our pickets. We did so instantly, and all marched out, except I and Ten men, the servants, and the band and Teamsters. We were left to pack up and strike tents, this we did in half an hour. They that once knew us knew us no more. It was seven at night, "dark as Erebus" raining heavily, and blowing a hurricane, but the Battalion double quicked out to the front and we double quicked to load our plunder & so went out into the outer darkness where death flashed from the red mouths of <u>the Carbines</u>. Many bit the dust, though it was but a false alarm some few of ours were wounded, none killed and so the skirmish ended but we lost our nights sleep & got very wet and my letter came to grief but we are quietly in camp again, as if nothing happened; and the fight still progresses in front, though it is today reported that the rebels are evacuating and retreating. I fear the news is too good to be true.

They are retiring while we are skirmishing forward to take new positions. The news from all other points, East, North, South & West, came in to us today first time for 10 days and seems to be very good which encourages us considerably. While we marched out last night the long looked for reinforcements came in and marched through town, 17,000 strong under Genl Reynolds. I hope the news is true all round if so, we will surely gain the day here and annihilate for the present the rebellion in the south & west, as far as large and organized armies are concerned. Of course, for years there may & probably will be Guerilla or Robber Bands and even new armies may be organized by their desperate leaders. But eternal vigilance we all know is the price of liberty and we must watch with arms in our hands, enforce the laws and prevent any rally.

Well in my notes I find worth mention on 27th Decr. a very wet day, continued rain with lightning, fog in the morning and a glorious sunset. On our hill it had set, but the Capitol and much of the city were illuminated with a golden halo of Glory, a flood of rosy sunlight while the valleys were dark and misty with vapor. This gradually crept upwards until nought but the top of Capitol & the American flag was embalmed in it. One golden window after another went out as the sunshine left it, like a lamp and at last all flitted to the red & golden tints of heaven with the young moon riding quietly in mid heaven, day passed quickly, much writing and reading to a late hour.

On Sunday 28th a very dense fog lasted to 11 oclock when it cleared off & left a fine warm afternoon. Went to the Episcopal Church again and home dining with some friends by the way, little to do and quiet.

On the 29th – very busy studying and writing. All our yearly returns and business begins to come in, fine warm Indian Summer kind of a day with fog at intervals. In camp and at work all the time nowadays. On the 30th – the fight begun as before reported – very busy up late, rumor with its thousand busy tongues makes us all anxious and uneasy as we here the cannons roar – while grape vine intelligence states how the Rebels are whipping us & taking prisoners whole Brigades. On the 31st muster day. The Major and I being the only field officers present mustered and reviewed the camp and Battalion. Men looked very well. Alarming reports all day, & with much truth in them – too much. Had to go to town to muster the guard at the Capitol, and to sate our curiosity and anxiety. Called on Genl Mitchell, Major Sidell & others, & then home to supper, and a jolly evening, as we invited all the Officers to partake off a great Bucket of Egg nogg at our quarters and to set the old year out and new year in as is wont. We did so – but about 8 P.M. had an alarm in camp which proved baseless & so after being under arms a few men were dismissed and we to our revels again. Much Cannonnading and Drumming after midnight made it an anxious night and we were out again in line of battle at 3 in the morning remaining in the Cold & Frost till daylight, & so ushered in the new year, river commences to rise, which has been much prayed for by Rosecrans & all.

On the 1st Jany 1863 remained awaiting events, quiet in camp, busy. Big dinner – Egg nogg after – a little cards & cigars after that, & a little sick before night. At 9 P.M. an order to have everything ready for march at a moments notice, Knapsacks packed, guns in hand – slept so until 3 A.M. when we fell in line as before all quiet, the fight is now so far off 25 or 30 miles. Cant hear it any more.

On the 2d Jany – News comes in fast, good & bad – citizens & soldiers all excited. We cannot rest, prisoners come in – wounded too. Guerilla cavalry all around picking up our stragglers and wagons – both armies suffering for eatables. They must steal from us. Very stormy and rainy day, stove smokes badly – much discomfort. Went down town at night. Stragglers & cowards from the field in crowds & our patrol arresting them – could not rest.

Moped around, seeking excitement & news, went to the theatre & found it crowded. Our patrols there too arresting officers and soldiers who should have been with their regiments. Home & to bed & forgetfulness at twelve M. I have much business on hand both early & late.

On the 3d Saturday – I have before told you part the story – all day busy – had to ride a little to the front. Saw Genl Woodruff as related & on returning proceeded to write to you. Started the first part on its route when the mail closed & commenced again on this second part to be interrupted as related.

To day very busy, all quiet. No chance to go to Church, though I did find time to relieve my discomfort in a bath and a complete change of dress from head to foot. With that exception I had not a breathing space from 6 A.M. to the present writing 9 P.M. as when duty was over, as it proved an hour ago, I returned to my interrupted narrative & my usual Sunday Evg amusements – a gossip with you.

We expect a large mail in tomorrow, and some Northern papers, a thing we haint seen for two weeks, telegrams we had today for the first time also provisions of all kinds. The inhabitants and officers want much. The soldiers unless where the fortunes or necessities of war prevents are well supplied so far and will be. But the officers buy their own rations & so fell the blockade in scarcity and in price.

I find my new mess very expensive. I will not save as much as before, such is the drawback on position.

I will send you a roll of two or three papers with local news here – in them that may be interesting to you or some of the Folks.

Happy New Year to them all. Love much love to you my dear girl, to Sallie, Mother, Aunt, and all. I am ever present in spirit, in the midst of the most pressing duties now. These times and scenes lead to seriousness and contemplation, to reviews of past life & happiness or the reverse, to the scenes we love – and the happiness we have enjoyed, in a life well spent, or to the sad record of opportunities wasted, of which we all have more or less and then it leads us on to a hereafter or ought too, to hoped for visions of home & happiness after war & carnage has subsided, to thoughts of what a future life & career may be – so hard as it is to guess just now, and so dark as the hereafter even when war is over now appears, & then on to death and judgement and a long hereafter of merited happiness or punishment. I say it leads to this, but I fear with but little effect on most for no where does crime & profanity so revel as on a battle field or in an army on an active Campaign. All senses seem blunted by the horrid scenes around & soon you look on even the dead with indifference, & contemplate your own probable fate in the same way – with the so usual wish to a soldier that if your turn comes it may be sudden death (unshrined & sinful as you are) <u>and not wounds</u>. Such is life in the army. Truly it is a wearing profession when an army and a Genl as ours the Gallant "Rosy" becomes in earnest. Night & day! Night & day! Sunday & Saturday!! holiday or otherwise!!! The horrid carnival of death goes on or more wearing still the horrid preparations before & after, to save yourselves, & make such the fate of your enemies.

Eliza I have killed no one yet. My hands are not red with any blood, and although I am heart & soul in the war & its success, God grant it may be so ordered I never may. If such cup however is presented to me – as in duty bound it will be Victory or Death! if I know myself.

Freedom must triumph and the World move on to the Millennium!

My Dear Molly will you do me the kindness to think of & write me about what I say in my last of date 26th Decr. It is written in serious, earnest, sober second thoughts, though it may seem in Jest. Decide for us & state your preference for a course, a place of future residence and work – and a time.

I feel I haint got the vantage ground to dictate or even suggest just now. Give me the cue. Mark out a point & a day if possible to look forward too, and then let us in sober seriousness work it out, so that it shall perforce be so <u>God willing</u> and let us without reservation have one thought in planning, discussing and working it out. My whole past history & present & past thoughts are open, & if there is or have been, I never intend to have any concealments in the future, whether near or distant. So let us work together! If we differ in all love & kindness stating the reasons and so arrangeing it for the best good of both as far as our light & reason will allow us – and if as will happen to poor human nature as long as we are frail & human – we cannot see things in the same light, Why agree to differ!! Acknowledging God's Providence in the exercise of which He has made no two alike whether human, animal or vegetable.

Think of it Molly Dear and with prayers & blessings on your head – Goodnight

I am as ever

Yours Sincerely

James E. Love

1st Lieut & Adjt. 8th Kans Vols

Nashville, Tenn.

To Miss Eliza M. Wilson St. Louis, Mo.

I have commenced a letter to Alexander several times but could make no progress under the circumstances. I can now write it with a clear conscience & will forthwith.

Love

Hd. Qts. 8th K.V.

Camp at Nashville

Jany 11th 1863

My Dearest Molly

In the feverish unrest consequent on a continued absence of our mails but partly because of a bad digestion and a very feverish state of the nerves, I am impelled again to address you, though I fear under such circumstances with but poor effect. My hand trembles dont it? Will my ideas come at will?

Our mail has gone to Murfreesboro, not once but half a dozen times and that is worse punishment than if there was no mail at all. It is aggravating! Positively!

To see the last frail plank, on which all your hopes of life had centred float on the billows top from your nerveless grasp is . . . faintest symbol to which I can liken it just at present!

Why do I craze about it? I hear you ask!

Well! Its one of our luxuries! A little excitement! A lottery ticket! In which you may have a blank! a forfeit!! or a prize!!! Mine are all prizes! The honey & manna on which I subsist. So I'm crazy as a bed bug this night. I wish I had a posset. Our luxuries are few. We live on excitement and are sometimes shut out from the world. We want to know! do tell!!

Him! I hear you say again! Mr. Curiosity! Well what of it? If I confess the soft impeachment?

But my <u>darling</u>, put it on better grounds? how are you? How have you been since 7th Decr. until this blessed moment. A cloud has obscured the Sun! The sun is probably enjoying itself and St. Louis is mayhap basking in its rays, your Smiles, but I don't see it.

Probably you can retort on me but if you get all my stationery at any time you will be answered even should it be late in the day, probably and I believe your longed for missives are "en route" for me, but I dont see it. They've not arrive yet!

Well we have passed a quiet week since the last holy Sabbath day. I have had a little less to do, & begin to pick up but I bless the Lord I haven't got to loaf around like some Officers or Soldiers. I honestly assure you I w'd be compelled to commit suicide within a week.

Rosecrans is yet at Murfreesboro. We defeated them utterly but under a less judicious leader they would have defeated us as badly! So we have not much to brag of in that way! But we have, at the results. A few more such victories just now would finish the war! Would leave them no army to fight with! And though it would cripple us dreadfully, would that not be a great result? And worth fighting for? Would it not save life? And Treasure? So mote it be!

We have had a cold wet dirty disagreeable week – with a single exception up to today. But today we have Spring and positively you can see the grass grow. It is green and beautiful already with one days sun. Warm & balmy, but with the excessive moisture around and no frosts of magnitude gone before – very unhealthy, and sickness must soon prevail. Thats whats the matter. The heat is unlooked for unseasonable, unhealthy and I am fidgetty from that cause or some other.

It wont last however and will probably ere you get this, turn in and freeze for two months, spoiling all the fruit & grain it coaxed to sprout before its time. I see you have had snow in St. Louis. Oh! Would I were with thee, just for one cold night in that ere wee front parlor. Wouldn't I sip nectar? In more ways than one & get my ears pulled perhaps for my pains, but a crowd comes in and bothers me, so I'll close, dismiss them, and to bed.

Goodnight! & joy be wee Yee a'
Love!

Jany 13th 62 [63]

Two days since I wrote the above, last night I got yours of the 25th Decr. very opportunely to hand. I suppose there are others on the way – and <u>in it</u> you do me but justice to suppose, that I have sent you letters & papers in quantity. Two or three long letters & 5 or 6 papers in that time, besides one or more to Alex & William and papers. I have had enough food, for a good imagination to write half a dozen of novels. I'm too lazy, if I had the brains to profit by it. I'm sorry to hear of Mrs. Morris's demise indeed and at such an unfortunate season. I had a very high opinion of her and always paid her the compliment of a call, amongst the very first of my friends which she was. She was a high spirited little woman, done her best to grace & dignify her position and was worthy of a better – if her good natured & worthy old man had had an education to qualify him to gain & hold it. Let her rest in peace!

Our sutler has not arrived yet; He has got caught somewhere on the shoals, or at a break in the railroads, if not worse luck. We have not heard of him, nor of the outer world <u>except</u> through the medium of the <u>Louisville Journal</u> to a later date than 1st Jany – so I have not heard of you by him or otherwise. I am so glad to hear that your Bazaar was a great success, and still more so that it is over for your sake. I'm sure you must need rest, will you take it? I congratulate you both on your Santa Claus present. Would I were there to see!

The weather continues fine & warm, though moist. A large fleet of boats have come up the river within a few days, but more than half are still anchored at the Harpeth Shoals 50 miles below – and the river is falling slightly but this south wind ought to melt some of the snows in the Alleghanies & send another freshet.

I have been down to the Levee looking for St. Louisans several times with but poor success so far. We have no news from the front of importance. All is quiet! The secesh have dissapeared and our army is being reorganized & recuperating.

I suppose there will be another fight when we least expect it at Shelbyville, Tullahoma or Chattanooga – or perhaps even sooner in East Tennessee if we follow the pack of mules.

With Love to you & all

I am my dearest Girl

Yours Sincerely

James E. Love

1st Lieut & Adjutant

8th Kans. Vols.

Miss E. M. Wilson

St. Louis Mo.

Jany 15th 1863

I feel as if I didnt wish to send this letter off until I got later tidings.

I send you two "*Independents*" today – a paper I have always liked much when I saw it at the Commercial Library or elsewhere. I wish I could send you the <u>Atlantic Monthly</u> for Decr. the first article on the procession of the flowers is so good & so readable. It is a real treasure for a resident of New England & w'd be a pleasant companion for a lover of flowers wild or exotic even in the West. I'll have a talk with the <u>Army Postmaster</u>. The secesh cavalry or "Guerillas" are indefatigable & have come back on our hands – annoying us daily and nightly. Three days ago they burnt a transport (small one). Yesterday they got bolder and at the shoals burnt Three steamers & when our little Mosquito Gun boat went to protect them they took it (a little Tug with one big Parrott Gun) and burnt it. The river is so low that boats get stuck occasionally and cant run away, & so suffer martyrdom. But Glory be to God. It has rained a regular water spout for 24 hours and has snowed and hailed constantly for 24 hours more – is hailing heavily now – and freezing. All the creeks are up, so will the river soon. And there is six inches snow to melt here yet and perhaps 2 or 3 feet in the mountains. Skirmishing constantly in the front, weather is no obstacle to our Western boys whether South or North – rather an incentive to exercise. I wish they had some energy in the East.

I am with Love ever

Yours

Love

Hd. Qts. 8th Ks. Vols.
Nashville, Tenn.
Jany. 18th 1863
My Dear Molly

I have got through another week — and such a change since last. Then all was fragrant with the breath of Spring. Now we are in mid winter again and sleighs abound. Snow & frost are dominant. On Wednesday before day it rained — so did it all day, and all night again it rained & blowed as if the windows of the great deep were again opened or broken up! Which is it?

Thursday morning it turned to sleet & a West Wind, then to hail & frost and finally by night a heavy snow storm. It snowed all night & all day Friday, same on Saturday clearing up in the afternoon, with a fine frosty winters day sun. Last night a fog & south wind & today a fine clear cool winters day. Sleigh bells mingling with the Church bells while down every hilly street (and this city as near as I can count must be like Rome built on seven hills) the little boys go on sleds as if by steam, at the risk of their necks and everybody else's shins.

So we progress in the sunny South.

The Creeks are up. The River is up. The fleet of Steamboats are up. Even the Gun boats are up this morning, and only the Bridges are down. Washed away.

Rumor is busy!

Grape Vine intelligence is plenty. Reliable news is scarce, an embargo being placed by the storm on Telegrams & papers. What you are doing in the North & West we know not but we expect a large mail tonight or tomorrow morning. May! we not be disappointed!

It is said with truth I fear that two or three St. Louis boats were burned by the Guerillas on Thursday last as they went down the river while aground temporarily ere the rise reached them. A little gun boat went to the rescue & got burnt also. It was a mere mosquito affair, a flat boat or tug with an engine on board & a big Parrott Gun. Now we have the mammoth and thirty feet water and over 20 Steamboats arrived today alone.

Isn't Uncle Sam considerable of a wholesale merchant?

Wheelers Cavalry went in chase of Mr. Guerilla and he skedaddled leaving 50 prisoners in our hands.

So they run!

Well from the front there is but little news, and no movement, both sides are taking breath and repairing damages, and both are now blockaded by the weather and the creeks. Our Pioneers are rebuilding the lost bridges their Cavalry are shooting at them to prevent it! Their Pioneers are busy on other bridges. If their friends and protectors take their eyes off a moment or lay their arms down to eat, our cavalry swoops in & takes a few prisoners or leaves a few dead behind them. So the war lingers. Glory none? Death or captivity plenty! That is what the balance sheet shows! All!!

Nothing is said of the mud & the Snow & the Rain & the frost & the wounds, and the weary weary days & nights passed in pacing up & down, a target for every chance shot of the enemy, a chance of passing to the great unknown hereafter unknown, unhonored & unsung and all for 13$ a month perhaps – and patriotism. It is terrible. This destruction of Gods Gift Life!!

What does "Orpheus"[1] the sweet singer say in a late letter, so sweet I cant help quoting! Did you see it?

"Yes," says the Chaplain, as softly as though he was speaking in a sick room, "they remain there, sleeping upon their arms, And O! my friends, they will never, never come back again."

He spoke truly, my boy; "And may a Kind Heaven see naught in the blood welling from their loyal hearts but the blush of a Soldier's honor; the glow of a patriot fire in which all their human efforts went up to God as the smoke of a glorious sacrifice.

"They sleep their last sleep upon the arms of their country; And whether those arms, with which she folds them into her heart, be white with the

---

1. American humorist Robert Henry Newell wrote a series of satirical articles using the pseudonym Orpheus C. Kerr, commenting on the war. The articles, published as letters from O. C. K., were widely read in newspapers and books.

ermine of winter, or green with the drapery of summer, the clasp shall be none the less strong with all a Mother's immortality of Love.["]

O.C.K.

But a truce to epigram, and the Sentiment of War.

I am well as you will suppose, happy as I can be at this distance from you, hoping to see you the same – against hope I fear.

I went to Church this morning & enjoyed the quiet and rest of the service and the walk & freedom of out of doors, after near a weeks confinement to the tent. Most the Camp has gone to the Levee to see the arrivals this afternoon and I have peace & quietness to think of you and a tete a tete (in spirit) is the result.

Wont you send me greeting

Sweet words! Kisses? Eh!

Conversation requires two

I pause for a reply

With much love and <u>kisses</u> & remembrance to all kind friends

I am ever yours

James E. Love

Hd. Qts. 8th Ks. Vols.

Nashville Tenn.

Jany 22d 1863

My Dearest Molly

I wrote on Sunday as usual but there was such a dearth of news, I did not send it off. I waited for a letter, for a paper, for the Sutler, none came. Also for a photograph I had taken last week. I enclose it. I think of having some others taken in a different style. When I do so, I will send you another, and also supply some of the other folks.

Nothing of interest has occurred since then, save that I recd a letter from Alex dated 5th inst. and one or two *Democrats* of about same date. It has rained & blowed continuously – freezing at times, so much of the deep snow is gone but we have deeper mud instead. I have employed my leizure time in reading "Fantine" & "Cosseth", the two first numbers of the "*Miserables*", very strange works they are, about very miserable people. The ideas all very French, the work exciting, but full of politics & the social necessities of the age.

We are able to purchase most things here now, but all at enormous prices. Six dollars a bushel for Potatoes, one dollar a pound for Butter, 25 cts a pound for Beef and 15 cts for a Northern Paper of late date. I send papers occasionally to you, Alex & William. I hope to hear from you soon. I am well.

Any news from Jim Morris yet?

Will they continue house keeping? I am interested you know to a small extent!

The Armies are <u>quiescent</u>. Stuck in the mud you might say – encompassed by the floods.

Love and remembrance to you and all friends

I am My Dear Eliza

ever yours

Love

Hd. Qts. 8th Ks Vols
Nashville Tenn
Jany 25th 1863
My Dearest Molly

It is again Sunday afternoon, and I have got the blues. Whats to be done, a one sided argument, or a one sided conversation soon drags. I like to argue you know and also to talk, but I want just now to be contradicted or something of that kind in order to infuse a little life into me. Wont you kindly do it for me?

I have passed a dull week. So dull that I can not record it. We have had a fine day or two and the rest miserable wet ones. We have passed the life of an oyster by day, with scarce spunk enough to read the magazines & papers we got. And then at night had some long dull games of whist and so time lagged and still no mail for me. Others were more fortunate. Whats the matter?

No letters, No Sutler, No Packages and no news!

I know it aint your fault but what then? Why I've got the blues thats all!

You know I've got no patience and I just wish this horrid war was over! There!

We hear rumors of what you are doing North, & what the army is doing elsewhere, but it seems all as distant and unreal as if it were in another land and year altogether. We seem at the bottom of a well — and when we get a paper 5 or 6 days old such strange things do we some times see, that I can scarce believe this is the 19th Century and the threshold to the millenium.

Have you seen how the rebels are shooting any of our Niggers they chance to catch? Oh dear! We see and hear of from Eye witnesses such sights. Why we in the army & you in the North feel bad, but in the South, all but the favored few, aye & even they suffer at times almost the torments of the damn'd.

I have not mustered courage to go to Church today. I have scarce been out for a week, there is nothing but mud inside and out. I am pretty well. I hope you are.

I send you papers pretty often. I will send you todays *Union*, a spicy little sheet. It contains an Irish Poem addressed to "<u>My Wife</u>", very sweet read it. That is why I send the paper.

Although I say I wish the war was over – and so do all my confreres in danger, yet none of us, feeling as we do the cold shade of the revolution in politics brought about by half secesh "Democrats" wish to quit until the war is ended – that is until the south is well whipped and willing for the future to live in peace and quietness with us northern mudsills and foreigners. This war ends in glory to us or our bones bleach on a southern soil.

Good night

Love

More anon

Love

Hd. Qts. 8th Ks. Vols.
Nashville, Tenn.
Feby 1st 1863
My Dear Molly

Last Sunday I wrote the foregoing, and then I didn't like it, and threw it aside and waited for a letter day after day. None came and I had nothing to write, so as its all true as gospel, I send it along anyhow. In the meantime first I got the *I.L.N.* for Decr 27th. I read that. I knew it had left you within a week. I read even to the advertisements and so it filled up all the spare time of one day & evening. Next day I got the Christmas No. Decr 20th, better yet then 3 or 4 *Democrats* as late as Jany 23d and finally Alex's letter of the 16th inst <u>with</u> enclosure. So you see how the mail operates, letters as old as Christmas or New Years we haint got yet while those of a week ago come to hand in good time. I hope none of them got burnt or captured By the bye. If you read any of those Love Letters of mine the other day in that parcel I suppose I may look for the mitten first mail.

Well, now I'm overpowered. Your candy, smoking cap and note came to hand first, and then your notes of the 15th & 16th. Still I look for more when the mail gets sorted, for you must have written I doubt not between Christmas & the 16th inst & also since that. I see the latest you have recd from me is the 3d. I wrote also on or about the 10th & 17th & now I enclose the 24th with todays. I hope you'll receive them <u>all</u>, if they only call forth such a charming response as those of Christmas & New Years <u>have done</u>.

For the Candy, a thousand thanks, the pleasure in eating is equal to a <u>New Sensation</u> and it reminds me so of old times when I used to help Miss Anna, Sallie & you to demolish it!

As to the Cap I wear it as proudly as Aladdin did his wishing Cap. It distances all competition at present in this Army! But I thought you had enough to do, working for that Bazaar, without worrying yourself about me. I am only too proud & Gratified at receiving favors from you! I could never say No! But pray let Alex fulfill my commissions or I shall be afraid to trouble him with them, in future.

The Sutler and his goods are yet in St. Louis. He sent this with a friend who came on in the fleet of over 30 boats which arrived two days ago. It is said to be the finest sight ever witnessed when the two fleets, one going down of 20 boats & this one met just above Fort Donelson. There was 4 or 5 Gunboats & 8 or 10 Barges in tow and each fleet advancing in two lines – the upward bound one opened its ranks to either Shore of the narrow river, while the other passed through in succession like arrows from Robin Hoods bow while cheers resounded and Flags floated on the air and shortly after the rebels 800 strong with 6 cannon attacked them but were soon shelled out by the bull dogs along, numbers slain, the rest ran as if from the avenging angel and left the aforesaid cannon in our hands.

The Army here, is just as on the Potomac, stuck in the mud, both sides are being reinforced. We have very exciting rumors from Memphis & Arkansas. I hope they are founded on fact! We had some from the Potomac during the week but they ended in a mad storm. Weather here fine & frosty with clear moonlit nights for two days. The rest endless rain. It commenced again last night.

On Thursday night our Band went out serenading. It visited The Union – Gov. Johnson and some Union Ladies refugees from the South. Two of them especially young & pretty (17 & 20) risked their lives several times during the last months fighting to bring us information from Murfreesboro riding 30 or 40 miles of a day (<u>or night</u>) through the trackless paths of the woods & mountains in order to pass the rebel pickets, who would have shot her at sight for so doing.

For months ere they were compelled to leave Home they were <u>ostracised</u> to such an extent that their most intimate friends and relatives would not visit or speak to them. One had sang in the Church quoir, until last Summer when she got a note stating the other singers, Male & Female, would leave if she came again. She went a week or two after and all did leave. She remained and sang until service was over, & left to return no more. Yet <u>they</u> have a brother in the rebel army. Being asked if they would return again, they said probably after our army had driven the rebels out but that they had no ties in the South or in Tennessee, their native state, but a Fathers Grave! Their mother is with them – a Buxom dame of about 40, a very superior woman – worthy to have lived in the days of the <u>revolution</u> or of <u>Jackson</u>.

But are we not making history now faster than even Jackson or the Revolutionary Fathers ever did – and are not the men & women of this Revolution as Self Sacrificing and as Brave.

I trow they are! And there are records as bright as any in history made <u>by a few</u> in this war already. Some alas sleep the last sleep! But many very many of the sufferers <u>never see the battle field</u>, but suffer a thousand deaths in silence while the loved ones are gone – whether to return any more for ever they know not.

Love

Well! As I said I got yours of the 15th! I think I must preserve and cherish it? A letter after all is but a poor conveyor of thought!

It runs flashing through my brain at least, faster than I can talk it, much less write it, and so only half the argument gets on paper and that is liable to be misunderstood, wanting as it does the context!

I had an argument with myself, fancying what you say in reply, and so you get my assertions as to what I wish to prove, without the necessary explanations.

Interpret my letters in that way, and perhaps they will be easier understood.

The mood I am in (very variable you know) also influences them much, and I have been in low spirits for two or three weeks, everything combined to make me so (The weather. The horrid sights and sounds. The bad news from other points. The want of letters and papers for near a month – and probably a little Jealousy or disappointed ambition combined) but I am glad that I wrote after all. It has done us both good. You answer many queries that when I pressed or hinted at them verbally you only laughed at me or parried otherwise. Now its just so with me. That I am very much influenced by what others wish or approve. Of course I would wish to be even more so by you. I have at the same time a strong will of my own. I am both Selfish and unselfish.

Now if for want of a hint I should when undecided go and do something contrary to your opinion or approval, I should be irritated, & liable to wreak my anger on somebody else – myself being probably alone to blame.

Love of approbation! <u>large</u>!! You Know.

So as I say – your letter has done us both good. Let us talk more of the future and give me your ideas as often as possible of anything concerning your own welfare or feelings, my welfare or that of both, and so I can shape my course to meet your approbation & my own pleasure. Whereas I might otherwise merit your displeasure and my <u>own</u> on sober second thought, I often hesitate a long time and then act rashly at last. A chance word or hint decides. Wont you sometimes give that hint. It is the most delicate flattery you can bestow on me. And mind you – even then I in all cases decide for myself. <u>I blame no one</u> if it turns out badly. On the contrary, I take heart of grace and feel reassured that Ive done all for the best.

If I worry about anything it is while it is undecided. The reality – bad though it may be when settled, always take all the weight off my mind.

Good night Love

Pleasant dreams & waking realities.

Love

Feb 2d 1863

The greater part of it. It is impossible to answer on <u>paper</u> – and much it is not necessary to answer directly. The prosecution of the whole subject at present requires time & deliberation, circumstances imperatively compel that but <u>time</u> will solve it all perhaps sooner than we expect.

The pecuniary part is in embryo as yet. Two thousand dollars would cover it all. Not enough for a rainy day but twice as much as I hoped to save from the wreck a year ago.

I must fight this war out. I am bound for three years perhaps in that case – say a year & a half from now!

Must we wait so long? Circumstances permitting I would rather not!

Well then suppose I should wish to persuade you to California? (No Gold hunt) or Kansas? After peace & Union or <u>Separation</u>! and could prove to your satisfaction that probabilities were better. Would that be too far away?

A thousand ideas float through my brain at times. None can be fixed for some time!

They above are the most radical, & for that reason I present them for consideration.

If I should be able to get leave of absence for a few days in summer and we could then or before decide on a fixed course, then all energies could be brought to bear to make it successful. A strong will, finds a way. I have a strong will, but it has never for any length of time together been directed to money making and why?

Because though I am the most domestic of animals in my tastes, I have never had a home on which to lavish my love or energies. As an incitement a little comfort, and no ambition with much love of ease satisfied me. It shall not be so longer if you say so and I can concentrate my energies on any of the thousand and one plans or places that would suit your wishes or my own.

What Castles in the air have you built and how were they tinted & colored, where situated?

Very practical they've been I've no doubt.

Were they located in the City? on the Prairies of say Illinois or Kansas? or would a prospect of the Pacific with beautiful plains & hills in the foreground and the snowy Nevadas in the distance be more of a home picture?

I love the Sea!

Do not you?

With much Love to you & all my dear girl. I wish to take your advice & be decided as soon as I have the date fully before me on which to base an opinion.

Ever yours,

Love

Hd. Qts. 8th K.V.

Nashville Tenn.

Feby 8th 1863

Well Molly Dear

What am I going to say to you now? Here you have been talking like a sage railing at me, and now poking fun at me all in a breath! All I can say is I enjoy the fun! I hope you do! The sage talk flattered me, so I told you in my last, and as to the scolding you give me, I think Ive often told you I liked that. I may change as I grow older though, and by the way Im a first rate scold (so said) myself.

Well the fact of the matter is I dont know much of what I said in my last or any other after I'm through, unless its something of permanent importance, or even then I explained about that too, in my last.

My moods are contradictory. I know it, and I try to warn you of it, but I hope it is more in seeming and from a lazy habit of writing or speaking without thinking, than in action.

Your afraid not! Are you indeed? Well so much the worse for me and for both if I dont try to mend.

In sober earnest Molly Dear pitch in. Any faults you see in me, tell me. I dont wish any one else to do so, but you I do! Be my Mentor! And even when I try most ingeniously to prove myself right you'll find I'll try to profit by it more or less.

This time I give it up at once. I'm wrong! All wrong!

Well the war here is very hot, our troops are moving and gaining small successes daily. Theirs are teasing and annoying us much also. I suppose you've heard of the 2d Fort Donelson fight by telegraph. Well to day and yesterday again they tried it with the Gun boats and fleet at the Shoals. It is said we killed over two hundred again – anyhow they were repulsed with heavy loss and our fleet is here safe – about fifty boats.

They also made a descent on the railroad, but were there repulsed and we are driving them slowly South daily – so it goes and every little while we take a batch of prisoners or a lot of Tennessee conscripts come and give themselves up.

The great fight is approaching – and it will be in this Mississippi Valley somewhere – this spring. Not one perhaps but a dozen – and somebody of course will get whipped. I dont think it can be postponed longer.

Starvation & despair tugs at the vitals of one party. A nest of peace preaching traitors try to sap the courage, and drain the hearts best blood from the other. So those in power and in the field are desperate and at last in a hurry and the army must fight whether Victory or Destruction be the result! May God defend the right?

I got a *Harper* of the 22d Nov. some days ago in which I see we are illustrious. Well, its an ever true tale. Can those be the caricatures you spoke of? I suppose so. *Harper* has some rather horrid illustrations lately. I'm sorry to say that I can endorse them all to the letter, true too true. Save only the Bull Run Story of "finger rings", "drinking bowls", and other horrid mementos, of those I know nothing, and hope for the sake of the poor erring human nature it is not so! I could never believe it; and although I could now if I tried, I've seen worse far worse right here. Yet I dont want too. I prefer blot the page – if our wayward sisters would only come back.[1]

I got yours of the 25th ult. today, also papers of the 26th & 30th – thanks my dear girl. I got a couple of pamphlets from Mr. Kinnear anent the Pine St. Church. I haint read them yet, but promise myself the pleasure today after Church.

The mud is nearly deep enough to swim a Gunboat but I think I shall be among the worshipers, business permitting. It has snowed and rained all week – and froze hard one or two nights of dreadful North wind. I guess the Confeds in their dirty rags, filth and scant shoe leather suffered some! We did! with Uncle Sam's best hap.

Now it thaws, and the river & creeks are booming. Ive got over my fit of the blues! Cause as I said close confinement, & little to do, being compelled to kill time in fact.

---

1. The February 7, 1863, issue of *Harper's Weekly* included an article regarding atrocities committed by rebels upon dead Union soldiers after the First Battle of Bull Run in July 1861. These atrocities included disinterring the dead to retrieve the bones, then making rings from the bones and drinking bowls from the skulls.

It dont agree with my temper as well as marching. Whatever it may do with my health. I'm sure its injurious however, though in a different way. I had an accident, & came near being forced to have a couple of fingers amputated. I had a pen knife ran an inch into my hand near my little finger & it cut an artery that runs about there – it bled but little. I kept my finger on the little hole, but it was almost impossible to stop it without amputation or nearly so – more like dissection I should say I suppose – with the help of Ice water in plenty I got through without injury I think. That was only three days ago and it is all cicatrised and healed already! Good healthy blood you see. I always astonish the doctors, when I get my flesh cut or torn, by a sudden recovery. It is a little numb, from the wrist to the end of the finger, circulation impeded and it feels as if asleep yet, that is all – fortunate its no worse. Aint I? Life's uncertain! Warnings many! I believe I was as badly scared as if a shell had taken off half a leg in the field!

The fleet to day brought it is said 25,000 reinforcements for old Rosy. I hope so. He'll use them to advantage if any one can! Oh! He is so devoted to the cause, sublimely courageous too, counts his own life as nothing.

Well he is our hero!

I can tell you of a heroine. Our Major (Schneider) a good and devoted fellow, honest and independent & a warm friend, had a friend, a Captain in an Ohio Regt. who was engaged for some years to his sister, his name James Wallace. He got his knee mashed by a cannon ball at Fredericksburgh, but would not have it amputated for weeks. He was reported dying and she prepared to go to see him but ere she started news came he was better and she did not go, her father did. In about ten days it was seen that amputation must be performed, and as soon as she knew it, she went on, to nurse him and keep his courage up. She arrived early one fine morning in January and soon it was amputated and he was doing well in good spirits, but she found that she could not wait on him as she wished not being a relative or nurse – so in order so to do, she was married to him before noon same day. Sitting by his bed, by a Washington divine there at hand. All went well under her kind care until nightfall. Then she left for supper. Five minutes after, the nurse saw a spot of blood. The knot on the artery had given way, and he bled to death instantly, before either his newly married wife or the doctor could arrive. Such is life; such is one of the many tragedies enacted daily now in our distracted country.

Truly those who die on the field suffer least! Badly wounded are many whom bullet or bayonet never reach! Thus Maid, wife & widow in one day. She and her father took the corpse home to Ohio and from her fathers house there was the largest funeral in that section ever known! Is she not a heroine?

With much love my dear Molly to self and all

I am

Ever Yours,

Love

Hd. Qts. 8th Ks. Vols.

Nashville Tenn

Feby 15th 1863

My Dearest Molly

I yesterday rec'd yours of 11th Jany & of 1st Feby also I.L.N. of Jany 10th and a letter of Wm's still older (Jany 6th) not to speak of a large bundle of useful official circulars from Mr. Kinnear. Quite a budget for one day aint it?

It put your humble servant in good humor with himself and all mankind out of Secessia! How long will it last say you? Well not long if this rain lasts for as I write it comes down with undiminished severity and the South Wind howls and runs riot, playing queer pranks both inside & out the sloppy tents! Jupiter Pluvius as in weeks past has wept an uninterrupted succession of Scotch Irish and Irish Spring weather all week since last you heard from me, save Thursday which was cold & dry & Friday a balmy old fashioned May day. Such is life in camp at Nashville.

In the front they are scouting and fighting daily, principally Cavalry or Mounted Infantry and some few pieces flying Artillery. There is but little movement forward – cause mud – but the amount of work done is enormous and in a few months there will be but few Guerrillas of the thousands in this dept. left to tell the tale. Morgan, Forrest, Wheeler and all the other dogs, are being chased to death, and find much trouble in saving their scalps as they run from day to day, while their men and horses are being killed, captured & scared so bad that they desert by hundreds daily.

I have no doubt but you read with avidity all that emanates from Rosecrans in the shape of orders or correspondence, so I need not mention particulars. It is all worthy of perusal from its high literary excellence and statesmanship displayed as well as from the sentiments enunciated.

The news you get from here is meager, but is reliable generally. He allows no Newspaper correspondents nor other strangers about camp. What is written is from Soldiers and they do not generally write to puff their comrades or to make fictitious reputations or news. Their time is fully occupied and they write with eloquence often of what they do know! I see Frank Blair &

Granny Grant keep paid correspondents to fill your papers with their names (Oh Sugar.)

Yours of the 11th Jany explains many matters left rather dim before, and accounts for all missing links to date in your interesting narratives. Glad to hear of the well being of your Peoria relatives. And as to your apologies for neglecting me, pray say no more about it. I know better. You stand for all time excused of any such negligence. If I was only half so busy I know I should be more remiss! But even in a rush of duties there is compensation, for a hurried letter is often the most felicitous in terms and agreeable to receive!

You will perceive that your fears as to my being overworked are needless. It soon passed away – and had it lasted I would have been spared the worst fit of the blues I ever had lasting for weeks pure ennui! Cause idleness, mud, rain, bad news, no mail, & nothing to read! Thank heaven all is changed and now we are on the flood tide to fortune & victory I hope!

Your enclosures also to hand about McPheeters & poor Mrs. Morris & Alex's carto. which I return. It is very good but too pale & death like dont you think.

Thanks for your hints, all good! Is it necessary to reiterate that I wish you at all times & seasons to criticize. Offend me! Never! Never! though I may not profit! In this case. If I can resist the temptation of showing a love of a bonnet, (Hat) I mean – I will profit by them all.

Glad to hear of your welfare and that of all the folks. Specially Sallie, your mother and aunt. I wish I could improvise a good Valentine for you or the Young Lady mentioned, fortune favoring me. I may do so yet. The day nearly escaped me but I cant forget old customs nor pass them by without regret.

I am well

I see that four companies of our Regt. were in your city on the 6th inst "en route" to join us. Why they stop there or what detains them, I cant say. We have expected them for two months. I suppose they dont wish to come. Our work is too hard. Uncle Sam gets some value for his money. He dont get much from the Army of the Potomac or Mississippi.

Adieu with much love, my dear girl

Ever Yours,

Love

It has turned out a fine afternoon and we are just about to have a dress parade, which has been impossible since three weeks. I arrested since writing Capt. Herd for being late at Guard Mount so often, and if it is pushed to investigation, his numerous acts of carelessness will cause his dismissal, for the honor of the Regt. We would rather not, but he must turn a new leaf or take his fate. Will you accuse me of vanity if I say that had I been in the Co. it would never have happened. I used to drive him up like a lazy mule – and get the Co. ready for my own credit as well as that of the boys. My successor dont do so, but I believe is working for his dismissal, so as to promote his own interest.

I must close. I will tell you the result again

ever yours,

James E. Love

James refers to Molly's Peoria relatives, which included her brother, R. B. M. Wilson, a doctor in nearby Washington, Illinois. *R.B.M. Wilson.* From *History of Tazewell County, Illinois* (Chicago: Chas. C. Chapman & Co., 1879).

Hd. Qts. 8th Ks Vols
Camp at Nashville Tenn
Feby 22d 1863

My Dear Molly

I recd yours of the 8th inst. a few days since I wrote you last Sunday & now I propose to do it again. I cant go to church. There is a rain and wind Storm and mud is knee deep, so I must worship at home. We have had the usual spell of weather since last. Warm, Cold, Dry, Mud, &c. Yesterday it poured down and every thing is under water, no drains, creeks or river beds are equal to the occasion. Several teams drowned in the suburban <u>Streets</u>, and the Carriages yet half under water, stand as warning monuments of the <u>Flood</u>. Nary rainbow have we had yet, neither has the sun appeared so I suppose our forty days are not over yet, and we cant hope for the waters abating.

Two months since the Rebels here said God was on their side because it had not rained for six months and the rivers were dried up. Now they are dumb and like drowned rats in a cellar – while we the Vikings of the North, go with our Gunboats & provisions whithersoever we will – quite in <u>our</u> element – but almost smothered in the blessing. The Army is in a high state of preservation and good morale, never so enthusiastic as now. They growl at the mud of course, but lie at their ease by a good fire at times and look for a dry spell next month when they will go on conquering and to conquer. If Grant cant take Vicksburg, we will march to his assistance and Gobble up Bragg by the way. The great struggle approaches & God Defend the Right. I am well. I had one of my nervous headaches during the week, but that has left me better than before as I fasted until it left me and drank strong Tea. There is some rheumatism and Typhoid Fever among the men caused by wet clothes and wet beds on the ground, but that is an inseperable concomitant of an Army in the field, and is not remarked – though it usual kills and disables twice as many as bullets.

Friend after friend departs. Who has not lost a friend.

Poor dear Ann Jane! I am so sorry to read your news. Not for her. Oh No! but for myself and her friends in St. Louis and elsewhere. Aye & for the community, for it has sustained a loss for it she was educating herself. She was one after your own heart. I mentioned once before how much I wished you knew her – and she so young. A stern sense of duty & right, immense perseverance, high principalled, pure, honest and innocent of guile yet shrewd withal, and though very modest and retiring yet equal to any occasion or duty to which she felt called, very quiet, & observing, yet when encouraged & drawn out as I tried to do occasionally quite a fund of interesting conversation, & no vanity, by far the best of the family. Though Mrs. Forsythe is a superior woman, the Timid Elizabeth is an estimable one – and Mina is very winning & my pet. Pshaw! Its too bad. The good die first! So tis said – Why?[1]

Well. If I dont go out in front and chuck myself away against a secesh bayonet, I'll die of a good old age. Consumption in the blood eh? I dont believe it! Its an imported malady never heard of in the family until after I was born. All the old folks live yet or died afflicted with Gray hair – while their children and Grand children die ere their time.

As you say – who next? Death seems as busy in the North as in the rebel section!

I have just got a copy of a telegram from Rosecrans. Very good thing – and to the point, commemorative of the day – Sunday and Washingtons birth day. You will see it in the papers or I may send a copy. I have read it at 4 P.M.

We will have a celebration tomorrow also by the citizens. What is St. Louis doing. She surpassed herself last year?

I finished the 5th Volume of the "*Miserables*" last night. It is a splendid work – as far as science, essays & politics are concerned, is written with a good motive for the elevation of all mankind & the benefit of the race but it is very Frenchy, introduces much immorality and should not be read by young folks.

---

1. James's cousin Anne Jane Forsyth graduated from the Normal School in St. Louis in 1861 and became a teacher at the school the following year. She died on February 2, 1863, at the age of eighteen.

I am my Dearest Girl with much love to you & all
Sincerely yours
James E. Love
1st Lieut & Adjt.
8th Ks. Vols.

Oh you dissipated people. How can you? When all the nice young men are in the army living like Monks or hermits without the light of the smile of any feminine & especially of those they love? What a bore.

I never can endure daylight or Gaslight, or <u>society</u> any more after this twilight tent existence, besieged by those pertinacious Rebels rain & mud.

I'll never be fit for conversation no more I'm sure!

Love

Hd. Qts. 8th Ks. Vols.
Nashville Tenn
March 7th 1863
My Dearest Molly

I seize the first opportunity to write again after a fortnights wearing work. Yours of the 8th 15th & Sallie's of the 22d Feby are unanswered. I have just got one from E.A.W. too of the 28th ult. I believe I wrote last on Sunday the 22d inst. Well next day our long looked for Co's came to hand & we have now one of the largest regiments in the army whether old or new, about 700 men for duty, all of which makes a deal of work for the undersigned.

We had a great celebration on the same day (23d) & were out in procession – considerable speechifying and singing. Our band also contributed much to the music of the procession & meeting. We have a fine Volunteer Band in which we take great pride. I as "Adjutant" am manager, disciplinarian & Chief Boss. It is composed of enlisted soldiers in our Regt. & costs us only a little trouble, whisky money, Instruments & new music for the performers, and Uncle Sam nothing – cause he wont pay for any more bands. We have had one or two fine days since heard from but as a general thing the rains descended & the floods came, but we are camped on a high rocky hill and so our tents still stand. The Cumberland & creeks are high & half Nashville is or has been under water. Rain & snow unending. Weather colder than for a month past.

I found a U.S. horse, saddle & bridle on the 23d & advertised him, but have not yet found an owner. He is a good young horse & I hope his owner wont call – so I can have the use of him during the war. Uncle Sam can have him after that as in honor & honesty bound too. Officers who are entitled to horses, can get a U.S. horse from a Q. Master & use him as long as required, but not sell them.

These Co's that rejoined us had something like a mutiny at St. Louis and about 50 deserted while 50 more came here in Irons but are now on duty at their own repented & earnest petition. They claimed that they had enlisted as Kansas Home Guards – it is all settled now & has been kept quiet and out of the papers by order of the Genl Commanding, on account of the honorable name for discipline & good conduct that <u>our</u> Battalion has <u>acquired down here</u>. It was some unfortunate misunderstanding as the men are of the best class and ardent in the cause.

Their arrival caused an immense amount of writing – as both officers and men were unacquainted with our way ("Rosecrans") of doing things here, quite different I assure you from their loose Kansas ways. The Col. being "Provost Marshall" and the Major sick all fell on me but with the assistance of two clerks I pulled through. Then on Saturday last came our usual bi-monthly muster for pay – with all its flood of writing taking up most of this week & including a Review of our Regt. by Genl Mitchell, & several Dress Parades & drills, so as to become accustomed to one another.

I have chaperoned a squad of the strangers to the Theatre once or twice & also to the Minstrels.

Genl R. B. Mitchell takes the field within a few days and wishes to take us with him as soon as Co. G. arrives but his successor Genl. Stanley objects and I dont think we will be in any fight prior to the middle of April or 1st May but <u>its mighty onsartain</u>. Everything at the Front is as usual with Rosy energy and activity scouting & foraging – and with uniform success and numerous Prisoners up till yesterday, when our brigade was overpowered & captured by an overwhelming force of the enemy.

All this however is attributable to the treachery, cowardice or incompetence – whichever he pleases of Genl Gilbert who has just arrived down here, and shown his usual stupidity or treason.

He it was that commanded our Corp. D. Armee from Louisville to Crab Orchard & back to Lebanon & to whom was largely due our disaster at Perryville & our want of brilliant success at Lancaster where Genl Mitchell had Morgans Brigade & a large wagon train almost surrounded (I wrote you of our skirmish in the evening & charge through the town & chase next day) when he ordered us to retire and not bring on a general engagement, & so gave them all night to prepare & run away. We lost about 700 to 1000 men in killed & prisoners.

You will hear stirring news as soon as the mud permits & especially if "Bragg" sends any Cavalry into Kentucky as he threatens to do.

What shall I say about that Spring St. affair. I dont know. I cant understand – besides had I not the Volunteer assistance of the said James & John Adams and their lawyer in examining title. Certainly I had – and if there is any fraud or loss about it – they have been more fooled than I was as they had had it in their eye for months before I came to town, and wished to purchase, but thought it w'd pay better to lend to me at 10 percent with all the profits of the building added. I aint a bit sorry. I wouldn't pity or bemoan myself if I was in their place – neither do I believe any body else in the business world would pity either me or them.

I am very much disappointed on account of my own future & yours for I had begun to calculate about St. Louis again. I always put it first you know & would live in it by preference when possible and as I said, I was looking about the ways and means to make it possible.

Now I dont know what to think.

I must congratulate Sallie on her great responsibilities. I had as I said an answer to my Valentine from her dated the 22d in which she states you are unwell – with a bad cold. Dear Girl Do take care of yourself. After these late parties with Hot air & dancing a night walk in the wet streets wants a good warm wrap & thick shoes at least – for the strongest constitution – much more so yours! Do so for me!

The mail is about to close, & I wish this off. So with warmest love & wishes to you my Dear girl & all friends.

I am in haste
Ever yours
James E. Love

Hd. Qts. 8th Ks. Vols.
Nashville, Tenn
March 22d 1863
My Dear Molly

I have procrastinated until I feel mean and guilty. I have allowed many little obstacles to prevent, when a strong will would have made a way & a time, & so I wont offer any excuses.

I got yours of the 7th about a week since, with enclosure.

Since last I wrote, we have been much as usual, with some fine weather for a change. Some have been luxuriating in the breath of summer as if the veritable June or September had come – but the buds & flowers & Green leaves are wanting. The grass is growing & today I saw the first blossoms of the Peach, so the spring is nigh.

I have not seen a flower save a bouquet the Colonel got up to yesterday when I got a small one tastily got up with red white & blue ribbons and flowers myself.

We are neither in the city nor the country, and the desolation & devastation caused by a large army of men & mules & wagons has caused nearly every green thing to disappear for some miles around, so I cannot snuff the breathe nor enjoy the beauties of spring as I did on the free prairies of Kansas. I am going to take a ride tomorrow perhaps I may make discoveries. I require it for I have been far too closely confined to tent life lately. I prefer roaming even when I walked, & now when I can ride, why I wish to move again. Twas said for some time past, that we would move to Franklin this week – but it is now said by the first of May we go to Columbia instead. Gossip I suppose. We shall see! The rivers are falling fast & the swamps draining – but this with warm weather has already brought much sickness. 50 new cases in our camp in a week – out of less than 300 men – a great deal of lung disease & Camp Diarhea – with some measles, Typhoid fever & congestion of Head, Lungs or liver.

I got some *Republicans*, & three *I.L.N.* from you within a day or two. Our British brethren are very severe on us still, but until we have a few more successes in the field we must grin & bear it. As soon as we have, our friends will be legion – are now growing in numbers.

Nice young men seem to be plenty in St. Louis. They are more favored than their brethren in the country, where they are cut by old & young if not warmly engaged on either side. There are no young men in the <u>south</u> – even the boys & old men are in the army. I hope the lists of deserters we are sending home to the Provost Marshalls in every town & county of the Union (<u>both officers & men</u>) & the <u>conscription</u> will change all that & put many of the cowards, shirks and swindlers who have taken government money, <u>with an oath</u>, into the army again, instead of sunning themselves at home against law, justice & morality.

The Army in the field calls loudly every day for the shooting of deserters, and the President promises to do so after 1st April. We have just completed our lists with a full description of every mans eyes, hair &c &c &c with his friends names, their residence his former residence his place of birth &c &c &c. All will be published, and their names gibbeted to the scorn of the world for ever with a chance of their being shot if found for 20 years to come. So Shoulder Straps & nice young men must look out.

Glad to hear of all them beaus, especially colonel – with town & country houses. Were I in your place, I dont think I could say no! Such are objects of honest ambition with all young ladies, of dishonest with some – and with all matchmaking mamas. Sorry I cant compete. I've waited four years to do so – shall I give it up. There is small prospect left of success.

When you've made up your mind let me know. For the present I dismiss the subject, until you send me your <u>cards</u>. The three small children I overlooked. I dont think you would undertake that part of the contract unless they had near & dear claims on you. I needn't explain further.

If you wish to strip the shoulders of some officers just give me a call, & I may allow you as a special favor. I have one or two jobs on hand – and some reprimands in front of the parade to make.

You can tell me anything or all you wish, under a charge of secrecy – depend on me – but as to this matter of 9th & Spring – Ive waited & scanned the papers but can see nothing & cant understand. My curiosity is excited. Otherwise I have no feeling in the matter – out of sight, out of mind. Glad I made the old man take it then – if he'd only got a few more papers on it & me I w'd have been his slave for life.

I haint had that photograph taken yet – cause want of funds. We merely live to eat & eat to live at present. Uncle Samuels green backs haint visited us for over seven months. Hope to hear from him next week – and then we'll have a pocket full of rocks again. The war progresses slowly southward – little fights daily. If I live two or three months longer I'll apply for a leave of absence – by that time I hope to have a claim that cant be refused. Heavy fighting & hot weather are before us. Who knows what may come of it. A little northern air will be useful anyhow – and now My Dearest Girl

With Love to you & all – cousin Wm. included

I am as ever,

Yours

James E. Love

James mentions the effects of "a large army of men & mules & wagons" on the grounds of his camp at the capitol building in Nashville. His camp probably looked similar to this one in Nashville a year later. The State House, Nashville, Tenn., 1864. National Archives photo no. 111-B-4732.

Hd. Qts. 8th Ks. Vols.

Nashville Tenn

March 31st 1863

My Dear Molly

I am still at Nashville notwithstanding your supposition to the contrary. "Man proposes God Disposes". So says the proverb. I have started to write half a dozen times and the press of business every time prevented. Now business must wait an hour while I bid a hurried Good Evening. Sunday or Saturday it has been all the same for over two weeks, and the overstrain & confinement has even made me sick – not of importance now; though it might have been & some of my best friends here have succumbed. Hale & Hearty they were to all appearance, <u>which I am not</u>, they withered like a leaf in the fall. This is the sickly season here in the Army at least; & I could not expect to escape altogether but fear not, my lifes insured, and I am coming home as soon as the war's over, as grey as a rat just to plague you.

Now I have had my little growl and apology I can come to particulars.

Its just so. Ive been under the weather – Liver &c, but I had to write & figure 5 or 6 hours up to 12 hours a day all the same, my business was in just such a snarl nobody else could do it, & it couldn't wait but that is past! Its all for glory you know?

I have had a horse for six weeks & rode him only three times yet, not much practice, considering how much I require it! Eh.

I have had a boquet or two notwithstanding & the early trees are just beginning to show their finest tints, some willows weeping & others are clad in the mildest of green.

The weather has been cold for March, but quite in character, blustering & raining, next day dust, very severe on tents. Our Regt. is united at last & we can show about 700 men – over 100 of them sick however.

This is the main cause of my labors at present & will soon cease.

We have been enlivened some by the presence of the Paymaster, who kindly paid us six months back dues on Saturday last. Preparing the rolls gave me much solicitude, as I had to see it all done correctly by over two dozen clerks – all at work for a week & so I can now sport some new clothes & hope to accomplish that Photograph first fine day.

I am your debtor in the meantime for two letters & much love & kindness. More than my crabbed nature can ever repay you I fear. I hope you have since got the letters you thought lost. I have been fortunate lately in getting all yours, sooner or later generally later. There was not much in it however!

We are again disappointed in respect to moving from here. General Mitchell can not be spared from here yet, & he will not spare us. We have a mutual affection for one another which will be beneficial to both – for reasons – among the rest – "<u>Rosecrans</u>" esteemed "<u>Mitchell</u>" – but the mud is drying up & we are all from "Rosy" down putting our houses in order for hot work in the sunny South as soon as the roads are practicable. We are just now employed in driving all "Secesh" south before us unless they give bonds on bonds & oaths on oaths & even that we do not allow <u>known Secesh to take</u>, but exchange them for Southern Union men in durance vile in the South & confiscate their property for the profit of Uncle Sam. Rosecrans intends to leave none but true blue behind him in this Department & "Burnside" will soon do the same for Kentucky as "Sumner" would have if he had lived for Missouri.[1]

The World moves & I hope more from day to day. Two or three terrible fights and then an end.

The very idea of that conscription will scare out the starving wretches opposed to us. Once the boasted chivalry of King Cotton, worshipped of all the Earth – now the most louzy ragged hungry set of demons you ever imagined & none so poor as do them reverence except for their national heir loom – Anglo Saxon pluck & endurance – base – yet <u>brave</u> sons of noble sires.

Tomorrow's "All Fools Day". Would I could play some pranks on you and Sallie.

---

1. Nashville residents had to take an oath of allegiance and pay a bond to insure the oath, or leave the city. As James explains, known supporters of the Confederacy were exchanged for Union men imprisoned in the south.

When I go to writing I go to thinking. I dont do much of it just now at other times on my own affairs and I go nearly crasy over the idea of a furlough to see you all once more – then I forget it again until next week & so time flies but I cant imagine what I would do – even I was in St. Louis to pass the time – unless I could be in your presence or close proximity & devour you with my eyes all the time. That wouldn't do would it? I'm afraid you aint ready for the denouement of such a catastrophe &c &c. You can fill out the picture & "Phansy My Pheelinks" – if you will – a man without a particle of patience beating the "devills tattoo" around one – whom he believed to be patience personified &c.

Always glad to hear of your dissipating & the gossip attendant but <u>pray my dearest love dont shut down on the little morsels you send me</u> – remember I am prudence personified – perfectly <u>mum</u> unless when you are around, & then I tell everything – but I promise to be a good boy & tell nothing for the future, & if you wont do everything I ask you too – just send me a flower in every letter & I'll forgive you.

Dont you think its nearly time though for us to have a big quarrel? I fear for the future if we dont have one soon! Just wait till I come to St. Louis & see if it dont come to that? Pshaw! I love your jokes, your fun, your scolding, or even your finding fault! I could not believe you honest & sincere if you didn't, for God knows I deserve to be found fault with often so dont make any apologies for your jokes.

I received about 40 papers, *Democrats* & others, within the last few days that had accumulated somewhere. Some from you also & a pamphlet. I send some papers – in the <u>Union</u> you can see much of us, as Genl Mitchell & our Regt. have a hand in every thing here & help to make all the local news. It seems more a part of us – more a Home paper at present than the "*Democrat*" or its compeers can be to a St. Louisian. It is our mouth piece, the voice of the Army of Rosecrans & Mitchell.

I have not been to New Zealand or the Chinchas but I was as near to them both as Belfast is to Glasgow – or St. Louis to Chicago. Closely connected in business & at this distance it almost seems to me as if I had been there & knew every green bay – every gold bearing river or grassy pasture of the one – the Queen of the South, as Britain is of the North & every rocky Egg & Guano covered bluff of the other, with its countless millions of water fowl & <u>divers</u>; Clouding the skies & covering the waters by day, & the rocks by night! And the Prince of Wales too is off the Hooks! Well I'm sorry for him! He wore such a shocking bad hat when in St. Louis, that it must have injured his eye sight! & he couldn't see <u>perfection</u>? Will that account for it? Dear me? How great events from little causes flow. Castles in the air versus Windsor Castle.

Castles in the air are for the most gorgeous you know. I take consolation? Do you?

How can McPheeters & those Secesh, sit & hear such heretical & political preaching as you must have now? There can be no religion in such action – no good motive that I or the world can see.

I would scorn to do it even were it a political or commercial row! In religion there is supposed to be some conscientious scruples left. In this case I dont perceive any!

Your billet doux of the 22nd to hand yesterday.

Im looking for another directly as the 29th has already faded into the future of misused Sabbath – unless you intend to come down & Surprise us – as did the young lady whose marriage is illustrated in a *Harper* I've just seen – to a Capt. (I wish I was a Capt) in the 7th New Jersey in Hookers Camp. Wasn't that gay? Give me a weeks notice; for we are not in daily communion with Washington & New York as are the aforesaid but out west in what was once the Sunny South but is now a desert, where potatoes are 10 cents a lb Eggs 60 to 75 cents a dozen. Common marketing not to be had for money & even Uncle Sam's boys who are well paid & fed are perishing for the want of it.

Our mess with a table as bare as poverty – stares at an expense to each daily at a Dollar.

I have filled this nearly with nonsense & so I'll go & read the papers & see if I can find any news to conclude with tomorrow. I've had so much to say at times – but I've forgotten it all & it wont come back to your afflicted correspondent at the late hour of 11 P.M. so Goodnight

Love

April 1st

What have you got to sing up North? Any new songs? The only thing sung by the Army is the "Battle Cry of Freedom" – "The Kingdoms Coming" and the "John Brown" Song. The first has created a perfect <u>furor</u>, everybody sings it at all times & places. Companies sing it; Regiments sing it; in camp & on the march. It seems as if it was the very echo of their <u>thoughts</u> or <u>wishes</u>, amid the excitement caused by the copperhead news we have got lately. Our band plays it! Of which by the bye, I am <u>boss</u> or director. I have a very good musician as leader, a hard working enthusiast, and it is now increased to 12 brass instruments, 3 fifes, 4 Bugles, 6 Kettle Drums, 1 Base Drum & <u>Cymbals</u>. Quite a force. When we have it all out, it forms two bands & plays alternately.

Today I am very well – No news – dreadful stormy weather. I have got a keg of beer & am proceeding to feed myself as per orders received from the Doctor. I have been down town & purchased some magazines – shoulder straps – New Hat &c &c &c including spurs. I have worn your "straps" every day almost to date. They are most as good as new yet and now I must go dress for Dress Parade.

I am with much love to you, Sallie, your Mother &c &c

Sincerely yours

James E. Love

1st Lieut.& Adjt.

8th Ks. Vols.

Hd. Qts. 8th Ks. Vols.

Nashville Tenn.

April 10th 1863

My Dearest Molly

You are a Jewel – and deserving of better treatment than I give you in my letters (more thought should I say) yes for better than my excitable temperament, would allow me too if present with you. One thing I'll tell you – that if more exacting – you would fare better. Know that the most exacting ladies are usually the best treated in this lazy, careless, selfish world – of which (world) I am a notable specimen.

I rec'd yours of the 22d March some days since and of the 30th yesterday both a long time "en route".

We are still at Nashville and as Bragg is largely reinforced, we look for a fight hourly. As I write news comes in of Guerilla raids on the Murfreesboro R. R., on the Louisville R. R., on the River and some hard fighting near Franklin. I sent out an hour ago 4 Companies to scout around & to go on the cars to the scene of disaster and see what is the matter. I was the only staff officer in camp when the order came from Genl Mitchell & had the boys & officers out on the <u>run</u> within five minutes thereafter.

If we go on the march or in the field, I will have more news for you – and more time to tell it than now and you will hear from me oftener instead of the reverse.

I will resume my tete a tetes at every halt by day or night as I used to last fall. Now I am over run with business. I expect to be relieved of part the pressure within a week – as it is ruining my health. <u>Then</u> I will have a ride out every day weather permitting <u>I hope</u>! So much my dearest Girl for yours of the 22nd.

And now as to that of the 29th March. Your presentiments are at fault, except that I have been an invalid from confinement – and unsuitable diet. I am in no danger from infectious diseases. That is to say – Not more than you or your brothers are in a large city. Dont be skeered for me. I never was half so safe – since I entered the army. No News from me is good News – for if anything happens you will hear by "Telegraph" – and besides I always keep my papers so arranged that a letter I have had written in my pocket over six months would go to <u>William</u> at once.

I got your paper of the 27th inst. with a fleet of others long delayed in the mail & so I overlooked Miss Kings marriage until yesterday!

Consolation is useless!

You dear girl, I wont laugh at you: but cease your anxiety! I am as safe from disease or death as in St. Louis. With Gods grace & permission more so.

You will see by my last letter that I had much the same thoughts about coming to St. Louis, its awkwardness &c, as you have had, but where else <u>could</u> I go & I ought to have a trip soon to restore the balance of my brain.

The only way to solve the difficulty would be an immediate marriage!

It would be the best!

But I am not prepared to recommend it!

Neither am I in a position to insist on it!

My position in the army is a small matter. Money would make that right. The difficulty to my view is pecuniary. I cant build that country house yet. You have the right to decide it!

I send ($400.00) Four hundred Dollars to William yesterday to use for me as before. I hope it got through safe. I must enquire in the morning! But my luck has changed since I entered the Army. I have no fear for it.

As you say! St. Louis has little claim on me – <u>only you</u> – and if I understand you you are willing to leave it with me at a future time.

Only my dear old Aunt Adams & perhaps my Cousins "Forsythe" do I care for as relatives.

I have many other dear friends in the city. If I was not too lazy to cultivate them.

I wish to be remembered to your Mother, Aunt & Sallie. Tell Sallie I was asking after her & David.

No more to night, peace & quietness reigns, so I'll to bed.

With kindest love and kisses dearest
Sincerely yours,
Love

April 12th

This cheery message hasn't skedaddled yet, so I begin again. I am yet in the land of the leal, business is brisk with us, I mean fighting business and patrolling, arresting drunken and dis-reputable officers & men.

Our companies came back all safe. News much exaggerated. We had the best of it at all points, but nothing to brag of as they skedaddled before we could hurt them much. You'll see a good deal of it in the papers – not all – 50 of the prisoners we took were citizens of Nashville. Our men brought in the wounded & saved the wreck as far as possible. Yesterday was quiet so far as heard from. Today there is more fighting and General Mitchell sent out at dusk a large train of ammunition, with one of our companies (50 men) to guard it, a dangerous business.

The "Eighth" has seen much bloodshed however, & has had nobody <u>killed</u> in their ranks yet, though many have been wounded & one or two disabled for life. We have been so lucky, most all the boys think as I do – that we bear charmed lifes. They say "God takes care of the Jayhawkers" – "The rebs all run away from us". We have passed often times where fighting has been before us, rebels all around us, often enough to gobble us up, but we passed safe through, & those who came after us were butchered. You can recollect numbers of places by name – and the last two instances I have just hinted at. On Friday 20 of our men went to Louisville. The train that followed them was fired into & destroyed.

Two companies I sent 12 miles out to Murfreesboro same day – 70 men only. The rebs had taken the train after a hard fight, burnt it, released 40 prisoners we had, took about 80 of our men prisoners – but when our little squad (the Eighth) came along – They ran like devils & left all their wounded over 20 in their hands – several of them killed, nobody hurt in our squad. The rebs actually shot two of their own men dead in the haste to get away; so we expect the company sent out tonight to Franklin back safe as usual – and will keep on daring & expecting like good luck until some fine morning we will be most awfully undeceived! I had a fine ride around the city & forts after being to church, both last Sunday afternoon & this along with Col. Martin & others. Today we called at a fine Union house where they have a fine conservatory, grapery &c &c & quite a botanical Garden for Nashville.

Some good looking young ladies, & one superb widow showed me around, & explained all the outdoor arrangements, down to asparagus & flower beds, then the Greenhouse, her birds, paintings &c &c. She has quite a studio & is really a good artist in oil color. Two hours passed easily with us all – and we left delighted but you see the widow would persist in taking me under her wing – Southern Chivalry too. She promised me a boquet & I've promised her a serenade. The Col. has got & given the same promise to & from one of the younger sisters. Major Schneider ditto with another. While Cap. Conover won golden opinions from the old man – their father. It would not be worth relating perhaps if we were out of Secessia & in some civilized country, but here it is like meeting the one just man in Sodom.

We had a nice parade this evening & quite a number of ladies to see us; among the rest the feminines of Gov. Johnsons household. And when I came off the Parade, what should I find but your favor of the 7th inst. Tuesday last. It came quick & safe for a wonder in these troublous times. I suppose my cash went through likewise.

I'll send you some more papers tomorrow & you must read them too, for there is much in them, and they are also "Eighth" Kansas institutions. If I wasn't a very modest young man, I would have my name put in too.

Flatterer I wont call you a witch; but I'll say you must have kissed the Blarney Stone. Dont fear the Beer barrel. I love a glass of beer dearly; but after one or two, I would as soon drink "Epsom Salts". Whisky I've quit for the present. Cigars I did quit, but Ive begun again, since Ive had some money. Now you know as much as I do myself. And I'll take a glass of beer for the Stomach's sake – an excellent tonic you know and I'd rather look like a dutchman than a lean lantern jawed Yankee.

We begin to need rain here also – so dry are the winds though the floods have scarcely subsided, & the mud is only skimmed over, and is soft as ever six inches down I find. I guess I had better write to "Sandy" or else retire so goodnight love.

Kiss me good bye – but say not farewell.

Sincerely yours,

Love

Hd. Qts.

8th Ks. Vol.

Nashville Tenn

April 16th 1863

My Dearest Molly

Since I wrote last all is quiet on the "Potomac"? We have had rain & spring has come in earnest. I wish I was in the woods to enjoy it or even in your 9th St. garden that "Alex" says is so much improved. By the bye I had that letter from him to day.

I wrote him two days since also. I envy you all your drives and flowers & glowing tete a tetes – though he says – Three is better company! Who ever heard of such a thing? Whats the matter with the young man? look after him or he'll do something desperate, not to say susaucide?

I'll give you on next page a piece of new poetry, the imagery of which your sea side education will I have no doubt cause you to appreciate; consider it dedicated to you, on the occasion at least.

We had yesterday a rather pleasant parade through the city. All went well, and everybody looked well, won golden opinions in fact from critical & curious eyes with the exception of when we were being presented to Genl R. B. Mitchell & Suite, when the noise & crowd of men, teams & horses, prevented the proper hearing of orders, and the manual of arms looked badly because not done "all together." The undersigned looked his best, & had a well behaved good looking horse which helped <u>much</u>! The Colonel and I headed the procession of course and were the cynosure of all eyes. I felt easy for once in my life under such circumstances, and so returned gaily to camp with bows from carriages and handkerchiefs and flags waved from doors, not to speak of certain strong minded rebel females who resolutely turned their backs on the show, & would none of it, but worked away at their <u>fancy work</u> as if we were but spectral phantasms, & "<u>they</u>" neither saw nor heard us; I could do naught but laugh at them, and they only punished themselves as but few observed their <u>martyrdom</u>.

We are having a warm spell just now, the first breath of summer, ere spring has come. The apple trees are all covered with blooms, some late peaches still retain all their wealth of color. The first lilacs have just partly opened and I have a boquet most as large as a half bushel right at my nose much of it sweet scented lilacs but also others more gaudy. I cant name them just now. The boys gathered & fetched it to me this morning. They have also brought several wagon loads of young cedars and other evergreens & planted them in camp each by his tent door and it already relieves the white glare of the tents & the limestone very much. I am very well at present, and if we finally get some old fashioned April or May weather will be better but even the summer heats in Dixie suit me better than winter & mud – hard labor & close confinement, in a dark tent with wet wood in the stove and its noxious charcoal fumes. So mote it be!

I have just rec'd yours of the 13th this moment, also Williams of the same date. Mignionette very sweet! Sweet as my ladies breath! I kiss it!

My letters have no regularity as today, but I send one a week and even allowing for irregularity of mails, you should get them in that way. I hope you'll take your summer trip whether Sallie does or not, and leave care and the sewing machine behind you. You require it I know. Where possible though keep away from barrack like hotels of the Saratoga Pattern, and give a preference to Nahaut, Long Beach & the ocean breezes.

I had my long talked of Photograph taken yesterday. I fear its a failure – in the first place my hairs too short. Secondly, just at the decisive moment he told me to close my lips. I will show my teeth you know, and I think it looks constrained. It is taken "en Vignette." I wont get it for two weeks or more, and if I dont like it, I'll make him try it again at half price.

Love!

Sunday Night 10 P.M.

All goes well, but I haint got this dockyment off yet. Oh it was so warm yesterday during the night a heavy thundergust & much rain, since which the thirsty Ground drank up and all nature smiles. A very dull day in camp, until evening when the sun shone out warm & clear. We had a bully dress parade, & many visitors, military celebrities, ladies & others. We have got our house in order – expect a fight, troop are moving in all directions – so look out for squalls. We stand fast, or do a little scouting as necessity may require. We are as usual not included in the general plan of attack or defense, but in case of extreme necessity, we rally on. The Capital depend on us and Rosy. I guess its only a big scare, as far as Nashville is concerned – but a fight is a necessity.

So good night, with love & remembrance to yourself, Mother, Aunt, Sallie &c

I am as ever

Yours sincerely

James E. Love

MY SHIP!

Mist on the shore, and dark on the sand,

The chilly gulls swept over my head.

When a stately ship drew near the land,

Onward in silent grace she sped.

Lonely, I threw but a coward's glance

Upon the brave ship tall and free,

Joyfully dancing her mystic dance,

As if skies were blue and smooth the sea.

I breathed the forgotten odors of Spain,

Remembered my castles so far removed,

For they brought the distant faith again

That one who loves shall be beloved.

Then the goodly galleon suddenly

Dropped anchor close to the barren strand,

And various Cargoes, all for me,

Laid on the bosom of my land.

Oh friend! her Cargoes were thy love,

The stately ship thy presence fair;
Her pointed sails, like wings above,
Shall fill with praises and with prayer.

Love

Hd. Qts. 8th Ks. Vols.

Nashville Tenn

April 25th 1863

Molly Dear

Suppose I commence a letter about nothing this fine Saturday afternoon. What have you got to say about it. All I can say is nothing new except a new camp, where we have a glorious pine & cedar plantation, & every man can sit under his own "pine or cedar tree," which is the nearest approach to the Millennium or the land of Judea we expect to approach while on this side "Louisiana or Georgy", where we will make bold to have a vine & Fig tree apiece, if Uncle Jeff permits.

I wrote to William & Alex, & now I am quits with all my correspondents. I am ready to march again. Our army is moving. It has occupied McMinn-ville, within the limits of East Tennessee, an important strategic point, without any incidents save the usual weekly list of Deaths, wounds, or capture on both sides.

We are doing a lively business in sending Secesh South, strange to say they dont like it, want to go North – so we compel them to visit their friends.

Any Ardent spirits in St. Louis that want a free pass & trip to Dixie, now's their time to apply, recommend them to visit Nashville & the 8th will attend to their case and kindly forward them to the clime so congenial to their souls. Copperheads[1] preferred as the most poisonous reptile of the two.

We have a new excitement to day, arresting everybody who wears military clothing without being in Uncle Sam's service. "Rosy" shoots all the Rebs he finds with arms in their hands and Uncle Sam's Clothes on. That is how "they" have been spying out all our doings & shooting our pickets, wolves in sheeps clothing, so to prevent mistakes neither friend or foe must wear our uniform unless in the ranks of Freedom.

White slavery here is the most horrid feature of the trade after all. I could give numerous stories to point a moral, but I will only enclose within a few

---

1. The term copperheads referred to Northerners who opposed the war and the abolition of slavery, and favored immediate peace.

days a photograph of a protogee of mine and some other Officers & let the little maids face speak for her, <u>trumpet tongued</u>. Her Mother is as white as any French Brunette in St. Louis. Her father an estimable citizen & member of the church <u>owns both</u> & lives in a palatial mansion, all right so far – but when death or disaster reaches him his slaves go to the auction block &c, &c. Alongside our camp also lives a daughter of the chivalry – poor white trash I suppose. Her husband a mulatto slave who owns his own time, and has grown up daughters as white as I am. Peachy complexion, fashionably wavy hair, good looking & well dressed. I helped to rescue one of them from insult & abuse two or three nights since. Such is slavery. Verily it is the sum of all villanies.

April 27th

Have passed a very pleasant Saturday & Sunday numerous visitors & time passed. To day down town on various business & found the streets thronged with parties rushing to take the Oath e'er the day of grace is past. It is comical & amusing to see them swallow this nauseous Yankee pill & swear its by their own free will.

I read last week a splendid story to my mind in "*Harpers Monthly*," "For Better For Worse" in the March, April & May Nos. 3 parts.

I recd two or three numbers of the *I.L.N.* since I last wrote. The prince & illustrations has not yet sickened me but the leading article on 1st page of last number was so stupid a misrepresentation of the origin & principles of our government, such as any schoolboy with reading propensities could controvert that I fear <u>it also</u> has fallen from grace & joined our enemies. <u>It</u> has made me sick. I must close it until it repents amongst our false or "Copperhead" friends.

It is excessively warm here to day – threatens rain. I can hear the deep mouthed music of the cannon somewhere down the river at <u>intervals</u> – don't know whats the matter, not much I suppose. And now my dearest girl with love now & forever to your sweet self and remembrance to all friends.

I am,
Sincerely,
James E. Love

James expresses his feelings on white slaves in the area. They probably looked similar to these children from a series of photographs circulated by abolitionists in the 1860s. "Rebecca, Augusta, and Rosa, emancipated slaves from New Orleans." Photograph by Kimball, 477 Broadway, N.Y., c. 1863. Library of Congress, LOT 14022, no. 121 [P&P].

Hd. Qts. 8th Ks. Vols.

Nashville Tenn.

May 3d 1863

Molly Dear

Tis a dreamy summer afternoon, and though still in the "land of the leal" I would visit you in spirit and present you as oft. before "The Master Key"! (For explanation read last poem in "*Harper*" for April.) The merry month of May has come around again. It smiles so far however mixed with April Showers, makes all nature delightful at last.

I am well and doing well as usually reported in an "Ameriky letter".

I wish I had some news to write, but all is prosaic stenogtyped business, exciting and interesting while passing, good for gossip these moonlit evenings, but impossible to pen.

I wish I could Photograph our camp for you – but our artist has left the service – been discharged like thousands of other patriots for disability contracted on duty and is now at Chicago. But as the next best thing I send my own ugly phiz so long looked for and talked of; even now I have only got one or two, and cant get more for a week. If they are any better I will send you another for exhibition.

Movements in the army are innumerable and with good results, but nothing decisive and no general engagement. Bragg & Co have all run away again, and we do not choose to follow them, (as they wish) on the direct road. Our troops have rode around them however and together with the Gunboats are 200 miles in their rear at Florence Ala. The rats around here are deserting the sinking ship. In other words, there is a tremendous rush to take the Abolition Oath by known rebs who give bonds "heavy" – and pray to be sent "North" if we wish not "South."

We live well now, vegetables & every thing plenty, but it costs nearly as much as a first class hotel.

So ended the first lesson and I went asleep to be waked by your letter of the 27th ult. just a week on the way. Glad to hear you are able to enjoy yourself. I haint been into any mischief. You've been reading the papers and supping at 6th St. or reading one of my letters where we expected a fight which didn't come off. When you have turned every thing out of doors, just waltz once or twice round the parlor for me, & drill a little & get Sallie to follow suit. You recollect one night John & I, joined you in doing so. Will those times ever come again. I am afraid that Tennessean has not improved me much. He is too busy & cant get materials from the North conveniently! Behold & judge!

Why should you skewer your heart in such a painful position? Am I the cause? I am proud to think it is with me – and has been. Your letters have kept me alive and well – those stories you see in the magazines of young men going to ruin because they seemed forgotten by the loved ones at home are only too true. Letters are like Manna to the famished affections – when a thousand devils as in the Army are tempting with blandishments – and threats. So tell me this heart is here freely and that the seeming sin is naught but Cupids dart and believe me Molly Dear with Love to you Sallie Mother &c

Sincerely yours,

Love

Hd. Qts. 8th Ks. Vols.

Nashville Tenn

May 10th 1863

Molly Dear

Yours of May 3rd to hand in good time. Very much pleased to hear how you are coming out and enjoying yourself. "Laugh and grow fat," is reputed a vulgar old Irish maxim, but full of sound sense. Cheerfulness and hope, prevents wrinkles. Keeps pleasant childlike lines on the face and figure and lengthens life – so says the good book & so mote it be.

We have had an excessively cold spell for <u>May</u>, but it is gone, and spring reigns again.

We had gooseberry pie yesterday & strawberries for dessert and I have three boquets on my desk and a Heliotrope putting out bountiful shoots, and perfuming the air around, under the "<u>cedar</u>" and only a few feet from my toes. All the poetry of camp life at once, except my ladye love, and yet I am "<u>ennuye.</u>" We have so much monotony, and so many exciting reports, that a little movement would be a relief. Under any commander but "Old Rosy" we would be dissatisfied. With him we know it is all for the best.

With earnest commanders in each Department, whose Souls are in the contest, and willing to fight for <u>success</u>, we have at last a good prospect of reaching a conclusion of some kind – and the more so as the fair ladies of the North by their sympathies actively displayed are neutralising all the schemes of the copperheads and cowards. Let them go South – where their friends are. There will their hearts be also – as well allow the Devil in heaven.

Why should we hear their sneers and submit to their deviltry – allow them to assassinate our government, our honor and our hopes of future welfare & happiness or ourselves from behind a fence or a tree.

In the name of all the outraged citizens of Missouri, Tennessee and Alabama whose blood calls to high heaven for vengeance, and the suffering of whose delicate women & children worse than a thousand deaths cry to all men for retribution. I say heap coals of fire on their guilty heads by sending them kindly south to their friends – while Uncle Sam uses their property for the benefit of the injured they can endure cold & hunger if need be with their brethren.

Good news from home! Good news from Fredericksburgh. Good news from Vicksburgh, from Louisiana, from North Carolina and from Kentucky; what more can we ask for. All things are valued by the cost – will we not value our Union – if again United.

Let England threaten – poor Ireland starves – and our Yankee gold is coming over in thousands to help us to till the soil and fight the battles of the promised land.

Aint you sorry you didn't come down to see me – before "Rosy" forbade it; you cant come now? Shall I go to you?

It is said Richmond is ours! I dont believe it just yet, but it will be, and soon thereafter or before, you shall hear of a fight here.

I received the *Republican* also & found Drake as eloquent as usual, and the Ladies "Shouting the Battle Cry of Freedom."[1]

What do you think of the photographs. I send three more. You can have first choice and imagine that the others came under cover to Alex, to be disposed of as he or you elect. I will send one to Morgan St.

Capt. Herd left for St. Louis on leave for 15 days last Tuesday cause sick wife. I suppose he'll call & see Wm or Alex, as he is acquainted with them. And now what more can I say.

I leave you to put it in the sweetest words or thoughts and so with Love to you Sallie, Mother &c

I am Molly Dear

Yours sincerely

Love

---

1. On May 2, 1863, the Loyal Ladies of St. Louis held a "Grand Mass Meeting" to form a National Ladies League, to "unite in an expression of their sympathies and sentiments in favor of the Union."

Hd. Qts. 8th Ks. Vols.

Nashville Tenn

May 20th 1863

My Dear Molly

I have waited a day or two expecting to hear from you or somebody else in your "burgh," but without success so I proceed. I rec'd three copies I.L.N. during the past week from you, very interesting they were indeed. Nothing of importance has occurred here. Weather has been fine & your correspondent in good health.

The Army has again turned in all its tents & baggage and is in the lightest marching order, immense fortifications will soon be completed here and it is evidently the intention to leave this place with a small guard behind them, the same at Murfreesboro, & then as soon as something is done at Vicksburgh & Fredericksburgh move boldly into Dixie.

We are ready for the march and are making efforts to do so, but the powers that be have arranged it otherwise, and have ordered us to leave our pretty camp and occupy some buildings in town. We are much disgusted, & dont wish to be cooped up and broiled in this dirty city during the summer. We shall see! Genl Mitchell has been removed and Genl Wood is in command. Genl Mitchell is home on sick leave and is assigned to the command of a Cavalry Brigade – he is a dashing Cavalry officer if his health & wounds will allow. Our Cavalry at present is doing good service all over Dixie.

We have at last had some military executions, very much needed they were.

I witnessed the shooting of a deserter on the 15th inst. It was very impressive. He died instantly without pain and was buried under a lone tree on a pretty Knoll alongside. It was witnessed by several thousand troops and citizens.

I had hoped the past week to be detailed to conduct some rebs to Alton, but Lt. Quin of Co. K. went instead and will have five days in St. Louis; so I cannot surprise you as I wished for the present my darling girl with much love I sign myself.

Sincerely yours,

Love

Have you got a good Photograph of Rosecrans? I have more than one!

On May 15, 1863, James witnessed the execution of Julius Mileka for desertion from the Tenth Michigan Infantry regiment. The scene probably looked similar to this drawing of the execution of a deserter from the Army of the Potomac. *The Execution of the Deserter William Johnson in General Franklin's Division, Army of the Potomac.* From *Harper's Weekly*, December 28, 1861.

2 P.M. 20th May

Molly Dear

I am rewarded by receiving this moment yours of the 10th inst. Glad you are so much pleased with the Photographs. In having it taken I tried to meet your ideas. I was aiming at another style. The result however proves your taste more correct. I enclose a proof taken since I wrote last. "Sallie" I remembered before.

Since I wrote in the morning I learn Genl Wood has been relieved from duty here, so our orders will not be enforced for the present if at all.

As to showing the Photograph whatever you do is right. I have no anxiety. The signature came there in this way. When we exchange among officers in the Army we usually put our signature at the bottom or on the back. I had done so on all six impressions ere I thought of it. I had six more since – I sent you three of them and since that another dozen. I enclose one that shows my appreciation of the plate! does it not? After drill this evening I called on a friend and I gathered Oh! such a pretty boquet – 20 or 30 varieties of roses.

Goodbye with kind love

Love

James mentions a photograph with his signature at the bottom, most likely this image included with the collection of letters.

Hd. Qts. 8th Ks. Vols.

Nashville Tenn.

May 28th 1863

Dearest Molly

Ere I am aware a week has passed. Another uneventful one, but anxious to us all, and breathless with excitement daily as it passed. We looked for later and yet later news from Vicksburgh, because on it so much depends. All our movements hinge on success or failure there and we are actively engaged preparing for it, be it good or bad. I have been cultivating the sulphur baths and drinking sulphur water trying to make believe I am at a watering place. I feel pretty spry over it and have a short ride to and fro. Our visitors (on business) to St. Louis are all returned safe, and report Alex looks jolly very busy and very gruff. Wm. absent, and the rest of the numerous Wilson & Adams families in good keeping order. <u>How does</u> that agree with the facts.

I have had so much late St. Louis gossip for a few days that I am satiated for the time being, but of course there is not a word specially of you or Ninth St. So dearest I have to look to you for all.

We have had a spell of cool weather and thunder showers for two days, which is rather agreeable than otherwise as this city of rocks is like St. Louis built on limestone, and alternates from clouds of dust to mud.

I had my heliotrope nicely placed in the half shade of my cedar, and some little curs come and eat it up a few days since, but I am forcing it out again. It is so dull & tiresome here now – or else my Bohemian propensities are craving for excitement once more. What would I not give for decisive news and a movement here. I rec'd two "*Democrats*" – contents noted. I am glad to see that "Drake" was elected.[1] I hope to write you a long letter soon.

Days pass now, not an event to note – no new faces – nothing – get up in the morning ½ p. 4 & drill – then breakfast. After that Guard mount, then write some long official reports all figures, then dinner. Then lie & read in the heat some light literature – or play some Backgammon for Lemonade, Cider

---

1. Charles D. Drake, a Radical Republican who wanted the immediate emancipation of Missouri's slaves, was elected to a state convention to decide the issue of emancipation in Missouri.

or Beer – then Drill again at 6 P.M. until after dark – then read all the papers – or play some more Backgammon or Muggins – or perhaps the Theatre – the day is passed – with no variation on yesterday. It soon gets dull – `and yet from the number around you have no privacy or time to yourself – although engaged in killing time half the day.

That is how our "Clique" works it. There is another Clique about equal numbers who eschew the reading & instead gamble and drink whisky all day and night when not on drill or duty – as above – believe me I never enter their tents unless on duty, and never stake a cent unless an investment in the aforesaid Lemons when I lose at Backgammon is called so by you – for Satan finds some mischief still for idle hands to do. Such is an interior view of camp life in a dull time. A little active duty changes all this & improves the minds, morals and health of the Majority as well as mine.

And now Molly dear I hope you continue well and happy and "when this cruel war is over" – I may be there to hear you sing about it, while I in return may give you the "Linkum Gunboats" &c &c and fold you in my arms as Safe, Safe, Safe at last.

With love and kisses, to your dear self – commend me to your friends.

I am ever yours

Sincerely,

Love

Charles D. Drake, senator from
Missouri. Steel engraving by
G. E. Perine, ca. 1870.

Hd. Qts. 8th Ks. Vols.
Nashville Tenn
May 29th 1863
Dear Molly

It was only yesterday I wrote you and yet I commence my eternal palaver again. Well this is Friday & my usual epistle is due you on Sunday and I wont mail this before that time, so thats settled.

I have just rec'd yours of the 24th last Sunday. It came through in very fair time, and I welcome it by trying to do likewise. With the most vivid memories of happy hours by your side in "ye olden time I thank you for the rose bud so mossy – but I am shocked and hold up my hands in holy horror at your perverse wish that I should be detained in this Sodom till this "Cruel war is Over." Well now to be even. I hope I <u>will</u> get 5 days in St. Louis this Summer or fall just to brighten my ideas & get out of this endless round of routine & red tape I am tied up in – and that when there you may be gallivanting at St. Paul or Montreal or the White Mountains (or whereever you most wish to be) There! Aint that Spiteful!!?

And now as a slight act of penitence for an unpardonable offence dont you think you ought to send me a Carte de visite – a late one – and if I cant see you – I really fear I wont – let me have a good counterfeit presentment as a slight balm to my wounded spirit. I know Ive got one. It lays before me as I write and looks as natural as life and as good as pie but we were both a year & a half younger then, think of that. Decr 1861 – sent as a valentine in Feby. 62 – so there's a dear girl send me another taken when you are as gay and happy as you describe and if I see it "thus" – why I'll be more contented to wait till Christmas or later, & hope when there to make my visit less "de trop."

Seriously I think I understand you perfectly – so be "Gay" and "God bless you"'!

I see mine of the 20th went through post haste – mail communication are in better order than ever before. Today it rains still. I could most fancy myself in Scotland – or Antrim. It is a dark cloudy windy chilly – Scotch misty day, but all natures smiles that the dry spell has ended and dust vamosed for a while. So I can be as lack-a-daisical as I please.

I wont make any such impertinent remarks about how you spend your time or the letters you write as you suggest. I know you are very good and never neglect me or forget me and I think this letter one of your best and kindest and full of news – so good bye till Sunday night.

Love

Sunday night

Herewith I enclose "Rosys" good natured Phiz.

I have no more to say. Weather stormy, exciting rumors of movements in front which I dont believe.

We are barricading the streets & building rifle pits. Bragg has left it is said and Rosy after him. We must defend ourselves against the roving cavalry.

Yours Sincerely

James E. Love

Lt & Adjt

8th Ks. Vols.

Sunday June 7th 63

On the march

To Murfreesboro

My Dear Molly

Aint you surprised. You cant be any more so than I am – at our movement and all the other movements here. On Tuesday last we moved our camp into the city in a vacant lot & began making ourselves very comfortable that day and the next, but that evening we were ordered to move into the Court House and Capitol at once. The C.H. was very dirty & we put a party to work cleaning it up for two days – though we growled a great deal. On Friday night I went to the Theatre & got home before twelve o'clock. Just as I came in a dispatch from Genl Rosecrans came to hand ordering us to Murfreesboro, to start by the Pike at daylight on Saturday. Here was the Devil to pay – but we slept on it & got up as usual & went leizurely about our arrangements. At six I was ready & proceeded to breakfast & by nine o.clock we started. It was near twelve ere we got out of town. We had quite an ovation, <u>city quite excited</u> as they expected to have us all summer. We marched until 3 o'clock nine miles where we camped for the night without Tents again as before. I will have a tent however to sleep and transact business in whenever I require it. This morning we started at 4 ½ o'c and got to camp here before noon. Men have sore feet, or we would have went 5 miles further – sixteen miles today.

We are near the scene of the battle of Stone river and graves abound. I intend going out later in the evening to reconnoiter. Tomorrow we go to camp two miles south of Murfreesboro and then I dont know what after.

We go back to the old division though and Brigade.

Address

8th Kansas Vols

3d Brigade

1st Division

20th A. Corps

Murfreesboro Tenn

It has been warm and pleasant since we started. A pleasant air stirring – no dust. It was wet early last week. I am very well & in good spirits as you may imagine at the change – though I could have wished a days warning – yet a good soldier is always ready. The country is very much devastated, but many fine residences are still standing, and crops and gardens planted – fences very scarce and no stock to be seen.

I have had a splendid dinner including Tomatoes, Green peas, strawberries, with fresh butter & butter milk – and since that a feed of wild raspberries and mulberries. The boys cut down a tree by our cook fire. Oh so pulpy and delicious bushels of them.

Another fortunate officer Lt. Brooks of our Regt. went to St. Louis & Alton with prisoners last week and I would have had a chance this week or next but it was not to be and the 18th Michigan reigns in our stead.

I cant forward this scrawl before tomorrow or Tuesday so for the present my dearest Girl fare you well. I hope to hear a good account from you soon.

Love and Kisses from

Yours Sincerely

Love

Wednesday

June 10th 1863

On Picket

My Dear Molly

After writing the above I went out to see the battle field – but little is to be seen – except the effects of the iron hail on the trees.

We marched at 4 o,clock on Monday and all the 5 miles we passed over up to Murfreesboro the evidences of bloody conflict were numerous and melancholy, rifle pits & trenches and fortifications with trees all torn and houses pounded into ruins and graves of men and bones of Horses and mules every where.

Murfreesboro looks much the same except that its inhabitants are all soldiers, officers and camp followers – fortifications of the greatest magnitude and strongest kind encircle it all and every house is stored with Crackers and Bacon. We went into camp after much counter-marching and contrary orders but soon found that everybody wanted to have us; and eventually the old Brigade carried the day, & we had to change camp and march half a mile next morning. One of the results of being popular – as soon as we got in camp we were ordered to the front on Picket duty where we found our old acquaintances the 25th & 35th Ill's and the 15th Wisconsin (Norwegian) Regiments 5 ½ miles from Murfreesboro. We arrived before nightfall and camped under the trees on a bluff, where we are now. Before we retired we heard several guns fire, & today we see the rebel vedettes plainly in sight on the Pike two miles off on the next hill. Stones River runs in a circle around Murfreesboro & is just half a mile behind us, between us and town. We are due south on the Shelbyville Pike and expect to be out for a week yet, when another brigade will relieve us, and we go back to camp. I suppose you understand what picket duty is. You are face to face with the enemy usually and at all times prepared for him – though all but a few sleep or lay around as they will with guns alongside night & day – nothing to encumber you but what you calculate to carry along save one tent for the Adjutant and Colonel to write in and transact business in. Rations are brought out in wagons every day or every third day by the quartermaster & cooked on the ground – men and officers carrying a blanket, a shelter tent, their gun &c, haversack with rations and an iron pail or kettle to every six or eight men – and so we are. The rebs advanced in force on our pickets every where same day as they attacked Franklin, having been informed that Rosy had reinforced Grant, & as he could not hold it, was evacuating Murfreesboro, and also Nashville. Now, as Rosy himself has been reinforced, our men soon showed them their mistake, and they again retreated with loss – although it was only good fortune saved Franklin – to us. Picket duty is very pleasant and exciting, except when it rains as it does today. And often for weeks both sides observe one another quietly without movement, when suddenly pop comes an attack when least expected. Any enterprising fellow can have a shot whenever he wants to, by risking more or less his own life – but we are not allowed to risk ourselves. We expect to advance – but I wont believe it, until we take Vicksburg and Port Hudson. Then we can have a good fight here and crush them if they dont run.

Col Martin is still in Nashville. They wont allow him to leave it is said. Numerous petitions have went in to that effect and to request we be sent back. I hope not. Though I know the risk – but I will be satisfied either way. We have had no mail since Saturday but I look for one hourly and if you wrote on the 31st I ought to hear from you by it. I must close this now however – and believe me Molly dear

Ever Yours Sincerely

James E. Love

Capt. Herd is going to resign. Would you like to see me Capt. Love. If so say so? If I wish it I can have it – either position has its advantages?

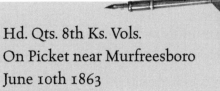

Hd. Qts. 8th Ks. Vols.

On Picket near Murfreesboro

June 10th 1863

My Dear Molly

I wrote you this morning and since I have nothing to relate, except the receipt of yours of the 4th inst.

Truly you give me news and how can I thank or love you enough. Pretend egotism as I will, the first & last thought present with me – with a full knowledge of myself too, is an overpowering sense of my unworthyness of the great treasure of love, you have entrusted me with – and the responsibility thus assumed by my <u>so far</u> unlucky self, to do likewise, refusing as you have others. I have no doubt better men with <u>better means</u> and <u>prospects</u> than poor me. The latest evidence you here just hint at.

What shall I say? Promises are not apropos – performances are what you require of me!

I shall write to William right away and enclose in an Envelope to you; as the mail is too slow to communicate with you first. I believe that for me is the most proper way, but I am bound to respect to the last your heretofore expressed wishes – so let it reach him or not as you wish, knowing how far you are committed, and how far our little romance has been suspected!

I think I ought to write to "Mother" also!

I am sorry I was not in St. Louis at the time!

I wait impatiently to hear from you again!

I wish I knew how to say what is necessary so as to tell the truth – and meet their views without injuring my or your cause; I respect both so much. I am nervously anxious to secure their cheerful consent. It was not necessary and I am sorry that you should assume the whole responsibility of concealment. I was first to blame – inasmuch as knowing your & their old country ideas. I should have spoken to Wm first; ere word had passed between us.

And if all goes well, would it not now be the best time to name a date after which if I can get "leave of absence" we could be united. I hinted in my last letter that I would not press matters until this "cruel war is over" supposing that to be your wish; if so say so to me, and have it understood with your friends or allow me to do so – that will be a year & a half.

My wishes would point to this fall or winter – as the longest time to which it would be adviseable for many reasons to postpone it.

When our time is out, I expect even if the rebellion is crushed, to be required a little longer. The south must be garrisoned by Soldiers or armed settlers for some years, so the time would pass, and valuable hours lost, matters unsettled and hope deferred.

But my dearest girl whatever happens depend on my warmest love, sympathy & good wishes for yourself and friends. They will do what is right. You will do what is right & I will try to do what is right, & I expect all will be as happy as a marriage bell in the end.

Mention the time now in consultation with your friends and with a clearly defined future before us, we will work together for good – in this world and with your sweet prayers in the world to come.

I am Molly darling

Yours Sincerely

Love

With a serious task before me for which I am unprepared. Goodnight Love.

Pleasant dreams

ever yours

J.E. Love

I enclose in another envelope two letters. Close them up, & enclose to Alex & forward or retain them for a more auspicious occasion as you wish.

Love

Hd. Qts. 8th Ks. Vols.

On Picket

Shelbyville road Tenn.

June 12th 1863

Molly Dear

Night before last after writing to you I dallyed with my task & left it incomplete. Yesterday I could find no time as I was out looking at the rebs. Quite pacific they were, and we tried to exchange papers without success. They evidently think we have Vicksburgh as they are able to get no news therefrom. "Alf Burnett" the "Celebrated" was along as correspondent of the "*Commercial*" of Cinti. and we had quite a pleasant trip. Genl Jeff C. Davis came out and joined us in our peaceful reconnoisance after we returned. "Alf" remained in Col. Heg's camp and invited officers and men over there, where he promised to amuse them. He did so with inimitable pathos fun and an India Rubber countenance.

This morning early yours of the 7th is to hand with its interesting budget. I gave it a right royal welcome.

This morning the sun is out and everything is steaming hot as midsummer dare be.

We keep early hours – up before 4 A.M. fill up the morning & evening hours with drill – during the noon heat, loaf or sleep if we can. After night be jolly and cool till the dew drives us home and to bed at 10 or 11 P.M. And before sunrise we nearly freeze again, standing in line of battle ready for attack or defence.

I enclose two notes in one to Alex – but you can deliver or suppress for the present as you wish (better not perhaps). When my mind is made up my temperament always prompts me to quick movements. I leave it to you to apply the curb. It is useful to man or beast.

Will write more fully soon; before or after I hear from you of this.

Kind love darling

Love

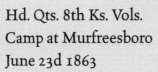

Hd. Qts. 8th Ks. Vols.

Camp at Murfreesboro

June 23d 1863

I recd yours of the 19th today. Bless you for the contents. We have just recd marching orders – with 12 days rations. I suppose it is into Dixie – as tis said the whole Army moves. Rosy is about to do something to skeer Bragg & Co. and stop Hookers advance into Pennsylvania &c &c. I hope you put that matter all right ere you left.

I claimed the Capts. Commission and will have it. It is a step up but I am sorry. I may get another on the battle field who knows? I have been paid the most flattering compliment – as the Col. has said to all that he would rather I wasn't promoted – that there is not another <u>officer</u> in the Regt. can fill my place. He will have to take a Sergeant!!! I hope to see you all O.K. as I said. The Col. & I are promised "leave of absence" <u>after this move</u>, as soon as the exigencies of the service will admit – by Genl Rosecrans himself – in writing.

I will write to you as usual every opportunity and if God in his providence wills that we never meet believe it all for the best.

I have no fears!

And now God bless you my love good bye

ever yours

James E. Love

8th Ks. Vols.

In the field

6 A.M. June 27th 1863

Dearest

We started just after I wrote you last, and if ever an army in the field was much in difficulties – we are – it has rained ever since. It commenced shortly after we got started in light marching order and we rode, walked & slept wet since. I am all right however – not even got a cold but my poor horse is used up, awful roads mud & rock, he has lost a shoe & a half.

The rebels have fought every inch of the way, but we have not got to the front yet. The country is so <u>hilly</u> and muddy that those behind cannot pass. We did not succeed in taking the first gap we came too on the Shelbyville Pike, 10 miles out, and so leaving a force there to watch – we started right & left over the hills to go round. The rebs done likewise and such hillside fighting is not often seen by a large army – only a few mountain Howitsers in play – all the rest musketry & bayonet. Several regiments in our Division have stumbled into hidden traps & had a bloody baptism – but on we go – and we are now only 8 miles from "Wartrace" where Braggs main army is posted to receive us. It is said he outnumbers us and was about sending men to help Lee – so Rosy pitched in – in order to keep them here. Our Regt. is as usual fortunate in escaping shot & shell – long may Providence favor us – for three days it has been a constant roar of cannon & skirmishing – but today it is quiet. We have heard one or two shells at a distance but there is either no fighting or it is at a distance too great. We hold all the gaps now, except one, and our army has passed through. A battle is expected on Monday unless Bragg runs away – or it rains all the time. I dont think Bragg will run. We are train Guard today – but by Monday it will be our turn in front. Then you may possibly hear from the bloody "Eighth".

We hear no news here – have to wait for the Nashville papers – and so you will get the news sooner than I will – certainly sooner by the papers than by any letter of mine. I received yours of the 19th before I started (on the 23d) – and hope that ere this you are enjoying yourself in Illinois. Take good care of yourself & depend on it, if I can dodge the balls I will – honestly doing the cause all the good I can – singing that feminine lyric – "When this cruel war is over" – that now is the rage. I hope you'll stay your two months and more & come back fresh as a daisy. I will direct until I hear from you as heretofore.

I am with kindest love to you & friends

Sincerely Yours

James E. Love

The Union army had to fight for control of three primary gaps through a range of high hills, shown on this map. *Skirmishes near Liberty Gap, Tenn., June 24–26, 1863.* From *Atlas to Accompany the Official Records of the Union and Confederate Armies.* Washington, D.C.: Government Printing Office, 1891–1895.

Camp at Beech Grove Tenn.

June 28th 1863

Dearest Molly

We started yesterday shortly after writing the aforesaid and soon it started to rain again. Roads knee deep in mud & from that upwards. You never saw such rocks & gaps – out of Ireland or Scotland. Soon we got on the Manchester Pike, but the heavy army wagons had cut it all up also. On it we passed through "Hoovers" & "Guys" Gaps where considerable fighting was done by the advance of our Division (Davis's) and "Johnstons". They gallantly charged on the rebs batteries & rifle pits & carried them with loss. I saw the graves of thirteen of the 125 Ills. These gaps are twelve miles long all Granite, flint & limestone rocks, one of natures strongholds where 5000 men could & should defy an army of 100,000 but they ran like whelps and it is said now are evacuating Wartrace & Shelbyville, falling back on Tullahoma.

Just after passing the gap we met a string of over a hundred butternut prisoners and heard that "Rosecrans" was in Manchester 18 miles. We have taken all their outposts or they have left mighty sudden on our approach. No news of our movements is allowed to go north – no letters – further than Nashville.

The settlers around here have all left. We made only seven miles, all we could through the Deep mud & camped at Beech Grove. It has rained all night. I slept in the mud & rain, got up stiff at 3 A.M. Now sitting in a thunderstorm on a deserted porch – where an old darky has been telling us ludicrous yarns of the skedaddle. "Lookee dar" she says "down to that old chesnut by the creek. The white folks sat round dar like so many poor darkies as I've seen them many a time chase with guards on horse back & bloodhounds & shake a pistol at them & strike them over the head – & now I seed them thar in the same fix. I'se so glad – you folks came so fast they hadn't time to saddle their horses. A Col that lived over at Massas said the Yankees could never come here no more & he had to leave on foot – the blue coats got his horse." An immense train is passing including pontoons.

Men & officers carry besides arms & ammunition – their tents, blankets & three days rations.

The Field & Staff ride & have a wagon. For the safe keeping of the papers I have a tent, the only one (save shelter tents) in the Regt. 5 P.M. I've just seen an old friend from Kansas, Dr. Hageboom. He left last Tuesday & this is Sunday. He had just reported to Genl Rosecrans at Manchester – we are 12 miles from it on the Pike. This country reminds me much of the North of Ireland or Scotland, hills, creeks, little patches of Farms, houses real stone & logs. Pine trees instead of Fir, very similar – & little garden plots of potatoes, cabbages, apples, cherries & plums, thickly settled with poor white trash who say "They are Union, but all the boys have been conscripted by the Rebs." They point out the conscripting officers freely – and we have burnt some of the houses already.

> Camp at Manchester
> June 30th 1863
> 12 o,clock Noon
> Molly Dear

After writing the last page we started again over the same execrable roads at 6 P.M. & marched to the creek near Manchester 12 miles, arriving at 1 o,clock in the morning. Oh! Such a weary wading through mud & water & climbing hills with wagons stuck every few yards. It was moonlit however & cool & no rain, so we lay down by a fire in the underbrush – jaded & weary with a saddle for pillow a horse blanket below & a rubber blanket above. Before we got to sleep it rained again – so we swam & slept in water all night soundly too, until reveille at 4 o,clock. Fighting today 9 miles in front towards Tullahoma – only skirmishing – as Rosecrans is still at Manchester while McCook has gone to the front. We are stuck in the mud & rain. Just before noon it cleared up a spell & quite a number of us went swimming in Duck River. Before we got dressed it rained again & it was 3 o,clock before we got breakfast having fasted save lunch since yesterday morning. At night our wagons came up – & we made ourselves comfortable

& had a good sleep. Today is muster day & a very busy one with me so many papers to make.

But my dearest girl I have time to write too, if opportunity offers – no matter what business is on hand. It is still raining thunder showers at intervals – but wet or dry we are busily preparing for future Marches & sending teams & useless baggage back to Murfreesboro. Which way we dont know! Suppose Rosy does!

I am hearty – never felt better or had better digestion!

As soon as mail opens I hope to hear good news from you darling – in the shape of a letter from your dear self!

Best wishes for your pleasure on the approaching 4th July – so for the present good bye.

Love

Hd. Qts. 8th Ks. Vols.
Camp at Winchester Tenn
July 5th 1863
Dearest Molly

I find it more troublesome to do any correspondence on this march than ever before, entirely on account of the rain. I wrote last on the 30th ult. a pencil sketch. I had been writing all that day on Regtl. business, and was so bothered by the figures in my head & the crowd around that I fear I scarce made it interesting. I had but one idea then and since, mud & rain. We heard much of skirmishing & fighting towards Tullahoma & Decherd, and we had orders to be ready to move at a moments notice with but one wagon to a Regt. – it to carry spades, picks, & officers blankets and 3 days rations – to be made to last 6 days if necessary and also orders from "Rosy" to fire low, and waste no shots, to have no artillery duels and no shelling of the woods, only to fire on masses of troops, & to rely on the bayonet. All of which smacked of hot work expected, & speaks volumes as to the impossible state of the roads. So early on July 1st we started with orders to form line of battle at a point named – three lines in fact – one within the other, but it was not to be. Our cavalry went ahead from all sides of the doomed city 12 miles off, and the rebels ran. They had been evacuating for 24 hours <u>before</u>, supposing that "Rosy" had them nearly surrounded and believing he had 100,000 men, when there aint half so many, and so ere we march two miles we heard that our advance was marching in, so we changed our course & marched in too, sending back for our wagons. We marched very slowly over mountain roads and streams, men suffering from heat which was excessive, between the showers, and some from Sunstroke. Skirmishing had been brisk in the advance but we saw none of it.

Slept well and off again at Sun up towards Winchester, heavy firing heard in that direction. Soon we came to Elk River, but found the Bridge burned & the stream flooded. Cavalry swam their horses and went on. We marched three miles to the railroad bridge only to find that in flames also, then back one mile to a ford – found water there 4 to 5 feet deep and running like a torrent. It took Sheridans Division all day & all night to cross. Men wading & swimming, with guns & clothes above their heads. Wagons had to be steadied with ropes thrown across, so that they shouldn't be swept down stream. There was a branch also to cross about 20 yards wide & from 2 to 3 feet deep. We spent the afternoon bathing & washing, and I had the misfortune to lose your ring, this time I suppose to be found no more. It fell in the deep water, and I and over fifty others hunted for an hour, but to no purpose. I have been a little superstitious about that ring. I fear I am yet, but I suppose I must just laugh at my folly. You know I held it subject to your call! What shall I do now? Wont you call for another soon? We have had several mails lately but no letters for me since yours of the 19th ult. I got three *I.L. News* from you however, that I read at each halt & gave away sheet by sheet as we marched. They were very welcome indeed and were worthy of preservation but if you could only see the thousands & thousands & thousands of Dollars worth of Uncle Sam's property thrown out and destroyed daily on these roads, you would be reconciled – aye even ammunition and food that may be badly needed even next day was dumped in the gulfs to lighten the wagons & to fill the holes. This day we made but 11 miles – short marches.

Next morning July 3d we marched at Sun up again, and crossed both creek & river & it took our Division all forenoon. The river had fallen 6 or 8 inches, but it was a ludicrous sight. I made my horse carry double, myself and a sick officer. I could scarce get him to navigate and at the same time keep the water out of my boot tops. As soon as we crossed we had a thunder shower of an hours duration, the heaviest we have yet had. Many men sat in it – among the brush with their clothes mostly under them – not on them. We got started again and after 5 or 6 miles came another river – very cold & over 3 feet deep – rapid & wide also, being over its banks. This we crossed in the same way and immediately after marched into Winchester with Colors flying, band playing, & but little trace comparatively of mud and water. We found some trace of a fight last night however – as our cavalry drove theirs from the ford & through the town and then invited themselves to a good warm meal & bed at the citizens expense – very expensive it was too. We camped in a fine old forest ½ mile S.E. of town for the night.

Yours,

Love

Winchester
July 5th 12. M.[1]
Dearest Molly

Next morning was the 4th and sorry to say it was the dullest I ever passed. At Corinth one year since it was just a shade better, while at Boonville Mo. the year before it passed gaily. We were busy cleaning up camp all morning & foraging for something to eat all afternoon from the natives bitter secesh the most of them are just here. Arrangements were made for a celebration in town at 12 Mi. which the rain busted. Genl Rosecrans came from Tulla-homa to participate but it only resulted in a Dinner at Genl McCooks at 4 P.M. All the Generals, their staff & a few Colonels were present over 60 – our Col. among the rest & our band discoursed sweet music. About 6 P.M. Genl Rosecrans & Staff departed to Tullahoma again. Another arrangement by our Brigade was to come off at 6 P.M. speechyfying by the Parsons & others, officers & men, music by several bands – song & glees & other amusements in a bower we had built & seated but again the inevitable rain ruined all and the men went to bed sulky. We could get no whisky or Beer for them even to mark the occasion. Finally the officers met & had a smoke at our quarters, and sang & told stories until after midnight.

So passed the 4th of July 1863.

And now another day is gone, and Sunday morning the 5th is rapidly pass-ing into the past. How many poor fellows here so gay or so sulky will live to see the next God knows. It is thundering and raining as usual, and we could hear cannon and musketry occasionally at some mountain passes from 5 to 7 miles off – which we wish to hold in order to make us safe here. We will not move further until the weather changes or the Railroad opens down to here. It is opened to Tullahoma already and the telegraph is open to Elk River so it wont be over a week or two ere the pioneers build the bridges, and then – What – I dont know. Bragg or Rosecrans may know what they intend, but God disposes. If this weather had not been a second deluge we should have

---

1. Based on the content, James wrote this letter at noon on July 5, 1863, after finishing the previous letter.

had Bragg's whole force surrounded "a la Vicksburgh" but it is now too late, adding another to the list of battles lost by the unpropitious elements.

I am very busy today again – writing all day. Army business can wait for Sunday or Fast Day – inexhorable necessity drives you on, same as a ship at Sea or a boat on the river.

I am gay and festive, healthy and happy as ever I was – or as I can be absent from those I love, but anxious just now for St. Louis news. You will know of the general movements of the army much sooner than I do. I can only learn of our Brigade, Division or sometimes as now of our Corp (McCooks) which is all here. For the rest we have to wait for Nashville papers and the Railroad perhaps. I expect news will go to you freely now, as long as we were stuck in the mud and the movements were in embryo, our letters and dispatches were all detained in Nashville.

If Grant, Meade & Foster send us good news, depend on "Rosy" making a desperate attempt on "Bridgeport" & Chattanooga on the Tennessee River and Railroad. If the news is bad we may not go so far from home, as it would then be unsafe – so one project depends on another for success in this immense struggle. By the Bye, let me know if you get the *Union* regularly. I have them sent direct now!

I hope you are enjoying yourself. My thoughts are with daily and nightly. Give my love and remembrance to all the folks. And with best Love and wishes to yourself I am my dearest girl

Yours Sincerely

James E. Love

P.S.

I address as before until otherwise instructed by you. You shall hear from me often as the mail permits. It is just about to close. Address to me as last.

Goodbye, now kiss me!

Love

Hd. Qts. 8th Ks. Vols.

Camp at Winchester Tenn.

July 18th 1863

My Dearest Molly

As I understand that part of our mails got lost or destroyed I suppose I had better commence two weeks back. I would fain hope that mine of the 28th & 30th June and 4th July went through safe – from which you would learn of my safety and good health and of our movements in rain, mud, short rations & misery – to be crowned however with success.

If not rec'd I cannot now replace it but must tell the story at a future time. I have not had a letter or paper from the North since we left Nashville except yours of the 18th June (previous to your leaving home[1]) and some I.L.N. papers you sent same time. I hope to get some daily but fear they are also lost. This under the circumstances is very trying to my patience, expecting as I am letters from you, from your Mother and William. Until I hear good or bad news I scarcely know how to write, but my dearest girl, basking in your favor I will go on the even tenor of my way & fear not for the result.

Do we not receive glorious news. Daily and hourly it comes to us, almost past belief it comes so rapidly from all points the compass under our continued and combined attacks at Vicksburgh, Port Hudson, Tullahoma, Bridgeport, Winchester, Chattanooga, Pennsylvania, & now Charlestown & Mobile. All have or will succumb, showing them overpowered, & with the Draft enforced, they can never rise again.

The N. York riots[2] are only for plunder and are over by this time, but the war is not over, neither will it be if we march all over the South. It may yet take a year or two to pacify them – and some fighting – though I now think the <u>great</u> battles are past all save one or two in Virginia or whereever "Lees" army goes to. Around it will now circle the last great struggle – and it is said "Rosecrans" is to leave us and take command East. God forbid "say I". We

1. Molly was again visiting her brother in Illinois.
2. The New York draft riots, by people opposed to the substitution and exemption provisions of the Conscription Act.

shall all protest unless it is clearly necessary for the good of the cause – but of that hereafter. I believe I could get leave of absence for twenty days now. If I wanted it. Others are trying & Lt. Col. Abernathy has succeeded. If you were at home I might be tempted and if I can I would wish to press our matters to a settlement at once or at a fixed time – but I wont try for it now – say what I shall do next chance between now and Christmas. Leaves will be easier obtained as the war progresses.

My dearest girl I cannot express how much I feel the loss of my mail at this time. I cannot rest. I cannot write. I cant settle to anything except pressing business and excitement so that it may drown thought. Suspense is weary and soul destroying; a positive refusal from your friends w'd be a relief, for then I could act to have it change – nerve myself for the contest – and think of ways & means. &c.

I am still Adjutant and date my letters from Hd. Qts. I am in no hurry to evacuate, but I have received my commission as Captain of Co. K. and will be mustered some day soon I suppose. I have now my choice. I expect of course to assume command of it – and if I can get a post of A.A.A.G with some General I will try for it. If Col. Martin again commands a Brigade, I expect to go with him as before. I had the most flattering letters written to the Gov. on my behalf by him and others – so I heard – from those who saw the documents. I did not.

I have since heard that it is expected that "McCooks Corp" will go to the Potomac with Rosecrans. That will suit us well if "Rosy" cant lead us to "Mobile" – I hope he may lead us to Richmond.

Outside of these Rumors all goes quietly with us. We are scouting around for guerillas & something to eat – and stay fast in camp. A pretty camp we have on a smooth grassy lawn or pasture with little groves scattered over it, in one of which our shelters are pitched, in another the Quartermasters train & Hd. Qts., in another the Hospital & doctors with the men. Shelters in nice lines stretching out right and left – and every thing kept as clean as a parlor – every leaf and chip picked up. We moved here on the 6th of July and soon got comfortable. On the ninth or tenth, we had news from

Vicksburgh & Pennsylvania, and our band with some others went to town to serenade Genl's Davis & McCook. Numbers of us went down also and there was quite a jollification. Genl Davis then ordered (as a favor) to go to the mountains next day and capture a large party of Guerillas there secreted. We went at two in the morning and got back before dark after the most disagreeable day we have yet had – the hardest work too. Came near ruining all our clothes and Horses. It was climbing rocks & descending cliffs all day – caves abounded – and in them we chased these desperadoes. We only caught three, six horses, 2 mules and some contrabands, found Bacon & provisions, clothes, fires burning &c &c – but the main body we missed in the caves – and as soon as we passed they started to the other side the mountains with all their splendid horses niggers &c and are now on the other side of the Tennessee River. We got back safe with our plunder & so tired we slept all next day, and did not recover for two or three days.

We had some pretty rifle shooting at them from a distance – but it was no use. Since that I have been excessively busy in camp with our half yearly papers & others that were up to that time neglected – and winding up all other business previous to the arrival of the expected commissions.

We have been inspected as a Regt. several times lately – and been highly complimented every time, on Wednesday last was the latest instance.

Day before yesterday the Paymaster also made his appearance and created much work for me, preparation and excitement. We hope to be paid tonight and if so will be the first Regt. in this army paid – if not pd tonight we will be tomorrow or Monday.

Our Chaplain (Mr. John Paulsen) has turned out to be a fine speaker, but is weakly – too much so for the service. Their work here is of a missionary character. They must have a robust constitution, and be able to rough it, and endure hardships. He is nearly worn out already – and has done nothing but travel with us – and speak once or twice. I fill a vacant hour this pleasant Saturday afternoon, not waiting for the morrow as usual.

If my last from this place on the 12th and the others mentioned reach you I will be pleased to hear.

Today is fine and Indian Summer like. Nights are cold and mornings foggy – even when it haint rained. We have no sun – and every thing gets mouldy whether out or in doors. Seems to me it is about as wet a time as has occurred since the flood. It has rained more or less for 24 days – but we look for Summer and a summer Sun yet.

What would I not give for a few hours or days by your side?

Aye even for that small boon? I need not try to say.

And how much more to have Molly by my side for the balance of my time on earth & for an eternity in the future – with the few comforts that a thousand or two a year w'd supply added thereto. I can picture bliss unspeakable – and Kisses – galore.

Good bye my dearest girl

Yours Sincerely

James E. Love

I suppose of course you are gone on your contemplated trip – but address this as usual hoping you will receive it in good time. I have been thinking often of your enjoyment and will be sorry to hear otherwise.

Love

Siege of Vicksburg. Chromolithograph by Kurz and Allison, 1888.

Hd. Qts. 8th Ks. Vols.

Camp at Winchester Tenn

July 25th 1863

Dearest Molly

Another week has passed and yet no letter. I say it not in reproach! No! No! No! but to note the fact of my great want and anxiety there anent!

Unless the mails are playing me false I know there is good cause for it all and no fault lies at your door.

I take it for granted now you went on the trip mentioned <u>with</u> and <u>to</u> Brother Roberts and that since that time you may be travelling with no time or privacy at your disposal and withal a wish to bell me the tale of your travels in a connected manner and at your leisure. Such being the case, or numerous similar reasons which I can imagine I shall be proportionably pleased, gratified & relieved when I hear from you as my anxiety is now great. I live in fear and trembling I assure you – for coward fears intrude of your sickness or other mishap. I need not enlarge on the catalogue of horrors a vivid imagination can supply when started – and then too I have not heard of your receipt of letters of importance to our future – neither from your friends – if you have given my proposals to them. So I am in a fever, and yet must keep cool in outward seeming all the time, for there is little or no privacy in the army – least of all to the Adjutant who is in turn every bodies servant and every bodies master.

I am yet Adjutant in name and reality. I am also Captain – in fact – though not ostensibly or in name – power is pleasant, pleasantest to me just so. I prefer being behind the scenes – but "Ntimporte". You understand all that for I believe and hope you understand me – with my many faults and few virtues.

No compliments now I command you. I always had a foolish fear of being suspected of fishing for compliments and so I complimented myself in order to secure the contrary from honest friends like you & others.

I do hope you are well and enjoying yourself.

And pray if the mails have on this occasion been in fault and your letters are lost – remedy the loss "An you love me."

Dearest Girl how I wish to see you words cant express.

Next to that is my wish to hear from you in answer to all my epistles since the 14th or 21st of June – let me know if a link is lost. Leaves of absence are now being granted. As soon as I can or will assume my position as Captain, I can obtain one. I feel strongly tempted <u>just now</u>, but mindful of what you have said in months past, I wont move until I hear from you. If I thought you were dangerously sick – I would go at all hazards. Otherwise miserly as I have become I will save the dimes until a later season.

Say When? You know the rest!

Love

Dearest Molly

For I will call you so once more. I cannot believe but it is all a cruel dream. I've just recd yours of the 26th June & 19th July (and an *I.L.N.*) a few hours since – and I am crazy – desperate.

I had written the foregoing during the afternoon. I was despondent (The influence of the ring I suppose). A presentiment of ill has been present with me for several weeks which I could not hide from you even in my letters.

I laid down my pen and went to sleep – to be rudely awakened by the arrival of the mail and your letters.

I send you all!

But is it true?

Surely you deceive yourself!

I know you well! I am sure you love me still! I cannot take no for an answer!

My life, my happiness! now and forever is at stake!

But I will not deal in words! I hope I love you too well to give you pain in any way!

I release you freely from all engagements! I will begin anew – but in mercy deal candidly with me – have no concealments! I have willingly had none! What have I done? What have I put in those letters that should change you so in one short week?

Or is it altogether the opposition of your friends? Surely that could be done away with?

But is it those in St. Louis or Washington?

I have my faults! No one is more conscious of them than myself! No one is more wishful of an honorable record! And I intend now as always to have it! So far if I have it not, it is my misfortune – and no one can accuse me of anything but of being in debt – or short of cash – at the very worst!!! All that must and shall change if a strong will can do it, and providence does not forsake me – so I always intended since I had an object. God knows I have worked hard for success too in my foolish blundering way!

But I ought to have addressed those letters to William & your Mother directly as you gave me leave too! In that I was wrong! But Oh Why – Why – did you not deliver them. A refusal from them would have sat lightly compared with this! I knew you would not act without their consent!

And I done wrong in accepting an engagement on any other terms!

I blame but myself – for you know I disliked secresy, and long engagements – yet I meanly allowed myself to be persuaded! So now I can only bow to your wishes and declare you free!

And yet I think it must have been something in those letters. I tried I know without doing violence to the truth to assume all blame in the matter! Was that it?

What <u>have</u> I done?

I am tempted to desert my post a few days & see you!

I am tempted to go see William & your Mother face to face – but no. Desertion is dishonor – is death and mine is to be an honorable one – an enemies bullet I suppose. You shall never have cause to blush for me. What I have learned of the world – of women – and of a hereafter from you and my mother has made that resolution a fixed one.

But without an explanation from you of this sudden change – and I am aware that it may be impossible for you to give it me! – my faith in human nature will be sadly shaken.

We shall always be friends. I shall however strive to be more – honorably – but you are free!!

Free as the Winds! released

I begin de Novo – that is all. And if I find it should be painful to you at a future time to resume our engagements, I hope I love you too well to insist! I will tell you now. I am tenacious of Love and hate! that is one of my faults.

Let it plead for or against me as it will.

Loving now I love for all time! But you are free! Use it well – to yourself, your friends – to me – and doing so – I <u>will</u> say as before with Gods help – it is all for the best.

That does not prevent me from trying to better it, in this world or the next.

If I do not convince you in time or eternity of my devotion to you (& my country) I very much mistake the amount of mulishness in my long head.

Think of me also in kindness for I will require it – rebelling as I intend to against your wishes – as I've not done heretofore.

Sunday morning

My letters may have shown vacillation of purpose, but never of love. Though usually I am chary of words – but that vacillation was from one motive only – the fear of not being able to place you in the position you were entitled to. Perhaps it was cruel to ask you tie yourself to poverty – to tie yourself to one who may be shot any day – but I had faith in the future. I have still. All must die – and in your love I feared not! If this is final – I fear less. I do not wish to live an old man – but I talk too much.

Let me hear from you ere you start for Superior, in kindness and in answer. Let me know too when you return.

I heard from William on Friday and wrote to him in answer.

I am well but have been rather bilious.

We are still stationary at Winchester. Rosecrans is at Nashville or Fort Donelson but will be here this week – until he comes we are idle.

Goodbye!

but Oh! Molly! Molly! dear I cannot give you up so

Very sincerely yours

James E. Love

128 Morgan St.

St. Louis Mo

August 10th 63

My Dearest Molly

I did not write on the 2nd inst. as I expected to start for the North next day. I did so and here I've been since Wednesday last, to find you started for the lakes – Sallie and Alex both gone. A sad disappointment to me, and I have foolishly postponed until this moment doing so. I hope however this will reach Washington to meet you on return. I could not rest on receipt of your letter, and so I at once made such strong influence & gave sound reasons, that I got leave for twenty days. I must leave here about the 21st and I must see you ere I go – as there is some sad mistake. Now that I am here I expect it is better you did not give those letters, as I can speak personally to all. If you have received my letters you will have learned that much as I suffer by it, I have released you freely. We are to each other as <u>friends only</u>. That we shall always be I hope – never otherwise by my action or wish. Whatsoever betides. So with <u>all</u> your <u>friends</u>, it will make no difference in my actions, demeanor, or words, so much I can & do freely promise.

But I cannot, will not give you up until you inform me that you love another better – or marry another.

I have talked love before and professed it too, but I never really loved another but you, <u>that I can prove</u> – it is so in all honesty. I never expect to love another. I have numerous faults, more than you know of, but I hope I can & would endow you with a wealth of love – more precious than a mine of riches. Feeling so I can proudly ask Wm & your mother for your hand. Aye every friend you've got, think it no trouble to conciliate all, & perhaps ere you receive this will have done so – in part or in whole – I will then learn I hope the reasons for their opposition which I take for granted as you see.

I never will blame you in the matter nor yet hold spite at them if from motives of prudence expressed or implied they refuse my suit. I shall demand an immediate union subject to your consent. They will probably laugh at that, yet I can keep a wife – absent to be sure like thousands of other poor fellows, but in case they do – badly as I may feel I will make haste slowly – and hold on the even tenor of my way so – for instance I will ask them if this war closes in a year – more or less – probably more and you are still free to love where you will may I address you. Of course I must present an honorable record, hold a good position, better than now – a Colonel or General if I can – and if I ever rise as I have no political friends Wm. knows it will only be by merit, <u>brains</u> or courage or both and besides all that I will covenant to be able to show means for a modest living. If I do this, as I swear I shall or die in the attempt, I cant see that <u>any</u> <u>one</u> has a right to <u>say</u> <u>nee</u> <u>nay</u> <u>except</u> <u>your</u> <u>sweet</u> <u>self</u> but if they do, I will apply to you all the same and tell them so in all candor.

I hold no claim on you, and if such be your determination also – I mean to postpone, I will hold none – except that I shall ask the boon of correspondence until you tell me you love – or are married to another. Until that time I will consider myself free.

When that sad fate happens to me, I hope to have stoicism enough to bear it, & accept what I shall consider the fiat of providence. Were I English, French or Dutch I might consult suicide, but as an Irishman or American I will see it out & wait till God calls for me, whether on the battle field or at a green old age.

I know with what feminine tenacity my heart clings to anything it loved, revered or respected in times gone by – be it small or great. I know how I will cling to your love to the last, be the circumstances of my live what they may. Aye I may make a "marriage de convenance," would probably – as it is not good for man to be alone, and I want a house angel to cling to – but I know as God is my judge I can never love again.

I fear at times I have used phrases that you did not understand – the slang of the army – such as "when this cruel war is over." I find it is not understood here – but for the future if you allow me correspond I will try to use English such as can be understood at all times & places – <u>and by all persons</u>.

I have not stated what I think from quiet observation here is the reason of this sad change in your wishes, and it is not necessary, but I hope I have formed correct conclusions. If so all will be well – and your action in the matter will be both justifiable, right, and fortunate in its results to us both.

For the present <u>you are free</u>, and I am I hope where I was ere a word to commit you passed. And now that I have defined my position, I will tell you I am well and enjoying myself at 15th & Morgan as well as can be expected under the circumstances. It is a sad wet time here however. I hope you, Sallie, Alex and Mr. & Mrs. R. W. &c have been & are doing likewise. I was surprised to find you had gone on a trip sooner than I was advised of, but I have improved the time, and hope to see at Washington or here ere I leave. If I have not heard from W within two days, I will start for that point or Chicago to meet you. I hope I shall not be "de trop" – even if received in only the light of a distant friend. Pray remember me to all the folks, Sallie & Alex especially. I hope to see them soon as I understand they intend returning at once, so mote it be – and also that you may come also but Washington will suit me as well as I will not intrude there longer than I am wanted or is necessary to a full & fair understanding of our present & future position to one another.

I have written in a hurry at Williams side and with his pen – which (the pen) dont suit me. I hope you can read it. I am with much love my dearest Molly

Yours ever

James E. Love

Address me here until the 19th August — afterwards as

Capt. Co. K. 8th Kans Vols.

Winchester, Tenn.

Office of the
UNITED STATES EXPRESS COMPANY
August 21st 1863
Dearest
I enclose Ivory Buttons, Birds & Ring. I hope all will reach you safe & soon, and please you as much to receive as me to give. I will write by this mail. I hope are well & safe my dear girl, and that you are not spoiling those bright eyes. I would have taken a much warmer adieu, were it not to spare you from remarks from envious eyes. I know who are my friends and I shall not forget them. Among them Wm & Jane stand first. I am well & in good spirits, will start in a few hours.
Goodbye
With much Love
dear dear Molly
Yours ever
Love

128 Morgan St.

St. Louis Mo

August 21st 1863

Dearest Molly

I sent per express today to Brimfield, the Ring & some other little things – but as I found it might not be safe I had care Dr. Murphy Peoria put on it where you will probably find it all safe & awaiting you by tomorrow night. 1 have just 5 minutes ere the bus arrives having forgotten until this moment – and not having the materials handy before. I am well and will write you as soon as I arrive. I hope you are not spoiling your bright eyes. I have heard nothing of the Colonel except that he wanted to see me. Folks are all well and quite cordial & pleased to have the matter settled so. My dearest love dont fret now – as you love me – and I will promise to get into no danger – more anon.

Yours Ever

Love

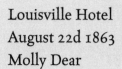

Louisville Hotel

August 22d 1863

Molly Dear

I hasten to take another opportunity to talk with you. I left yesterday and supposed I would be far on my way now – but the cars were overloaded with soldiers from Vicksburgh & so 2 hours too late this morning, and I missed connection. All is activity here. Our army is moving and I expect to be detained 24 hours. I have been passing such a nice lazy day – had a bath & a complete clean outfit – <u>feel</u> good looking for once in my life, but I would give my right hand to have "Molly" by my side. I dont know where I'll catch the "<u>8th</u>" – it looks very much here as if the war was over every where except in unfortunate "Virginia" and that all we will have to do will be to march in and take the country – it is a large country however – and we will get away from post offices at once – so you may be longer in hearing from me than expected – and I write <u>now</u> to say so. I will write as heretofore. You must do the same if it is only a word of blessing and to say you are well. Keep your eyes bright & your courage up and the twelve months will be short – very short – for I am coming home long before that time I believe as <u>surely</u> as I wish it <u>truly</u>.

I hope you found your friends at Brimfield well especially your friend "Mary" & my friend "Annie C." I wrote you a miserable note in a hurry yesterday and sent a pacquet for you care Mr. Church and Dr. Murphy. I suppose it got there today to find you gone, and will safely await your return to that "burgh" (Peoria). I want to hear from you very soon & never again wait because of reported Army movements, letters will come to us daily, even when mine cant get to you. We will now be away from Post Offices, and as it was last winter all will be irregular but safe & sure to arrive sometime – recollect that not <u>one day in a month am I in danger whatsoever</u> – usually I am as safe as you. I am interested now a thousand fold more than ever In Keeping myself so. I will do so – <u>there is my word</u>. I look no more <u>for fame</u> – save in your eyes & heart.

"No News" – will always be "Good News". Bad news travels fast and if anything happens to me you will hear by telegraph a week before any letter could reach you. You will hear worse than the reality too. Now recollect all this & read this letter over & over <u>disappoint the world</u> by allowing me to show it a stout bright eye'd, clear headed, warm hearted wife in the happy days soon to come and if after that "people will talk" what care we. Our happiness is within ourselves – and depends not I <u>know</u> – <u>positively know</u> – not on outsider, or on circumstances dear dear dear girl. I strain you to my heart & kiss you good bye once more.

Ever yours

Love

Address in all cases

Capt. Co.K

8th Kansas Vols. 20th Army Corp

Army of the Cumberland

I will write again as soon as I overtake the 8th – and address to Peoria once, then to St. Louis.

Over the mountains
Across the Tennessee
Near Trenton Alabama[1]
Sunday August 30th 63
Dearest Molly

I last wrote you from Louisville and since that I have been so busy it was impossible.

I left Louisville on Sunday morning and at Nashville that night learnt that our Regiment had crossed the mountains to Stevenson, Ala – such a wild trip – they had to pull up all the wagons by hand. All got over safe – except some dangerous fall by those on <u>horseback</u>. I continued on by rail and arrived late on Monday night, and soon found the Regt. 2 miles South. Tuesday I had for rest but I worked at papers all day & late at night fearing another move. On Wednesday & Thursday I was on Picket duty near the river 3 miles from camp & my sentinels could see and hear those of the enemy on the other side, and sometimes talked with them. On Friday again I was very busy with papers – had four clerks at work besides myself – and intended to write you after night – but such is human calculation. At 5 P.M. we were ordered to move – "to change Camp." We did so and camped at 9 P.M. some 5 miles down the river in a Thicket. At 3 in the morning an order came for <u>fifty oarsmen</u> from each Regiment – and our Pontoons were all moved to the front and placed alongside the river in a row – hidden from the other side by the underbrush – and on the top of the bank we now guessed what was to be done – all was secret before. At daybreak our Brigade was ordered out & each company marched down – each Captain got charge of a boat. At the word of command – the axe men cut down the brush in front & the boats were at once launched down the steep bank & into the water. It was reported a battery was posted opposite & we could see cavalry pickets on guard – so we were all braced for Death & hot work. I had extra oarsmen named, & had all my officers instructed, so that if any one fell, the others should go right straight along without delay. We got the word at once and

---

1. James wrote this letter from the vicinity of Trenton, Georgia, not Alabama.

soon rushed the heavy pontoons down in the water & aboard & then rowed for dear life. My boat was first in the water but I did not wish to be over too soon – so I waited & took a fair start with some half dozen – but my men being from St. Louis and boatmen soon got ahead & we were first across. It was an anxious moment and all that could lay down close to the bottom, in the water that leaked in – fifty or sixty large boats were crossing at once a river as wide as the Mississippi opposite St. Louis, (but with little current). A grand sight to those who looked on, but all was quiet save a few scattering shots & nobody hurt. We had batteries & sharpshooters on the North bank ready to open on the rebs, as soon as they showed themselves, but they were surprised and skeered so that they rode & ran off as fast as they could go.

I was first across with my company. We climbed the bank – formed behind a fence then charged over it & through a heavy corn field after the flying Rebs – & so to a road where we were to form in line of battle as fast as we got across. About the time I got there the "Colonel" arrived and took command. Within 5 minutes several other companies came up and Regiments formed right & left. Then skirmishers were ordered out, and I got the post of honor – so went out bushwhacking on the Chattanooga road. We chased our cowardly friends over a mile – took a position on a ridge & watched for four hours while a pontoon bridge was built and our horses & teams crossed over. The rest of the Regiments were similarly engaged or else at work assisting the Pioneers in building or our teams in crossing. The river here passes through a gap in the mountains and we were ordered to double quick to the top of those in our front and camp for the night, until the rest of the Army could cross and the trains climb the hills. We did so – dreadful steep & rough they are. We got up in good time last night driving the rebs before us. We had some good shots at them but they never returned any after we got well across – but ran watching us. Our teams have not come up yet. We had a light frost last night. I slept under an apple tree in an orchard by a fire & without a blanket. I made a good bed with Pine tree tops & got along very well. It is now noon and our teams are just in sight so we will get a cooked meal directly – so far for 48 hours our bill of fare has been honey, apples, peaches, roasting ears corn, and crackers from our haversacks – and a cup of coffee and now darling I have told you all the news just as it happened. I am well & feel stronger than when I left. I did not expose myself needlessly – I never will – but where honor calls I will not be last. It is generally safest to push on in such cases – and I did so being well supported by my men. I was surprised at my coolness. I thought of everything however & muttered a prayer as we marched & rowed across. And now I hope my dear girl you got my other letters & pacquet and that I will soon hear that you are well and happy – and have enjoyed yourself much at Brimfield. We will be here yet for a few days. The Rebs are retreating to Atlanta, Georgia, and I think evacuating Chattanooga, which if we have not to day – will have by Tuesday next. We go to Chattanooga & then all East Tennessee is ours. Isn't it glorious. Where next I cant tell you – but will give you all news as it happens.

We are in a fine healthy country – cool too for the season. And now my own love I must close. Our fighting here is all over for a month or two again – so keep your mind easy. Give my love to all the folks when you can – and accept a large share of love and kisses yourself.

I am

Yours Sincerely

James E. Love

Miss E. M. Wilson

Peoria,

Ills.

Detail from *Map Showing the Army Movements around Chattanooga, Tenn.* Plate 97 in *Atlas to Accompany the Official Records of the Union and Confederate Armies.* Washington, D.C: Government Printing Office, 1891–1895.

Camp at Winston's Valley head Ala.

Near Rome Georgia

Sunday Afternoon

August [September] 6th 1863[1]

Molly Darling

I seize this hot and quiet hour in camp as aforesaid to commune with you. I am well and jolly – let me hear that you are the same. We are having a pleasant time easy marches & long halts in the mountains, a pretty place it is to ruralise and no sign of an enemy – many of the folks we meet are evidently Union and are seizing the opportunity to escape to Illinois – as if from the plague – leaving most their household goods behind them, and of course their farms and improvements – and fleeing to a land of Freedom or refuge. Our troops are swarming down here, only McCook's Corp of infantry however and Stanley's Corp of Cavalry. Stanley's boys are regular dare devils and avengers, and are going if not gone to the heart of Georgia – bent on destruction to railroads there. We are merely supporting them, and protecting their base and rear.

We are about 40 or 50 miles south of Chattanooga in the mountains. Our division in the advance. We suppose we are only on Picket duty here, in order to stop Bragg if he attempts to run this way and also to prevent re-inforcements reaching him from the region west of us. While Genls Burnside, Thomas, Crittenden and others do the fighting and maneuvering in East Tennessee and other points north of us – and drive Buckner and the other Confederates to Chattanooga or into North Carolina. If they concentrate at Chattanooga it will be another Vicksburgh siege for it is very strong by nature (no place more so) and Bragg cant afford to run further unless he wishes to give up all the South and have the war concentrated in Virginia and the Carolinas. This is our supposition based on what we see and hear. Time will soon reveal.

I see your papers dont know much if anything of what we are doing here in this department. We know but little ourselves, but guess a good deal of

---

1. James dated this letter August 6, but, based on the content, he actually wrote it on September 6.

what is intended. Our army is now extended in a line from Kentucky to Georgia – through East Tennessee, all working on a general plan and Bragg, Buckner & Johnston retiring before us, perhaps concentrating. Each Division of ours connects with the next in some way and they support each other and can concentrate as soon as necessary to fight the rebel army when we reach it.

We left camp on Sand hill Mountain on the 2nd & went south 15 miles to camp at Youngs in a fine valley south of Trenton Ga. On the 4th we came 6 miles further South over another range to this valley. Pretty mountain farms and valley orchards with pleasant vistas up and down opening through the timbered ranges, a sight sometimes like a North Country sea coast scene with the fog looking like river or sea as needs be.

I have seen some pretty plants and flowers on the creeks that are new to me already, but now are preservable or transportable with present facilities.

Lookout Mountain & range lays between us and Georgia and we are camped partly on its western slope and in a narrow valley at its foot. It runs due North until it ends abruptly at the Tennessee behind Chattanooga. Such is the condition of things with our end of the right wing of this army. About 25 to 30,000 crossed the Tennessee since we did & they are scattered on these mountains & valleys for 20 miles to 30 – each way awaiting orders from our old War horse who never yet made a miscalculation "Rosy".

The mail is disjointed now as I warned you it might be and it comes and goes when opportunity offers – so this will close not until notified thereof.

I have sometimes an hour in the hurry at present upon me to think of you dear girl, and of the times when I shall be again at your side. I so long to hear from you, but I did not look for a letter before this time, or even for a week yet; so I possess my soul in patience and hope that you safely recd my last notes by the way side. Sorry they were not more presentable to critical eyes – but I hope and know you wont criticize.

I have written to Alex twice since I left, so they are posted St. Louis ward. I suppose you are back at Dr. Murphy's now, or even at Washington, in a week or two more we can look for some cool fall weather, then you can venture to St. Louis without fear of being stewed. We had quite a cold spell down here since I left you, but it is past some days since, and only cold foggy and dewy nights remain to be followed with hot winds and sun in day time as if a furnace blast.

I have got a gay shelter from the Southern & Western sun stuck up on the hillside on 3 poles and have written (with my clerk) under its friendly shade all yesterday and today, such moments have to be used while marching zealously; or you fail to perform important duties in time – but a company commander is not much harassed – like an adjutant, and I expect soon to have my house in order and then have much comfort with my company and mess.

At present I am house cleaning after the outgoing dirty & lazy tenant. Thats all. I have been reading the story of the Guard on the March and am much pleased with the sad story. I foolishly did not bring with me a stock of magazines to beguile the hours when long halts try our patience by the way – but it is too late now, as we are far from express facilities. All goes comfortable and pleasantly with me at present and when it changes you shall hear. And now I hope your enjoyments with Miss Church and her sisters married or single have equalled your expectations and that all goes pleasantly with you. You know you must tell me all. Theres a dear good girl – don't be so reticent (<u>with me</u>) hereafter.

I try to lay my thoughts, actions and wishes transparently before you! Will you reciprocate? but I know you will.

So with dearest love & kisses to yourself, with Love to Sallie, Jane – your Mother, Aunt and the rest I am for the present

As ever

Sincerely Yours,

James E. Love

recollect address to the 8th Kansas 20th Army Corp.

no more is necessary at any time

Love

Sept. 7th 63

Nothing new today in camp. All quiet yesterday and today. Weather warm. I am well. Good news from "Burnside." I believe he has fought Buckner and is marching to join us. Mail closes at 4 P.M.

Love and all good wishes to my own darling Molly & her friends from

Love

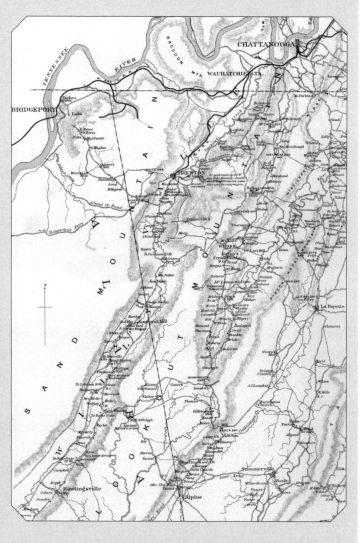

This map shows the topography in the region, where James marched from the crest of Sand Mountain into Will's Valley, and south to Valley Head, Alabama, near the B in "Alabama." Detail from *The Chicka-mauga Campaign*. Plate 48 in *Atlas to Accompany the Official Records of the Union and Confederate Armies*. Washington, D.C: Government Printing Office, 1891–1895.

Camp near Alpine
Chattooga Co. Georgia
Sept. 12th 1863
Dearest Molly

When last I wrote we were on the other side of Lookout Mountain. On the 8th we changed to a pretty camp in the woods. On the 9th we got marching orders. We started at 8 A.M. on a reconnaissance. Several Brigades each on a different [line illegible]. It was said Bragg was evacuating Chattanooga and it was desirable to find out what way he was going, so that we could follow to advantage. Our Brigade went 14 miles towards Broomtown & then found the road down hill blockaded with trees felled across – went to work to clear them but found the enemy in force on the other side. Meantime our Cavalry sent 80 men [line illegible] and had a skirmish. Their advance of 80 men were roughly handled by the rebels on whom they had come unawares but the main body coming up drove the rebels six miles, taking prisoners. We had two or three killed & eleven wounded. Next morning (10th) we had orders to return to the South, which we did along the ridge road. We got down hill at last away down, down, down, marching only 10 miles – but the two last miles was down hill & round about so steep it was rather tiresome. All our troops are coming across this road. It is on the way to Rome & to Atlanta Georgia where Bragg is concentrating all the Southern & Western Armies for a final stand. He dont understand and dont like Rosecrans flank movements – so when we have all arranged for a fight, so as to get in his rear & surround him, he has always run away so far.

Lookout Mountain is very high & has fine precipitous sides at places where you can get extensive views of the valleys below & the mountains beyond for 20 or 30 miles. Several of these views I had the pleasure of seeing within the last three days. I got my first sight of the Blue ridge on the 10th that is clear into both North & South Carolina of which states they in part form the boundaries.

We camped at the foot of the hill by a large spring and branch where we yet remain. Although we marched 24 miles to get here we are only 15 miles from Winstons. We found our Brigade here ahead of us, & all day yesterday other troops are coming in, down hill in a continuous stream. Horse, foot & artillery. We run amid in camp all day – sending out foraging parties – as our trains had not come up and we had nothing to eat or sleep on except what we had carried along. I have my horse yet & made him very useful in carrying Blankets & rations so I was comfortable compared with some. My Darkey "George" rides him, as of course I am not allowed to and in fact if the march is only 10 to 14 miles – I would as soon walk now. So here we are in Georgia – with the enemy close at hand – marching past our front. We are only 10 miles from his railroad – which we may perhaps go and take possession of today. I suppose in fact we will march soon as our trains arrive. An immense train is now coming down & has been all night – so I suppose ours is at hand.

We have had no mails now for ten days. It is said a large mail is at hand but we may not get it for several days from the amount of movement and confusion around.

It is said our whole army is in Georgia & close at hand, while Burnside has Chattanooga & East Tennessee about cleared of the Traitors — so we go marching on. I am in a hurry to see that mail, as I expect several Billet Doux from you in it.

I hope my dearest girl is well and happy – but to realise it fully, I want to know – never mind the uncertainty of the mails. Let that only be an incentive to more frequent writing – some if not all will arrive here in time & when it comes you know it is always "<u>latest news</u>". I am well & hopeful. So God bless you darling. With Love to all the folks – I am dearest Molly

Ever yours Sincerely

James E. Love

Camp on Trenton Road
Winstons Valley, Ala.
Sept. 15th 1863
My own dear Girl

Here we are back again & Northward bound I fear. We have been marching back & forth ever since for what object I dont know – threatening the rebels and they us at all points. Now up hill, now down again. Now up the valley, now down again. All ways in motion. We are going toward Trenton or Chattanooga now which is a change. After writing you on the 12th I went on Picket and there I heard the news and found the movements of which I speak – where we are moving so. Picket is not dangerous as the troops who are seeking a fight or making a movement go outside our lines at such times and unless they are whipped or driven back very badly – no one can trouble the pickets. The pickets in fact keep citizens in from communication with the enemy – and straggling soldiers from danger.

We are now two miles north of our old camp at "Winstons Valley head" and just so much nearer Chattanooga – and this after all our "Corps" was within ten miles of Rome. It is very strongly defended however by Mountains – Rivers & Troops. It is said the rebels have attacked us a little to the North – but there is no danger from that. I am well – got a glorious appetite for Pork & Coffee & hard bread.

We found or met a small mail awaiting us here – but there is evidently much more for us somewhere. I have not heard from you dear girl. How I long for some of your sweet words. I heard of you however as I had several letters of the 2nd 3d & 4th among them one from Alex. in answer to one of mine from Stevenson last month. He said Sallie & he were enjoying themselves in St. Louis "horseback" and that you were at Churchfield &c – having a good time & no word of return. I hope so – but did you get my letters & Express package. Echo answers not! but I suppose so dear dear girl. If we get to Chattanooga then we will have good communication again and I shall hear of you often again – only to think I have passed nearly a month

without a word from you – but it is no fault of yours. So as the mail closes
just now I bid you good bye – enclose a kiss & best wishes to you & all.

I am dearest

Yours ever

James E. Love

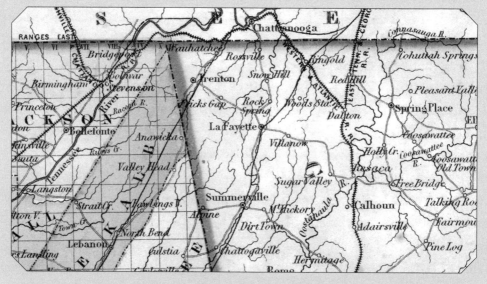

Since last writing, James marched from Alpine, Georgia, to just north of Valley
Head, Alabama. General William S. Rosecrans was gathering his forces, which had
been spread out between Chattanooga and Alpine, while General Braxton Bragg
concentrated his forces at Lafayette, Georgia. Section of map of Alabama. From
George W. Colton, *Colton's Atlas of the World Illustrating Physical and Political Geography*
(New York: J. H. Colton & Co., 1856).

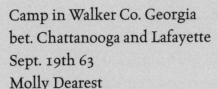

Camp in Walker Co. Georgia
bet. Chattanooga and Lafayette
Sept. 19th 63
Molly Dearest

All is changed since last I wrote you. We have marched and counter-marched every day since, and two days ago came suddenly in front of the enemy, very near where Negley was driven back a week ago in Michelmores Cove, between Stevenson's Gap & Dug Gap. I am very well, although very cold this morning, sitting in the sun by a fire, with a blanket over my shoulders. I slept last night on corn stalks cut down <u>where I lay</u>. I crouched in the furrow, to escape as far as possible the frosty night air, with the fire alongside. Such is the Sunny South even in Northern Georgia.

Yesterday at this time I was hungry, but today I am well fed. We have been lying for two days in line of battle, or as skirmishers, but have only heard a little distant firing. Bragg has evidently been reinforced and is coming back again. Only a short distance will he venture for the "Army of the Cumberland" is once more before him. Altogether I enjoy it, and will grow fat directly, but I miss my regular letters and morning paper!

How are you dearest? Still at Churchfield? Pale and interesting as ever? I hope not! You ought to be getting stout and sunburnt now! I mean comparatively Dear!

On the evening of the 13th to which date I believe my record reaches we marched up, up, up Lookout Mountain again two miles and camped at a spring. Next day across it to Winston's Valley and down again, then up the valley towards Trenton, where I wrote you. Next day we lay in camp till evening, then marched back to our old camp. Next morning at Sunrise up the mountain again and so Northwards to Stevensons Gap 25 miles. The last 15 miles we suffered for water and fasted all day – a good feed in camp at night made us forget that and sleep soundly. In the morning early down the <u>gap</u> to where "<u>Thomas</u>'" train was coralled. Thomas moved out and his train after him, when Presto in dashed some of Wheelers Cavalry, to cut it off. I fear we surprised them and cut a few of them off instead. We went out skirmishing and flanking the train 3 miles, and at night back again to a fine spring. Camped in line of battle at 10 P.M. during the night and day some firing, and had we been later the train would have been burnt but nobody was hurt on our side excepting one slight wound; several of the impudent Cavalry bit the dust including the Colonel of the 3d Confed Cavalry. Our darkeys lost us in the melee and so I had to sleep without blanket and without supper. Very cold it was, but I did so cheerfully – and in good spirits – all were preparing for the long looked for fight. I had no fears whatsoever, nor have I today but the fight didn't come, although we were in sight of their camp fires on the Mountain side. We camped in Negley's camp. The Rebel Cavalry drove him from here a week ago, & now in turn they run from us (17th). All day yesterday we waited an attack but Bragg moved to the North, and we slowly and sullenly followed him to prevent his flanking us and cutting us off from Chattanooga and the North. After dark we came to this place where we found "Thomas," fires all burning brightly, probably as a blind to cover his movement on Chattanooga.

The whole army has moved and is rapidly concentrating in front of Chattanooga. All is again in motion this morning as far as the eye can see is Rosy's troops or Braggs Camp fires. We expect to move momentarily and all are equipped and horses saddled for a rapid march or a fight if Bragg wishes it so! It is yet cold, dusty, dirty and stormy, and the air is loaded with the smoke of houses, miles of fences and tons of valuable Army stores, so it is hard to compose an interesting letter to a lady.

I only hope my dear girl is well and happy! If she is not so, the time will feel long to me until I join her to part and pain her no more – but if I am assured she is it will pass quickly and to I hope good purpose and a happy issue at last! Fear not! The Rebels hold not <u>my life in their hands</u>! I long to see you again already and count the days! Why it is four weeks since I bade you a sorrowful goodbye, and now I am at the other end of this great country; but happen what may, I feel that in a few more months I will be with you again a new man! And then? Will we separate much for a long time? Not with my will I assure you? Unless by your advice! but hark the <u>bugle blows</u>

the assembly for a march and perhaps a fight, so I bid you a hurried adieu, but hope with Gods help to address you again soon with glorious news for the good cause.

With Love and Remembrance to all at Churchfield, Peoria & Washington and St. Louis, I am my dearest Love.

Yours Sincerely

James E. Love

When James wrote this letter, he was camped near Crawfish Spring. Photograph by M. E. Kodner, 2013.

Sept. 23d 1863

Mollie Dear

I am laying out in a cotton field & doing well. I am at present within Bragg's lines but hope to be exchanged at once, as thousands of others are today and yesterday. We have just got some rations sent by Rosecrans, the first since the fight. When I closed this note, we started and marched rapidly 8 miles or more, and all at once got into a most terrific fight. I was under fire several hours, and rallied the men of my company and of others several times. I brought the flag back more than once when we were driven – but it was of no avail. The enemy overpowered us and drove us back.

At the crisis I fell headlong among them, shot through the thigh in two places, and my clothes riddled besides. I am doing well, and I am I assure you in good spirits and suffered no pain – neither when wounded or since. I am weak as it bled freely – and the sinews are cut and bone jarred very much. I expect to forward this from Chattanooga – will write whenever I can; believe me I will suffer less from pain than you will from pity.

Yours ever

Love

James lay in these woods after being shot during the Battle of Chickamauga. Photograph by M. E. Kodner, 2013.

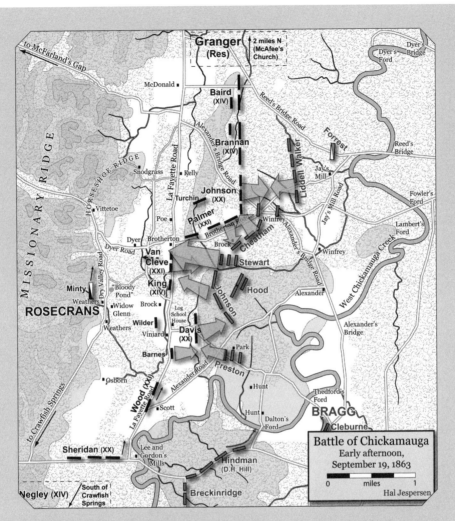

James's division, led by Major General Jefferson C. Davis, marched across the Lafayette Road and fought the Confederate forces on the other side. The thick arrow with Davis's name, in the center of this map, shows the movement. *Map of the Battle of Chickamauga, early afternoon September 19, 1863.* Map by Hal Jespersen, www.posix.com/CW, December 11, 2008.

Section 3

PRISON

October 1863–February 1865

On October 21, 1863, James arrived at Libby Prison in Richmond, Virginia. Over the next sixteen months, through the remainder of his letters, he was moved from one Confederate prison to another. Conditions for Union officers in these prisons, while not as bad as those in prisons for enlisted men, deteriorated as they became overcrowded and the Confederates ran out of resources to provide adequate supplies. Exchange or escape became the two primary topics of James's letters—and his only hope of getting out of prison.

James remained at Libby Prison until May 1864, when citizens of Richmond became concerned about escaped prisoners threatening their security. On May 6, James was moved from Libby to a prison in Danville, Virginia, then to Camp Oglethorpe in Macon, Georgia. By the end of July, Union general William T. Sherman and his army had fought the Battle of Atlanta and laid siege to that city. Sherman then sent some of his forces on raids to destroy railroads between Atlanta and Macon. As the raids moved closer to Macon, Confederate officials moved the prisoners to Charleston, South Carolina. In early October 1864, due to the spread of yellow fever among prisoners at Charleston and the movements of Sherman's army, the prisoners were moved from Charleston to a prison camp in Columbia, South Carolina. In one of his letters, James described Camp Sorghum, as it would come to be called, as "a fine healthy place," but that was not true. The camp had no tents or barracks, and the men received meager rations of rice, salt, cornmeal, and sorghum. Conditions at the camp were so bad that prisoners escaped nightly. In mid-December 1864, the Confederates moved the prisoners from Camp Sorghum to Camp Asylum, a walled enclosure located on the grounds of the South Carolina Lunatic Asylum.

Throughout all of these moves and many months in prison, James remained hopeful that he would be exchanged. Unofficial prisoner exchanges had occurred since 1861, when commanders on the field agreed to exchange equal numbers of prisoners. Federal government officials refused to formally exchange prisoners because they did not want to recognize the legitimacy of the Confederate government. As the prison populations increased and the public became more outraged, the two sides finally, on July 22, 1862, agreed to the Dix-Hill Cartel, which established a man-for-man, rank-for-rank system of exchanges. Unfortunately, the system quickly fell apart; general exchanges stopped on May 25, 1863, but special exchanges continued. Shortly after the Battle of Chickamauga, Union general William S. Rosecrans and Confederate general Braxton Bragg exchanged prisoners who were well enough to be transported, but, for some reason, James was not included. In his letters, James repeatedly mentions that several of his friends and family, including Molly's brother William, tried to obtain a special exchange for him but never succeeded.

Since James was unable to obtain an exchange, his only other option was escape, which he attempted three times. During the move from Macon to Charleston by train, the prisoners cut large holes in the floor of the freight cars. While the train was stopped in the woods just before Charleston, James and 150 other men got out below the cars and ran. James came within sight of Union gunboats, but there were too many Confederate pickets in the area to communicate with them. While on the run, he raided cornfields for food and was caught by a farmer, who turned him over to a regiment of Home Guards. In November 1864, he escaped from Camp Sorghum. He reached the Savannah River, at which point he was not far from Sherman's army. Sherman was in the midst of his March to the Sea, or Savannah Campaign, marching from Atlanta to Savannah, Georgia. Unfortunately, there were also many Confederate guerrillas and pickets in the area, and James was recaptured on December 4 and returned to Camp Sorghum.

In early February 1865, Sherman began his Carolinas Campaign, starting in Savannah and heading north. During the several days that James wrote his last letter, Sherman's army got closer to Columbia. On February 15, the Confederates moved the prisoners from Columbia to Charlotte, North Carolina, where James wrote the last entry of his letter, "Tonight I intend to go if possible, with a party of eight for East Tennessee . . . With love farewell till I see you."

Atlanta Ga.

Oct 10th 1863

Dear Alex

Here I am a prisoner & <u>wounded</u> in the leg twice. I am doing well – and will be as good as new – if I live to see you. I fear I am reported <u>Dead</u> – but I am far from it. I assure you – this is <u>not</u> <u>spirit</u> <u>land</u>. I hope to be exchanged some day & refresh you with my experience. I am well treated as possible – under the circumstances – and my wounds promise to heal soon. Meantime it is dull – my supply of writing & reading matter being limited. I hope this will go through – to make sure I will try again in a few days.

Love & Remembrance to all

I am ever yours

James E. Love

After several days in a field hospital, James was transported to Atlanta, Georgia. *View of Atlanta, Georgia*. From Harper's Weekly, November 26, 1864.

Libby Prison Hospital

Richmond Va

Oct. 24th 1863

My Dear Eliza

I have not written heretofore until assured it would go through. I wrote to Alex. I was shot twice in the leg – both wounds are doing well – a buck-shot is supposed to be inside yet. I hope to be around soon. The bone was not injured – but I can not use it at all at present. Too much exposure & fatigue before and since the fight injured my health considerably, but now I am under treatment. I am improving fast and as soon as I get strength, I am informed I will be good as new. I lost much blood on the field. The fight continued to rage over me at intervals on Saturday and Sunday, and when removed I was laid in a cotton field for 10 days or more – which proved fortunate, as we were kept cool and had plenty of room – attendance we couldn't get. On the whole I've done well – bad treatment was exceptional, and scarcely ever from a soldier. So I feel now in good spirits. I have been here three days, and I scarce know myself. There is no prospect of Exchange at present, so I must content myself here for a while.

Write to me – address simply to

Capt. James E. Love

Prisoner of War

Libby Prison Hospital

Richmond Virginia

Enclose in two envelopes & let the inside one be open (both addressed) so that it can be examined here. I hope to hear good news of you – <u>all</u> will be news – as I've got no letters since I saw you. I am probably supposed <u>dead</u> at the Regt. I have hoped & prayed such would not be the case in St. Louis or with you – but I fear – and so I hastened to write to Alex. I have thought daily & hourly of you & other kind friends in St. Louis.

So God bless you

With much love

Sincerely

James E. Love

Capt. Co. K. 8th K.V.

Remembrance to Mother – Aunt – Sallie – &c &c

"Libby." From Robert S. Lanier, ed. *The Photographic History of the Civil War in Ten Volumes*, Vol. 7 (New York: The Review of Reviews Co., 1911).

CATON LINES

ILLINOIS & MISSISSIPPI TELEGRAPH COMPANY[1]

Peoria Oct 31st 1863

By Telegraph from Washington, Oct 31st 1863

To Dr. Murphy

Love is wounded in leg – doing well

Prisoner at Atlanta

R. B. M. Wilson

---

1. Telegram from Molly's brother Robert B. M. Wilson, in Washington, Illinois, to his friend Dr. Murphy, in nearby Peoria.

Libby Prison Hospital
Richmond Va
Nov 8th 1863
My Dear Eliza

I hope long ere this you have received my first brief epistles. Time passes even in the Libby, and I can show so far a daily improvement. I can move around easily with crutches and use my left foot a little at times. I pass the time in playing backgammon & chequers or cooking, in fact very lazily – smoking some & if I can get exchange by Christmas (no hope I fear) I will be able to walk easily without help. We had two large cases in the hospital yesterday from the Sanitary Commission – so we live well again & comfortably. Thanks to pillows, comforts & clean clothing, besides eatables.

If I could hear from you & could feel I was not a prisoner I am as comfortable as my wound would permit, but this uncertainty annoys. I hope to hear from you or Alex in a day or two – and I think of it hourly, daily & nightly. I have only your Photograph with me now for three months, and I find it not half so eloquent as the original – but would get along if I could hear from you. I hope all goes well with you and that you are at home easy in mind & in good health. I try to act as if no news was good news. That is usually the case where the army is concerned, and is what I wish you always to recollect where I am concerned.

Give my Love and Remembrance to your Mother, Sallie, Mrs. Rogers, Aunt, William &c and dont forget to write me whenever you can. I can give you but little news here. One of our number – Major Slough of Ohio died of his wounds and another of Pneumonia during the week. About a dozen have recovered so far as to leave the Hospital for the Prison. Provisions are scarce in Richmond & Rations very short with the Prisoners generally. The Officers are allowed to send out and buy whatever they can afford to – but the Privates are not allowed such Privileges. I wrote you a long letter last week but could not get it sent.

I hope you will get this. I will write every week & some will reach you – with much love good bye.

I am
Sincerely yours
James E. Love
Capt. Co. K. 8th Ks. V.

James mentions on the following page that he was busy manufacturing fancy bone work, probably similar to this item carved by a Confederate prisoner. Horse charm carved by a prisoner at Rock Island Prison, 1863–1865.

Libby Prison Hospital
Richmond Va
Dec'r 5th 63
Molly Dear

Another week has passed into eternity and I am still inactive here. I expect to be here for months yet. I pass time pleasantly enough much as I would aboard ship – of which our present position often reminds me. I am still slowly improving, and hope to enjoy a very jolly Christmas here if the eatables ordered come through in time. I am so glad to hear that you remained in Illinois for I have no doubt it will add to your health and strength, and has protected you from impertinent observation and remark. I hope Mr. & Mrs. M. are in good health, also your friends the Church's and Mr. & Mrs. W. Give them my kindest regards and remembrance when you write them and all the seasonable compliments. The same to Sallie, Mother, Aunt and all the rest.

I have been busy for two weeks manufacturing fancy bone work. It is the fashionable method of killing time here, gives room for considerable display of ingenuity and patience, a small nic nax takes days in filing and rubbing. Very pretty things are made by those expert as engravers or sculptors but I am not one of them. Any little thing however is valuable as a memento of Libby or Chickamauga. You will get this before the holidays so dearest "<u>Merry</u> <u>Christmas</u> and a <u>happy</u> <u>New</u> <u>Year</u>". Think of me as very <u>comfortable</u> and <u>contented</u>. Be so yourself and dissipate as much as your health will allow and in so doing you will do more to make me feel happy and contented than you can in any other way, and write me the news every Sunday as I promise to do to you. I could give you much news – but it is all contraband.

With much love and high hopes for a future not distant
I am Mollie Dear
Yours Sincerely
James E. Love

Libby Prison Hospital
Richmond Va
Decr 13th 1863
My Dear Molly

As I have received all your letters, I hope you will some time receive all mine. I have written every week since 1st Nov; before that I <u>could</u> <u>not</u>, but I wrote to Alex; and the course of mail is sometimes slow. Glad to hear how you enjoy yourself. Give my kindest remembrance to Brother "John." I can rejoice with Mrs. North sincerely too, and I hope she has not been disappointed. Patience is a virtue. I suppose this will find you at Ninth St. I hope you will find Mother and Aunt recovered and all enjoying the Holidays. Love and remembrance to all! Did E.A. write? but of course it ended in talk! As to Mr. & Mrs. John A. I am not surprised. I knew it would come soon. When I was in St. Louis, she told me as much. She is a most unhappy mortal. I w'd say they are, but then he can avoid it if he wishes. He is in fact the cause! Along with her bad "early training" and present shiftlessness! I thought it a little Paradise, and was so foolish as to envy them and hope to buy it or another like it cheap some day! Will that day ever come? My Ambition is becoming so lowly, that such a place in St. Louis, with a clerkship or <u>a small business in town w'd fill it up for years to come</u>. I am anxious in this feeling and earnest, as I have long known that without such a home spot to be truly a <u>home until death</u>, I w'd never be contented. That is all I ever worked for. The only goal I set before me. A small Orchard & Vineyard and a large garden, with strawberries, other berries and all kitchen stuff! Will you help me, now and in future to carry out such an ideal. Near or in St. Louis if you will? If not there why in California, or anywhere South, East or West – not North?

I w'd I believe after all prefer St. Louis, other things being equal! Think of this and find out Mr. J's ideas of price, time of payment &c &c. It will be a guide to what <u>others</u> might want for a similar place. I will be worth very little when my debts are paid, unless somebody pay's me but I w'd like to be in St. Louis early in Spring so as to look around and settle at once. What say you? Mollie Dear?

Yours Sincerely
James E. Love
Capt. Co. K. 8th Ks. Vols.

When he returned to St. Louis, James hoped to have a home with
"a small Orchard & Vineyard and a large garden." The city had open
green spaces for such plans, even near where Molly lived on Ninth
Street in the bottom right corner of this image. America's Center
and the Edward Jones Dome are in this area today. Upper right
center detail from *Bird's-Eye View of St. Louis, Mo.* Lithograph by
Middleton Strobridge and Co., Cincinnati, after J. T. Palmatary, 1858.

Libby Prison Hospital
Richmond Va.
Dec'r 14th 1863
My Dear Girl

I have been so happy since I rec'd yours of the 22d ult. on Tuesday last. I wished to answer at once but found I must needs wait until today, ere I could give you a correct one. It was reported that <u>our boxes was stopped</u>, but it proved to be only the "money" contd therein, or in letters (if found?), and so we can still receive <u>good</u> <u>things</u> and good news from home. I can make no suggestions, besides "Christmas" comes too soon, it will be holiday season ere you get this! I hope it will find you as happy and contented as it leaves me, that I am so, I assure you. I am well, (except when I eat too much), and I get stouter daily. Ere the New Year is fairly inaugurated, my limbs I hope will be as good as new, equal to light exercise anyhow. And so the world moves, even if Libby Prison dont, and I am satisfied to <u>remain here a little longer</u> if our Government does its duty in the case. If it does not! Woe to it! It alone is responsible! As we know "Stanton"[1] can get us out of here tomorrow!! So let the winter pass and be sure and enjoy yourself whenever you can with <u>no regrets</u> for me, like a dear sensible girl, as you <u>once were</u>! And I will come and see you with or before the first flowers of spring!

You see I hope and I am content in that hope, and even if disappointed in it, I will still be easy in mind, as "<u>it is all for the best</u>"

Love and Remembrance to your dear self and all <u>your friends and mine</u>.
I am dear Mollie
Yours Sincerely
James E. Love
Capt. Co. K. 8th Ks. Vols.

I expect a <u>box or two</u> from William every day – certainly before "Christmas"

---

1. Secretary of War Edwin M. Stanton.

Libby Prison
Richmond Va.
Decr. 18th 1863
My Dearest Mollie

For general news I must refer you to my note to Alex. I received yours of 29th Nov'r two days ago. I am in good health, and keep improving daily up to this time. I am so glad to hear good news from you, that I almost forget I am imprisoned. On comparison, I find I am no worse off now, than if I was in the field, so I take heart of grace and hope on as usual.

I tell you the <u>truth</u>, as far as <u>these</u> short letters will permit, so dont fret so much for me! If I was out of here even now, I would still be much of a house plant. Though I can walk well, without perceptible "limp" on these floors – I soon tire, the sinews not being sound yet. I loose command of my knee joint, and then perforce must sit down. Since I wrote you an order has been issued to receive no more food or clothing for us from <u>our</u> Gov't or people. Whether that includes private boxes is not yet certain, but I yet hope not. And I hope Alex has sent me a large supply ere this time as we will soon be in need. I expected to get them for Christmas but I must dismiss that thought now. You will see all this news, and all about our exchange or non exchange in the papers I suppose long before I can write it to you. I hope you have got my weekly notes, since 1st Nov'r although they seem long on the way. I have no St. Louis news from Sallie yet, but I hope it is on the way. I can only send you this and a Kiss for New Years Gift at present but hope to follow soon! I have full confidence and trust in your patience yet! You are right about time spent in games! I soon tire – and a word in your ear, I never stake money though Mr. John A. often tempted me.

Ere that Photograph is lost, <u>I will be</u>! It is safe and will return to plague you I have no doubt. What about Mr. J's house & Garden? I had a letter from Alex same time as yours, but no news in it save than all went well.

Weather has been gloomy and wet here several days, but is now clear and cold. So mote it be.

With Love and Remembrance to Sallie, your Mother, Mrs. Rogers and all the rest I suppose I must say for the present goodbye Mollie dear

Yours Sincerely

James E. Love

Capt. Co. K. 8th Kans. Vols.

Miss E. M. Wilson

St. Louis, Mo.

On December 11, 1863, Confederate colonel Robert Ould sent a letter to Brigadier General Sullivan A. Meredith, Union Agent of Exchange, informing him that the Confederates would no longer allow the delivery of food and clothing sent by Union authorities and people to prisoners of war. "Colonel Robert Ould, Confederate Agent for the Exchange of Prisoners." From Robert S. Lanier, ed., *The Photographic History of the Civil War in Ten Volumes*, Vol. 7 (New York: The Review of Reviews Co., 1911).

Hotel DeLibby
Richmond Va
Jany 4th 1864
My Dear Molly

If you have got any of my letters, you will have discovered that I do get your letters (<u>all of them</u>), some two or three weeks after their date. I have supposed until today that you have been receiving mine likewise some three weeks old, but I fear now that some do not reach you! Why I cant guess, unless I make them too long, or write something contraband? I write as usual every Sunday and I have sent Duplicates of some letters, so there should be no danger of them reaching you. I intend to <u>continue so</u>.

I received yours of the 13th ult. Today! Glad to hear of your continued health, and that of your Peoria and Washington friends! Have you ever met Charley or Mrs. DeWitt in Peoria? Charley saw my name in some list of Prisoners here, and at once sent me a box of Sanitary Goods, for my use and that of the needy in general.

I am in good health; and I manage to pass the days pretty well, monotonous though they be. We have preaching and prayer meeting of a Sunday – but there is need of a revival. Libby is very profane in its practice!

We had another dance on New Years Eve. Of course I was there, and temped to practise, though I came away early through fear of hurting my leg! Exchange news is rather unsatisfactory.

And now my Dear Girl, as I wish this to go through quick, and have really nothing to say, I will end here with Love and Remembrance to your Mother, Aunt, Mrs. R., Sallie &c &c (<u>I suppose you are in St. Louis</u>) and your dear self.

I am
Yours Sincerely
James E. Love
Capt. Co. K. 8th K.V.
Miss Eliza M. Wilson
Box 1573 P.O.
St. Louis, Mo.

Libby Prison
Richmond Va.
Jany 10th [1864]
Molly Dear

As usual now I have no news but that I am well and growing stout for want of exercise! Libby becomes very dull. Hopes of Exchange have vanished into thin air, and we pace our few feet of plank like caged <u>Lions</u> or disconsolate Eagles. In bone work I can make no Chef de'Euvres, and so it drags it slow length along devoid of interest except as a device to kill time or as a "<u>Labor of Love</u>" occasionally, even reading wearies and food palls on the taste unless something new and spicy is served up. There has been no "<u>flag of Truce</u>" for fourteen days so I fear I wont receive my usual letter, but the darkest hour is just before the perfect day, and patience exercised for months past, is as much a virtue as ever! What think you of the homily? As true as sermons in general, and as hard to practice, as easy to preach! You will say? Weather here now is bitter cold and a heavy snow has lain for several day's. Fancy the condition of our poor enlisted men on Belle Isle in tents exposed to the weather and short of food and clothing and firewood. They receive the soldiers ration issued by the C.S.A. of course but that is all. Small Pox is still rife both in this city and in "Danville" among them.[1] There is none of consequence among the "Officers" in Libby. Genl Morgan visited us yesterday and I had a word with him! He is quite a "Lion" here now!

And now Molly dear as I have nothing to write about I cant enlighten any other correspondents so give my Love and Remembrance to Alex, Sallie and all and tell them I am well and in good spirits for though the above is a quiet Sunday evening statement of the case, I am encouraged every morning on reading the papers! The Southern Confed is decidedly <u>blue</u> just now and if it ever had any chance of longevity, its present Congress would Kill it by their insane Legislation in a short time it is so far gone that a Great

---

1. In November 1863, only half of the six thousand prisoners at Belle Isle Prison had tents for shelter during a brutally cold winter, and smallpox killed more than one hundred prisoners at Danville Prison.

Warrior and Dictator (or tyrant) like Ceasar or Napoleon is its only hope of Salvation! It <u>may</u> soon have one! Will it save it? We shall see! The pinch is to hold on now to next June – Corn is King! Cotton has abdicated and a very imperious Monarch he is <u>we can see</u> from our prison windows – where ragged children gather the corn bread and scraps we throw away for our amusement but all this is as well known North as South of the Potomac.

I am with Love

Yours Sincerely

James E. Love

Capt. Co. K. 8th K.V.

James mentions the "enlisted men on Belle Isle in tents exposed to the weather." "Belle Isle: The Confederate Commandant in the Foreground, The Capitol of the Confederacy in the Distance." From Robert S. Lanier, ed., *The Photographic History of the Civil War in Ten Volumes,* Vol. 7 (New York: The Review of Reviews, 1911).

Hotel De.'Libby
Richmond Va
Jany 13th [1864]
Molly Dear

I wrote on the usual day, but I afterwards suppressed the letter as I thought it w'd not go through, so outside of the fact that I am well & in good spirits I have no news to tell. I will write you as usual, but other correspondence will be small until this scarcity of items is done away with. I hope my dear girl you are well and enjoying yourself in St. Louis, and that all goes well with you and your friends.

We are I fear for a while cut off from our letters and you may not even get this for some time, as there has been no "flag of Truce" boat for over two weeks, and no Northern News of course. How or why we know not? Letters, boxes and every thing is of course stop'd by this for the present.

I hope you will get a note occasionally of what I have and will send weekly and for that reason I will make them short and uninteresting as to stirring or current news with us.

It has been very cold for two weeks and snow has been deep for about a week. It promises to thaw tonight. I hope the cold will abate as some of our prisoners are poorly provided with clothing. I am all right for a siege now, and fear not – but as I become more active, I suffer more and more from ennui, and <u>bone</u> <u>work</u> and cooking from repetition loses interest and becomes distasteful. I lack the patience and skill of hand to produce any Chef de'euvres in bones and all the common effects I have mastered. What remains is more in the province of a sculptor or engraver – for which my nervousness unfits me.

All hopes of Exchange here seems to have died out. A month ago we were all bouyed up with hope, now some are despairing.

And now my dearest girl with Love and Remembrance to all your friends and yourself I must adieu by the bye. Our old opponent Genl Morgan called on us on Saturday last, and I had a word with him, as had many others.

I am sincerely yours
James E. Love
Capt. Co.K. 8th Ks.Vol.

James suffered more and more from boredom in Libby Prison, shown here as it appeared from the James River. "Libby Prison: A Unique Photograph." From Robert S. Lanier, ed., *The Photographic History of the Civil War in Ten Volumes*, Vol. 7 (New York: The Review of Reviews, 1911).

Libby Prison
Richmond Va.
Jany 17th [1864]
Molly Dear

I have no letters as yet but I expect a budget on Tuesday for a "<u>Flag of Truce</u>", has at last arrived. What it purports we have not yet learnt but as I have given up all hopes of exchange for some months to come, or until the present state of affairs has changed either for better or worse. I see both North and South signs of preperation for a more desperate struggle than ever in the Spring and until it is decided I fear the causes of quarrell over us poor prisoners will not be decided by one or other party giving way. I hope to hear that you have received my letters up to Christmas at least and that my last are on their way! What are you doing? How are you? I suppose quite <u>used up</u> with the number of Balls and parties since your return to St. Louis, for I see and hear that St. Louis is gayer than ever before; well I hope so, for I wish well to The Mound City, and hope all I have ever prophesied or said for it may come true, whether I remain a citizen of it or not after the war! After the war! When will that be? Nine months or Nine years? Which? Who knows? Well I'll tell you when I see you? Perhaps!

And Sallie the dear little minx. What is she about? Why what a stranger I will be when I return! In these short letters you can neither <u>learn</u> or <u>communicate</u> anything but mere common place.

Weather here is fine bright and cold now for some weeks past. I am well of course. Contented as possible under the circumstances and as a consequence hearty and <u>Stout</u>. I weigh more than I have done since 1853. <u>Thirty pounds</u> more than when I saw you last, but then I was in marching and fighting trim and able for any fatigue! Now I am an Epicurean! And my most profound thought is daily and nightly on good eating and drinking! However a few weeks march or active life will reform all that and reduce superflous weight! I hope I may have that privilege in the spring, for if I dont have that chance then when the flowers and grass is coming, I am afraid my much vaunted patience will evaporate, and I will be as ready to climb a rope or run against a bayonet as others are now.

Love and Remembrance to all and especially Dear Molly yourself.

I am sincerely yours,

James E. Love

Capt. Co. K. 8th Kans. Vol.

A flag of truce boat, like the one shown here, finally arrived at Libby Prison. In James's case, the boat brought letters but no hope of a prisoner exchange. "The White Flag Boat That Carried Prisoners to Freedom." From Robert S. Lanier, ed., *The Photographic History of the Civil War in Ten Volumes*, Vol. 7 (New York: The Review of Reviews, 1911).

Libby Prison
Richmond Va
Feby 14th 1864
My Dear Eliza

Your letters have all been rec'd up to 24th Jany. Mine may be delayed, but I expect you will get them all eventually. This is a dull valentine. It has the advantage of brevity. Libby is dull now – but we had excitement enough during the week. We have been digging a Tunnel for 47 nights and on Tuesday night 110 officers escaped through it, ere it was discovered – probably one half will be caught.[1] Weather was very cold, or I w'd have risked my wound also. I am well and though dissapointed still hopeful – something good to eat and to read would make us more contented.

With much love
I am ever
Yours Sincerely
Love
Miss E. M. Wilson
Box 1573 P.O.
St. Louis Mo.

---

1. On the evening of February 9, 1864, 109 prisoners escaped from Libby through a tunnel eight feet below ground, sixteen inches in diameter, and fifty to sixty feet long. The escape was one of the largest prison breaks during the war.

Libby Prison
Richmond Va.
Feby 14th 1864
Wm. C. Wilson Esqr.
Dear Sir

I rec'd safe the box ship'd by you on the 7th Decr and acknowledged it at the time; Have you sent any since? If so what did it contain? If not send me one at once <u>same as last</u>! If <u>you find they are coming through and being delivered to us</u>: To include 10 lb Star Candles = some Beans = Letter Paper & Envelopes = Butter instead of Lard = <u>No Clothing</u>. Send per Adam's & Co. I am well – my leg is healed and will soon be as stout as ever; I hope to hear from you soon

With Love and remembrance to you and all friends

I am

Sincerely yours

James E. Love

Libby Prison
Richmond Va.
Feby. 21st 1864
Mollie Dear

I expect to hear from you again about Tuesday as a mail has arrived but is not yet distributed, but I must write today or lose a week – as we are only allowed to write one letter of six lines each Monday. I am well, thank God but it has been excessively cold during the week, and much suffering is the consequence among us. It is now moderating and I suppose Spring will soon be on hand. Nothing new here. Glad to hear such a good report from St. Louis.

So with much Love to you and to all friends
I am
Sincerely yours
James E. Love
Capt. 8th Kansas Vol.
Miss E. M. Wilson
Box 1573 P.O.
St. Louis Mo.

Hotel DeLibby
Richmond, Va.
Feby. 28th 1864
My Dear Mollie

Yours of the 4th and 7th just Rec'd safe. Accept a thousand thanks for its kind tenor and <u>contents</u>. The "Chapter" attached was perused with interest, and I hope to profit thereby. The "enclosure" is a sprited likeness. I prize it much! I think you improved since <u>August</u>! Not so thin! I can give no cause why my letters should not reach you except their length – or accident. It is amazing but as I wish you to get them all, I will be more careful! I am right well myself, and as resigned as possible to the prospect of remaining here another summer. This is a Spring like day, and if its influence extends Southwards, we may expect to hear of battles fought and won soon – "May Heaven defend the right"! I cant send list of wants now but tell Wm I want <u>everything</u> but Clothing and Corn Bread and to send a box soon and often say monthly.

I am
My Dear Mollie
Ever Yours Sincerely
James E Love

Hotel DeLibby
Richmond Va.
March 6th 1864
Mollie Dear

Yours of the 14th Feby to hand since you last heard from me, and I now write this glorious Sunday afternoon. We have passed since a most exciting week. We knew our friends were raiding around the city,[1] and that all the Militia were out to receive them, and on this small foundation, many tongued rumor built a thousand exciting reports possible and impossible of rescue for us, and disaster for the Confed's. And so we waited daily and nightly so nervously and wishfully but Alas in Vain. Our hopes are now again excited by the fact of a boat load (near 900) Officers & men being sent by "<u>Butler</u>"[2] for Exch. I fear only to be dissapointed again, though I have the best authority for supposing it is the commencement of a general Exch. I am still in good health, and glad to hear such a good report from St. Louis. The "Truce boat" now comes weekly.

And now with much Love to you and all your friends
I am
Sincerely Yours
James E. Love
Capt. 8th K.V.
Miss E. M. Wilson
Box 1573 P.O.
St. Louis Mo.

---

1. On March 2, Union brigadier general H. Judson Kilpatrick, with three thousand troops, raided Richmond, but was forced to retreat.
2. Union general Benjamin F. Butler, special agent for the exchange of prisoners.

Hotel De'Libby

Richmond Va.

March 13th 1864

Dearest Mollie

Yours of the 21st and Wm's of the 25th ult. just to hand. We live in the midst of such a mass of rumors that I scarce know what to write you! Some Special Exchanges have been made, more are in progress, but whether it will become general or not I cant say. As I have not made myself prominent here in any way, I do not expect a chance as yet, unless some kind friends North may have made application without my knowledge. My wounds are quite healed up! I assure you! And I feel but few bad effects. I am so sorry I was not in St. Louis with Co.K. but I hope I will live to follow it there.[1] No use looking at or talking to "Rosy" unless you are prepared to turn a <u>good</u> <u>Catholic</u>! And I know when that will be. I am well and wish to be in the fields again this fine spring day. Hope you are in better humor ere now. If so – I <u>assure</u> <u>you</u>

    I am My Dear Mollie

    With much Love to you & all

    Sincerely Yours

    James E. Love

    Capt. Co.K.

    8th Ks.Vol.

    Miss E. M. Wilson

    St. Louis Mo.

---

1. The Eighth Kansas arrived in St. Louis on February 20, 1864, and remained for a few days before returning home to Kansas.

Hotel De' Libby
Richmond Va.
March 20th 1864
Mollie Dear

"Hope deferred maketh the heart sick." While I w'd not have grumbled to stay here six or twelve months for principle, I do grumble loudly at the system of favoritism and Special Exchanges, as it appears to be instituted now. For <u>six months</u> I have written of contentment & even pleasure here, but all that is gone, all amusement, all study, all rational employment is at an end, & in their place only the feverishness of hope or despair, as rumor elates or depresses us. Our Gov't assumes a great responsibility in keeping us here, now <u>there is no</u> principle involved. I received yesterday yours of the 28th ult: must I repeat that I get all (have got all I believe) letters sent me – whether long or short.

I envy my friends in the "<u>Eighth</u>" their pleasant hours at home, but I suppose I must say at the bottom of my heart, I expect to be in St. Louis soon also – and if I have missed the grand reception there & at Alton & Leavenworth, Do I not hope for a private one from my friends that will be far more real and refreshing to me after this wide desert of pain and prison life. Is not my Mollie's smile more to me than an ovation? I trow it is! And will be I hope when Co."K" is no more!! It was a joyous meeting I have no doubt between the boys and "Rosy" – for I think their respect for each other was mutual, not to speak of love and admiration.

And now Mollie Dear give my love to your Mother, Aunt, Mrs. Rogers, Sallie, Wm & accept a large share for yourself. And with remembrance for all friends

I am ever
Sincerely yours
James E. Love
Capt. Co.K. 8th K.V.
Miss E. M. Wilson
St. Louis Mo.

Libby Prison
Richmond Va.
March 27th 1864
Mollie Dear

Whether I precede or follow to your city this missive, I will as long as the present uncertainty lasts, continue to write, and if any hitch occurs in the Exch. I wish that much wanted and long looked for box of supplies forwarded as soon you learn the fact.

I will write or telegraph as soon as I get through the lines; I received yours of the 6th inst. yesterday. I hope that no rumors will cause you or my other friends to quit writing, letters are the one <u>excitement</u> often of our dull weeks and I could ill spare them. I am well with an alarming appetite, and an Aldermanic tendency, it will take me a month or two, to train down to light marching order again. You say no word of yourself, but I presume you are well or you would not be so actively engaged on "<u>Fair</u>" work.[1] Glad to hear of friend Kinnear, &c, &c. What of Miss Love. He seems to be waiting until this "cruel war is over" also. How does Sallie's acquaintance with "<u>Rosy</u>" prosper – tell her to be on her good behavior for he never forgets a face or a name. I cant for the life of me understand why so many of my letters fail to reach you.

We have had a cold dark week with frost and a heavy snow (six inches) so that traffic by rail was impeded. Today is a cool sunny spring out doors – with the incipient buds to be seen on the trees across the "James River" which runs rapidly past, muddy from a slight freshet as the snow melts, interrupting the fishermen, who have just begun to cast their seines for the first Spring Shad. Ere next Sunday dawns I hope to know whether I am entitled to liberty or a prison, dear! dear! I <u>would so</u> wish to drop in on you with the daisies or <u>first</u> <u>flowers</u> of spring, but I am not sanguine of any such luck.

---

1. Women in St. Louis started preparations for a fair to benefit the Western Sanitary Commission, which provided hospital supplies for sick and wounded soldiers. The Mississippi Valley Sanitary Fair was held in St. Louis in May 1864.

Love to Mother, Aunt, Sisters & friends
I am as ever
Sincerely yours,
James E. Love
Capt. 8th K.V.
Miss Eliza M. Wilson
St. Louis Mo.

Libby Prison
Richmond Va.
April 3d 1864
Mollie Dear

I have no letter to acknowledge this week. There has been no "Truce Boat" for two weeks. It is said, "an arrangement is being made at Fortress Monroe," but how truly I cannot learn. We are yet in hopes, but some disagreement may occur any moment that w'd consign us to the Custody of these walls for the summer, so I hope until the certainty that <u>I am out</u> flashes to you from F. Monroe, that you will not on any such newspaper rumor as you mention intermit writing or sending the needed supplies. My Chum, had a fine box delivered to him last week – so I am at present well provided for but we have been much in want, of butter, ham, sugar & Candles for two months, and of literature for a longer time. We have had some cold weather again during the past week & much rain or snow daily. There has been and is still quite a flood in the "James River" in consequence. We have a good sermon now in Libby nearly every Sunday. The Revd Mr. Converse, formerly of Philadelphia officiated last Sunday and today. He gave us in a mild, persuasive, logical manner, good sound Evangelical truth, pointedly applied. I should judge he is a Presbyterian of the "Old School" & with his fine white head & beard his words have much weight.

I am well. My wounds are whole & painless. There are only about <u>2000</u> prisoners now in Richmond, of whom nearly <u>900</u> are officers, and the rest enlisted men, of these last some <u>800</u> are sick. All the rest have been sent to Georgia & N. Carolina.

This is my last sheet of paper and envelope & Money is out for months, however it is not much needed here – where we are well supplied with boxes. And now my dear girl with love to you, Sis, and all friends, I am with you in spirit this Sunday Afternoon, and some hopes of an early meeting.

I am ever
Sincerely Yours
James E. Love

8th K.V.
Miss E. M. Wilson
St. Louis Mo.

Libby Prison
Richmond Va
April 10th 1864
Mollie Dear

It is Sunday once more and of course I must write if it is only to pass time but what to write is the question. I am so dreadfully dispirited and Home-sick that I fear I shall become sick in reality. The weather has its depressing influence. It is balmy and springlike at times, but April Showers are almost continuous and heavy. The grass begins to come out green under the influence of Sun & Showers, and the Willows across the "James" to sprout. But "Why cannot I come out"? If an Exchange is arranged for! The river is at its highest flood, and is over the low meadows opposite the Prison & the city, and also running into the canal and streets alongside the Prison, aye even several feet in our cellars, and it is said that boats at this stage cannot pass the obstructions safely, and so for the present Providence stops our exit, but how truly I cannot say. Rumor at whose mercy we are has deceived us so often. We are now a race of unbelievers. The <u>prison</u> was never so irksome as now when we cherish some hopes of leaving it soon. The cold weather and good spirits that we have heretofore kept up, has kept us all in good health, but if our hopes are to be dashed now when heat & damp weather intervenes, there will soon be much sickness in Libby, we are just in the condition when an epidemic would make a clean sweep. We have had no letters for three weeks. There is a mail at "City Post" but it cannot <u>reach us</u> in less than a week under present circumstances – my last date is 7th March. I have had the blues dreadfully all last week. I am so impatient of this delay. I said I knew not what to write and here I have nearly filled my sheet with our prison fancies. I will hope that only the weather prevents me from joining you and if so I will steal a kiss on May ere yet. Who knows? I may anticipate this grumbling missive and be doubly welcome when present in "body" as well as "in spirit".

So with Love to Mother, Aunt, Mrs. Rogers, Sis & Brothers and a treble portion to your sweet self

I am Dear Mollie

Sincerely Yours,

James E. Love

Capt. 8th K.V.

Miss E. M. Wilson

St. Louis Mo.

Libby Prison
Richmond Va.
April 17th 1864
My Dear Mollie

Sunday evening finds me as usual pen in hand. We are at last quite sanguine of an early Exchange and so I have got over the blues for the present. I have therefore but little news for you, and only write to say I am coming, and I love you and hope to steal a kiss and hear your merry laugh ring out very soon and in the merry May days <u>then</u> to come. I hope soon to get a clean bill of health from Dr. Marshall – and enjoy a season of rest, fresh air and peace of mind, that I want so much.

I desire very much to hear from you as we have had no mail for three weeks. If we do not leave early this week we expect to have a mail ere Saturday, as one came up yesterday I learn. I have passed a quiet day.

Monday

Hoping I knew not what, I postponed closing this until the latest moment. I have nothing new however. We were surprised yesterday afternoon to see a large number of boxes for us, landed from a Canal boat. I hope there is one for me – unless I should be fortunate enough to leave within a day or two. Tomorrow will be seven months since I was wounded – Four months since I entered Libby. Capt. Chase (a hostage) has just returned from Salisbury, N. C. Penitentiary and reports that he was better treated there than we are here.

A thousand loving words to you! Love also to Sallie, Mrs. R., Mother, Aunt & brothers. I would write to some of the Morgan St. folks, if I had any news but you see how it is, and if you do not make my excuses – I must need make them in person – or neglect you next week.

Adieu my love
Sincerely yours,
James E. Love
8th Ks.Vol.

Miss Eliza M. Wilson
Box 1573 P.O.
St. Louis Mo

James writes that Capt. Chase returned from prison at Salisbury, North Carolina, and "that he was better treated there than we are here." From C. A. Kraus, *Bird's Eye View of Confederate Prison Pen at Salisbury, N.C., taken in 1864* (New York: J. H. Bufford's Sons Lith., ca. 1886). Library of Congress Geography and Map Division, Washington, D.C.

Libby Prison
Richmond Va.
April 24th 1864
My Dear Mollie

I on Thursday rec'd yours of the 15th, 20th and 27th March and words cannot express how welcome they were, or what a tonic they proved from failing health, and repeated dissapointment in our hopes of Exchange. I was almost despairing, while the beautiful Spring weather tantalized me so I felt I w'd go crazy. All this is gone, and I can look back on it to day as a dream of the past, and were it not for the spring fever yet raging in my veins, it w'd seem no more real than a nightmare. Truly I have to thank Providence for my trip in August again and again – for thanks to that and its results I am now alive. I rec'd yesterday the <u>boxes</u> ship'd by William on the 17th ult. in good order, and will probably find them a useful addition to our store; as Exchange seems again to have moved into the hazy future of next month. I wish I could swell the crowd at your "<u>Fair</u>" for I have some pleasant memories of benefits rec'd in the Hospital; a debt I must strive to repay. We expect a boat and a mail today or tomorrow, when I expect to have some two or three weeks later news from you. Depend on me, you shall have a weekly bulletin as long as I stay here, and am allowed to write: but I desire intensely to return to you.

With loving words to you, and Love to all your friends
I am ever
Sincerely Yours,
James E. Love
8th K.V.
Miss E. M. Wilson
Box 1573 P.O.
St. Louis Mo.

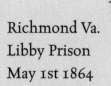

Richmond Va.
Libby Prison
May 1st 1864
My Dear Mollie

I am still looking for letters from you. A "Truce Boat" came up on Thursday, but the mail is not yet delivered to us. A few officers (Thirty) and men were paroled, and more are expected daily. The Exch thus you will see progresses very slowly and I have again postponed the good time I expected when liberty again w'd be my portion. The weather has been fine and spring-like but showery. It is very pleasant inside and out, but the season is so late or it appears so to me. The trees are only putting out their leaves, and are not yet well covered. The routine of the prison is much as usual, some are fretting, but most are in confident expectation of an early release.

We get accessions to our numbers every week – last week some twenty officers joined us, including Genl. Wessells, who was the first Colonel of our Regiment in 1861, and with whom of course I have claimed an acquaintance. He is very quiet and unassuming, and feels his capture <u>very</u> <u>much</u>. The majority of the officers captured with him have not yet arrived. I am well, and pass away the time reading and dreaming as best I can. I am so glad to hear of your continued health, and of your exertions for the benefit of the fair. I hope and expect it to be a grand success, an honor to St. Louis and the great West. A visit to it, and the exercise and change there – anent would recruit my health and spirits; but potent medicine and pleasure as it would be, I must shut my eyes to hope, or the reaction if I still found myself pining here in June, w'd be too severe.

A thousand loving words to you. Love to Sis, Mother, Aunt, &c, &c. I received a nice box of Groceries from Wm last week. I wrote to you and E. A. then, so now

Adieu my love   To
Yours Sincerely   Miss E. M. Wilson
James E. Love   St. Louis. Mo.
Capt. 8th Ks.Vol.

Libby Prison
Richmond Va
May 5th 1864

Dearest Mollie

I rec'd yours of the 3d, 10th and 17th yesterday, and I proceed to answer at once, for fear of <u>interruptions</u>. "Blessed are they who have no expectations, for they will not be dissapointed," is the proverb most applicable to "Life in Libby"; I assure you I have none at present on the Exchange question and I must be contented so, but it is hard work. I cherished hopes of getting out of here all last month but "kissing you by favor," and I have no friends here or in Washington who interest themselves in my behalf. I am well but would like to have a talk with Dr. Marshall before I attempted any more hard work. I am fleshy, <u>corn fed</u> – it agrees with me – but I am not fit for the field.

The content, I have so often spoken of – and which so puzzles you is as usual comparative – arising equally from the absence of hope of better, and the fact that I am no worse. If I have an enemy in the confederacy, and I know I have no personal ones, I wish him no worse than to be placed in my position, and as hopeless of bettering it, as I am today. "<u>What is the</u> matter that Exchange progresses so slowly?" I am glad to hear that you have been so free of colds. It is even more incumbent on you to be careful now in spring – so continue to care of yourself my dear.

Pray inform my inquiring friends that the <u>proper</u> way to show their interest in me is to procure a Special Exchange for me through some of our Senators.

Libby is now much as usual time hangs heavy. The days spent in Chess and reading but especially in <u>cooking</u>, in the hot and smoky atmosphere around the stoves. You wait & wait your turn, and can expend all your surplus ill temper. While every evening is occupied with a dance – a prayer meeting – a Lyceum with a debate or a Lecture or a sermon on Sunday night. The long nights are passed in bed but not in Sleep – lights are put out at 9 P.M. so from half past 8 to 7 A.M. when the kitchen is opened and we bundle up to cook again and to answer at roll call the time is divided between singing, telling stories, hideous noises, practical jokes all in the dark. There is much excitement inside and out to day on account of the advance of Grant and reported fighting on the Rapidan and the report that a large fleet is coming up the "James." A flag of Truce with a few prisoners for Exchange is also reported. Meantime Good bye. Loving words to you and Love to all.

Yours Sincerely

James E. Love

Capt. 8th K.V.

Miss E. M. Wilson

St. Louis Mo

Libby Prison, Union Prisoners at Richmond, Va. Lithograph by Coupil & Company. Virginia Historical Society.

Prison No. 3
Danville Va.
May 10th 1864
Dear Molly

I rec'd yours of the 3d 10th & 17th April on Thursday. I wrote you on the 1st May and again on the 6th from Libby but through accident neither letter got off, so I make another attempt. At midnight on the 6th we were ordered to prepare for a march to Petersburgh but all night was spent calling the roll while we stood in the street. At daybreak we marched across the "James" to Manchester and there took the cars for <u>Danville</u>. We got here on Sunday morning after a hot and tiresome ride, and now occupy the buildings formerly filled with our men. We are even more crowded than in Libby, and all the comforts which we had gradually accumulated around us there we left behind – so far we are much worse – but we are much better fed. The weather has suddenly become very warm.

If we had some exercise and a chance to bathe or wash our clothes, we would content ourselves awhile. I am well as usual, and I intend to keep <u>contented</u> and <u>good</u> tempered even if it should puzzle you for some time yet.

Why should I cry over spilt milk? Or repine because I cannot attain an <u>impossibility</u>.

I am glad to hear you have been so free of colds during the winter. It is incumbent to be equally cautious during the Spring so take care of yourself dear – and with many Loving Words – and Love to all your friends.

I am
Sincerely yours,
James E. Love
Capt. 8th K.V.
Miss E. M. Wilson
Box 1573 P.O.
St. Louis, Mo.

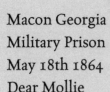

Macon Georgia
Military Prison
May 18th 1864
Dear Mollie

We were moved from "Danville" on the 12th inst. and arrived here yesterday after a most unpleasant ride and a short march in mud and rain. We are camped inside what was the fair grounds, in rather warm quarters, and exposed to the weather, but we expect to build sheds in a day or two and then I will much prefer it for the summer and fall to Libby. We have no longer any hopes of immediate Exchg. unless all our friends in the North unite to bring pressure to bear on our Government.

I am in good health at present. My last letter from you was dated 17th April. If our mails come to us I should soon have two weeks later. I fear this will be long on the way. There is so much interruption to the travel on the roads at present. I was glad to hear of your good health and that of your friends.

I must keep as hopeful as possible, but I do not fancy being here six months longer or more. I protest against it loudly and will so continue. We have been made believe by our "<u>Commissioners</u>" directly and officially for three months past that Exchange would go on immediately and generally – had we <u>not</u> been; <u>half</u> of us <u>could</u> and <u>would</u> have escaped at the risk of our lives. The present uncertainty will be death to many.

With much Love my dear girl to you and all – I am as ever
Yours Sincerely
James E. Love
Capt. 8th K.V.
Address
"Camp Oglethorpe"
Macon Ga.
Miss E. M. Wilson
Box 1573 P.O.
St. Louis Mo.

Camp Oglethorpe
Macon Georgia
June 2d 1864
Molly Dear

I wish to write, but what can I say. I am in as good health as usual, getting well. Sunburnt again and as much unlike the pale stout Libby Prisoner of a month ago as possible. If we had boxes coming in freely we would be better off than in Libby. We have built ourselves comfortable Summer quarters sheds or shanties. We are crowded for room of course, but can have a game of ball or wicket when we please – and some do please to keep the balls in motion all day.

I have not heard from you since I left Richmond – but hope to soon – if mails are allowed to come to us. I hope you continue to enjoy good health – have had a <u>grand</u> fair – and are determined enjoying the prairie breezes same as last summer. I fear I shall have to content myself here this summer. We do not expect any Genl. Exchange during the campaign though there may be Special Exch so it is no use fretting; and when ever any news is to be had regarding us you have the chance to see it first. My dear girl must not get despondent. <u>There is no cause</u> and I promise I will not. When I banished the <u>blues</u> in <u>Libby</u> two months ago – it was for at least a year.

A thousand loving words to you. Love to Sis, Mother, Aunt, Mrs. R. and all friends.

I am
Sincerely yours,
James E. Love
Capt. 8th K.V.
Miss E. M. Wilson
Box 1573 P.O.
St. Louis Mo.

Camp Oglethorpe
Macon Ga.
June 6th 1864
Molly Dear

I understand a mail will leave to day so I hasten to improve the opportunity. We hope to hear from St. Louis soon. We get news from our armies every day, but none from home for over a month.

I hope you are well and as I expect to be here all year now, that you are enjoying yourself in Illinois. It would please me to hear so. I look for news of a successful fair, and to hear of the conquest you and Sis have made. I had set my heart on being there, but our movements <u>here</u>, and other matters pressing, distracted our thoughts from it. How long we will stay here I cannot guess. We may be moved any day again. I hope to gain renewed health and strength with care. We have (part of us) good shelters now from Sun and rain but as we must have exercise, we are all getting burnt pretty brown. In all my long imprisonment, I felt much the want of an acquaintance. Nearly every officer had troops of friends, but it is only the other day that any officer from our brigade or Div. was captured, save one who came with me – most the prisoners are from the Eastern Armies few from the West, except "<u>Chicamauga</u>." We get plenty of corn meal at present with a little bacon. We are all in high spirits and will endeavor to keep so.

With much love to you – and Love to Mother, Aunt, & all.
I am My Dear Girl
Sincerely Yours,
James E. Love
Capt. Co. K. 8th K.V.

St. Louis June 22/64[1]
My Dear E. M.
Got the accompanying letters today & will write to him tomorrow.

---

1. Molly's brother William C. Wilson added this note.

We are all pretty well & kept this week quite busy
As ever
Wm
Miss E. M. Wilson
Box 1573 P.O.
St. Louis Mo.

Charleston S.C.

August 3d 1864

My Dear Molly

I hear that I can send a letter through, so I hasten to inform you of my change of residence. We left Macon in haste on the 27th ult. and got to Savannah next day – changed cars and went on to Charleston. On the road I made several attempts to escape and at last succeeded just at Charleston. I was out six days, made over 30 miles through the swamps, & was within 8 or 10 miles of our pickets, when an old farmer whose corn field I had visited being out coon hunting found my track, put his dogs on it, and caught me in 10 minutes more, ere I dreamt of danger. I was well treated, and I got here again by rail last night. We are at present in Jail but expect to move tonight to the Marine Hospital.

I am in better health than usual. I got covered with mosquito bites and chiggers, but that is a very minor evil and was scarcely noticed at the time; though painful now. I hope to get a mail soon and thus hear from you. I hope my dear girl is well and in good spirits. Some 50 high officers are to be specially exchanged today. When will my turn come – none of these have been in prison so long as I have. What chance there is for Exchange or boxes Wm. can learn better than I. When there is a chance be sure he embraces it. In good hopes and with love to you and all friends I am my dear girl

Yours sincerely

James E. Love

Capt. 8th K.V.

Miss E. M. Wilson

Box 1573 P.O.

St. Louis Mo.

Charleston S. C.
August 6th 1864
Molly Dear

I hope the present note will reach you. I fear those I have sent for some time past from Macon Ga. would not go through for lack of opportunity. I wrote weekly however and used up all my paper. I am in good health, now I have recovered from the fatigues of my trip in the country. We are considerably crowded and dirty here, but expect to be moved to better quarters daily. I do hope that our case will come up for Exchange soon. Some Fifty Officers of high rank lately captured were exchanged here this week, because they were under fire. Why should not we? I am much discontented with this matter. All those who fell with me at Chicamauga have been at home now a year while I am in <u>Charleston</u>. I'd rather live in the Swamp like a fugitive Nigger but everything must have an end – even this War! And then if no Special Exchange has released us a General Exchange will release those alive – most of us however will never be able for the field again. Of the News, you will know from the papers more than I. I look impatiently for a mail as I expect many letters long on the way. If we remain here, I will need a full outfit of clothing, unless we can draw some from the fleet and if boxes can come to us. I want everything heretofore sent besides a large lot of Apples, Onions, Potatoes, and Saurkraut, as sanitary stores, and reading matter old or new, — <u>money</u>, <u>too</u>, if <u>it can</u> be <u>sent</u> <u>safe</u> <u>in</u> <u>gold</u>!! with these alleviations we will manage to exist. But what is my dear Mollie doing all this hot weather. My imagination is so dull that I sometimes fancy I have none left. While in the swamps the other day however I was undeceived, for I caught myself dreaming many day and night dreams as of old. I feel very stupid here nevertheless, and fear I am growing as old as I am growing grey. One year ago I was in St. Louis; what a change there is in me since and what a long and momentous year it has been to me and many, and yet I have much to be thankful for; and do thank God often for his Kindness and preservation through danger and sickness. Our cosy sermons, lectures and prayer meetings at Macon are all at an end, and there is at present no room or chance to hold any here, all our preachers are left behind us too.

Remember me to the folks at Washington and Peoria, and all your friends in St. Louis, Sallie, Mrs. R., Mother Aunt &c. We are in the midst of the sickly season but it has touched us very lightly, and I hope will pass without much danger to life and without epidemic.

And now my dear Mollie I hope you keep your mind easy. When you do not hear from me, it is caused by the exigencies of an active campaign. Take care of yourself dear, and enjoy yourself while you can. My turn will come. Meantime I am in good hands – and with Gods help will yet see you safe and well

I am ever yours sincerely

James E. Love

Capt. Co.K. 8th K.V.

Miss E. M. Wilson

Box 1573 P. O.

St. Louis Mo.

Bursting of a Shell in the Streets of Charleston, South Carolina. From Harper's Weekly, January 9, 1864.

Charleston S. C.

August 20th 1864

Dearest Mollie

I wrote you last week. Also to Wm and Mr. Kinnear but lest accidents should happen, I will continue my weekly jottings, in fact I write weekly ever since I left Libby. I have had none from you, since May 15th but I expect a mail soon. I wrote for a box last week to include underclothing &c and to be sent Via Hilton Head Care Genl Foster. I continue in good health, and I hope for an Exchange this fall, but will not be much dissapointed if it fail. I do hope however that some of my friends will procure me a Special Exchange and that very soon, for I have had enough of prison life, so much as to be willing to risk my life on any plan of escape. I have done so and failed, been recaptured, so when a parole was offered me in common with six hundred other Officers a few days since, escape from these swamps walls and guards seemed so hopeless that I took it, in return for privileges to be received. And in consequence I am now with Two hundred others an inmate of the "Marine Hospital", formerly the property of U.S. It is a fine airy building with Three Story Piazza all around, with a good yard, built on the center of the lot, and encircled with fine Shade trees – Crape Myrtle, Fig, China and White Mulberry. The Fig trees loaded with Figs fast ripening and the beautiful "Crape" covered with its fairy like plumes and sprays of living Pink. You cannot appreciate the improvement but I can, and as long as I am doomed by Government to be a prisoner, I must be contented here – on Parole within the Grounds attached. Eleven months have passed to day since I was wounded and captured. Who is responsible?

I hope very soon to hear of your health and welfare, also of all your friends, and that you have enjoyed the summer as it ought to be, in the country. A thousand Loving words to you my dear Girl, and Love and Remembrance to all friends from

Yours Sincerely,
James E. Love
8th K.V.
Miss E. M. Wilson
Box 1573 P.O.
St. Louis Mo.

Since his last letter, James was moved from the jail, the building on the left side of this sketch, to the Marine Hospital, the building on the right. *Jail and Marine Hospital, Charleston, S.C.* From Ballou's *Pictorial Drawing-Room Companion*, August 8, 1857.

Marine Hospital
Charleston S. C.
Sept. 10th 1864
My Dear Molly

I today propose to write to you as usual though news I have none. I keep in moderate health and strength considering time and place. The city is said to be remarkably healthy, and so are we. Our daily routine of cooking, eating and sleeping goes dully and evenly on, weather now cold then hot, and occasionally to wash our clothes and clean up our quarters the only variation or heavy duty. I write on our airy and pleasant Verandah. The church going bells sounding in my ears. Our imprisonment is much mitigated since we were paroled. I borrowed some money a month since, and I have milk morning and evening with my rice and bread – which is quite a grateful addition to our rations. A few days ago we were furnished with gas in the evenings which has added much to our cheerfulness and sociability. If we could only hear from our loved ones at home our minds would be easier than they have been for months past. I look daily for an answer from you to my first letter from here. How I do hunger and thirst after it, be the news it contains old or new would matter little. The sight of a letter, the bodily presence it brings along with it, the magnetism in the lines, something there is that fills a want far greater than any words the few lines it may contain can do. Perhaps it is, what other eyes cannot see, but that from its receipt I know, that you live, and I unworthy dog that I am, am thought of loved and prayed for still? But where have your tiny notes been wandering for months past? To what Dead Letter Office consigned? Or have you known better about the mails than I! I hope so! For if not I know how my dear girl has suffered from anxiety. Would to God I was near today, as I am in spirit, to chase away the tears and weary sighs, and cheer the sad heart that I fear you must carry under your smiling exterior. I am the prisoner, but I feel Guilty whenever my thoughts wander homeward for I know that I am not the most to be pitied. I know the worst here, and I can see you at home with kind friends &c, &c, so my mind can be comparatively easy! But you are fearing you know not what and dont believe half what I say to cheer you in my letters! But you are wrong, I tell you only the truth, not half the truth perhaps because much of it is contraband and what I do tell is shown in the best light, but what then. I live am in health and have enough to eat, for the rest I can endure for a season, and trust in God for a deliverance at some time. I cannot see why it should be long delayed either! as all the difficulties in the way seems settled but I have written for money and boxes, and clothing so as to be prepared for winter. Meantime with much Love to you, [two lines cut out of letter]

Love to all your friends, and Remembrance to all the true, Lovely and brave hearts in St. Louis:

I am, Molly dear,

Yours Sincerely

James E. Love

Marine Hospital
Charleston S. C.
Sept. 18th 1864
My Dear Mollie

I was agreeably surprised last night on receiving yours of the 26th July, the first since date of May 15th which I rec'd in Macon in June. Such a long three months as it has been. I am glad to hear that some of my letters reached. I hope ere this you have rec'd others from "Macon" as well as from this place. I am now encouraged to expect others from you daily, written during August or Sept.! It was a pleasure also to see my oft express'd hopes and wishes gratified by hearing from you in Ill's! Of your health and pleasure there, and also of the welfare of your friends there, including your prime favorite "Charlie"! From the dates you mention I find my longest and most interesting letters have been intercepted. You can imagine what a severe trial it is thus to know that all my eloquence is lost, and that I must refrain from much news or many words for the future. Knowing that many failed to reach, many of my letters were almost repetitions of former ones. At present I will only tell you that I am well, that I have every prospect of continuing so, as I am comfortably situated, that I live well, being just at present in funds, and we have the privilege of buying in the market what we want. We have managed to get some books too, something we have never had since we left Libby. So if it were not the Irksome Knowledge that we are here compulsorily, we could enjoy a lazy mans paradise, and eat & drink, read, smoke and sleep to the end without much danger to life or morals. So fear not. All we want is clothing and that we hope soon to get from the fleet or home! If our government has any reason for not exchanging us, so long as there is no special Exchanges as heretofore, we shall be satisfied, but not otherwise. So long as we are allowed to remain here we will be comfortable, but if the military operations, or other causes, compel our removal, it will be to our pain and discomfort. Our hopes of Exchange have all died out for the present. Sunday quiet reigns around me, it is usually pretty well spent, at Macon we had sermons morning & evening, and prayer meeting nearly every evening but since we came here, all our <u>Preachers and Doctors</u> have been exchanged, so there is no service in our Hospital at present, but we can see and hear that there still is in some of the others – it was a great pleasure and boon to us I assure you and I was a regular attender! Letters will follow us even if removed – <u>when allowed to come at all</u>! Sorry I cant join you today in your Cherry pie, but I will make it up in Rice Pudding. With much Love, dear Molly and remembrance to all your friends

I am ever yours sincerely,

James E. Love

One year a prisoner tomorrow!!!

Miss E. M. Wilson

St. Louis Mo.

Marine Hospital
Charleston S. C.
Sept. 24th 1864
My Dearest Molly

I have a chance (I hope) to smuggle a letter to you this morning if I write quick, by an Officer returning to his regiment! I have had much suffering there is no doubt in person, but not the agony of mind that you must have had so I have a right to pity you in turn, for your kind thoughts hitherward – but now and I hope for the future (my future long or short) here I will be pretty comfortable. I have got some money, I am on Parole, about 700 Officers out of 1800 are also paroled – if a box with a liberal amount of under clothing arrives soon I will have nothing to fear, unless by the accidents of War around the city. The rebs are compelled to remove us to the interior, that would be very unfortunate for us, but I scarce expect to be moved this Winter, unless our Government takes compassion on us and allows a General Exchange next November and so we can move home. I dont know what to think however of the probability, and I fear I may remain longer unless through some special arrangement.

I have been so fortunate during my imprisonment in the speedy recovery of my wounds and health, while others with <u>less</u> wounds and stouter Physique linger long and linger yet, so fortunate in having money, clothing and boxes when in greatest need that I think and with reason I have been all the time under a special providence, indeed I do. Is it not in answer to your prayers my dear girl?

It certainly cannot be mine! Though I hope I have learned to be better in that respect than when I saw you last! Providence has been so kind to me many a time and oft. that did I not acknowledge it and worship I would deserve a double punishment. While thousands around me have been suffering greatly and heroically, I as one of a few have measurably escaped. While our poor men have died in thousands, I and those with me have enjoyed very fair health. Truly I thank God and trust with some confidence that the future will not belie the past in his care and kindness, but if suffering comes ought I to expect to be the only exempt, and must I not endure, with my small stock of patience as best I can. <u>God helping me</u>. Amen.

I would so wish to be with you, and united with closer ties, but I do not wish to give any hopes. If all goes well to that time, I will leave the Army early in the spring. My time is up and I have tried to be a faithful servant, but something is due to myself and much more in my estimation to you so I will if others can be found to fill my place and ease my conscience as regards the good work in the cause I have so near my heart, for truly I and millions others could never live in peace and contentment, in the western country if this vile imposture of a Military Despotism should success, and the hope of the freedom of Nations and millions in Europe and elsewhere should be so driven back and obscured for ages, providence in his kindness and love for man would never permit it, unless as a temporary punishment for our many national sins.

I am so longing to get to home and quietness however that I would make many sacrifices of <u>opinion</u> and comfort to do so. I hope I may soon do so and join you on or near the Prairies is what I nightly and daily pray. I received yours of July 26th a few days since and answered it by Flag of Truce. I look for others daily, and hope to hear that you have received some, and now will receive all of mine, so I will be saved repetitions and can study to make my letters more interesting.

I wish to be remembered to your friends at Washington and Peoria, also to Sallie, Mrs. Rogers, John, your Mother and all others at St. Louis when you write. I have just written to William. I hope both will reach soon, and if <u>I could follow</u> I w'd, remain at home for some time at least, even if I judged it well to hold my commission for a few months longer. Keep a good heart all will yet be well. All things will work together for good I hope although we may for the time be disappointed. Meantime adieu my Love

I am ever

Yours Sincerely

James E. Love

P. S.

As far as I can ascertain the Southern Press and People expect to give in if they cannot <u>prevent Lincoln's election</u> or gain some decisive advantage soon, that is ere we can draft fresh troops, signs of exhaustion are very apparent. Men and money are scarce, boys of 13 & 14 and old men of 50 and 60 are all in arms, while so little faith have they in their cause that a dollar is worth but 4 cents in specie and a bond with interest on it not worth more if as much. Dreadful fighting must ensue soon at Richmond and also in Georgia. They are about to stake all, so a decisive defeat to them would be worse than a <u>Waterloo</u> – and not to gain a great Victory would be as bad as defeat has heretofore been. Will my dear Girl be prepared to see me soon and to grant me any moderate requests I may make – or be resigned to my absence for a lengthened time if such is necessary for the cause of justice and the Government! This may be the case but I fear a dreadful reckoning will be against some one in our Government who has been careless of our sufferings and our cries, and who has caused this dilatory policy to be pursued.

Yours

Love

P.P.S.

A large invoice of clothing and Sanitary goods have just arrived. I hope I shall be fortunate.

Yours

Love

Marine Hospital
Charleston S. C.
Sept. 28th 1864
My Dear Molly

I asked Capt. Austin to send you a letter when he reached Atlanta which would give you the news more in detail than I can by the "Truce Boat." I think I told you before of Capt. A. (of the 8th) being captured on the 4th of July last. Well he was one the fortunate ones under the arrangement made between Genls. Sherman & Hood at Atlanta. So also was Lt. Hale, who was wounded at Chicamauga about the same way and time as myself, and who has been my messmate and companion ever since.

So I am solitary indeed and now mess alone, but it has its advantages too and company is only too plenty around. I hoped to be one of the "fortunates" myself but was as usual ignored or forgotten, along with hundreds of other good men, and old prisoners. Two anniversaries have passed since I wrote you, and so quietly that I scarcely noticed them myself. I was a year a prisoner on the 20th Inst. and my Birthday passed yesterday. Verily time flies even in prison, but he leaves his mark <u>deeper</u> <u>here</u> than at "<u>Home</u>". You should see how gray I am becoming as well as many others here, it is astonishing indeed what effect this confinement and low spirits has on some! The weather now is delightful, but still very warm. Prison healthy, as am I. No letters since my last, and no boxes yet. We have good news from the Armies, and if all goes I begin to expect to see you before or at Christmas yet. Who knows what may happen then. Meantime my dear Girl, with a thousand loving words to you and Love and Remembrance to all your friends.

Prayers for your comfort, health and Peace of mind.
I am
Yours Sincerely
James E. Love
Miss E. M. Wilson
Box 1573
St. Louis Mo.

Camp near Columbia S. Ca.
October 10th 1864
My Dear Molly

In consequence of sickness I believe principally, we were all moved out to this place on Thursday last quite unexpectedly.

I have been in good health so far, and as we are now camped in a fine healthy place, with common care I hope to continue so. I have not yet received a letter, but I received a box about one fourth full of clothing, tin ware &c. No groceries or money. These were taken out (it is said) by order of Genl. Foster. At any rate I did not get them. As it is I can get along fairly to January next before which time there should certainly be an exchange effected, else I shudder to think of the suffering and death that will ensue among the old prisoner's, from cold, want and the loss of hope; whether we are well or ill treated by our Confederate guards. There are and has been so many exchanges going on that in Gods name I cannot see any reason why all should not be exchanged soon. There is a large mail awaiting us some where, and I expect a letter from you. Pray write at every opportunity, for I am nearly crazy for a letter, without reference to news.

I pray often for your health, welfare and peace of mind. With much love to you my dear girl, and a kind remembrance to all friends, this cold weather.

I am as ever
Yours Sincerely
James E. Love
Capt. 8th K.V.

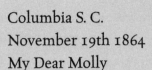

Columbia S. C.

November 19th 1864

My Dear Molly

I have waited several days hoping to be fortunate enough to secure an Exchange as I am one of the Oldest Prisoners but it seems Exchanges are postponed again to a future day, and I must be patient. I would have escaped a month ago, only for this expectation. Now it is too late. I rec'd your letter of Oct. 4th yesterday. I was very glad indeed to hear of your health, and that you were still enjoying quiet in Hoosier Land, and had not yet ventured to Missouri. Of course my dissapointment was great to hear that Wm. failed to procure a Special Exchange but the news we have had here led me to anticipate that much. The weather is again warm here, today it rains, and then we look for winter. I wrote to Wm. a few days since for a box to arrive at Christmas and we have begun to prepare our Shanty for cold weather; so you can judge that my hopes at present as to being in St. Louis this winter is small. I enter on the winter campaign in good health I assure you, and with the aid of a little money and warm clothing I have sent for will come out in good condition next spring, "so <u>let not</u> <u>your heart</u> be <u>troubled</u>." Trust in me. There is much to say always that cannot be mentioned in these short notes. I look for later news from you daily by way of <u>Savannah</u>. Give my love and remembrance to Sallie, Mrs. R., Mother, Aunt and all the others when you reach St. Louis. We are much pleased with the election news we receive; sorry to dissapoint the "Doctor" and his allies, but MacClellan has now sunk beneath the surface never to rise, and the Chicago Copperheads will be <u>jibbeted</u> in history with the torries of the 1st revolution.[1] Better far better for them to have come out as <u>honest</u> <u>rebels</u>, if they look for future name and fame!

I could give you much news but I dare not, so read the papers, and I must keep my budget until that time I so long for, when I can see you again face

---

1. In the 1864 presidential election, Union general George B. McClellan was the candidate of the radical Peace Democrats, or Copperheads, who believed that the war was a complete failure and wanted an immediate end to the conflict even without securing a Union victory. This platform offended many Union soldiers, who believed it invalidated all of their sacrifices.

to face, when probably the war will be over and peace again dwell in our glorious land. The prospect at present to me looks bright. May I not be disapointed is my constant prayer. I know you join with me daily, so I greet you with a thousand loving words and kisses.

I am, as ever,
Yours Sincerely
James E. Love
Capt. 8th K.V.

James was moved to "Camp Sorghum," so named for its meager supplies of rations. *Camp Sorghum, opposite Columbia, South Carolina. From* Harper's Weekly, *April 1, 1865.*

Columbia S. Ca.

Dec'r 5th 1864

My Dear Mollie

Since I last wrote to you, I have been out on a trip to meet Sherman, or visit East Tenn. but I failed to do either, was recaptured and am now back at the old place. We had a hard time out, but a little exercise and starvation even is a change from the monotony of Prison life; and very few feel worse for the trip. All goes on in camp as usual. The weather is again warm and favorable.

I am in my usual health would have nothing to complain of, if I <u>was</u> <u>free</u>. I wrote to Wm. C. last week and intend to send him a parcel for safe keeping till I come myself. I suppose you are now enjoying the winter season in St. Louis; and ere you have received this will have passed the usual quiet Christmas and New Year. I did expect to show my face at the festive board about that season but I am born to dissapointment and to be a thorn in the side of all my best friends; but with your good help and prayers I hope this programme will be changed, when this cruel war is over. I <u>must be patient</u>! I know <u>how long suffering</u> <u>you are</u>; and think it needful to again remind you, that your imagination makes me suffer more than I do in reality, and that you are really the Martyr and hero, <u>not I</u>. Pray believe it! It is so I assure you! I suffer but what thousands of poor unfortunates at home and abroad suffer daily and live! And God Willing I will live and meet you in happiness yet. The sick and badly wounded are to be exchanged! Would you rather see me on that list, or in health here?

News I have much, but it is contraband. I wish to be remembered when you can kindly to all. With love dearest to yourself and every kind thought

I am as ever

Yours Sincerely

James E. Love

Capt. 8th Ks. Vol.

Miss E. M. Wilson

Box 1573

St. Louis Mo.

Camp Asylum
Columbia S. Ca.
January 29th 1865
My Dear Molly

As no mails have left the camp that I could hear of, for several weeks I have failed to write as usual. The last rec'd from you is over three months old and so I indite the first Epistle of the year not knowing when it may reach you. We have had a spell of very cold weather for The Sunny South. Cold enough in fact for St. Louis and making me wish very much for a box at times, but it seems that the days of boxes have gone by, and our imprisonment becomes thus more sombre, dreary, and hard as it progresses. Under Providence I have enjoyed the blessings of good health so far, with the exception of a slight cold and some other little ailments to which I am liable from time to time. Our spirits are kept up from day to day by the good news, and progress that we hear the cause is making North & South. We have been excited and amused by rumors of Peace and Armistice lately but put little faith in them as we fully expect another summer of hard fighting ere that happy day can yet arrive!

I hope you received all safe my letter of Decr. first and the parcel of Nick Nax, letters &c I sent by Lt. Reynolds, for <u>safety</u>, and safe keeping. As I told you when I made up that parcel containing all my effects I had made arrangements for escape. I did escape, but as before failed to make it good and was recaptured. We are too closely confined now, to permit any such dreams, even if the weather was favorable. All hopes of Exchange for the present has died within us, though we know not what a day may bring forth, and we have yet failed to understand the cruel order by which our Government stop'd our boxes while it allowed Rebel Prisoners North to receive all manner of comforts that could be purchased by Cotton.

I hope my dearest girl is well, and enjoying the seasons parties and Sleigh rides. Let not your heart be troubled on my account. I am in good hands.

Trust in God and in me. All is I hope for the best, and in Gods good time my release will come. Love to all. Much love to you ever darling.

Yours Sincerely

James E. Love

Capt. 8th K.V.

In December 1864, James was moved from Camp Sorghum to Camp Asylum, both in Columbia, South Carolina. *Asylum Camp, Columbia, South Carolina.* Courtesy of the South Carolina Confederate Relic Room and Military Museum, Columbia, SC.

Camp Asylum
Columbia S. Ca.
January 29th 1865
My Dearest Molly

The former sheet as you will perceive was written for the open mail and is full of half truths. I can still preach as you see, but I cannot practice resignation even yet and at times I feel as blue as of Old. We have at last got into a building but it is cold and poor comfort, not half enough firewood is supplied us for comfort barely enough for two meals a day while the free air of heaven careers through a thousand cracks and crannies. Per consequence we are compelled to exercise to keep warm, and to wear all our clothes at once, numbers lay in bed half the day to keep warm. I am much better off than most. I am comfortable just now in that great overcoat I recd last spring from Wm. and I have yet got my watch left, with which I intend when next there is a partial Exchange to try to purchase my way out, that is the way (I have only lately found out) that half the Exchanges are procured here. I believe I told you before that I had a letter from Col. Martin dated in October last, stating that he had taken steps to procure me a Special Exch. but you see even his influence has failed to free me, and yet my name may be on the list here for months and I be oversloughed by others who have more money; so if I get a chance away goes my watch. It is evident to me that there is a Providential purpose in my detention, perhaps time is thus given me to repent of my past follies and sins, perhaps my life is to be thus saved for future usefulness. It was seemingly a mere accident by which I missed my Exchange on the field of Chicamauga, and many such accidents have seemingly detained me since. God knows how bitterly I relish it, and how much I would prefer fighting the battles of my Country in the field, but it is only too probable, I will now remain to the end of the War, and if God smiles on the cause during the present as he has during the past year, the closing scene of this wicked rebellion will be seen during the present Summer or Fall.

I have managed to keep some money on hand up to the present time. At present it takes nearly $5.00 Confed each per day to keep us from Starvation. Our rations (Corn meal and Sorghum) are not sufficient. I drew on William for $50.00 last Decr. but the Officer who negotiated it for me, went off with the proceeds, and I sent a note through to stop it. I hope it was in time. I may draw on him again, but better not pay until he hears from me, as rascality is at a premium here – and numbers have been swindled – as we only get about 10 or 12 cents on the dollar in this worthless trash, and we are so desperately needy at times it is too bad to lose good gold besides I cant afford it as you know?

A little more firewood and something to read would make time pass quickly even here, half my time is passed in cooking, washing and Baking for be it known I am Baker to our mess. I am too restless to lay in bed more than 10 or 12 hours, and so I do much solitary promenading up and down quarter deck fashion.

An acquaintance of mine, Capt. Hescock of the 1st. Mo. Artillery has been and is very sick from Pneumonia or consumption, and I have been trying to keep up his spirits by staying with him a little. I fear he will not reach home as his lungs are in a bad state. He is a Virginian but an old resident of St. Louis. We are at present enclosed in a part of the grounds of the State Lunatic Asylum closely guarded and no present chance to escape, but if from any cause we are moved, say Sherman or Kilpatricks progress thither wards – I will assuredly try again, in these escapades the niggers are invaluable, they guide us, feed us, hide us, and give us a chance to sleep warm when they can. They are now well posted as to the cause and result of the war, and will prove a bad investment to their masters for the future I think let the war result as it may.

Much money has come to officers lately. I often wonder whether William sent me any or not. In exchanging it now we get Fifty-seven dollars Confed for one Dollar in gold – and still it depreciates.

Of course I did not get the last box sent me (in October). I suppose it must have been sent back from Hilton Head. None have been allowed through the lines since November by our Government as we understand it. I hope there is a good cause for this. I do not doubt it in the least, but our sufferings in consequence make us liable to be prejudiced against (Staunton say).

There are still nearly twelve hundred Officers here, besides Five hundred at Salisbury and Danville, and numbers of others scattered all over the Confederacy in solitary torture. The thousands of Privates who suffer and die from cold, hunger and exposure and torments unnamable and inconceiveable at various places I need not here enlarge on. Poor fellows they die unhonored and unsung; martyrs to a <u>deadly</u> policy, for which some one will have to answer at the bar of the nation and of God – better far better, had they died a lingering death from wounds or fever on the field. Our sufferings are pleasures in comparison; our prison sumptuous and comfortable to describe, when beside their lazar house. I subscribed in Libby for some Books descriptive of our life there. If they should come by Express I hope Wm. will receive them and pay charges. I have lately subscribed also for several Books and plates illustrating our life in Macon, Charleston, Savannah and here, which will give our friends North a better idea of our circumstances here than I can. I have kept a Diary however of my personal experiences and feelings of which I may read you extracts if I should ever be so fortunate as to see you again. The weather here must soon moderate, and when it does, we will be able to have a little enjoyment again at times. We have lately found it impossible to read or write or play cards even. Today is yet cold but a warm sun shines which has moderated the temperature enough to allow me to write this scrawl.

Sherman's progress has alarmed and scared the Rebs more than anything that has happened to them yet, and they all consider him our best General. I hope that nothing will stop his course, no diplomacy or orders from the North. I dont think any force the South can bring to bear can stop him, and that you will continue to hear of him proceeding conquering and to conquer until he has overan at least all South Carolina – which place we here hold responsible for most the miseries that have befallen us. The Niggers sing Hallelujahs for him every day, and so do we nightly. We have a new song set to new music both composed in camp, which is the latest sensation in that respect. It is entitled "<u>Shermans March to the Sea</u>"!! and we have enjoyed it much; while the Rebs are proportionably bored when they hear it.

All sorts of businesses and professions are carried on in camp. Our string band when the weather permits discourses most excellent music, while Carpenters, Shoemakers, tailors, cap makers, and mattress makers find plenty of work. We have numerous glee clubs, whist clubs, chess clubs, and Gambling Banks of every kind and description where monies are staked from 25 cents to over one <u>hundred dollars</u>. You know I dont indulge; an occasional game of chess, whist or backgammon is my only failing in that way, but even were I so disposed I have had to be too economical, to spread my little money too far to risk a cent, when I might lose a dinner thereby. We have preaching occasionally the last was last Monday, none to day (Sunday) as it happens probably from the inclemency of the weather during the past week. Since I commenced a small mail has come in, but no letters for me, and none later than the beginning of Decr.

With Prayers for your happiness & Welfare,

Goodbye

Love

Feby 4th 1865

Dearest Molly

As rumors of an early Exch. of sick still continue to prevail, I resume my notes, hoping they may reach you and cheer you a little in my absence. I have found that our letters accumulated at Hilton Head, in consequence of Sherman's movements, have been since sent to City Point and Richmond for transmission but I fear the lazy Rebs will scarcely trouble themselves to read them and let us have them. As they are too lazy to read ours to send away several thousand letters have accumulated in their hands for friends at home so far and that is the reason we have quit writing.

We have heard of an attack on Grant by Lee in which the latter was repulsed with Loss of Men and Gunboats. I hope it is true as it disproves the rumors of Armistice. Also that Grant is appointed Comr. of Exch. in lieu of Butler disgraced, and that he has had an interview with Ould from which some expect great results. I do not.

Feby. 12th 1865

We have passed another wet & frosty and so to us miserable week. Many rumors however are current to cheer us, all tending to a favorable result to our arms, or towards an early Exch. for some of us. I have had a cold and occasional sick headache, but nothing of moment, even to my idea and you know I am rather fearful of colds. Fortunately I had just got possession of "Jane Eyre" and "Very Hard Cash" and I laid abed and sweat it off. I am now quite free. I have just got a letter from our old Lt. Col. (Schneider) from Ohio, where he is at home sick, and he states that Col. Martin being out of the Service had called on him and shown him a letter of mine dated 9th Decr. that he had taken immediate steps in some quarter where they had the will and the power for my Exch. that he hopes if possible to procure it and also assure's me that all will soon be at home. That ought to put me in good spirits you would say but still I doubt. We have been promised the same from the highest authority and deceived. I have no faith left. I am much pleased and gratified at the receipt of the letter, and will try to wait the issue patiently but meantime the crisis in the shape of Sherman is upon us and we are under momentary expectation of being ordered to move out of the way of our friends again, like the dove from the Ark. We can find no where to rest. All is commotion outside. All the Old men and all the boys above fourteen are out, in fear of a raid from this Cavalry – while his main force is said to be at or near Augusta, and another column at or near Charleston. We go to _____. I'll tell you perhaps when we get there. On the merest grounds of humanity our government should Exchange us. I fear they <u>can not rescue us</u> – until we are marched to death, or killed by cold and exposure, being driven before the advance of our friends like so many cattle. Columbia today, by the bye, is like a fair. It is full of men, women, children, horses, cattle, furniture and supplies and wagons of all kinds, just flocked in, in order to escape the clutches of the victorious Sherman.

I sent a letter by and same time as the one I have just mentioned (9th Decr.) to you. I happened to have it written but not mailed, also one to Wm asking him not to pay a certain <u>Bill of Exchange</u>. I wonder if either reached. I have now some hopes they did, as one has, why not all. They must unless some unfortunate accident prevented. If so you will have heard from me – though you will feel annoyed at the scanty amount of news contained therein. If I had known of any certain opportunity, I would have prepared as I am now doing and given you as much truth as paper and pen will convey, but a chance is so problematical and paper is so scarce, and &c, &c, &c. Why I may actually carry this through myself. I have no doubt that ere May day several hundred of us will rejoice our friends with our personal presence. Why should not I? Well I might were I not a Jonah!!! So dont expect me. Today is a beautiful Spring day, warm sun and balmy wind. Yesterday was almost as fine, and so I washed all my clothes. They were much in need and made all preparation for a march to a new prison or <u>camp</u> – so <u>called</u> a <u>Prison</u> or to Sherman & Liberty, for if I can fool the guard so as to get off without a shot in the back I will run for it, and so will the majority of us. While I was busy there was service held in camp by a preacher who has visited us for that purpose before – so I was not present, but to day a Lt. Gunn of Ky. preached and we had a very pleasant service indeed at which I was present and I hope I profited. I now fill up the interval before our dinner (or supper rather) in writing to you.

Oh! I so pray and pine to hear from you my dear girl. I hope you keep up heart and enjoy yourself for after all in a troubled mind and suspense you must suffer more than even I do from these few evils of the body – believe me I suffer more in mind than in body myself even now and also in the long months gone by. When my mind was easy I made light of our sufferings and extracted as I ought many sunbeams from my Cucumber. It was only when at times I got the blues from dissapointed hopes that I gave in to our tormentors; I hope for so little now, that I can scarce be dissapointed again, but I feel it much that I do not get a letter from you occasionally. I know you write.

For months no letters came in camp from the North! Now they come again, but I am not fortunate as yet. I may be tomorrow! I pray to God I may! A large mail came in to day and yesterday, the balance comes tomorrow.

I made out a draft on Friday on Lawyer Evans, who owes me money, but I do not expect him to pay it. I dont wish him to pay it until I return home, or write to request it. I have not got any money on it yet, and I do this to prevent rascality. I got such a fright last time when I drew on William that I resolved not to do so again if I could help it; unless I wished it paid at once which I know he would do. If he paid the first one I sent (in Decr.) why I must only trust to repaying myself by taking from some Reb, according to the laws and rules of war, a thing I have not done as yet, but the provocation is so strong in this case that I have almost sworn it! And why not? such has been the way of the world since time began!! The bluest blood of the English Aristocracy, hold their rank, wealth and title by the good old rule that he should take who had the power and he should keep who can – so of all <u>rank</u> – the world over! Save a few of late day by merit, and a few by legal or illegal gains in trade! Only think if I had been out of here, I would be Major or Lt. Col of our Regt. Yes even if I had got out when Austin did in Sept. last, or even when I escaped in Novr. I could yet have been Major but because I am a prisoner I am yet plain Capt. Love – but in that respect I suffer along with 40 or 60,000 other prisoners so I do not grumble at what may perhaps be a necessary regulation.

I do want to get out of here however, so as to secure any such windfall and then leave the service if I want to. I would like to be promoted once or twice first. I assure you, vanity and a sense of justice would then both be satisfied but dinner is now ready, and as that is the main event of our day, it brooks no delay, or evasion so for the present my dearest girl goodbye. With much love to you and all friends – and more gossip anon

from yours truly

James E. Love

Capt. 8th K. Vet. Vol.

Feby. 14th 1865

Well my Love, I have just received a valentine from you, it was dated 27th Nov but what of that. It is to remind me that there is more and better things to come, and it was full of Love too, and of your ardent hopes nay expectations of my early Exchange. In fact you puzzle your brains! why I am not released ere now? Now on that subject I can enlighten you now, though I could not have done so six months ago. And first I am in a Kansas Regt. Thats Bad! Then I am from Mo. Thats worse!! And both together is quite damnable in all rebel eyes! Then although I have been wounded and badly, I was turned out of the Hospital over a year ago, so that counts against me, when an Exchange of sick or wounded is in progress, and probably accounts for the dissapointment of the Washington authorities in part. But not altogether for with about two dozen exceptions, and they mostly General & Field officers the U.S. Govt. have not got anybody they wanted exchanged since last May.

The Rebels send who they please, and always those who are traitors to us, or who pretend to be so, also those who have most money, in hand to <u>Bribe them with</u>!!! Now I have none to spare in that way! And I never ask any favors of them! Nor never will, unless I am starving. I hope it wont come to that, for I w'd almost prefer it, to stooping to them. And <u>thats</u> whats the matter!

Bless your dear heart. Almost every officer here has a promise of an Early Exchange, and yet few believe in being Exchanged before the end of this year or of the War! There will be a few fortunate ones of course and that soon but the sick and the <u>monied ones</u> only. Our Governt professed to be anxious to Exchange us all, but that I should say it. <u>It is false</u>! And only said to keep you quiet at home. They hope to capture us – not Exchange us! and all the movements are in that way, but they cannot capture many of us, for the Rebs will move us quicker than our army can move! All is pretence, and this will be the result, a number of thousands will be exchanged within a month or more perhaps, and then Grant and Sherman will capture their Railroads, and stop Exchange by their movements, as they did last year, and on this pretence, for it is only a pretence, Exchange will stop again until the fall. Ere which time as I said they hope to capture us – and so give no equivalent! As I said I have no such hope.

But if the cause prospers I forgive it all, what after all is my little mite of suffering, when weighed against that of the Nation at large!? Therefore I pray for its success and dont wish the war to stop until in Gods good Providence all its citizens are free and all our wishes granted by a reestablishment of the Union that will be as lasting as it is glorious!

I wish to be with you so much however that I will give my watch to any Reb who will take me out; and I will escape by any tunnel or other means that offers. The Rebels have just discovered a Tunnel, but others are in progress that they wot not of; and if they move us, why numbers will escape as usual. Well my Love I am sorry I cant send you a better Valentine, but when I reach home I will try and do better. I will try and do and be all you want of me!

I look for some more letters from you daily, for we have not got half our mail yet. Meantime do be disheartened and above all things – write to me.

Love

Feby 16th 1865
After writing the above we were notified to pack for a move. We were marched to the cars and found all Columbia in excitement, cause Sherman

was coming. We soon found we were bound for Charlotte and after a tiresome ride of 18 hours arrived here last night. It was an awful day and night rain sleeted and froze hard until the ground and trees were covered with an inch of ice. It was so rough I would not escape though I had a good chance last night we slept by a large fire in an open field. It was cold and foggy but dry, today the same. Tonight I intend to go if possible, with a party of eight for East Tennessee. Exchange news is good, but we have no faith and would rather cheat the rebs if we can, and carry our own letters. I have just got one from Wm. dated 25 Decr. announcing a box – none from you. With love farewell till I see you

Sincerely

James E. Love

By the time General William T. Sherman entered Columbia, South Carolina, James had been moved to Charlotte, North Carolina. *General Sherman's Entry into Columbia, South Carolina, February 17, 1865*. From *Harper's Weekly*, April 1, 1865.

Epilogue

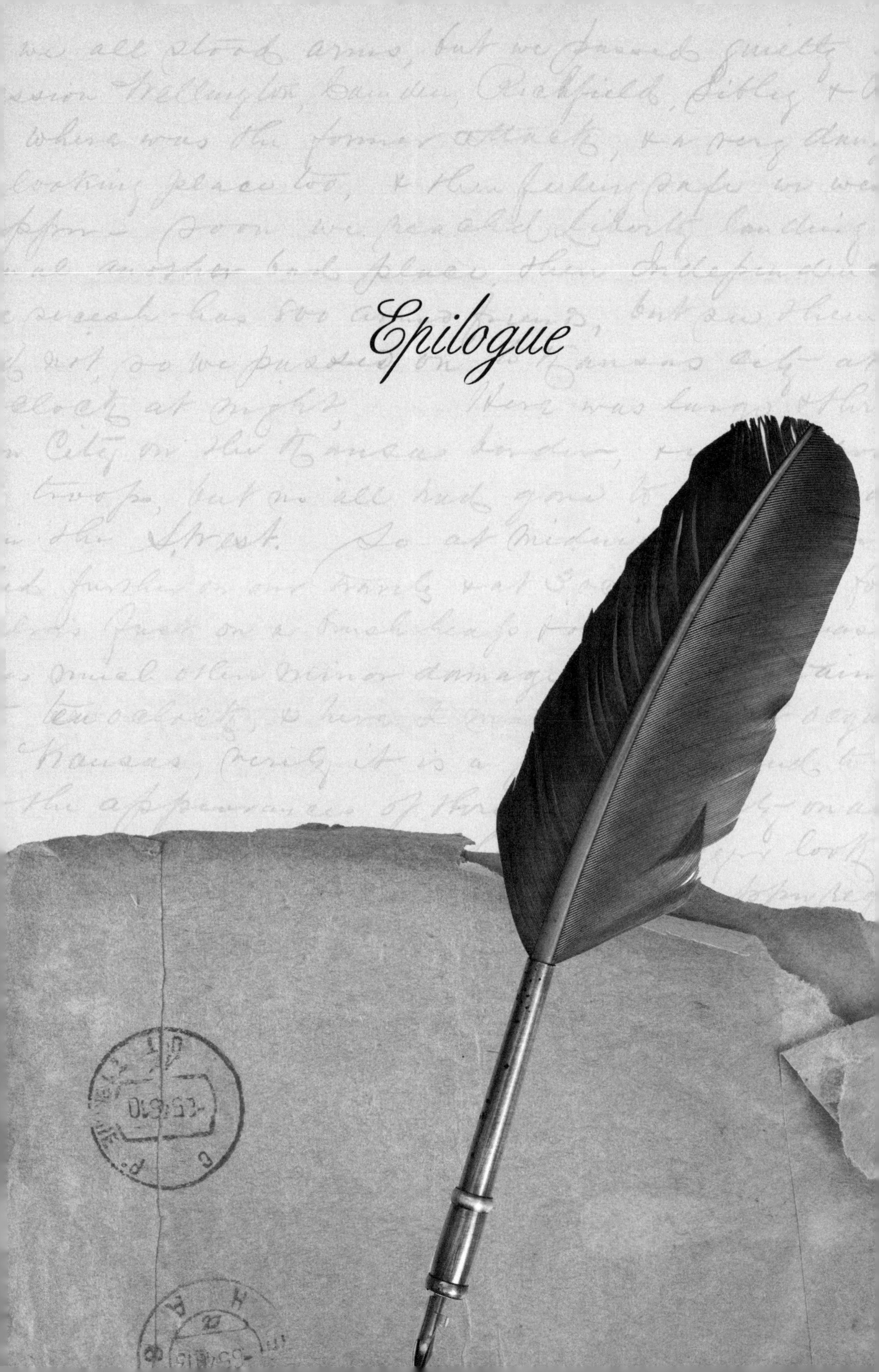

On February 16, 1865, after writing his last letter to Molly, James finally escaped from his Confederate captors while camped in a field near Charlotte, North Carolina. He and seven other Union officer prisoners received rations of hard tack and bacon, paid a fee to their North Carolina guards, and then ran. They were fired upon and chased, but they moved quickly across a bridge over Long Creek. They next came to a bridge over the Catawba River, where a guard stopped them. James and the other men fabricated a story to get past the guard—then ran for it. The guard fired his gun, and soon a whole picket chased the men, quickly capturing one, and then two more a few hours later. The next morning, some boys out hunting saw the rest of the group. The men learned that the boys' mothers had helped Union officers before, and they arranged to be hidden in an empty shanty for a day or two until the threatened search was over and they could get a guide. As James recalled in his reminiscences, they could "never repay their kindness and watchfulness day and night."

On February 20, after three days of rest, the men started with their guide, Manuel, a free black man, at 6 p.m. To avoid guards, they traveled a circuitous route of twenty miles but gained only six miles. They reached the only unguarded bridge across the south fork of the Catawba River at the Pin Hook Factory, a textile mill near present-day Belmont, North Carolina. At that point they had to decide whether to go down the river to find General William T. Sherman, or up and across the mountains into Tennessee. They met secretly with several Union men and learned that twenty escaped prisoners had just been captured nearby, so they decided to go west.

Along their way to Tennessee, the men received directions and rations from white men and women who supported the Union, free blacks, and slaves. During the evening of February 21, the men lost their way, but they met a free black man who guided them to the old Charleston Road. They spent February 22 in a deserted cabin with a man that James described as "energetic, well read, a practical miner, [though] Union, a native Southern Abolitionist, energetic and quoting Jefferson." This man helped the group find Alec, a "brave Negro pilot," according to James. The men were assured that they were already safe, because they had only fifty miles to the Blue Ridge Mountains, where an underground railroad for prisoners and refugees commenced. After their guide arrived at 8 p.m., they started and made twenty miles to camp. They passed through Shelby, North Carolina, at 4 a.m. and then crossed the Broad River, with their "brave guide prospecting the way." After resting during the day in a tent, James and the others moved again after dark. In heavy rain, they waded knee deep for miles and asked for directions at a miserable shanty of two Confederate soldiers. James wrote, "They knew us at a glance . . . and they bid us God Speed, if we wished to travel such a horrible night." By 2 a.m., they camped two miles west of Sandy Run, after a night of grueling travel. James wrote, "We were only 6 miles on our way but more fatigued than in travelling 30 miles." Their guide Alec left them so he could move ahead and prepare to meet them at Broad River, nine miles ahead, at sunset. However, the men had to move around so many plantations that they traveled twenty-five miles before they reached the bridge over the river. Once they crossed the bridge, Alec gave them a canteen of whiskey, and James wrote, "never was whiskey more needful or beneficial." After resting for a few hours, the men started again at midnight, passing Rutherfordton, ten miles ahead, before morning. Along the way, they found a soldier at home with his wife. She baked some bread and boiled some eggs, for which the men paid, and gave them a piece of bacon. At 4 a.m., Alec returned to conduct the men to the residence of their next guide, Lewis. The men paid Alec and were sorry to part. James recalled that Alec was a slave who hired his time and had accumulated three thousand dollars in property, the price of his freedom. He also made trips of one hundred miles to sell iron and other goods. Alec believed that General William Sherman would free him without cost and he could save his iron and other goods for Yankee gold. According to James, Alec's advice to other slaves was to stay where they were and wait, so they could continue living in their old homes as free people.

The men started again at 6 p.m. and made six miles to land owned by Jim Hamilton. He gave the men a good dinner and had the men's shoes soled and mended. They next crossed three flooded creeks with Jim, riding a mule, as their guide. Because of rain, they traveled only seven miles, all uphill. The next day, they slept in a loft until 11 a.m. During the day the men heard many visitors discussing Sherman and the early end of the war. At night they started again with their guide but turned back after they heard of some troops near Asheville. Their next guide came early and conducted them, before daylight, to an old schoolhouse in the mountains. At midnight, they started again to ascend the mountains, reaching the top after a climb of five miles in four hours. Since the next stage was across the Blue Ridge and Black mountains, they had to wait several days for the weather to clear, so they would not become lost in fog or snowdrifts.

When the sun finally came out on March 5, the group started at 11 a.m., reached the top of the Blue Ridge at 4 p.m., and were down in the valley, on the west side, at sunset. Then they had a very rough march to the foot of the Black Mountains, which they reached at 1 a.m. on March 6. After a rest, they started early to climb the mountains, which had no trail and were very steep over rocks, stumps, and fallen timber. The group reached the top, six thousand feet high, at 1 p.m. After a good dinner, they crossed over to the headspring of Caney Creek and passed rapidly down the stream. At daylight, they started again to the Asheville road. After traveling another three or four miles, and a rapid march over a steep range, James and the rest reached "Egypt" at the foot of Bald Mountain. The next day they reached the summit of Bald Mountain, then descended rapidly and reached the valley for dinner at 3 p.m.

Unfortunately, James did not recount the rest of the trip, but after traveling 350 miles in twenty-eight days, James reached the Union lines and reported at Knoxville, Tennessee, on March 14, 1865. Two days later, he requested a leave of absence. The exact date of his arrival in St. Louis is not known. However, James and Molly were married in St. Louis on May 2, 1865, and later that month he was honorably discharged. After almost four years of military service, including seventeen months as a prisoner, and 160 letters to his fiancée, James was home and starting his life with his beloved Molly.

After an extraordinary story that included immigrating to the United States from Ireland, traveling to Australia and living there for four years, and then surviving four years of war, James had an ordinary, presumably happy, life. Unfortunately, he did not leave behind any correspondence, diaries, or other papers to document the rest of his life, but city directories, the census, and other sources at least provide information on where he lived and worked.

In 1866, James and Molly lived in their first home at 927 North Twentieth Street in St. Louis, and James worked as a bookkeeper for wholesale grocer Francis Lepere, the same place where he worked when he first came to St. Louis in the early 1850s. On May 20, 1867, James and Molly had their first child, and only son, William S. Love. In 1868, James started to work as a cashier for the Union Savings Association, where his brother-in-law William C. Wilson was the vice president. The following year, James and Molly's first daughter, Maude, was born. In 1871, James and Molly moved to a new home at 1916 Wash Street, and on March 23 of that year, their daughter Jessie was born. James continued to work as a cashier for the Union Savings Association until 1877, and on January 19 of that year, James and Molly's final child, Edith, was born. For the rest of his life, James worked as a cashier, clerk, or bookkeeper for various businesses. In 1884, James and Molly moved to 1818 Wash Street and remained in that house until 1898, when they moved farther west to their final home at 5714 Maple Avenue. James died on December 27, 1905, and was buried at Bellefontaine Cemetery in St. Louis.

Captain JAMES EDWIN LOVE

Left: Captain James E. Love from Military Order of the Loyal Legion of the United States memorial sketch, ca. 1905. Military Order of the Loyal Legion of the United States Records. Right: Molly Love in her home at 5714 Maple Avenue, ca. 1910s. Courtesy of Steve Stuart.

James and Molly lived in this house at 5714 Maple Avenue from 1898 until their deaths in 1905 and 1924, respectively. Courtesy of Steve Stuart.

Molly remained in the house at 5714 Maple Avenue for the rest of her life. Her daughters and grandchildren lived with her for many years. According to her great-grandson, Molly was a fervent prohibitionist. Molly died on April 1, 1924, after falling down the stairs at her house. She was ninety years old.

Left: William S. Love, 5 months, October 14, 1867. Middle: Maude Moore Love, 2 ½ years, October 1871. Right: Jessie Wilson Love, 6 months, October 1871. All from James E. Love Papers, Missouri Historical Society, from originals in care of Dr. Arthur Love.

Left: William S. Love as an adult. From memorial biography. Courtesy of Steve Stuart. Right: Edith Rogers Love Sevier, early 1900s. Courtesy of Jennifer Rosier.

William S. Love attended school in St. Louis, including Smith Academy and the Manual Training School of Washington University, from which he graduated in 1883. He then worked for a year as a railroad surveyor for the Texas and Pacific Railway in Arkansas before returning to St. Louis to attend Washington University. William graduated from that institution with a degree in mechanical engineering in 1888. Immediately after graduating, William started to work for the Pond Engineering Company, engineers for power plants, and eventually took charge of the company's Chicago branch in 1892. That same year, William married Martha Ann Archibald, daughter of James Miller and Alice (Gilson) Archibald. He remained in Chicago, working for various engineering companies, until 1906, when he moved to New York to work in the home office of the Wheeler Condenser and Engineering Company of New York. He died on December 11, 1907, at East Orange, New Jersey, leaving behind his wife and an adopted son, Douglas Love. William is buried with his parents and his wife at Bellefontaine Cemetery.

Maude M. Love lived with her parents at 5714 Maple Avenue as late as 1900. In the late 1890s and early 1900s, she worked as a teacher and stenographer. By

1910, according to the census, Maude was still single, lived in Sundance, Crook County, Wyoming, and worked as a stenographer for the U.S. Land Office. At some point between 1910 and 1920, she married a man with the last name of Kise, because on the 1920 census she is listed as Maude M. Kise, widowed, living in Converse, Wyoming, and still working as a stenographer for the U.S. Land Office. However, in the 1930 census, Maude is listed as divorced. At that time she was living at Our Lady of Lourdes home in Dubuque, Iowa, and she continued to live there until at least 1940. Maude died on June 26, 1958, at the St. Francis Home in Dubuque. She is buried with her parents at Bellefontaine Cemetery.

Edith R. Love still lived at 5714 Maple with James and Molly in 1900 and worked as a teacher. In 1904, she married Joseph R. Sevier, and in 1920 they lived in Augusta, Georgia, where he was a Presbyterian minister; they had two children. Around 1924, Joseph purchased Fassifern School, a private girls' school in Hendersonville, North Carolina. According to the 1930 and 1940 censuses, Edith and Joseph lived in Hendersonville and Joseph was principal of the school. Also in the mid-1920s, Joseph purchased land for a Christian summer camp for girls. Camp Greystone continues to operate today in Tuxedo, North Carolina, not far from the area that James Love passed through after escaping from prison. The camp has remained in the family throughout its history, and the current director is James and Molly's great-great-grandson. Edith Love Sevier died in Hendersonville on April 11, 1945.

Jessie W. Love was the third of James and Molly's four children. On February 20, 1895, in a small ceremony in the parlor of her parents' home at 1818 Wash Street, Jessie married Lewis B. Stuart. He was born in St. Louis in 1870, the son of John L. and Mary Stuart. Lewis's grandfather, James Stewart (he changed the spelling of his last name when he came to America from Scotland, but his son John L. retained the original spelling), arrived in St. Louis in 1866 and established the firm of James Stewart & Co., engineers and contractors. The firm had projects all over the country, including a powerhouse at Niagara Falls, and in 1894 had contracts totaling $1.5 million. In 1880, John L. Stuart, his wife, Mary, and their five children, including Lewis, lived at 2600 Wash Street, just a few blocks from James and Molly. As an adult, Lewis worked for his family's firm. In May 1896, Lewis and Jessie had their first son, Lyall. Two years later, when the

James and Molly's daughter
Jessie Love Stuart, ca. 1930s.
Courtesy of Steve Stuart.

family was living in Fort Wayne, Indiana, while Lewis led construction of the county courthouse, their second son, Lewis B. Stuart Jr., was born on March 14, 1898. Sadly, the elder Lewis died in a train accident on October 11, 1899, at the age of twenty-nine, while supervising a construction project in Owego, New York.

Following the death of her husband, Jessie brought her two young sons back to St. Louis. In the 1900 census, they are listed as living with Jessie's father-in-law, John L. Stuart, at 5346 Maple Avenue. The following year, Jessie and her sons moved in with James and Molly at 5714 Maple Avenue. In his reminiscences, Lewis B. Stuart Jr. recalled that his first memories were of his life at that house, watching delivery trucks and wagons from the front porch and listening to his Grandfather Love's war stories. Lewis attended Dozier School through the eighth grade and then Soldan High School. His studies at Princeton University were interrupted by World War I. He enlisted with the Marine Corps Air Service but never served overseas. After graduating from Princeton University, Lewis began his career at Ralston Purina. He was a longtime friend of Donald Danforth, son of the company's founder, William H. Danforth. Lewis started in

Left: Lewis B. Stuart Jr. lived with his grandmother for many years. Molly Love and Lewis B. Stuart Jr., ca. 1905. Courtesy of Steve Stuart. Right: Lewis B. Stuart Jr. enlisted with the Marine Corps Air Service during World War I.

the production department and eventually became executive vice president of the company.

In the mid-1930s, Jessie, Lewis, and his wife and children moved out of St. Louis city to 22 Fair Oaks Drive in Ladue, a suburb in St. Louis County. Fortunately, the family moved James's letters with them. At some point, Lewis had someone make typed copies of all of James's original handwritten letters. In November 1949, Jessie donated twenty of James's letters to the Missouri Historical Society, and in August 1965 her son Lewis donated the rest of the letters. These letters have been part of the Archives collections ever since, certainly used many times over the years by people researching the Civil War.

In 1997, after graduating from the University of Michigan with a degree in history, I started as an intern in the Archives department at the Missouri Historical Society. My job was to help Dennis Northcott, one of the archivists, compile a guide to the Civil War manuscripts in the Archives, so I read letters, diaries, and

Graves of James Love, Eliza Mary "Molly" Love, Maude M. Kise, William S. Love, and his wife, Annie A. Love, at Bellefontaine Cemetery, St. Louis. Photo by Ira Kodner.

other papers of various Civil War soldiers, researched the soldier and the content, and wrote a brief biographical sketch and general description of the documents. During college, I had focused primarily on twentieth-century American history, except for one survey course on the nineteenth century. For some reason, I'd always thought the nineteenth century was boring. As I read these first-person accounts of the war, I realized that I had been completely wrong. I had just been reading the wrong sources. During the course of the project, Dennis asked me to write a description for the James E. Love Papers, and I was hooked, not only on the idea of becoming an archivist, but on these letters and this couple, James and Molly. James had such an extraordinary life before the war, and he wrote such wonderfully descriptive letters about his war experiences. Of course, he also wrote deeply emotional, romantic letters to his "dear Molly." I was a young, single woman with the same name, which obviously contributed to my profound interest in these letters. The first time I read them, I was convinced that these letters, out of all the many Civil War collections that I read, needed to be shared, somehow, with a wider audience.

By 2011, I was a full-time associate archivist at the Missouri Historical Society, and the Civil War Love Letters project became a reality. To commemorate the sesquicentennial of the Civil War, we started posting the text of each letter, 150 years after James wrote it, on our blog. I began to do more in-depth research into the content of the letters, and James and Molly's genealogy, including their ancestors and descendants. Through my research, I discovered links between a few of my parents' friends and James and Molly's descendants.

First, when I found the obituary for Lewis B. Stuart Jr., who died in 1985, I learned that he had been a member of Ladue Chapel, a Presbyterian church in St. Louis. I knew that my parents' dear friend Marie Oetting was also a member of that church, and I found out that she had known him and had fond memories.

Shortly after learning of this connection, I had the great pleasure of getting in touch with James and Molly's great-great-grandson, Steve Stuart, who has supported this project from the beginning. He kindly sent scans from the reminiscences of his grandfather, Lewis B. Stuart Jr. In these pages, while explaining his friendship with Donald Danforth and the trips he took with Donald and William H. Danforth, Lewis mentioned seeing Gordon Philpott. I could not believe my eyes! My parents are great friends with the son of Gordon Philpott.

The discovery of these two connections was amazing enough, but the third link was astounding. Several of the photographs in the James E. Love Papers are copies of originals in the care of Dr. Arthur Love from Brisbane, Australia. He is a direct descendant of James's uncle Robert Love, who went to Australia around the same time as James, in the 1850s, and remained in the country. In order to use the images on our website, I had to contact Dr. Love to request permission. Around this same time, my parents were on vacation in Florida and saw their friend Dr. Ian Lavery, who was originally from Australia. My father met Dr. Lavery in the mid-1970s when both were doing a medical fellowship in Cleveland, Ohio. During their visit in Florida, my dad mentioned my project and that I had contacted Dr. Love. To my surprise, Dr. Lavery and Dr. Love had gone to school together in Australia!

These links across time and geography only deepened my dedication to James and Molly, and to this project. I hope people have enjoyed reading these letters and getting to know James and Molly as much as I have. More important, I hope I have honored the lives and memory of James, an ordinary man who lived an extraordinary life, and his dearest Molly.

Acknowledgments

Thank you first to Eliza Mary "Molly" Wilson Love and her descendants: to Molly for keeping James's letters; to her daughter Jessie Love Stuart for keeping the letters and deciding to donate them to the Missouri Historical Society; to Molly's grandson Lewis B. Stuart Jr., for getting typescripts of all of the letters; to James and Molly's great-great-grandson Steve Stuart for supporting this project from the beginning and providing family photographs and documents; to James and Molly's great-great-great-granddaughter Jennifer Keyton Rosier for providing information and photographs of her branch of the family; and to Dr. Arthur Love in Australia for providing several family photographs, especially the only photograph of Molly from the Civil War period.

Nevin Taggart is a current resident of James's hometown of Bushmills and compiler of the North Antrim Local Interest List blog. I got in touch with him in early 2012 after discovering that he posted information about the online Civil War Love Letters series on his blog. Since then, Nevin has kindly answered many questions about the Love family genealogy and the history of northern Ireland. Thank you for sharing James's story with people in Bushmills.

Eric Alessi and Alyssa Cliffe, my interns in 2010, scanned all the letters so we could post the images on the Missouri History Museum's blog, History Happens Here (www.historyhappenshere.org).

Gerry Allen, Park Ranger–Interpretation, Chickamauga & Chattanooga National Military Park, helped me find the marker for the location of the Eighth Kansas on September 20, 1863.

Julie Hoffman, Stark County (OH) District Library, for sending the obituary of James Wallace.

Many people at various repositories provided images: Mack Linebaugh, Director of Digital Services, Nashville Public Radio; Jay Richiuso, Assistant Director for Manuscripts Services at the Tennessee State Library and Archives; Holly Reed, National Archives & Records Administration Still Picture Reference; Lisa Jacobson, Presbyterian Historical Society; Nancy Sherbert, Curator of Photographs and Acquisitions Coordinator, Kansas State Historical Society; Joan Albert and Jamison Davis, Virginia Historical Society; and Kathryn Conley and Rachel Cockrell, South Carolina Confederate Relic Room and Military Museum.

Dr. Earl J. Hess, Stewart W. McClelland Chair in History, Lincoln Memorial University, kindly agreed to check for any inaccuracies in the introductions.

This book and the Civil War Love Letters series on the Missouri History Museum blog never would have happened without the three fabulous women in the Publications department: Victoria Monks, Director of Publications, who enthusiastically supported this book from the beginning; Keri McBride, Editor, who edited and posted all of the letters on the blog over the past four years; and Lauren Mitchell, Senior Editor, who kindly walked me through the final writing stage and edited and designed the book.

My family has always been a tremendous source of support, through my life and this project. Thank you to my sister, Beth, her husband, Jeremy, and their children, Henry and Zoe, for listening when I needed to talk and making me laugh when I needed a break. Thank you, especially, to my parents, Ira and Barbara Kodner, for always encouraging my interest in history, from driving out of our way so I could see John Adams's house when I was eight, to trudging through hot and buggy Civil War battlefields as I followed in James's footsteps.

Sources

Books

Burke, W. S. *Official Military History of Kansas Regiments during the War for the Suppression of the Great Rebellion.* Leavenworth, KS: W. S. Burke, 1870.

Dyer, Frederick H. *A Compendium of the War of the Rebellion.* [Wilmington, NC]: Morningside Press, 1994.

Gerteis, Louis S. *Civil War St. Louis.* Lawrence: University Press of Kansas, 2001.

Hesseltine, William Best. *Civil War Prisons: A Study in War Psychology.* Columbus, OH: Ohio State University Press, 1930.

Hewett, Janet B. *Supplement to the Official Records of the Union and Confederate Armies.* Wilmington, NC: Broadfoot Publishing Company, 1996.

Lanier, Robert S., ed. *The Photographic History of the Civil War.* New York: Review of Reviews Co., 1911.

McFarland, Bill. *Keep the Flag to the Front: The Story of the Eighth Kansas Volunteer Infantry.* Overland Park, KS: Leathers Publishing, 2008.

Speer, Lonnie R. *Portals to Hell: Military Prisons of the Civil War.* Mechanicsburg, PA: Stackpole Books, 1997.

War of the Rebellion: A Compilation of the Official Records of the Union and Confederate Armies, The. Washington, DC: Government Printing Office, 1880–1901.

Welcher, Frank. *The Union Army, 1861–1865: Organization and Operations.* Vol. 2: The Western Theater. Bloomington: Indiana University Press, 1993.

Winter, William C. *The Civil War in St. Louis: A Guided Tour.* St. Louis: Missouri Historical Society Press, 1994.

Woodworth, Steven E. *Jefferson Davis and His Generals: The Failure of Confederate Command in the West.* Lawrence: University of Kansas Press, 1990.

Newspapers

Harper's Weekly

Illustrated London News

St. Louis Daily Missouri Republican

Daily Missouri Democrat

Nashville Daily Union

Manuscripts

James E. Love Papers, Missouri Historical Society, St. Louis

Compiled service record of James E. Love, Eighth Kansas Infantry, National Archives

Index